TABLE OF CONTENTS

*"This book aims to **guide product managers,** business leaders, and anyone interested in the future of technology through the dynamic landscape of AI and its impact on product management. By exploring key concepts, practical strategies, and real-world examples, readers will gain valuable insights into navigating the future where AI and product management converge."*

INTRODUCTION

DEFINING THE LANDSCAPE

In the ever-evolving terrain of technology, the convergence of artificial intelligence (AI) and product management has become a defining feature of the contemporary business landscape. The symbiotic relationship between these two domains has ushered in a new era of innovation, challenging traditional paradigms and reshaping the way products are conceptualized, developed, and delivered to users.

As we stand at the crossroads of technological advancement, it is crucial to understand the intricate interplay between AI and product management. Product managers are no longer mere architects of features; they are orchestrators of intelligent systems, harnessing the power of machine learning, data analytics, and automation to redefine user experiences and business processes.

This journey into the future of product management and AI is not merely a forecast but a roadmap that navigates the complex terrains of opportunities and challenges. It requires a keen understanding of the profound changes AI introduces to the product development lifecycle, the impact on user-centric design, and the transformative nature of data-driven decision-making.

The landscape we traverse is marked by the fusion of human ingenuity with the capabilities of machines. It's a realm where algorithms augment creativity, where data becomes the currency of innovation, and where products evolve dynamically in response to real-time insights. As we embark on this exploration, it is imperative to grasp the significance of

AI not as a standalone entity but as an integral force shaping the future trajectory of product management.

This book seeks to unravel the intricacies of this evolving landscape, offering a comprehensive guide for product managers, business leaders, and enthusiasts who aim to harness the potential of AI to propel their products into the future. We will delve into the collaborative synergy between human expertise and machine intelligence, explore ethical considerations in design, navigate the challenges of agile methodologies in AI projects, and decipher the critical role of continuous learning in staying ahead of the curve.

Join us on this expedition as we define the landscape where the pulse of AI harmonizes with the heartbeat of product management. Through insights, strategies, and real-world case studies, we aim to empower you to not only adapt to this changing landscape but to thrive within it, creating products that resonate with users in a world where the only constant is relentless innovation.

THE EVOLUTION OF PRODUCT MANAGEMENT

In the annals of business history, the role of product management has undergone a metamorphic transformation. From its humble origins as a function primarily concerned with overseeing product development, today's product management stands as the linchpin in orchestrating innovation, customer satisfaction, and organizational success. This evolution has been a dynamic journey, shaped by changing consumer expectations, technological advancements, and the relentless pursuit of delivering value in a rapidly shifting marketplace.

In the early days, product management was a nascent discipline, often confined to coordinating the various stages of a product's life cycle without a distinct strategic focus.

However, as markets expanded, and competition intensified, the need for a holistic approach to product development became apparent. The product manager emerged as a vital link between engineering, marketing, and sales, wielding influence over the entire product journey.

The evolution gained momentum with the recognition that successful products were not merely the result of technical prowess but required a deep understanding of customer needs and market dynamics. Product managers transitioned from being taskmasters to strategic visionaries, championing user-centric design principles and advocating for products that transcend mere features to become solutions aligning seamlessly with customer desires.

As technology advanced, so did the challenges and opportunities for product managers. The advent of the internet era brought with it a digital revolution, transforming how products were conceptualized, developed, and delivered. The role of product management expanded to navigate the complexities of online platforms, e-commerce, and digital marketing, demanding a new set of skills and a heightened focus on adaptability.

In recent years, the evolution of product management has been significantly influenced by the rise of artificial intelligence (AI) and data-driven decision-making. Product managers are no longer solely stewards of tangible products; they are orchestrators of intelligent systems, leveraging machine learning algorithms to anticipate user needs, optimize experiences, and drive innovation at an unprecedented pace.

This book seeks to unravel the layers of this evolutionary tapestry, providing insights into the historical context that shaped modern product management and forecasting the trajectory that lies ahead. Through the exploration of key milestones, industry shifts, and the infusion of emerging technologies, we aim to equip product managers, aspiring professionals, and business leaders with a nuanced understanding of the evolution that propels this dynamic discipline into the future.

Join us on this journey through time, as we trace the path from product management's humble beginnings to its current state, and peer into the horizon where innovation, customer-centricity, and technological prowess converge to define the next chapter in the evolution of product management.

THE RISE OF ARTIFICIAL INTELLIGENCE

In the realm of technological progress, few phenomena have captured the imagination and transformed the landscape as profoundly as the ascent of Artificial Intelligence (AI). Once relegated to the realm of science fiction, AI has emerged from the confines of imagination to become an omnipresent force shaping the present and defining the future. Its rise marks a pivotal moment in the evolution of human-machine interaction, disrupting industries, challenging conventional wisdom, and heralding an era where machines not only mimic human intelligence but, in many ways, surpass it.

As we stand on the precipice of this transformative age, it is essential to delve into the genesis, development, and implications of AI. The story of AI is one of relentless pursuit — an ongoing quest to imbue machines with cognitive abilities that were once considered exclusive to human intellect. From the pioneering days of symbolic reasoning to the current era of machine learning and neural networks, the trajectory of AI is a testament to the insatiable human appetite for pushing the boundaries of what is possible.

The rise of AI is inseparable from the exponential growth in computational power, the vast accumulation of data, and breakthroughs in algorithmic efficiency. It is a story that intertwines technological innovation with an unwavering determination to unlock the mysteries of intelligence. The result is a tapestry of advancements that have given rise to intelligent systems capable of speech recognition, image analysis, natural language understanding, and decision-making – tasks once reserved exclusively for the human mind.

In the business landscape, AI has transcended novelty to become a strategic imperative. From optimizing operational processes and enhancing customer experiences to revolutionizing product development and decision-making, organizations across industries are harnessing the power of AI to gain a competitive edge. The rise of AI is not just about automating tasks; it's about augmenting human capabilities, fostering innovation, and redefining the very fabric of work and industry.

This book seeks to unravel the layers of the AI narrative, offering a comprehensive exploration of its rise, impact, and potential future trajectories. Through an examination of key milestones, ethical considerations, and the convergence of AI with product management, we aim to provide readers with a nuanced understanding of this unprecedented technological revolution. Join us on a journey through the annals of AI's ascent – from its conceptual roots to the present-day algorithms reshaping our world – and contemplate the profound implications as we navigate the intricate interplay between human ingenuity and machine intelligence.

1. THE CONFLUENCE OF PRODUCT MANAGEMENT AND AI

UNDERSTANDING THE INTERSECTION

In the dynamic landscape of technological innovation, the intersection of Product Management and Artificial Intelligence (AI) represents a pivotal convergence that transcends traditional boundaries and reshapes the very essence of how products are conceived, developed, and delivered. This chapter embarks on a journey to unravel the intricate interplay between these two domains, exploring the synergies that arise when human ingenuity meets the transformative power of intelligent machines.

The Collaborative Synergy

Product Management has traditionally been characterized by its focus on understanding customer needs, envisioning solutions, and guiding the product development process. However, with the advent of Artificial Intelligence (AI), the landscape of Product Management has undergone a transformative shift. This shift is marked by the emergence of a collaborative synergy, where human intuition, creativity, and strategic thinking intersect with the analytical prowess, automation capabilities, and predictive insights offered by AI systems.

At its core, this collaborative synergy represents a fusion of human ingenuity with machine intelligence, resulting in a dynamic partnership that amplifies the strengths of both entities. Human Product Managers bring a deep understanding of market dynamics, user behaviors, and strategic vision to the table. They possess the ability to empathize with users, identify unmet needs, and envision innovative solutions that resonate with their target audience.

On the other hand, AI systems offer a wealth of capabilities that augment and enhance the traditional Product Management framework. These systems are adept at processing vast amounts of data, identifying patterns, and extracting actionable insights at scale. Through machine learning algorithms, AI systems can analyze historical data, predict future trends, and optimize decision-making processes in real-time. Additionally, AI-powered automation tools streamline repetitive tasks, enabling Product Managers to focus their time and energy on high-impact activities such as strategic planning, creative ideation, and stakeholder engagement.

The collaborative synergy between human Product Managers and AI systems transcends the boundaries of traditional product development approaches. It enables teams to leverage the complementary strengths of both entities, leading to the creation of innovative, adaptive, and intelligent products that meet the evolving needs of users and businesses alike.

In this symbiotic relationship, human Product Managers act as orchestrators, guiding the strategic direction of AI-powered products and ensuring alignment with overarching business objectives. They provide context, domain expertise, and qualitative insights that inform the design and implementation of AI algorithms and systems. Meanwhile, AI systems serve as invaluable allies, offering predictive analytics, automated decision-making, and personalized recommendations that enhance the user experience and drive business outcomes.

Together, human Product Managers and AI systems form a collaborative partnership that transcends the limitations of traditional product development paradigms. They represent a new frontier in Product Management, where the fusion of human creativity and machine intelligence gives rise to groundbreaking innovations, transformative experiences, and sustainable competitive advantages in the digital era.

Redefining Product Capabilities

The integration of Artificial Intelligence (AI) into products heralds a paradigm shift in their capabilities. No longer bound by static functionalities, products infused with AI exhibit a dynamic responsiveness to user behavior, learning patterns, and environmental changes. This transformative potential fundamentally alters the way products interact with users, adapt to their needs, and deliver value in real-time.

For Product Managers, understanding and harnessing this transformative potential requires navigating the complexities of AI technologies such as machine learning algorithms, natural language processing, and predictive analytics. It entails embracing AI not merely as a tool but as a fundamental enabler of product evolution and innovation.

At its core, redefining product capabilities with AI involves several key principles:

1. Dynamic Responsiveness:
AI-powered products can dynamically respond to user interactions, preferences, and contextual cues. Through machine learning algorithms, products can analyze user behavior patterns, identify trends, and adapt their functionalities and content in real-time. This dynamic responsiveness enables products to provide personalized experiences, anticipate user needs, and deliver relevant recommendations that enhance user engagement and satisfaction.

2. Continuous Learning:

AI empowers products to learn and improve over time through continuous feedback loops. By ingesting and analyzing large volumes of data, products can iteratively refine their algorithms, models, and predictions to become more accurate, effective, and adaptive. Product Managers play a critical role in facilitating this continuous learning process, ensuring that products evolve and adapt to changing user preferences, market dynamics, and technological advancements.

3. Anticipatory Intelligence:

AI enables products to go beyond merely reacting to user inputs and instead anticipate user needs and preferences proactively. Through predictive analytics and pattern recognition, products can forecast user behavior, anticipate future trends, and preemptively offer relevant solutions and recommendations. This anticipatory intelligence enhances the user experience by streamlining decision-making processes, reducing friction, and delivering value ahead of user expectations.

4. Real-time Adaptation:

AI-powered products excel in adapting to changing environments, contexts, and user requirements in real-time. Whether it's adjusting content recommendations based on current browsing behavior or optimizing pricing strategies based on market demand, AI enables products to dynamically adapt their strategies and tactics to maximize effectiveness and relevance. Product Managers leverage AI-driven insights and automation capabilities to orchestrate these real-time adaptations, ensuring that products remain agile, competitive, and responsive to evolving market conditions.

Redefining product capabilities with AI involves leveraging its transformative potential to enable dynamic responsiveness, continuous learning, anticipatory intelligence, and real-time adaptation. Product Managers play a pivotal role in driving this transformation, guiding the strategic integration of AI into products and orchestrating their evolution to meet the ever-changing needs and expectations of users in the digital age.

The Impact on Product Development Lifecycle

The integration of Artificial Intelligence (AI) into the realm of Product Management heralds a profound transformation in the traditional product development lifecycle. Agile methodologies, which have long been the cornerstone of nimble and iterative product development, now intersect with AI-driven processes, ushering in a new era of accelerated innovation and adaptability.

At the heart of this transformation lies the need for Product Managers to adapt to the accelerated pace of development facilitated by AI. Gone are the days of linear and sequential product development cycles; instead, Product Managers must embrace a more iterative and dynamic approach that leverages AI to enhance efficiency, reduce time-to-market, and continually iterate based on data-driven insights.

Key aspects of the impact of AI on the product development lifecycle include:

1. Integration of AI into Agile Methodologies:
Agile methodologies, with their emphasis on flexibility, collaboration, and rapid iteration, provide an ideal framework for incorporating AI into the product development lifecycle. Product Managers collaborate closely with cross-functional teams, including data scientists, engineers, designers, and stakeholders, to integrate AI-driven capabilities seamlessly into the development process. Agile ceremonies such as sprint planning, daily stand-ups, and retrospectives adapt to accommodate the iterative nature of AI development, with a

focus on delivering value incrementally and responding quickly to changing requirements and feedback.

2. Accelerated Iteration and Experimentation:
AI enables Product Managers to accelerate the pace of iteration and experimentation throughout the product development lifecycle. Machine learning algorithms analyze vast amounts of data to generate insights, identify opportunities, and inform decision-making in real-time. Product Managers leverage AI-driven analytics and experimentation tools to conduct A/B tests, optimize features, and validate hypotheses rapidly. This accelerated iteration cycle allows teams to iterate on product features, refine user experiences, and address pain points more efficiently, leading to faster time-to-market and improved product-market fit.

3. Continuous Learning and Adaptation:
AI-powered products can learn and adapt continuously based on user interactions, feedback, and environmental changes. Product Managers leverage AI-driven insights and analytics to monitor user behavior, track key performance indicators, and identify trends and patterns in real-time. This continuous learning loop enables teams to adapt their product strategies, prioritize feature development, and pivot quickly in response to evolving market dynamics and user needs. Product Managers play a crucial role in facilitating this continuous learning and adaptation process, ensuring that AI-powered products remain agile, competitive, and relevant in the ever-changing digital landscape.

4. Data-Driven Decision Making:
AI empowers Product Managers to make data-driven decisions throughout the product development lifecycle. Machine learning algorithms analyze large volumes of data to uncover actionable insights, predict outcomes, and inform strategic decision-making. Product Managers leverage AI-driven analytics dashboards, predictive models, and

recommendation engines to prioritize product features, allocate resources, and optimize product strategies based on quantifiable metrics and performance indicators. This data-driven approach enables teams to make informed decisions, mitigate risks, and maximize the impact of their product development efforts.

The integration of AI into the product development lifecycle revolutionizes the way Product Managers conceive, build, and iterate on products. By embracing AI-driven methodologies, Product Managers can accelerate innovation, enhance efficiency, and drive continuous improvement throughout the product lifecycle, ultimately delivering more valuable and impactful products to market in less time.

Beyond Features

In the era of Artificial Intelligence (AI), the role of products transcends traditional notions of mere features. Instead, products evolve into intelligent companions, capable of adapting to individual user preferences, personalizing experiences, and offering solutions that extend beyond the expected functionalities. This paradigm shift challenges Product Managers to move beyond conventional feature-focused thinking and embrace a holistic view of product development.

At the core of this transformation lies the concept of the product as an evolving ecosystem, responsive to the ever-changing needs and expectations of its users. Rather than viewing products as static entities defined by a fixed set of features, Product Managers must adopt a dynamic mindset that recognizes the fluid nature of user interactions, preferences, and contexts.

Key aspects of this shift include:

1. Personalized Experiences:

AI enables products to deliver highly personalized experiences tailored to the unique preferences, behaviors, and contexts of individual users. By leveraging machine learning algorithms and predictive analytics, products can analyze user data in real time to anticipate needs, make recommendations, and adapt their functionalities accordingly. Product Managers play a critical role in defining the parameters of personalization, identifying relevant data sources, and ensuring that personalized experiences align with broader product goals and user expectations.

2. Adaptive Functionality:

In the era of AI, products possess the ability to adapt their functionalities dynamically based on changing user requirements and environmental factors. Through techniques such as reinforcement learning and contextual awareness, products can learn from user interactions, optimize their performance, and evolve to better meet user needs. Product Managers collaborate with engineering and data science teams to design adaptive algorithms, define feedback mechanisms, and establish governance frameworks that enable products to adapt intelligently to user feedback and environmental changes.

3. Ecosystem Integration:

AI-powered products exist within a broader ecosystem of interconnected services, devices, and platforms. Product Managers must adopt a systems thinking approach that considers the interdependencies and interactions between various components of the ecosystem. This involves collaborating with external partners, third-party developers, and API providers to integrate seamlessly with complementary services and leverage external data sources. By fostering an open and interoperable ecosystem, Product

Managers can unlock new opportunities for innovation, extend the reach of their products, and deliver enhanced value to users.

4. Continuous Evolution:
AI-driven products are not static entities but dynamic systems that evolve in response to user feedback, market trends, and technological advancements. Product Managers facilitate this continuous evolution by establishing feedback loops, monitoring performance metrics, and prioritizing feature enhancements based on user insights and business objectives. By embracing a culture of continuous improvement and experimentation, Product Managers enable their products to remain relevant, competitive, and adaptive in the ever-changing landscape of AI-powered innovation.

In the era of AI, products transcend mere features to become intelligent companions that offer personalized experiences, adaptive functionality, and seamless ecosystem integration. Product Managers play a pivotal role in shaping this evolution, guiding their teams to embrace a holistic view of product development that prioritizes user-centricity, adaptability, and continuous evolution. By embracing this mindset, Product Managers can unlock new opportunities for innovation and deliver transformative experiences that delight users and drive long-term success.

Navigating Ethical Considerations

In the rapidly evolving landscape of AI-powered product development, Product Managers are confronted with a myriad of ethical considerations that demand careful navigation. As products become more intelligent and pervasive in users' lives, issues related to privacy, bias, and transparency come to the forefront, necessitating a proactive and conscientious approach to ethical decision-making.

1. Privacy Protection:
With the proliferation of AI-driven technologies, concerns surrounding data privacy and user consent have become increasingly prominent. Product Managers must prioritize the protection of user privacy by implementing robust data governance frameworks, ensuring compliance with relevant regulations such as GDPR and CCPA, and obtaining explicit consent for data collection and usage. By adopting privacy-by-design principles and incorporating privacy-enhancing technologies, Product Managers can mitigate privacy risks and build trust with users.

2. Bias Mitigation:
AI algorithms are susceptible to biases inherent in the data they are trained on, leading to potential discrimination and unfair treatment of certain user groups. Product Managers must proactively address bias in AI-driven solutions by implementing rigorous data validation processes, diversifying training datasets, and regularly auditing algorithmic decision-making to detect and mitigate bias. Additionally, fostering diversity and inclusion within product teams can help uncover and address unconscious biases throughout the development lifecycle.

3. Transparency and Explainability:
The opacity of AI algorithms poses challenges in terms of understanding how decisions are made and explaining them to users. Product Managers must advocate for transparency and explainability in AI-driven products by designing user interfaces that provide insights into algorithmic decision-making, disclosing the sources of data used for training models, and enabling users to understand and control the use of their data. By promoting transparency and empowering users with meaningful information, Product Managers can enhance trust and accountability in AI-powered products.

4. Responsible Use of AI:
Product Managers bear a responsibility to ensure that AI-driven solutions are deployed and used in a manner that aligns with ethical principles and societal values. This involves establishing clear guidelines and policies governing the ethical use of AI, conducting ethical impact assessments to evaluate potential risks and unintended consequences, and engaging with stakeholders to solicit feedback and address ethical concerns. By fostering a culture of responsible innovation and ethical leadership, Product Managers can uphold the integrity and credibility of AI-powered products while maximizing their positive impact on society.

Navigating ethical considerations in AI-powered product development requires a proactive and holistic approach that prioritizes user trust, fairness, and responsible use of data. Product Managers play a central role in championing ethical principles, advocating for user rights, and ensuring that AI-driven solutions are developed and deployed in a manner that respects the dignity and autonomy of individuals. By embracing ethical considerations as integral to the product development process, Product Managers can foster trust, enhance accountability, and drive positive societal impact through AI-powered innovation.

AI'S IMPACT ON TRADITIONAL PRODUCT MANAGEMENT

In the ever-evolving landscape of technological innovation, the integration of Artificial Intelligence (AI) with traditional Product Management practices marks a paradigm shift, transforming not only how products are managed but challenging the very foundations of established methodologies. This chapter delves into the profound impact of AI on traditional Product Management, exploring how intelligent systems are reshaping roles, processes, and expectations within the discipline.

Rethinking Decision-Making Processes

The integration of Artificial Intelligence (AI) into the realm of Product Management catalyzes a fundamental rethinking of decision-making processes. Traditionally reliant on human intuition, experience, and qualitative analysis, decision-making in Product Management now undergoes a transformative shift as AI injects a dose of intelligence into the process.

1. Data-Driven Insights:
AI-driven data analysis and predictive modeling provide Product Managers with unprecedented access to actionable insights derived from vast volumes of data. Machine learning algorithms sift through diverse data sources, uncovering patterns, trends, and correlations that may elude human observation. By leveraging these insights, Product Managers gain a deeper understanding of user behavior, market dynamics, and competitive landscapes, enabling more informed decision-making.

2. Real-Time Adaptability:
AI enables Product Managers to make decisions in real-time based on up-to-the-minute data streams and user interactions. Through techniques such as predictive analytics and anomaly detection, AI algorithms identify emerging trends, anticipate changes in user preferences, and alert Product Managers to potential opportunities or threats. This real-time adaptability empowers Product Managers to respond swiftly to market shifts, adjust product strategies dynamically, and capitalize on evolving customer needs.

3. Personalized Recommendations:

AI-powered recommendation engines offer Product Managers personalized insights and suggestions tailored to their specific roles and objectives. By analyzing historical data, user preferences, and contextual information, recommendation systems deliver targeted recommendations for product features, marketing strategies, and optimization opportunities. Product Managers leverage these personalized recommendations to prioritize initiatives, allocate resources effectively, and drive strategic decision-making aligned with business goals.

4. Augmented Decision-Making:

AI augments, rather than replaces, human decision-making processes in Product Management. While algorithms provide valuable insights and recommendations, Product Managers retain the final authority and accountability for decisions. AI serves as a tool for enhancing decision-making capabilities, enabling Product Managers to consider a broader range of factors, scenarios, and outcomes in their strategic deliberations. By integrating AI-driven insights with their domain expertise and strategic vision, Product Managers make more informed, data-driven decisions that drive business growth and innovation.

AI-driven decision-making in Product Management represents a paradigm shift towards data-driven, real-time, and personalized approaches to strategic planning and execution. By harnessing the power of AI to unlock actionable insights, facilitate adaptive strategies, and augment human decision-making capabilities, Product Managers navigate a dynamic landscape with confidence and agility, driving value creation and competitive advantage in an increasingly complex and fast-paced digital environment.

Accelerating Iterative Development

Agile methodologies have long served as the cornerstone of nimble product development, enabling teams to iterate quickly and respond to changing requirements. However, with the infusion of Artificial Intelligence (AI), the pace of iterative development accelerates to unprecedented levels. Machine learning algorithms, in particular, play a pivotal role in facilitating rapid prototyping, testing, and refinement, empowering Product Managers to adapt and evolve their products at a pace previously unimaginable.

1. Rapid Prototyping:
AI-driven tools and frameworks expedite the prototyping phase of product development, allowing Product Managers to explore and validate new ideas quickly. Machine learning algorithms enable the generation of prototypes based on user input, historical data, and design specifications, streamlining the iterative design process. With AI-powered prototyping tools, Product Managers can experiment with different concepts, gather feedback, and iterate rapidly to refine their product vision.

2. Agile Testing and Validation:
AI accelerates the testing and validation phase of product development by automating repetitive tasks and providing predictive insights into product performance. Machine learning algorithms analyze user feedback, engagement metrics, and usability data to identify potential issues and opportunities for improvement. Through techniques such as A/B testing and multivariate testing, Product Managers can evaluate alternative designs, features, and user experiences in real-time, iterating based on data-driven insights to optimize product performance.

3. Continuous Improvement:

AI fosters a culture of continuous improvement by enabling Product Managers to leverage real-time data and feedback loops to refine their products iteratively. Machine learning algorithms monitor user interactions, behavior patterns, and market trends, identifying areas for optimization and enhancement. Through iterative experimentation and optimization, Product Managers can fine-tune product features, user interfaces, and performance metrics, driving incremental improvements that enhance user satisfaction and drive business value.

4. Agile Deployment and Scaling:

AI streamlines the deployment and scaling of product iterations by automating deployment pipelines, scaling infrastructure dynamically, and optimizing resource allocation. Machine learning algorithms optimize release schedules, identify bottlenecks in deployment processes, and predict infrastructure requirements based on demand forecasts. By automating repetitive tasks and optimizing deployment workflows, Product Managers can accelerate the delivery of new features and updates to the market, maintaining a competitive edge in a rapidly evolving landscape.

The integration of AI accelerates iterative development processes, enabling Product Managers to prototype, test, and refine their products at an unprecedented pace. By leveraging machine learning algorithms to automate tasks, analyze data, and optimize processes, Product Managers foster a culture of agility, experimentation, and continuous improvement, driving innovation and delivering value to customers in a fast-paced digital environment.

The Rise of Intelligent Automation

As Artificial Intelligence (AI) continues to permeate various aspects of Product Management, one of its most profound impacts lies in the realm of intelligent automation. AI-powered systems and algorithms are increasingly adept at performing routine and repetitive tasks that were once the domain of human workers. This transformative shift not only streamlines operations but also frees up human resources to focus on higher-value activities such as strategic thinking, creativity, and the nuanced aspects of product development.

1. Task Automation:
AI excels at automating repetitive and mundane tasks that consume significant time and resources within the product management process. From data entry and reporting to scheduling and administrative duties, AI-powered tools and bots handle these tasks efficiently and accurately, allowing Product Managers to allocate their time and energy to more strategic endeavors.

2. Process Optimization:
Intelligent automation goes beyond task-level automation to optimize entire processes within the product management lifecycle. AI-driven workflows and decision-making systems streamline processes, eliminate bottlenecks, and ensure smoother collaboration across teams. By automating repetitive processes and standardizing workflows, Product Managers can enhance efficiency, reduce cycle times, and accelerate time-to-market for new products and features.

3. Personalized Insights and Recommendations:
AI-powered analytics platforms generate personalized insights and recommendations tailored to the specific needs and objectives of Product Managers. Machine learning algorithms analyze vast volumes of data, identify patterns, and surface actionable insights that inform decision-making and drive product innovation. By leveraging AI-driven insights, Product Managers gain a deeper understanding of user behavior, market dynamics, and competitive landscapes, enabling more informed and data-driven decision-making.

4. Augmented Decision Support:

AI augments the decision-making capabilities of Product Managers by providing real-time insights, predictive analytics, and scenario modeling. Machine learning algorithms analyze complex datasets, identify trends, and generate forecasts that aid in strategic planning and risk assessment. By leveraging AI-driven decision support tools, Product Managers can make more informed decisions, mitigate risks, and capitalize on emerging opportunities in a rapidly evolving market landscape.

The rise of intelligent automation through AI revolutionizes the way Product Managers approach their roles, enabling them to focus on strategic thinking, creativity, and value-added activities. By leveraging AI-powered tools and algorithms to automate routine tasks, optimize processes, and augment decision-making, Product Managers enhance efficiency, drive innovation, and unlock new opportunities for growth and success in the digital age.

Enhanced User-Centric Design

User-centric design has always been a central focus for product managers, emphasizing the importance of understanding and meeting user needs and preferences. With the integration of Artificial Intelligence (AI) into product development processes, user-centric design takes on a new dimension, characterized by hyper-personalization and dynamic adaptation to individual user behaviors and preferences. AI-powered tools and algorithms enable products to anticipate user needs, deliver tailored experiences, and continuously evolve based on user feedback. However, this enhanced level of personalization also raises important considerations related to privacy, transparency, and ethical use of data.

1. Hyper-Personalization:

AI-driven personalization algorithms analyze vast amounts of user data to create highly tailored experiences for individual users. By leveraging machine learning models, products can dynamically adapt their content, features, and recommendations based on factors such as browsing history, past interactions, demographic information, and real-time behavior. This level of hyper-personalization enhances user engagement, satisfaction, and loyalty by delivering relevant and contextually appropriate experiences that resonate with each user on a personal level.

2. Continuous Evolution:

AI enables products to continuously evolve and improve over time through iterative learning and adaptation. Machine learning algorithms analyze user feedback, engagement metrics, and performance data to identify areas for optimization and refinement. By iteratively testing and refining product features, interfaces, and content, product managers can ensure that their products remain aligned with evolving user needs and preferences, driving ongoing user satisfaction and retention.

3. Balancing Customization and Privacy:

As products become more personalized, product managers must navigate the delicate balance between customization and privacy concerns. AI-driven personalization raises important questions about data privacy, consent, and user control over their personal information. Product managers must prioritize transparency, provide clear explanations of how user data is used, and offer robust privacy controls to empower users to make informed choices about their data. By implementing privacy-by-design principles and adhering to regulatory requirements, product managers can build trust and confidence among users while delivering personalized experiences.

4. Ethical Considerations:

Product managers must also consider the ethical implications of AI-driven personalization, ensuring that their products adhere to ethical guidelines and principles. This includes addressing issues such as algorithmic bias, fairness, and accountability in the design and implementation of AI systems. Product managers should proactively assess the potential impact of AI-driven personalization on diverse user groups and take steps to mitigate any unintended consequences or biases that may arise.

AI enhances user-centric design by enabling hyper-personalization and continuous evolution of products based on individual user preferences and behaviors. Product managers play a crucial role in navigating the complexities of AI-driven personalization, balancing customization with privacy concerns, and ensuring ethical use of data to deliver personalized experiences that delight users while upholding trust and transparency.

Data-Driven Insights as Core Assets

In traditional Product Management, decisions often rely heavily on the experience and intuition of seasoned professionals. However, with the integration of Artificial Intelligence (AI) into the product development process, data emerges as a central and invaluable asset. Product managers must not only embrace data-driven decision-making but also foster a culture where data is recognized as a strategic resource that drives innovation and informs strategic direction.

1. Embracing Data-Driven Decision-Making:

AI enables product managers to leverage vast amounts of data to gain valuable insights into user behavior, market trends, and product performance. By analyzing data from multiple sources, including user interactions, transaction histories, and market research, product managers can make informed decisions based on empirical evidence rather than relying solely on intuition. Data-driven decision-making enables product managers to prioritize features, allocate resources effectively, and optimize product strategies to better meet user needs and business objectives.

2. Fostering a Culture of Data Literacy:
With the growing importance of data in product management, product managers must prioritize building a culture of data literacy within their teams. This involves not only acquiring the necessary technical skills to analyze and interpret data but also promoting a mindset where data-driven insights are valued and integrated into everyday decision-making processes. Product managers should provide training and resources to help team members develop their data literacy skills and encourage collaboration between cross-functional teams to leverage data effectively.

3. Integrating Analytics into Product Development:
Data-driven insights should be integrated into every stage of the product development lifecycle, from ideation to launch and beyond. Product managers can use data analytics to identify user pain points, validate product hypotheses, and measure the impact of new features and initiatives. By incorporating analytics tools and metrics into product development processes, product managers gain visibility into user engagement, conversion rates, and other key performance indicators, allowing them to iterate and optimize product strategies in real-time.

4. Leveraging AI for Advanced Analytics:
AI-powered analytics tools enable product managers to go beyond traditional data analysis techniques and uncover deeper insights from complex datasets. Machine learning algorithms can identify patterns, trends, and correlations that may not be apparent through manual analysis alone, enabling

product managers to uncover hidden opportunities and address emerging challenges. By leveraging AI for advanced analytics, product managers can gain a competitive edge in the market and drive innovation through data-driven decision-making.

Data-driven insights emerge as core assets in the era of AI-driven product management, empowering product managers to make informed decisions, foster a culture of data literacy, integrate analytics into product development processes, and leverage AI for advanced analytics. By embracing data as a strategic resource, product managers can drive innovation, optimize product performance, and deliver exceptional user experiences that drive business success.

Adapting to Uncertainty and Complexity

The integration of Artificial Intelligence (AI) into product management introduces a new layer of uncertainty and complexity. Unlike traditional product development processes, where outcomes are often predictable and static, AI-powered products operate in dynamic environments where algorithms continuously learn, evolve, and adapt based on new data and feedback. Product managers must navigate these challenges and embrace uncertainty as a core aspect of AI-driven product development.

1. Dynamic Nature of AI:
AI algorithms are inherently dynamic and adaptive, continuously learning from new data and evolving their behavior over time. This dynamic nature introduces uncertainty into the product development process, as the performance and behavior of AI-driven products may change unpredictably in response to new inputs or changes in the environment. Product managers must be prepared to embrace this uncertainty and adapt their strategies and plans accordingly.

2. Continuous Learning and Evolution:
AI-powered products require a shift from traditional, static planning approaches to a more agile and iterative mindset. Product managers must recognize that the very nature of the product may evolve as AI algorithms learn and improve. This requires a continuous feedback loop where product managers monitor performance, gather insights, and iteratively refine product features and strategies based on real-time data and user feedback.

3. Flexibility and Adaptation:
Adaptability becomes a core competency for product managers operating in AI-driven environments. Product roadmaps and plans must be flexible enough to accommodate changes in AI algorithms, market dynamics, and user preferences. Product managers must be willing to pivot quickly in response to new information or unexpected developments, adjusting priorities and strategies to align with evolving business objectives and user needs.

4. Experimentation and Iteration:
Experimentation becomes a key strategy for managing uncertainty and complexity in AI-driven product development. Product managers should embrace a culture of experimentation, where hypotheses are tested, and outcomes are measured in a controlled environment. By conducting experiments and gathering empirical data, product managers can gain valuable insights into the performance of AI algorithms and make informed decisions about future product enhancements and optimizations.

Adapting to uncertainty and complexity is a fundamental challenge for product managers in AI-driven product development. By embracing uncertainty as a core aspect of AI-powered products, adopting agile and iterative approaches, and fostering a culture of experimentation and adaptation, product managers can navigate the dynamic landscape of AI-driven product management and drive success in an ever-evolving marketplace.

As AI integrates seamlessly with traditional Product Management practices, the impact is profound and multifaceted. This chapter sets the stage for a comprehensive exploration of the evolving dynamics, presenting a landscape where intelligent systems augment the capabilities of product managers, redefine established processes, and herald a new era in product development. The journey into the confluence of Product Management and AI requires an understanding not only of the potential benefits but also the challenges and nuances that come with this transformative integration.

NEW HORIZONS: OPPORTUNITIES AND CHALLENGES

As the realms of Product Management and Artificial Intelligence (AI) converge, a new frontier of possibilities and challenges emerges, reshaping the landscape of innovation and product development. This chapter explores the horizons that unfold at this confluence, presenting a dynamic interplay of opportunities that beckon product managers to innovate and challenges that demand a strategic response.

The Era of Intelligent Innovation

The integration of Artificial Intelligence (AI) into Product Management marks a pivotal shift towards an era of intelligent innovation. Product managers are now empowered to conceive and develop products that transcend conventional boundaries, leveraging the capabilities of machine learning, natural language processing, and predictive analytics to create intelligent solutions that evolve and adapt in real-time.

33

1. Expanding Possibilities with Machine Learning:

Machine learning algorithms enable product managers to create products that continuously learn and improve over time. By analyzing vast amounts of data, machine learning models can identify patterns, trends, and correlations that may not be apparent to human observers. This opens up new possibilities for product innovation, allowing product managers to develop solutions that adapt to changing user preferences, market dynamics, and environmental factors.

2. Enhancing User Experiences with Natural Language Processing:

Natural Language Processing (NLP) technologies enable products to understand and interact with users in natural language, opening up new avenues for personalized and intuitive user experiences. Product managers can leverage NLP to create conversational interfaces, virtual assistants, and intelligent chatbots that engage users in meaningful conversations and provide valuable assistance and insights.

3. Predictive Analytics for Anticipatory Solutions:

Predictive analytics empower product managers to anticipate user needs and preferences before they arise, enabling proactive and anticipatory solutions. By analyzing historical data and user behavior patterns, predictive analytics models can forecast future trends, identify potential opportunities, and recommend personalized recommendations and actions. This enables product managers to create products that anticipate user needs and deliver value proactively.

4. Disruptive Innovation and Market Transformation:

The prospect of intelligent products powered by AI opens up new opportunities for disruptive innovation and market transformation. Product managers can leverage AI technologies to create solutions that redefine industries, revolutionize user experiences, and drive market growth. From personalized recommendations and adaptive interfaces to autonomous systems and intelligent automation, AI-driven products have the potential to reshape entire markets and create new paradigms of value creation.

The integration of AI into Product Management heralds an era of intelligent innovation, where product managers have the opportunity to create products that transcend traditional boundaries and deliver unprecedented value to users and businesses alike. By harnessing the capabilities of machine learning, natural language processing, and predictive analytics, product managers can drive transformative change and shape the future of technology and society.

Hyper-Personalization and User Engagement

In the era of AI-driven product management, one of the most significant opportunities lies in the realm of hyper-personalization. AI technologies enable product managers to create highly tailored experiences for individual users, leveraging insights from data to understand and anticipate their preferences, behaviors, and needs.

1. Dynamic Personalization:
With AI, product managers can create dynamic and adaptive experiences that adjust in real-time based on user interactions and feedback. By analyzing user data such as browsing history, purchase patterns, and demographic information, AI algorithms can personalize content, recommendations, and interactions to match each user's unique preferences and interests. This level of customization enhances user engagement and satisfaction, leading to higher retention rates and increased customer loyalty.

2. Real-Time Recommendations:
AI-powered recommendation systems enable product managers to deliver personalized recommendations to users at the right time and in the right context. By analyzing user

behavior in real time, AI algorithms can identify relevant products, content, or actions that are most likely to resonate with each user. Whether it's suggesting products based on past purchases, recommending articles based on browsing history, or providing personalized offers and promotions, AI-driven recommendation engines enhance user engagement and drive conversion rates.

3. Contextual Interactions:
AI technologies enable products to understand the context of user interactions and tailor responses accordingly. Natural language processing (NLP) algorithms allow chatbots and virtual assistants to interpret user queries and provide relevant answers or assistance in real time. By understanding the context of the conversation, AI-powered chatbots can deliver more personalized and helpful responses, leading to improved user satisfaction and engagement.

4. Balancing Customization and Privacy:
While hyper-personalization offers significant benefits in terms of user engagement, it also raises concerns about privacy and data protection. Product managers must strike the right balance between customization and privacy, ensuring that user trust remains paramount. This involves implementing robust data privacy measures, obtaining user consent for data collection and usage, and being transparent about how user data is being used to personalize experiences. By prioritizing user privacy and trust, product managers can build long-lasting relationships with their customers and differentiate their products in a crowded marketplace.

Hyper-personalization powered by AI presents product managers with an unparalleled opportunity to create highly engaging and tailored experiences for their users. By leveraging AI technologies to understand user preferences, deliver real-time recommendations, and contextualize interactions, product managers can drive increased user engagement, loyalty, and satisfaction. However, product managers must prioritize user privacy and trust, ensuring that hyper-personalization efforts are conducted responsibly and ethically.

Data-Driven Decision-Making at Scale

In the realm of AI-driven product management, data takes center stage as a powerful driver of decision-making. Product managers have access to vast datasets containing valuable information about user behavior, market dynamics, and product performance. By leveraging AI technologies such as machine learning and predictive analytics, product managers can extract deep insights from this data to inform strategic decisions and drive product innovation.

1. Leveraging Big Data:
AI enables product managers to harness big data at scale, allowing them to analyze large volumes of structured and unstructured data from diverse sources. This includes user interactions, transactional data, social media activity, and market research insights. By aggregating and analyzing this data, product managers can uncover patterns, trends, and correlations that provide valuable insights into user preferences, market dynamics, and competitive landscapes.

2. Predictive Analytics:
AI-powered predictive analytics empower product managers to forecast future trends and outcomes based on historical data and machine learning algorithms. Predictive models can anticipate user behavior, market demand, and product performance, enabling product managers to make proactive decisions and mitigate risks. Whether it's predicting customer churn, forecasting sales trends, or identifying emerging market opportunities, predictive analytics provide product

managers with valuable foresight to guide strategic decision-making.

3. Real-Time Insights:
AI enables real-time analysis of data streams, allowing product managers to gain immediate insights into user behavior and product performance. Real-time analytics dashboards provide up-to-date information on key metrics such as user engagement, conversion rates, and revenue trends. This real-time visibility enables product managers to identify emerging issues, capitalize on opportunities, and make data-driven decisions on the fly, ensuring agility and responsiveness in an ever-changing market landscape.

4. Streamlining Decision-Making Processes:
While AI empowers product managers with vast amounts of data and insights, it also presents the challenge of managing and interpreting this information effectively. Product managers must implement robust data governance frameworks and analytics processes to ensure that decision-making processes are not overwhelmed by complexity. This involves defining clear metrics, establishing data quality standards, and leveraging AI-driven tools and technologies to automate data analysis and reporting tasks.

AI-driven data analytics transforms data from a passive asset into a proactive force driving decision-making in product management. By leveraging big data, predictive analytics, and real-time insights, product managers can gain deep insights into user behavior, market trends, and product performance, enabling them to make informed decisions and drive product innovation at scale. However, product managers must implement robust data governance and analytics processes to streamline decision-making and ensure that data-driven insights are translated into actionable strategies effectively.

Continuous Learning and Adaptation

In the dynamic landscape of AI-driven product management, continuous learning and adaptation are paramount. As intelligent systems evolve and learn from user interactions and changing environments, product managers must adopt an iterative mindset to keep pace with these advancements. This shift represents a departure from traditional, more rigid development methodologies and demands a culture of agility, experimentation, and ongoing improvement within product management teams.

1. Iterative Development:
AI-driven product development thrives on iteration and experimentation. Product managers must embrace a mindset of continuous improvement, where products are developed, tested, and refined in iterative cycles. This iterative approach allows teams to adapt to changing user needs, market dynamics, and technological advancements, ensuring that products remain relevant and competitive in a rapidly evolving landscape.

2. Experimentation and Innovation:
Continuous learning encourages experimentation and innovation within product management teams. Product managers should create an environment where team members feel empowered to explore new ideas, test hypotheses, and take calculated risks. This culture of experimentation fosters creativity, drives innovation, and enables teams to discover novel solutions to complex challenges.

3. Data-Driven Insights:
AI provides product managers with access to vast amounts of data, which can be leveraged to gain actionable insights into user behavior, market trends, and product performance. By analyzing this data, product managers can identify areas for

improvement, validate assumptions, and make informed decisions about product direction and features. Data-driven insights serve as a foundation for continuous learning and adaptation, enabling teams to iterate on product iterations based on real-time feedback and data-driven experimentation.

4. Agile Mindset:

Embracing an agile mindset is essential for continuous learning and adaptation in AI-driven product management. Agile methodologies, such as Scrum and Kanban, promote flexibility, collaboration, and responsiveness to change. Product managers should foster a culture of agility within their teams, where rapid iteration, cross-functional collaboration, and feedback-driven development are prioritized. This agile mindset allows teams to quickly adapt to evolving requirements and market conditions, driving continuous improvement and innovation.

5. Lifelong Learning:

The field of AI is constantly evolving, with new technologies, techniques, and best practices emerging at a rapid pace. Product managers must commit to lifelong learning and professional development to stay abreast of these advancements. This may involve attending industry conferences, participating in online courses, and engaging in peer-to-peer learning networks. By investing in continuous learning, product managers can deepen their understanding of AI technologies, expand their skill sets, and drive innovation within their organizations.

Continuous learning and adaptation are essential principles for success in AI-driven product management. By embracing an iterative mindset, fostering a culture of experimentation, leveraging data-driven insights, embracing agile methodologies, and committing to lifelong learning, product managers can navigate the complexities of AI-driven product development and drive continuous improvement and innovation within their organizations.

Ethical Considerations in the AI Era

As AI becomes increasingly integrated into product management, ethical considerations take center stage, requiring careful navigation by product managers. The ethical implications of AI touch on various aspects, including transparency, fairness, accountability, and privacy. Product managers play a crucial role in ensuring that AI-driven systems are developed and deployed responsibly, prioritizing user trust and societal well-being.

1. Transparency:
Transparency is essential in the deployment of AI systems, as users have the right to understand how their data is being used and how decisions are made. Product managers must ensure that AI algorithms and models are transparent and explainable, allowing users to comprehend the logic behind recommendations and decisions. By providing transparency, product managers can build trust with users and mitigate concerns about the opacity of AI-driven systems.

2. Fairness:
Fairness is a critical ethical consideration in AI, as biased algorithms can perpetuate discrimination and inequality. Product managers must actively work to identify and mitigate biases in AI systems, ensuring that they treat all users fairly and impartially. This may involve conducting bias audits, implementing fairness-aware algorithms, and establishing diverse and inclusive development teams. By prioritizing fairness, product managers can help build AI systems that promote equity and justice.

3. Accountability:

Accountability is another key aspect of ethical AI, as it ensures that developers and users are held responsible for the outcomes of AI-driven systems. Product managers must establish clear lines of accountability for AI products, defining roles and responsibilities for all stakeholders involved in their development and deployment. Additionally, product managers should implement mechanisms for auditing and monitoring AI systems, enabling timely intervention in the event of unintended consequences or ethical violations.

4. Privacy:

Privacy considerations are paramount in the era of AI, as intelligent systems often rely on vast amounts of personal data to make predictions and recommendations. Product managers must prioritize user privacy and data protection, adhering to stringent privacy regulations and industry standards. This may involve implementing robust data governance frameworks, obtaining informed consent from users, and adopting privacy-preserving technologies such as federated learning and differential privacy. By safeguarding user privacy, product managers can build trust and confidence in AI-driven products.

5. Responsible Innovation:

Ultimately, product managers must embrace responsible innovation, ensuring that AI-driven products are developed and deployed in a manner that aligns with ethical principles and societal values. This requires a proactive approach to ethical decision-making throughout the product lifecycle, from design and development to deployment and beyond. Product managers should engage with stakeholders, including users, policymakers, and advocacy groups, to solicit feedback and address concerns related to ethical AI. By prioritizing responsible innovation, product managers can help shape a future where AI benefits society while minimizing potential harm.

Ethical considerations are paramount in the AI era, and product managers play a pivotal role in navigating these complex ethical landscapes. By prioritizing transparency, fairness, accountability, privacy, and responsible innovation, product managers can build AI-driven products that enhance user trust, promote equity, and contribute positively to society.

Reskilling and Collaborative Teams

As the realms of Product Management and AI converge, there arises a pressing need for reskilling and upskilling teams to navigate the complexities of this integration effectively. Product managers and their teams must embark on a journey of acquiring new skills, embracing emerging technologies, and fostering collaborative environments conducive to innovation and growth.

1. Acquiring New Skills:
Product managers and their teams must embark on a continuous learning journey to acquire the necessary skills for navigating the AI landscape. This includes developing proficiency in data science, machine learning, and other AI-related technologies, as well as gaining insights into the ethical, legal, and societal implications of AI. Product managers may need to undergo training programs, attend workshops, and engage in self-study to stay abreast of the latest developments in AI and their implications for product management.

2. Embracing Emerging Technologies:
With AI becoming increasingly integrated into product development processes, product managers must embrace emerging technologies and tools that facilitate AI-driven innovation. This may involve leveraging AI platforms, frameworks, and libraries to streamline development workflows, automate repetitive tasks, and enhance decision-

making processes. Product managers should stay informed about emerging trends and best practices in AI, experimenting with new tools and techniques to drive product innovation and competitiveness.

3. Fostering Collaboration:
Collaboration is essential in the AI era, as product managers and their teams must work closely with data scientists, engineers, designers, and domain experts to develop AI-driven solutions that meet user needs and business objectives. Product managers should foster a culture of collaboration and cross-functional teamwork, encouraging open communication, knowledge sharing, and idea generation. By breaking down silos and leveraging the diverse expertise within their teams, product managers can harness the full potential of AI to drive product innovation and success.

4. Bridging the Gap:
One of the key challenges in reskilling teams for AI integration is bridging the gap between technical and non-technical stakeholders. Product managers must ensure effective communication and understanding between data scientists, engineers, and domain experts, translating technical concepts into business terms and vice versa. This may involve organizing cross-functional training sessions, facilitating knowledge exchange forums, and fostering a culture of learning and collaboration across the organization.

5. Nurturing a Learning Culture:
Lastly, product managers should nurture a learning culture within their teams, where continuous improvement, experimentation, and knowledge sharing are encouraged and celebrated. This involves creating opportunities for skill development, providing access to resources and training programs, and recognizing and rewarding team members for their contributions to learning and innovation. By fostering a

learning culture, product managers can empower their teams to adapt to the evolving demands of the AI landscape and drive sustainable growth and success.

Reskilling and collaborative teamwork are essential components of navigating the intersection of Product Management and AI. By acquiring new skills, embracing emerging technologies, fostering collaboration, bridging the gap between technical and non-technical stakeholders, and nurturing a learning culture, product managers can position their teams for success in the AI era and drive innovation and growth in their organizations.

As we venture into these new horizons, the opportunities are vast, promising a future where intelligent products redefine industries and user expectations. Simultaneously, the challenges are nuanced, demanding a strategic and ethical approach to navigate the complexities of this transformative confluence. This chapter sets the stage for a comprehensive exploration of the dynamic landscape that unfolds as Product Management and AI converge, inviting product managers to seize the opportunities and tackle the challenges on this exciting journey of innovation.

2. AI-POWERED PRODUCT DEVELOPMENT

ACCELERATING INNOVATION WITH AI

In the dynamic landscape of product development, the infusion of Artificial Intelligence (AI) brings forth a transformative wave, reshaping the very essence of how products are conceived, created, and brought to market. This chapter delves into the realm of AI-powered product development, exploring the myriad ways in which intelligent systems accelerate innovation, redefine processes, and open new frontiers in the quest for groundbreaking products.

The Intelligent Ideation Process

In the realm of Product Management, the ideation process serves as the cornerstone for innovation and product development. With the integration of AI, this process transforms, becoming more dynamic, data-driven, and creatively charged than ever before. The emergence of intelligent algorithms and machine learning models opens up new avenues for generating novel ideas and uncovering innovative opportunities.

1. Harnessing Data Insights:
AI empowers product managers to leverage vast datasets and analytics tools to gain deep insights into market trends, user behavior, and competitor activities. By analyzing this wealth of data, product managers can identify emerging patterns, detect latent needs, and uncover untapped opportunities for innovation. Whether it's mining social media feeds for consumer sentiment or analyzing customer support

46

tickets for pain points, AI-driven data analysis provides a rich source of inspiration for the ideation process.

2. Uncovering User Needs:
One of the key benefits of AI in ideation is its ability to uncover latent user needs and preferences. By analyzing user interactions, feedback, and engagement metrics, AI algorithms can identify gaps in existing products or services and suggest potential areas for improvement or innovation. For example, sentiment analysis tools can parse through customer reviews to uncover common pain points or desires, providing valuable insights for product enhancement or new feature development.

3. Enhancing Creativity:
AI injects a surge of creativity into the ideation process, offering tools that go beyond traditional brainstorming. Intelligent algorithms can analyze diverse sources of inspiration, from consumer trends to cultural movements, to generate novel ideas that resonate with target audiences. Whether it's generating product name suggestions, designing user interfaces, or conceptualizing marketing campaigns, AI-driven creativity tools provide product managers with a wealth of possibilities for innovation.

4. Mitigating Bias:
Another advantage of AI in ideation is its ability to mitigate human biases and preconceptions that may limit creativity. Unlike humans, AI algorithms are not influenced by personal biases or subjective opinions, allowing for a more objective and data-driven approach to idea generation. By relying on AI-driven insights and recommendations, product managers can ensure that the ideation process is inclusive, unbiased, and focused on addressing genuine user needs and market opportunities.

5. Iterative Refinement:
The intelligent ideation process is not a one-time event but rather an iterative journey of exploration and refinement. Product managers leverage AI to continuously generate, evaluate, and iterate on ideas, refining them based on user feedback, market validation, and business objectives. Through rapid prototyping, user testing, and data-driven experimentation, product managers can validate and prioritize ideas, ensuring that only the most promising concepts are pursued further.

the integration of AI transforms the ideation process into a dynamic and data-driven endeavor, empowering product managers to uncover new opportunities, unleash creativity, and drive innovation. By harnessing the power of AI to analyze data insights, uncover user needs, enhance creativity, mitigate bias, and iteratively refine ideas, product managers can unlock the full potential of intelligent ideation and create products that truly resonate with users and drive business success.

Rapid Prototyping and Iterative Refinement

In the dynamic landscape of product development, speed and agility are paramount. Rapid prototyping, facilitated by AI, has emerged as a cornerstone of modern product management practices. This approach enables product managers to swiftly translate ideas into tangible prototypes, iterate on them based on user feedback, and refine them iteratively to meet evolving user needs and market demands.

1. Accelerated Development Cycles:
AI-driven rapid prototyping expedites the product development lifecycle by streamlining the process of creating and testing prototypes. Traditional methods of prototyping often involve time-consuming manual processes and require extensive resources. With AI, product managers can leverage

automated tools and algorithms to generate prototypes rapidly, reducing time-to-market and enabling faster iterations.

2. Simulation and Prediction:
AI-powered prototyping tools enable product managers to simulate various scenarios and predict outcomes with a high degree of accuracy. By feeding historical data, user inputs, and environmental variables into machine learning models, product managers can anticipate how users will interact with the prototype and predict the potential impact of design decisions. This predictive capability empowers product managers to make informed decisions and refine prototypes more effectively.

3. Real-Time Feedback Loops:
AI facilitates real-time feedback loops that enable product managers to gather user feedback promptly and incorporate it into prototype iterations. Through features such as sentiment analysis, user behavior tracking, and A/B testing, AI-driven prototyping tools provide actionable insights into user preferences, pain points, and preferences. Product managers can use this feedback to refine prototypes iteratively, ensuring that the final product meets user expectations and delivers value.

4. Continuous Improvement:
The iterative nature of AI-driven prototyping fosters a culture of continuous improvement within product development teams. By embracing a mindset of experimentation and iteration, product managers can leverage AI to explore alternative design options, test hypotheses, and refine prototypes incrementally. This iterative approach allows product managers to evolve their prototypes based on user feedback and market insights, leading to more robust and user-centric final products.

5. Agile Responsiveness:

AI-powered rapid prototyping enables product managers to respond swiftly to changing market dynamics, competitive pressures, and user needs. By iterating on prototypes quickly and efficiently, product managers can adapt their product roadmap in real time, seize emerging opportunities, and address evolving challenges. This agile responsiveness allows product managers to stay ahead of the curve and deliver products that remain relevant in a fast-paced and competitive market environment.

Rapid prototyping facilitated by AI revolutionizes the product development process by accelerating cycles, simulating outcomes, gathering real-time feedback, fostering continuous improvement, and enabling agile responsiveness. By embracing AI-driven prototyping tools and techniques, product managers can streamline their development workflows, mitigate risks, and deliver innovative products that meet the ever-changing needs of users and markets.

Predictive Analytics for Market Insight

In the realm of product management, staying ahead of market trends and understanding consumer behavior are essential for success. Predictive analytics, powered by AI, has emerged as a game-changer in providing valuable insights into future market dynamics and consumer preferences. Product managers can leverage predictive analytics to anticipate market shifts, identify emerging trends, and make data-driven decisions that steer product development efforts in the right direction.

1. Historical Data Analysis:

Predictive analytics relies on analyzing vast amounts of historical data to identify patterns, correlations, and trends. Product managers can use AI algorithms to mine historical sales data, customer demographics, online interactions, and other relevant datasets to uncover valuable insights into past market behavior. By understanding historical trends, product managers can gain insights into potential future developments and prepare their products accordingly.

2. Real-Time Market Monitoring:
AI-powered predictive analytics tools enable real-time monitoring of market dynamics, allowing product managers to stay abreast of changing consumer preferences, competitor actions, and industry trends. By aggregating and analyzing data from various sources such as social media, online forums, and industry reports, product managers can detect early signals of market shifts and adjust their product strategies accordingly. Real-time market monitoring empowers product managers to make proactive decisions and seize emerging opportunities.

3. Consumer Behavior Prediction:
Predictive analytics algorithms can also forecast future consumer behavior based on historical data and current trends. By analyzing past purchase patterns, browsing behavior, and demographic information, product managers can predict which products or features are likely to resonate with different customer segments. This insight enables product managers to tailor their product offerings, marketing campaigns, and pricing strategies to meet the evolving needs and preferences of their target audience.

4. Demand Forecasting:
AI-driven predictive analytics can help product managers forecast demand for their products with greater accuracy. By analyzing historical sales data, market trends, and external factors such as seasonality and economic indicators, product managers can predict future demand patterns and adjust their production and inventory levels accordingly. Accurate demand forecasting minimizes the risk of stockouts or

overstocking, optimizing inventory management and maximizing revenue potential.

5. Competitive Intelligence:
Predictive analytics provides product managers with valuable insights into competitor strategies, market positioning, and product performance. By analyzing competitor data, customer reviews, and industry benchmarks, product managers can identify gaps in the market, benchmark their products against competitors, and develop strategies to differentiate their offerings. Competitive intelligence enables product managers to stay ahead of the competition and capitalize on untapped market opportunities.

Predictive analytics powered by AI empower product managers with valuable insights into market trends, consumer behavior, demand forecasting, competitive intelligence, and real-time market monitoring. By leveraging predictive analytics tools and techniques, product managers can make informed decisions, mitigate risks, and capitalize on emerging opportunities, ultimately driving the success of their products in the dynamic and competitive marketplace.

Automating Repetitive Tasks

In the realm of product development, numerous tasks are repetitive, time-consuming, and prone to human error. Intelligent automation, facilitated by AI technologies, revolutionizes the way these tasks are handled, freeing up valuable human resources to focus on higher-level strategic initiatives. Here's how intelligent automation transforms various aspects of product development:

1. Data Entry and Processing:
Data entry and processing tasks, such as manually inputting data into spreadsheets or databases, are prime candidates for automation. AI-powered systems can extract data from

various sources, including documents, emails, and web forms, and automatically populate databases with accurate and structured information. By automating data entry and processing, product teams can minimize errors, streamline workflows, and ensure data consistency and integrity.

2. Testing and Quality Assurance:

Testing and quality assurance (QA) are critical stages of the product development lifecycle, ensuring that products meet high standards of performance, reliability, and user experience. AI-driven test automation tools can automatically execute test cases, identify bugs and defects, and generate detailed reports, significantly accelerating the testing process. Automated testing allows product teams to detect issues early, iterate quickly, and release high-quality products to market faster.

3. Customer Support and Service:

Customer support and service operations often involve repetitive tasks, such as responding to frequently asked questions, troubleshooting common issues, and handling routine inquiries. AI-powered chatbots and virtual assistants can automate these tasks, providing instant responses to customer queries, guiding users through troubleshooting steps, and escalating complex issues to human agents when necessary. Automated customer support enhances efficiency, improves response times, and enhances the overall customer experience.

4. Content Generation and Personalization:

Content generation and personalization are essential aspects of product marketing and user engagement strategies. AI-driven content generation tools can automate the creation of personalized marketing materials, product recommendations, and user communications based on individual preferences and behavior patterns. By leveraging AI to automate content generation and personalization, product teams can deliver highly relevant and engaging content to users at scale, driving user engagement and conversion rates.

5. Workflow and Process Automation:
AI technologies enable the automation of various workflow and process management tasks, such as project scheduling, task assignment, and progress tracking. AI-powered project management tools can analyze project data, predict potential bottlenecks, and dynamically adjust project schedules and resource allocations to optimize efficiency and productivity. Workflow automation streamlines collaboration, enhances visibility, and enables product teams to focus on high-priority tasks and strategic initiatives.

Intelligent automation powered by AI revolutionizes product development by automating repetitive tasks, accelerating processes, enhancing efficiency, and freeing up human resources to focus on strategic thinking, creativity, and innovation. By embracing intelligent automation technologies, product teams can streamline workflows, improve productivity, and deliver high-quality products and services to market faster and more efficiently than ever before.

Dynamic Adaptation to User Behavior

In the era of AI-powered product management, dynamic adaptation to user behavior emerges as a game-changer. Traditional products often offer static experiences, providing the same features and content to all users regardless of their preferences or behaviors. However, AI technologies enable products to evolve and adapt in real time based on user interactions, feedback, and contextual cues. Here's how dynamic adaptation to user behavior unfolds in the AI-driven product landscape:

1. Personalized Recommendations:
AI algorithms analyze user behavior, such as browsing history, purchase patterns, and engagement metrics, to generate personalized recommendations tailored to each user's preferences and interests. Whether it's suggesting relevant products, articles, or content recommendations, AI-driven recommendation engines dynamically adapt to user behavior, ensuring that users receive personalized experiences that resonate with their unique preferences.

2. Adaptive User Interfaces:
AI-powered user interfaces can dynamically adapt their layout, content, and functionality based on user behavior and contextual factors. For example, an e-commerce website may adjust its navigation menu, product listings, and promotional banners based on a user's browsing history, location, or past interactions with the site. Adaptive user interfaces enhance usability, streamline navigation, and optimize the user experience for each user.

3. Context-Aware Interactions:
AI enables products to understand and respond to the contextual cues and environmental factors surrounding user interactions. For instance, a smart home device equipped with AI capabilities may adjust its behavior based on factors such as time of day, user preferences, and sensor data. By leveraging context-aware interactions, products can anticipate user needs, provide timely assistance, and deliver seamless experiences tailored to the user's current situation.

4. Continuous Learning and Improvement:
AI-powered products continuously learn from user behavior, iteratively refining their recommendations, predictions, and responses over time. Through techniques such as reinforcement learning and adaptive algorithms, products adapt and improve based on feedback loops, user interactions, and evolving preferences. Continuous learning

enables products to stay ahead of changing user needs and preferences, ensuring ongoing relevance and engagement.

5. Predictive Personalization:
AI-driven predictive analytics enable products to anticipate user preferences and behavior, proactively personalizing experiences before users even express their needs. For example, a music streaming service may curate personalized playlists based on a user's listening history, mood, and preferences, anticipating their musical tastes and mood preferences. Predictive personalization enhances user engagement, satisfaction, and loyalty by delivering tailored experiences that exceed user expectations.

Dynamic adaptation to user behavior powered by AI technologies revolutionizes product management by creating personalized, context-aware experiences that evolve with each user interaction. By leveraging AI-driven capabilities such as personalized recommendations, adaptive user interfaces, and context-aware interactions, product managers can deliver highly engaging, relevant, and tailored experiences that delight users and drive business success.

Augmented Collaboration in Cross-Functional Teams

In the realm of AI-powered product management, augmented collaboration within cross-functional teams emerges as a cornerstone of success. Traditional product development often siloes teams based on their respective roles and expertise, leading to communication barriers and inefficiencies. However, AI technologies serve as a catalyst for augmented collaboration, enabling product managers, data scientists, engineers, and designers to work together seamlessly toward common goals. Here's how augmented collaboration unfolds in cross-functional teams:

1. Shared Understanding and Language:

AI serves as a common ground for cross-functional teams, fostering a shared understanding and language around data-driven insights, predictive analytics, and machine learning algorithms. Product managers, data scientists, engineers, and designers gain a deeper appreciation for each other's expertise and perspectives, facilitating more effective communication and collaboration.

2. Data-Driven Decision-Making:

AI empowers cross-functional teams to make informed decisions based on data-driven insights and predictive analytics. By leveraging AI-powered tools and technologies, teams can analyze large datasets, uncover patterns, and extract actionable insights that inform strategic decisions and product development initiatives. Data-driven decision-making ensures that cross-functional teams align their efforts with business objectives and user needs.

3. Iterative Experimentation and Learning:

AI facilitates iterative experimentation and learning within cross-functional teams. Product managers, data scientists, and engineers collaborate to design experiments, test hypotheses, and iterate on product features based on real-time feedback and insights. By embracing a culture of experimentation and continuous improvement, teams can optimize product performance, enhance user experiences, and drive innovation.

4. Coordinated Execution and Delivery:

AI streamlines coordination and execution within cross-functional teams, ensuring that product development initiatives are delivered on time and within budget. Project management tools powered by AI enable teams to allocate resources, track progress, and manage dependencies effectively, minimizing delays and bottlenecks. Coordinated execution and delivery are essential for meeting deadlines, achieving milestones, and delivering high-quality products to market.

5. Agile Adaptation to Change:
AI fosters agile adaptation to change within cross-functional teams, enabling them to respond rapidly to evolving market dynamics, user preferences, and technological trends. By embracing flexibility, resilience, and agility, teams can pivot quickly, adjust strategies, and course-correct as needed to stay ahead of the competition and deliver value to customers.

Augmented collaboration in cross-functional teams powered by AI technologies enhances communication, decision-making, experimentation, execution, and adaptation. By leveraging AI as a catalyst for collaboration, product managers, data scientists, engineers, and designers can harness the collective intelligence and creativity of their teams to drive innovation, deliver exceptional products, and achieve business success.

Enhancing Quality Assurance with AI

In the realm of AI-powered product management, the role of AI in quality assurance (QA) emerges as a transformative force, revolutionizing traditional testing methodologies and approaches. Here's how AI enhances quality assurance in product development:

1. Automated Test Case Generation:
AI algorithms can automatically generate test cases based on requirements, specifications, and historical data. By analyzing past testing scenarios and identifying common patterns, AI-driven test case generation accelerates the testing process, ensuring comprehensive coverage and minimizing manual effort.

2. Intelligent Test Prioritization:

AI-powered QA tools prioritize test cases based on their likelihood of uncovering critical defects or vulnerabilities. Machine learning models analyze historical data on bug severity, code changes, and test results to intelligently prioritize tests, focusing resources on areas of highest risk or impact.

3. Real-Time Anomaly Detection:

AI enables real-time anomaly detection during testing, allowing QA teams to identify deviations from expected behavior or performance metrics. By monitoring system logs, user interactions, and environmental variables, AI-driven anomaly detection algorithms can flag potential issues early in the development process, reducing the likelihood of critical defects slipping through the cracks.

4. Predictive Maintenance and Monitoring:

AI facilitates predictive maintenance and monitoring of software systems, proactively identifying potential issues before they escalate into full-blown problems. By analyzing historical data on system performance, resource utilization, and user feedback, AI models can predict when and where failures are likely to occur, enabling preemptive action to mitigate risks and ensure system reliability.

5. Intelligent Test Result Analysis:

AI-powered tools analyze test results and identify patterns, trends, and correlations that may indicate underlying issues or areas for improvement. Natural language processing (NLP) algorithms parse test logs, error messages, and user feedback to extract actionable insights, empowering QA teams to diagnose problems more efficiently and make data-driven decisions.

6. Adaptive Testing Strategies:
AI enables adaptive testing strategies that evolve in response to changing requirements, user feedback, and environmental conditions. Machine learning algorithms continuously learn from testing outcomes and adjust testing strategies dynamically, ensuring that QA efforts remain aligned with evolving project goals and priorities.

7. Continuous Improvement and Learning:
AI fosters a culture of continuous improvement and learning within QA teams, leveraging feedback loops and historical data to refine testing processes and methodologies over time. By embracing experimentation, iteration, and collaboration, QA teams can optimize their workflows, enhance testing effectiveness, and deliver higher-quality products to market.

The integration of AI into quality assurance processes enhances testing efficiency, effectiveness, and reliability. By automating test case generation, prioritizing tests intelligently, detecting anomalies in real time, and facilitating predictive maintenance, AI empowers QA teams to deliver high-quality products that meet or exceed user expectations.

Ethical Considerations in AI-Powered Development

The integration of AI into product development introduces a host of ethical considerations that demand careful attention and proactive management. Product managers play a pivotal role in navigating these complex issues and ensuring that AI-powered systems adhere to ethical standards and principles. Here are some key ethical considerations in AI-powered development:

1. Bias and Fairness:
AI algorithms are susceptible to bias, reflecting and potentially amplifying societal biases present in the data used

for training. Product managers must proactively identify and mitigate bias in AI models to ensure fair and equitable outcomes for all users. This involves conducting bias assessments, diversifying training datasets, and implementing algorithmic transparency and explainability measures to mitigate bias-related risks.

2. Transparency and Explainability:
Transparency and explainability are essential for building user trust and confidence in AI-powered systems. Product managers must ensure that AI algorithms are transparently designed, documented, and communicated to users, enabling them to understand how decisions are made and why certain outcomes are produced. This fosters transparency, accountability, and user empowerment in the use of AI technologies.

3. Privacy and Data Protection:
AI-powered systems often rely on large volumes of user data to train and optimize models, raising privacy concerns related to data collection, storage, and usage. Product managers must prioritize user privacy and data protection, implementing robust data governance frameworks, encryption mechanisms, and access controls to safeguard sensitive information. Additionally, product managers should obtain informed consent from users regarding data collection and usage practices, ensuring compliance with relevant privacy regulations such as GDPR and CCPA.

4. Accountability and Liability:
As AI systems autonomously make decisions and take action, questions of accountability and liability arise in cases of system failures, errors, or unintended consequences. Product managers must establish clear lines of accountability and responsibility for AI-powered systems, defining roles and procedures for addressing issues such as algorithmic errors, biases, and ethical violations. This involves collaborating with

legal and compliance teams to develop policies, procedures, and risk management strategies to mitigate liability risks associated with AI deployment.

5. Societal Impact and Ethical Use Cases:
Product managers must consider the broader societal impact of AI-powered products and prioritize ethical use cases that align with societal values and norms. This involves conducting ethical impact assessments, engaging with diverse stakeholders, and soliciting feedback from impacted communities to ensure that AI technologies are deployed responsibly and ethically. Product managers should prioritize applications of AI that benefit society, promote social good, and mitigate potential harms while being cognizant of the unintended consequences and ethical dilemmas that may arise.

Ethical considerations are paramount in the development and deployment of AI-powered systems. Product managers must proactively address issues of bias, transparency, privacy, accountability, and societal impact to ensure that AI technologies are deployed responsibly, ethically, and in alignment with user expectations and societal values. By prioritizing ethical considerations throughout the product lifecycle, product managers can build trust, foster innovation, and create positive societal impact with AI-powered products and services.

This section illuminates the transformative impact of AI on product development, presenting a landscape where innovation is not just accelerated but redefined. As product managers embrace the opportunities afforded by AI, they simultaneously grapple with the responsibility of navigating ethical considerations and ensuring that the acceleration of innovation is aligned with user needs and societal expectations. In the ever-evolving journey of product development, AI emerges as a catalyst, propelling us into a future where the boundaries of innovation are continually pushed and new possibilities unfold at an unprecedented pace.

INTELLIGENT AUTOMATION IN PRODUCT LIFECYCLE

In the dynamic landscape of product development, the infusion of Artificial Intelligence (AI) heralds a new era characterized by intelligent automation. This chapter delves into the intricate ways in which AI transforms the product lifecycle, introducing efficiencies, reducing manual overhead, and elevating the entire development process to unprecedented levels of adaptability and innovation.

Automating Ideation and Conceptualization

In the realm of product development, the ideation and conceptualization phase marks the inception of innovative ideas and solutions. With the advent of AI, this phase undergoes a significant transformation, leveraging smart algorithms to automate and enhance the ideation process.

1. Data-Driven Insights:
AI-powered systems can analyze vast amounts of structured and unstructured data, including market trends, competitor strategies, consumer preferences, and historical product performance. By processing this data, AI algorithms can uncover valuable insights and patterns that inform the ideation process. For example, natural language processing (NLP) algorithms can analyze customer reviews, social media sentiments, and online discussions to identify emerging trends, pain points, and opportunities within the market landscape.

2. Predictive Modeling:

AI algorithms excel in predictive modeling, forecasting future trends and outcomes based on historical data and patterns. Product managers can leverage predictive analytics to anticipate market demands, consumer behavior shifts, and competitor strategies, enabling them to conceptualize products that are not only relevant in the present but also future-proofed against evolving market dynamics. By extrapolating insights from predictive models, product managers can make informed decisions about product features, functionalities, and positioning strategies.

3. Automated Generation of Ideas:

AI algorithms can generate a plethora of innovative ideas by synthesizing insights from data analysis, market research, and user feedback. Generative models, such as generative adversarial networks (GANs) and variational autoencoders (VAEs), can produce novel concepts, designs, and product features that align with predefined objectives and constraints. Product managers can explore a wide range of potential ideas generated by AI algorithms, selecting and refining those that hold the most promise for further development.

4. Rapid Prototyping and Validation:

Once conceptualized, AI-powered systems can facilitate rapid prototyping and validation of product ideas. Machine learning algorithms can generate prototypes based on user requirements, design specifications, and feedback, accelerating the development process and reducing time-to-market. Moreover, AI algorithms can simulate user interactions with prototypes, enabling product managers to gather real-time feedback and iterate on designs iteratively. This iterative approach fosters agility and responsiveness in the product development lifecycle, ensuring that final products meet user needs and expectations effectively.

5. Personalized Recommendations:

AI-driven recommendation engines can provide personalized suggestions and insights to product managers based on their preferences, past decisions, and performance metrics. By analyzing product manager behaviors and interactions, recommendation systems can offer tailored guidance and recommendations for ideation and conceptualization processes. This personalized approach enhances productivity, creativity, and decision-making effectiveness, empowering product managers to make informed choices and drive innovation within their organizations.

AI automates and enhances the ideation and conceptualization phase of product development by leveraging data-driven insights, predictive modeling, automated idea generation, rapid prototyping, and personalized recommendations. By harnessing the power of AI in this critical phase, product managers can unlock new opportunities, accelerate innovation, and create products that resonate with users and thrive in dynamic market environments.

Accelerating Design and Prototyping

Intelligent automation plays a pivotal role in expediting the design and prototyping phases of product development, revolutionizing traditional approaches, and enhancing efficiency. Through the integration of AI-driven tools and techniques, product managers can accelerate the design process, iterate on prototypes rapidly, and ultimately deliver a more refined end product. Here's how AI accelerates design and prototyping:

1. Automated Design Generation:

AI-powered design tools leverage machine learning algorithms to generate design alternatives automatically. These algorithms analyze design patterns, user preferences, and brand guidelines to create a multitude of design options tailored to specific objectives and constraints. By automating the design generation process, AI enables product managers to explore a broader range of possibilities and iterate on designs quickly.

2. Predictive Prototyping:
AI algorithms can predict user responses to different design elements and features, allowing product managers to anticipate usability issues and refine prototypes accordingly. By analyzing user behavior data and historical performance metrics, predictive modeling techniques enable product managers to optimize designs for enhanced user experience and engagement. Predictive prototyping accelerates the iteration cycle, reducing the time and resources required to refine prototypes.

3. Real-Time Feedback Loops:
AI facilitates real-time feedback loops between designers, product managers, and end-users, enabling rapid iteration and refinement of prototypes. Intelligent analytics tools track user interactions with prototypes, identify pain points, and surface actionable insights for design optimization. By incorporating real-time feedback into the design process, product managers can iterate on prototypes iteratively, ensuring that final designs align closely with user needs and expectations.

4. Generative Design:
AI-driven generative design techniques leverage algorithms to explore and evaluate countless design permutations based on predefined parameters and objectives. Generative design algorithms simulate evolutionary processes, generating innovative design solutions that optimize for specified criteria, such as performance, cost, or aesthetics. By automating the generation of design alternatives, AI empowers product

managers to explore unconventional design concepts and identify optimal solutions more efficiently.

5. Collaborative Design Platforms:
AI-powered collaborative design platforms facilitate seamless collaboration and communication among cross-functional teams, streamlining the design process and accelerating prototyping efforts. These platforms integrate AI-driven features, such as version control, design suggestion engines, and real-time collaboration tools, to enhance productivity and foster creativity. By providing a centralized hub for design collaboration, AI enables product managers to coordinate efforts effectively and drive the prototyping process forward.

AI accelerates the design and prototyping phases of product development by automating design generation, predicting user responses, facilitating real-time feedback loops, enabling generative design, and supporting collaborative design platforms. By harnessing the power of AI in design and prototyping, product managers can streamline workflows, iterate on designs rapidly, and deliver innovative products that meet user needs and exceed expectations.

Streamlining Development Processes

The integration of AI into development processes revolutionizes traditional workflows, enhancing efficiency, reducing errors, and accelerating the overall product development timeline. Here's how AI streamlines various aspects of the development process:

1. Automated Code Generation:
AI-powered tools automate the process of code generation, translating high-level specifications and requirements into executable code. By leveraging machine learning algorithms and natural language processing techniques, these tools analyze project requirements, design patterns, and best

practices to generate efficient and error-free code automatically. Automated code generation eliminates the need for manual coding, significantly reducing development time and minimizing the risk of human errors.

2. Intelligent Testing and Quality Assurance:
AI-driven testing tools enhance the efficiency and effectiveness of quality assurance processes by automating test case generation, execution, and analysis. Machine learning algorithms identify patterns in code changes and user interactions, predicting areas of potential defects and prioritizing test cases accordingly. Automated testing frameworks simulate user behavior, system interactions, and edge cases, ensuring comprehensive test coverage and early detection of bugs. By automating testing and quality assurance processes, AI accelerates the identification and resolution of defects, improving product quality and reliability.

3. Code Optimization and Performance Tuning:
AI algorithms analyze code repositories and runtime data to identify opportunities for code optimization and performance tuning. By detecting inefficiencies, bottlenecks, and resource-intensive operations, AI-driven optimization tools suggest code refactoring techniques and performance enhancements to improve application speed, scalability, and resource utilization. Automated code optimization streamlines the development process, enabling developers to deliver faster, more responsive, and resource-efficient applications.

4. Intelligent Bug Detection and Resolution:
AI-powered bug detection tools leverage machine learning algorithms to analyze code repositories, user feedback, and error logs, identifying potential bugs and anomalies in real-time. These tools prioritize bug reports based on severity, impact, and frequency, enabling developers to focus their efforts on critical issues first. By automating bug detection and resolution, AI accelerates the debugging process,

reducing the time and effort required to identify and fix software defects.

5. Predictive Maintenance and Monitoring:
AI-driven monitoring and maintenance tools analyze system performance metrics, user behavior patterns, and historical data to predict potential issues and proactively address them before they escalate. Machine learning algorithms detect anomalies, deviations from normal behavior, and impending failures, triggering alerts and automated remediation actions. Predictive maintenance streamlines the development process by minimizing downtime, preventing service disruptions, and optimizing resource allocation.

6. Continuous Integration and Deployment (CI/CD):
AI facilitates continuous integration and deployment practices by automating code integration, testing, and deployment processes. AI-driven CI/CD pipelines automate the building, testing, and deployment of software updates, ensuring rapid and reliable delivery of new features and enhancements. By automating repetitive tasks and minimizing manual intervention, AI accelerates the development lifecycle, enabling product managers to release updates more frequently and respond to user feedback more agilely.

AI streamlines development processes by automating code generation, testing, optimization, bug detection, maintenance, and deployment tasks. By leveraging AI-driven tools and techniques, product managers can accelerate the development timeline, improve product quality, and deliver innovative solutions more efficiently.

Predictive Analytics for Resource Allocation

Predictive analytics in resource allocation revolutionizes how product managers manage project resources throughout the product lifecycle. Here's how AI's predictive capabilities enhance resource allocation:

1. Forecasting Resource Needs:
AI analyzes historical project data, including resource utilization, task durations, and project milestones, to forecast future resource needs accurately. Machine learning algorithms identify patterns and trends in resource consumption, allowing product managers to anticipate staffing requirements, equipment needs, and budget allocations for upcoming projects or phases. By leveraging predictive analytics, product managers can proactively allocate resources based on expected demand, minimizing the risk of shortages or overages.

2. Optimizing Resource Utilization:
AI-driven predictive models optimize resource utilization by identifying opportunities to streamline workflows, reallocate resources, and eliminate bottlenecks. Machine learning algorithms analyze resource allocation patterns, identify inefficiencies, and recommend optimization strategies to improve productivity and efficiency. By optimizing resource utilization, product managers ensure that resources are allocated judiciously, maximizing their impact and minimizing waste.

3. Budget Forecasting and Management:
AI's predictive analytics capabilities enable accurate budget forecasting and management throughout the product lifecycle. Machine learning algorithms analyze historical project data, cost estimates, and budget allocations to predict future project costs and financial requirements. Product managers can use these insights to develop realistic budgets, track expenditures, and adjust spending priorities as needed to stay within budget constraints. By forecasting budget requirements with precision, AI empowers product managers

to make informed financial decisions and allocate resources effectively.

4. Identifying Risks and Mitigating Challenges:
AI analyzes historical project data and external factors to identify potential risks and challenges that may impact resource allocation. Machine learning algorithms predict project risks, such as delays, resource shortages, or scope creep, enabling product managers to proactively mitigate these challenges. By identifying risks early in the project lifecycle, product managers can develop contingency plans, allocate additional resources as needed, and adjust project timelines to minimize the impact on project delivery.

5. Real-time Monitoring and Adjustments:
AI continuously monitors project progress, resource utilization, and external factors to provide real-time insights into resource allocation. Machine learning algorithms detect deviations from planned resource allocations, alerting product managers to potential issues or opportunities for optimization. With real-time visibility into resource utilization, product managers can make timely adjustments, reallocate resources dynamically, and optimize project workflows to ensure project success.

6. Improving Project Performance:
AI's predictive analytics capabilities drive continuous improvement in project performance by identifying opportunities for optimization and efficiency gains. Machine learning algorithms analyze project data, performance metrics, and historical trends to identify areas for improvement and recommend actionable insights. By leveraging AI-driven recommendations, product managers can optimize resource allocation, streamline project workflows, and enhance project performance over time.

Predictive analytics for resource allocation enables product managers to forecast resource needs, optimize resource utilization, manage budgets effectively, identify risks, and improve project performance throughout the product lifecycle. By leveraging AI's predictive capabilities, product managers can make data-driven decisions, allocate resources judiciously, and ensure the successful delivery of projects on time and within budget.

Real-Time Data-Driven Decision Making

Real-time data-driven decision-making powered by intelligent automation revolutionizes how product managers navigate the complexities of the product lifecycle. Here's how AI facilitates real-time decision-making at every stage:

1. Continuous Data Analysis:
AI algorithms continuously analyze vast datasets from various sources, including user interactions, market trends, and performance metrics. By processing data in real-time, AI provides up-to-date insights into user behavior, preferences, and emerging trends, allowing product managers to stay informed about the evolving landscape and make data-driven decisions promptly.

2. Dynamic Performance Monitoring:
Intelligent automation enables dynamic monitoring of product performance metrics in real time. AI algorithms track key performance indicators (KPIs), such as user engagement, conversion rates, and revenue generation, providing instant feedback on the effectiveness of product features and initiatives. Product managers can quickly identify areas of improvement or optimization and adjust their strategies accordingly to maximize performance.

3. Personalized User Experiences:

AI-powered personalization algorithms analyze user data in real time to deliver personalized experiences tailored to individual preferences and behaviors. By leveraging real-time insights, product managers can dynamically adjust content, recommendations, and user interfaces to enhance user engagement and satisfaction. This real-time personalization enables products to adapt to users' evolving needs and preferences, driving increased user retention and loyalty.

4. Agile Iterative Development:

Real-time data analysis empowers agile iterative development by providing instant feedback on product features and updates. AI algorithms monitor user feedback, usage patterns, and performance metrics, allowing product managers to iterate rapidly and prioritize enhancements based on real-time insights. This agile approach enables product managers to respond quickly to user feedback, market changes, and competitive pressures, ensuring that the product remains competitive and relevant in a fast-paced environment.

5. Adaptive Marketing Strategies:

AI-driven analytics enable adaptive marketing strategies that respond to changing market conditions and user behaviors in real time. By analyzing real-time data on consumer trends, competitor activities, and market dynamics, product managers can optimize marketing campaigns, adjust messaging, and allocate resources dynamically to maximize impact and ROI. This real-time optimization ensures that marketing efforts are targeted, relevant, and effective in driving user acquisition and engagement.

6. Proactive Issue Detection and Resolution:

AI algorithms proactively detect issues and anomalies in real time, allowing product managers to address them promptly before they escalate. By monitoring system performance, user feedback, and other relevant metrics, AI identifies potential issues, such as technical glitches, user dissatisfaction, or declining performance, enabling product managers to take corrective actions swiftly. This proactive approach minimizes downtime, mitigates risks, and enhances the overall user experience.

Real-time data-driven decision-making facilitated by intelligent automation empowers product managers to stay ahead of the curve by leveraging up-to-date insights to inform strategic decisions, optimize product performance, personalize user experiences, and adapt marketing strategies dynamically. By harnessing AI's real-time capabilities, product managers can drive continuous improvement and innovation throughout the product lifecycle, ensuring the long-term success and competitiveness of their products.

Agile Integration with AI Automation

The integration of AI with agile methodologies represents a powerful synergy that enhances the adaptability and efficiency of product development processes. Here's how AI seamlessly aligns with agile principles to drive iterative development and rapid responsiveness:

1. Continuous Feedback Loops:
Agile methodologies prioritize continuous feedback loops, allowing product teams to gather input from stakeholders and users throughout the development process. AI automation complements this approach by analyzing feedback data in real time, extracting actionable insights, and providing recommendations for iterative improvements. By integrating AI-driven feedback analysis into agile workflows, product managers can ensure that development efforts remain aligned with user needs and market demands.

2. Dynamic Prioritization:

Agile development relies on dynamic prioritization to focus efforts on delivering the most valuable features and functionalities first. AI-powered algorithms analyze user data, market trends, and business metrics to inform prioritization decisions in real time. Product managers can leverage AI-driven insights to adjust feature backlogs, reprioritize tasks, and allocate resources based on evolving project requirements and strategic objectives. This dynamic prioritization ensures that development efforts remain agile and responsive to changing priorities and market conditions.

3. Predictive Planning:

Agile teams often face challenges in accurately estimating project timelines and resource requirements. AI introduces predictive planning capabilities that leverage historical data, machine learning algorithms, and predictive analytics to forecast project outcomes and identify potential bottlenecks proactively. By integrating AI-driven predictive planning tools into agile workflows, product managers can anticipate resource needs, mitigate risks, and optimize project schedules to ensure the timely delivery of high-quality products.

4. Automated Testing and Validation:

Agile development relies on automated testing and validation to maintain product quality and accelerate release cycles. AI-powered testing tools use machine learning algorithms to automate test case generation, identify edge cases, and detect defects with greater accuracy and efficiency. By integrating AI-driven testing solutions into agile development pipelines, product managers can streamline the testing process, reduce manual effort, and accelerate time-to-market while ensuring the reliability and robustness of their products.

5. Adaptive Resource Allocation:
Agile teams often need to adjust resource allocation dynamically to respond to changing project requirements and priorities. AI-driven resource allocation models analyze project data, team performance metrics, and external factors to recommend optimal resource allocations in real time. Product managers can leverage AI-driven resource allocation tools to optimize team productivity, minimize bottlenecks, and allocate resources effectively to maximize project outcomes within agile frameworks.

6. Intelligent Iterative Improvement:
Agile methodologies emphasize iterative improvement through continuous iteration and refinement of product features and functionalities. AI-powered iterative improvement tools analyze user feedback, usage data, and performance metrics to identify areas for optimization and innovation. By integrating AI-driven iterative improvement mechanisms into agile workflows, product managers can accelerate the pace of innovation, enhance product quality, and deliver greater value to users with each iteration.

The integration of AI with agile methodologies enhances the adaptability, efficiency, and effectiveness of product development processes by enabling continuous feedback loops, dynamic prioritization, predictive planning, automated testing, adaptive resource allocation, and intelligent iterative improvement. By leveraging AI-driven capabilities within agile frameworks, product managers can drive innovation, accelerate time-to-market, and deliver products that meet evolving user needs and market demands.

Enhancing Quality Assurance with Intelligent Systems

Integrating intelligent automation into quality assurance processes enhances the efficacy and efficiency of testing efforts across the product development lifecycle. Here's how AI-driven systems enhance quality assurance:

1. Automated Test Case Generation:
AI-driven testing tools leverage machine learning algorithms to automatically generate test cases based on historical data, code analysis, and user interactions. These tools analyze patterns in code changes, user behavior, and system interactions to identify critical test scenarios and generate test cases that cover a wide range of functionalities and edge cases. By automating test case generation, AI-driven systems accelerate the testing process and ensure comprehensive test coverage, reducing the likelihood of undiscovered defects.

2. Intelligent Test Prioritization:
AI-powered testing tools prioritize test execution based on factors such as code changes, defect history, and business impact. Machine learning algorithms analyze historical test results and project data to predict the likelihood of defects in specific areas of the application and prioritize test cases accordingly. By focusing testing efforts on high-risk areas and critical functionalities, AI-driven systems optimize resource utilization, accelerate defect detection, and minimize time-to-resolution.

3. Predictive Defect Detection:
AI-driven testing tools employ predictive analytics and anomaly detection techniques to identify potential defects before they manifest in production environments. These tools analyze historical defect data, code changes, and system performance metrics to detect patterns indicative of impending failures or performance degradation. By proactively identifying and addressing potential defects during the testing phase, AI-driven systems mitigate the risk of post-release issues, enhancing the reliability and robustness of the product.

4. Dynamic Test Environment Provisioning:

AI-powered testing tools automate the provisioning and configuration of test environments based on project requirements and resource availability. These tools leverage machine learning algorithms to optimize test environment configurations, allocate resources efficiently, and scale infrastructure dynamically to accommodate fluctuating testing demands. By automating test environment management, AI-driven systems reduce manual effort, accelerate test execution, and ensure consistent testing conditions across different environments.

5. Adaptive Test Case Maintenance:

AI-driven testing tools employ natural language processing (NLP) and pattern recognition techniques to analyze test case documentation, identify redundancies, and suggest optimizations. These tools analyze test case descriptions, execution results, and user feedback to detect patterns indicative of outdated or ineffective test cases. By automating test case maintenance, AI-driven systems streamline test case management processes, improve test coverage, and facilitate ongoing optimization of testing efforts.

6. Real-Time Performance Monitoring:

AI-driven testing tools monitor system performance in real-time during test execution, capturing performance metrics, and identifying performance bottlenecks. These tools employ machine learning algorithms to analyze performance data, detect anomalies, and predict potential scalability issues or resource constraints. By providing real-time insights into system performance, AI-driven systems enable proactive performance optimization, ensuring that the product meets scalability and performance requirements under varying workload conditions.

The integration of intelligent automation enhances quality assurance processes by automating test case generation, intelligently prioritizing tests, predicting defects, dynamically provisioning test environments, facilitating test case maintenance, and enabling real-time performance monitoring. By leveraging AI-driven testing tools, organizations can improve the efficiency, effectiveness, and reliability of their quality assurance efforts, ultimately delivering higher-quality products to market faster and more confidently.

Ethical Considerations in AI-Powered Automation

Ethical considerations in AI-powered automation are paramount as intelligent automation becomes increasingly integrated into various aspects of product development and decision-making processes. Here's a deeper exploration of the ethical considerations that product managers must address:

1. Bias Mitigation:
AI algorithms are susceptible to bias, reflecting the biases present in the data used to train them. Product managers must proactively identify and mitigate biases in AI models to ensure fair and equitable outcomes. This involves conducting thorough bias assessments, diversifying training datasets, and implementing bias detection and correction mechanisms. By addressing bias in AI-powered automation, product managers uphold principles of fairness and prevent discriminatory outcomes.

2. Transparency and Explainability:
Transparency is essential to foster trust and accountability in AI-powered automation. Product managers must ensure that AI algorithms and decision-making processes are transparent and explainable to users and stakeholders. This involves providing clear documentation on how AI models operate, disclosing the factors influencing automated decisions, and offering users insights into the rationale behind AI-driven recommendations. Transparent AI-powered automation

promotes user understanding and acceptance, fostering trust in the product.

3. Accountability and Oversight:
Product managers bear responsibility for the ethical use of AI-powered automation within their products. They must establish clear accountability structures and oversight mechanisms to monitor the behavior and impact of AI algorithms. This includes implementing audit trails, conducting regular ethical reviews, and establishing channels for reporting and addressing ethical concerns. By promoting accountability and transparency, product managers ensure that AI-powered automation aligns with ethical standards and regulatory requirements.

4. User Consent and Control:
Respect for user autonomy is essential in AI-powered automation. Product managers must obtain informed consent from users regarding the use of AI-driven features and automation, especially in contexts involving sensitive data or significant decision-making. Additionally, product managers should provide users with meaningful control over AI-driven functionalities, such as the ability to opt out of automated decision-making or adjust personalization settings. Empowering users with control enhances transparency and promotes the ethical use of AI-powered automation.

5. Fairness and Equity:
AI-powered automation should strive to promote fairness and equity in decision-making processes. Product managers must assess the potential impact of automated decisions on different user groups and ensure that AI algorithms do not disproportionately disadvantage certain demographics or communities. This involves implementing fairness metrics, conducting bias audits, and incorporating fairness-enhancing techniques such as algorithmic transparency and fairness-aware training. By prioritizing fairness and equity, product

managers uphold ethical principles and mitigate potential harms associated with AI-powered automation.

6. Continuous Ethical Evaluation:
Ethical considerations in AI-powered automation are dynamic and evolving. Product managers must engage in continuous ethical evaluation and reflection, staying informed about emerging ethical issues and adapting their practices accordingly. This involves fostering a culture of ethical awareness within product teams, promoting ethical education and training, and actively engaging with stakeholders to address ethical concerns. By embracing a proactive approach to ethics, product managers ensure that AI-powered automation remains aligned with ethical principles and societal values.

Ethical considerations in AI-powered automation are essential for promoting fairness, transparency, accountability, and user trust in automated decision-making processes. By addressing issues related to bias mitigation, transparency and explainability, accountability, and oversight, user consent and control, fairness, and equity, and continuous ethical evaluation, product managers uphold ethical standards and promote the responsible use of AI-powered automation in product development.

This section illuminates the profound impact of AI-powered intelligent automation on the entire product lifecycle. As product managers navigate these transformative changes, they must not only leverage the efficiencies offered by automation but also remain vigilant in addressing ethical considerations to ensure that AI becomes a responsible and value-driven partner in the journey of product development. The confluence of AI and intelligent automation unfolds as a catalyst for unprecedented efficiency, adaptability, and innovation throughout the product lifecycle.

ENHANCING DECISION-MAKING WITH PREDICTIVE ANALYTICS

In the ever-evolving landscape of product development, the fusion of Artificial Intelligence (AI) with predictive analytics emerges as a potent force, reshaping decision-making processes and propelling innovation to new heights. This chapter delves into the transformative impact of predictive analytics powered by AI, exploring how it enhances decision-making at every juncture of the product development lifecycle.

The Predictive Power of AI

The predictive power of AI revolutionizes how product managers anticipate market trends, user behavior, and product performance. Here's a detailed exploration of how AI's integration with predictive analytics empowers product managers:

1. Analyzing Historical Data:
AI algorithms excel at analyzing vast amounts of historical data to identify patterns, trends, and correlations. Product managers leverage AI-powered predictive analytics to delve into historical market data, user interactions, and product usage metrics. By examining historical trends, product managers gain insights into past performance and potential future trajectories, guiding strategic decision-making processes.

2. Forecasting Market Dynamics:
AI-powered predictive analytics enable product managers to forecast market dynamics with greater accuracy and granularity. By analyzing historical market data and external factors such as economic indicators, competitive landscape,

82

and consumer trends, AI algorithms can generate forecasts for future market conditions. Product managers leverage these forecasts to anticipate changes in demand, identify emerging opportunities, and adapt product strategies accordingly.

3. Anticipating User Behavior:
Understanding user behavior is critical for product success. AI-driven predictive analytics analyze user interactions, preferences, and engagement patterns to anticipate future behaviors. By leveraging machine learning algorithms, product managers can predict user actions such as purchasing decisions, content consumption patterns, and engagement levels. This foresight enables product managers to tailor product experiences, content recommendations, and marketing strategies to align with anticipated user behaviors.

4. Optimizing Product Performance:
Predictive analytics powered by AI help product managers optimize product performance by forecasting outcomes and identifying optimization opportunities. By analyzing historical performance metrics and conducting scenario analyses, AI algorithms can predict the impact of potential changes or interventions on key performance indicators (KPIs). Product managers use these insights to prioritize initiatives, allocate resources effectively, and drive continuous improvement in product performance.

5. Guiding Strategic Decision-Making:
AI's predictive capabilities guide strategic decision-making processes across various aspects of product management. From product roadmap planning to resource allocation and market positioning, predictive analytics inform decision-making by providing data-driven insights into future outcomes and potential risks. Product managers leverage AI-powered predictions to make informed decisions that

maximize opportunities, mitigate risks, and drive sustainable growth.

6. Enabling Proactive Adaptation:
Predictive analytics empower product managers to proactively adapt to changing market conditions and user preferences. By anticipating future trends and potential disruptions, product managers can take preemptive actions to stay ahead of the curve. Whether adjusting product features, revising marketing strategies, or exploring new market opportunities, product managers leverage AI-powered predictions to drive proactive adaptation and maintain competitive advantage.

The predictive power of AI-driven analytics equips product managers with invaluable foresight into market dynamics, user behavior, and product performance. By leveraging AI-powered predictions, product managers can make informed decisions, optimize product strategies, and drive proactive adaptation to capitalize on opportunities and navigate challenges in an ever-evolving landscape.

Forecasting Market Trends

Forecasting market trends is a crucial aspect of strategic decision-making for product managers, and AI-powered predictive analytics greatly enhance their capabilities in this regard. Here's a detailed exploration of how AI enables product managers to forecast market trends:

1. Data Analysis and Pattern Recognition:
AI algorithms excel at analyzing large volumes of historical market data to identify patterns, correlations, and trends. By processing data from diverse sources such as sales figures, customer demographics, social media interactions, and industry reports, AI algorithms can uncover insights that might not be apparent through traditional analysis methods.

Product managers leverage these insights to gain a comprehensive understanding of market dynamics and identify emerging trends.

2. Identifying Emerging Patterns and Signals:
AI-powered predictive analytics enable product managers to identify emerging patterns and signals that may indicate shifting market trends. By monitoring changes in consumer behavior, preferences, and sentiment, AI algorithms can detect early indicators of emerging trends or shifts in market demand. Product managers use these insights to stay ahead of the curve and proactively adjust their product strategies to capitalize on emerging opportunities or mitigate potential risks.

3. Predicting Future Market Conditions:
AI algorithms leverage historical data and advanced statistical modeling techniques to predict future market conditions with greater accuracy. By analyzing historical trends and extrapolating patterns into the future, AI-powered predictive analytics can forecast market growth rates, demand trends, and competitive dynamics. Product managers rely on these predictions to make informed decisions about product development, pricing strategies, and market positioning.

4. Scenario Planning and Risk Management:
AI-powered predictive analytics enable product managers to conduct scenario planning and risk management exercises to assess the potential impact of different market scenarios on their products. By simulating various market conditions and outcomes, AI algorithms help product managers anticipate potential risks and develop contingency plans to mitigate them. This proactive approach to risk management ensures that product strategies are robust and resilient in the face of uncertainty.

5. Adapting Product Strategies in Real-Time:

AI-powered predictive analytics provide product managers with real-time insights into changing market dynamics, allowing them to adapt their product strategies promptly. By continuously monitoring market trends and consumer behavior, AI algorithms can alert product managers to shifts in demand, emerging competitive threats, or opportunities for innovation. Product managers leverage these real-time insights to make agile adjustments to their product strategies and stay responsive to evolving market conditions.

6. Enhancing Competitive Advantage:

By leveraging AI-powered predictive analytics to forecast market trends, product managers can gain a competitive advantage by being proactive rather than reactive. By anticipating market shifts and aligning their product strategies accordingly, product managers can position their products more effectively, capture market share, and outmaneuver competitors. This proactive approach enables product managers to stay ahead of the competition and drive sustainable growth in dynamic market environments.

AI-powered predictive analytics empower product managers to forecast market trends with precision, enabling them to make informed decisions, mitigate risks, and capitalize on emerging opportunities. By leveraging AI algorithms to analyze historical data, identify emerging patterns, and predict future market conditions, product managers can develop proactive product strategies that drive competitive advantage and long-term success.

Anticipating User Needs

Anticipating user needs is a fundamental aspect of product management, and AI-powered predictive analytics significantly enhance a product manager's ability to foresee user preferences and behaviors. Here's a detailed exploration of how AI enables product managers to anticipate user needs:

1. User Behavior Analysis:
AI algorithms analyze vast amounts of user data, including interactions, feedback, and historical usage patterns, to gain insights into user behavior. By examining how users engage with a product, AI can identify recurring patterns, preferences, and trends that indicate their needs and preferences.

2. Predictive Modeling:
Using advanced statistical modeling techniques, AI can predict future user behavior based on historical data. By extrapolating patterns and trends into the future, AI algorithms can anticipate how users are likely to interact with the product, what features they may find valuable, and how their needs may evolve.

3. Personalization and Recommendations:
AI-powered recommendation engines leverage predictive analytics to personalize the user experience and make tailored recommendations. By analyzing a user's past behavior and preferences, AI algorithms can predict what content, products, or features are most relevant to them, thereby anticipating their needs and enhancing their overall experience.

4. Understanding User Intent:
Natural language processing (NLP) and sentiment analysis algorithms enable AI to understand user intent and sentiment from textual data such as customer reviews, support tickets, and social media interactions. By analyzing the language and context of user communications, AI can infer their underlying needs, desires, and pain points, allowing product managers to address them proactively.

5. Iterative Feedback Loops:

AI-powered predictive analytics facilitate iterative feedback loops, where user feedback is continuously analyzed to refine predictions and improve the accuracy of anticipatory models. By incorporating real-time feedback into predictive algorithms, product managers can iteratively adjust their strategies to better align with evolving user needs and preferences.

6. Proactive Product Development:

Armed with insights from AI-powered predictive analytics, product managers can take a proactive approach to product development, anticipating user needs before they arise. By introducing features, enhancements, or innovations that address anticipated user needs, product managers can stay ahead of the curve and deliver products that resonate with users on a deeper level.

7. Enhanced User Engagement:

Anticipating user needs enables product managers to create more engaging and meaningful experiences for users. By delivering features and content that align with users' expectations and preferences, products can foster stronger connections with their audience, drive user satisfaction, and increase retention and loyalty over time.

AI-powered predictive analytics empower product managers to anticipate user needs by analyzing user behavior, predicting future interactions, and personalizing the user experience. By leveraging AI algorithms to understand user intent, make tailored recommendations, and iterate based on feedback, product managers can develop proactive product strategies that resonate with users and drive long-term success.

Optimizing Feature Prioritization

Optimizing feature prioritization is essential for product managers to ensure that development efforts are focused on delivering the most impactful features to users. Here's how AI augments this process through predictive analytics:

1. Data-Driven Insights:
AI analyzes vast amounts of data, including user engagement metrics, market trends, and historical performance data, to gain insights into the potential impact of each feature. By examining patterns and trends in the data, AI algorithms can identify which features are most likely to drive user satisfaction, retention, and overall product success.

2. Predictive Modeling:
Using advanced statistical modeling techniques, AI can predict the potential impact of each feature based on historical data and user behavior patterns. By extrapolating trends into the future, AI algorithms can estimate how users are likely to respond to new features, helping product managers prioritize those with the highest predicted impact.

3. User Feedback Analysis:
AI-powered sentiment analysis algorithms analyze user feedback, including reviews, surveys, and support tickets, to understand user sentiment towards existing features and potential new ones. By identifying common themes, pain points, and areas for improvement, AI enables product managers to prioritize features that address user needs and preferences effectively.

4. Market Analysis:
AI algorithms can analyze market trends, competitor offerings, and industry developments to identify emerging opportunities and threats. By understanding the competitive landscape and market dynamics, product managers can

prioritize features that differentiate their products, capitalize on market trends, and address unmet user needs.

5. Iterative Optimization:
AI facilitates iterative optimization of feature prioritization by continuously analyzing feedback and performance data to refine predictions and recommendations. Product managers can use AI-driven insights to adjust their prioritization strategies dynamically, ensuring that development efforts remain aligned with evolving user needs and market conditions.

6. Resource Allocation:
By optimizing feature prioritization, AI helps product managers allocate resources more effectively, ensuring that development efforts are focused on features with the highest potential impact. This maximizes the return on investment and minimizes the risk of investing resources in low-impact or redundant features.

AI augments feature prioritization by providing data-driven insights, predictive modeling, user feedback analysis, market analysis, iterative optimization, and resource allocation guidance. By leveraging AI-powered predictive analytics, product managers can prioritize features more effectively, driving user satisfaction, retention, and overall product success.

Dynamic Pricing Strategies

Dynamic pricing strategies are essential for industries where pricing flexibility can lead to significant revenue optimization and market competitiveness. Here's how AI-driven predictive analytics revolutionizes decision-making in dynamic pricing strategies:

1. Market Analysis:

AI-powered predictive analytics algorithms analyze market conditions, including supply and demand dynamics, competitor pricing strategies, and consumer purchasing behavior. By continuously monitoring market trends and data, AI can provide product managers with real-time insights into changing market conditions, enabling them to adjust pricing strategies accordingly.

2. Competitor Pricing Intelligence:

AI algorithms scrape data from various sources, including competitor websites, e-commerce platforms, and price comparison engines, to gather intelligence on competitor pricing strategies. By analyzing this data, AI can identify pricing trends, competitive positioning, and pricing gaps, helping product managers make informed pricing decisions.

3. User Behavior Analysis:

AI analyzes user behavior data, including browsing history, purchase patterns, and response to pricing changes, to understand how users respond to different pricing strategies. By segmenting users based on their price sensitivity and willingness to pay, AI enables product managers to tailor pricing strategies to specific user segments, maximizing revenue while minimizing churn.

4. Predictive Modeling:

Using historical data and machine learning algorithms, AI can build predictive models that forecast the impact of different pricing strategies on key performance metrics, such as revenue, profit margins, and customer lifetime value. By simulating various pricing scenarios and analyzing the predicted outcomes, product managers can identify optimal pricing strategies that maximize revenue potential.

5. Real-time Adjustments:

AI enables real-time adjustments to pricing strategies based on changing market conditions, user behavior, and competitor actions. Product managers can set rules and triggers that automatically adjust prices in response to predefined criteria, such as changes in demand levels, inventory levels, or competitor price changes. This dynamic pricing approach ensures that prices are always optimized to maximize revenue while remaining competitive in the market.

6. Iterative Optimization:

AI facilitates iterative optimization of pricing strategies by continuously analyzing feedback and performance data to refine predictions and recommendations. Product managers can experiment with different pricing strategies, monitor the results, and adjust their approach based on the insights gained from AI-driven analytics.

7. Revenue Maximization:

Ultimately, AI-driven dynamic pricing strategies enable product managers to maximize revenue potential by setting prices dynamically based on real-time market conditions and user behavior. By leveraging AI-powered predictive analytics, product managers can achieve optimal pricing strategies that balance revenue generation with market competitiveness and customer satisfaction.

AI-driven predictive analytics revolutionizes decision-making in dynamic pricing strategies by providing real-time market insights, competitor pricing intelligence, user behavior analysis, predictive modeling, real-time adjustments, iterative optimization, and revenue maximization guidance. By harnessing the power of AI, product managers can implement dynamic pricing strategies that drive revenue growth and market success.

Streamlining Resource Allocation

Streamlining resource allocation is crucial for product managers to ensure efficient and effective product development processes. Here's how predictive analytics, powered by AI, can guide resource allocation in various aspects:

1. Human Resources Allocation:
AI-driven predictive analytics analyzes historical project data, team performance metrics, and project requirements to forecast human resource needs throughout the product lifecycle. By considering factors such as project complexity, skill requirements, and team capacity, AI can predict staffing needs for different project phases and allocate resources accordingly. This ensures that the right people with the right skills are assigned to the project at the right time, maximizing productivity and efficiency.

2. Budget Allocation:
Predictive analytics helps product managers forecast budget requirements for various project activities, including development, marketing, and infrastructure. By analyzing historical spending patterns, market trends, and project scope, AI can predict future budget needs and recommend optimal budget allocations. Product managers can use these insights to allocate resources effectively, ensuring that budget constraints are addressed while still meeting project objectives.

3. Development Timelines Optimization:
AI-powered predictive analytics can forecast development timelines by analyzing historical project data, team velocity, and potential bottlenecks. By identifying critical path activities, resource dependencies, and potential risks, AI helps product managers optimize development schedules to meet project deadlines. Predictive modeling allows product

managers to simulate different scenarios and assess the impact of resource allocation decisions on project timelines, enabling them to make informed decisions to ensure timely delivery.

4. Resource Utilization Efficiency:

Predictive analytics provides insights into resource utilization efficiency by analyzing resource allocation patterns, utilization rates, and productivity metrics. By identifying underutilized resources, overallocation issues, and inefficiencies in resource utilization, AI helps product managers optimize resource allocation to maximize productivity and minimize waste. This ensures that resources are allocated effectively to tasks that deliver the most value to the project.

5. Risk Mitigation Strategies:

AI-driven predictive analytics can identify potential risks and bottlenecks in resource allocation and recommend mitigation strategies. By analyzing historical data and project performance metrics, AI can predict potential resource shortages, skill gaps, or budget overruns and recommend proactive measures to address these issues. Product managers can use these insights to implement risk mitigation strategies and ensure that resource allocation decisions are aligned with project objectives and constraints.

6. Continuous Improvement:

Predictive analytics enables continuous improvement in resource allocation processes by providing feedback loops and performance metrics. By monitoring resource allocation decisions and their impact on project outcomes, AI helps product managers identify areas for improvement and optimize resource allocation strategies over time. This iterative approach ensures that resource allocation processes evolve to meet the changing needs of the project and maximize overall efficiency and effectiveness.

AI-powered predictive analytics guides resource allocation by providing insights into human resources allocation, budget allocation, development timelines optimization, resource utilization efficiency, risk mitigation strategies, and continuous improvement opportunities. By leveraging predictive analytics, product managers can make informed decisions to ensure optimal resource allocation throughout the product lifecycle, ultimately leading to successful project outcomes.

Real-Time Data-Driven Decision-Making

Real-time data-driven decision-making is a critical capability facilitated by the integration of AI and predictive analytics in product management. Here's a detailed exploration of how this integration empowers product managers:

1. Continuous Data Analysis:
AI algorithms continuously analyze vast streams of data in real-time, including user interactions, market trends, and product performance metrics. This continuous analysis ensures that product managers have access to the latest insights and trends, allowing them to make informed decisions based on up-to-date information.

2. Timely Insights Delivery:
Predictive analytics processes real-time data streams to generate actionable insights promptly. Product managers receive timely notifications and alerts regarding significant changes in user behavior, market conditions, or product performance, enabling them to respond quickly and adapt their strategies accordingly.

3. Dynamic Decision-Making:
Real-time data-driven decision-making enables product managers to make dynamic decisions that reflect the rapidly changing nature of markets and user preferences. By leveraging AI-powered insights, product managers can adjust

product strategies, marketing campaigns, and feature priorities in real time to capitalize on emerging opportunities or mitigate potential risks.

4. Agile Response to Market Changes:

With access to real-time insights, product managers can adopt an agile approach to respond swiftly to market changes. Whether it's adjusting pricing strategies, optimizing marketing messaging, or pivoting product development efforts, real-time data-driven decision-making allows product managers to adapt their strategies in real time, ensuring that their products remain competitive and relevant.

5. Personalized User Experiences:

Real-time data analysis enables product managers to deliver personalized user experiences by leveraging AI-driven insights into individual user preferences and behaviors. By dynamically adjusting product features, content recommendations, and marketing messages based on real-time user interactions, product managers can enhance user engagement and satisfaction.

6. Performance Monitoring and Optimization:

Real-time data-driven decision-making facilitates continuous performance monitoring and optimization of product initiatives. Product managers can track key performance indicators (KPIs) in real time and adjust strategies or tactics as needed to optimize outcomes and maximize ROI.

7. Risk Mitigation:

Real-time data analysis helps product managers identify and mitigate risks proactively. By monitoring real-time data streams for anomalies or deviations from expected patterns, product managers can detect potential issues early and take corrective actions to prevent adverse impacts on product performance or user experience.

8. Iterative Improvement:

Real-time data-driven decision-making enables iterative improvement of product strategies and initiatives. By analyzing real-time performance data and user feedback, product managers can identify areas for improvement and iterate on their approaches continuously, driving continuous innovation and enhancement of product offerings.

Real-time data-driven decision-making, facilitated by AI and predictive analytics, empowers product managers to make dynamic, agile, and personalized decisions that drive product success in today's fast-paced and data-driven business landscape.

Addressing Uncertainty and Mitigating Risks

Addressing uncertainty and mitigating risks is paramount in product development, and AI's predictive analytics capabilities offer a powerful solution to these challenges. Here's a detailed exploration of how AI helps product managers navigate uncertainty and mitigate risks:

1. Risk Assessment and Prediction:

AI-powered predictive analytics assess historical data and current trends to identify potential risks and predict future outcomes. By analyzing patterns and correlations in data, AI algorithms can anticipate potential pitfalls, such as market fluctuations, user behavior shifts, or technical challenges, allowing product managers to proactively address them.

2. Proactive Risk Mitigation Strategies:

Armed with predictive insights, product managers can develop proactive risk mitigation strategies to address potential challenges before they materialize. Whether it's adjusting product features, reallocating resources, or refining go-to-market strategies, AI enables product managers to take preemptive actions to mitigate risks and safeguard project success.

3. Scenario Planning and Sensitivity Analysis:
AI facilitates scenario planning and sensitivity analysis by simulating different scenarios and assessing their potential impacts on project outcomes. Product managers can use AI-powered predictive models to explore various what-if scenarios, evaluate their potential consequences, and develop contingency plans to mitigate risks associated with each scenario.

4. Early Warning Systems:
AI-driven early warning systems monitor key performance indicators (KPIs) and alert product managers to deviations from expected norms. By detecting anomalies or trends indicative of potential risks, these systems enable product managers to intervene early, address emerging issues, and prevent them from escalating into more significant problems.

5. Data-Driven Decision-Making:
AI's predictive analytics capabilities enable data-driven decision-making, even in the face of uncertainty. By relying on data-driven insights rather than intuition or guesswork, product managers can make informed decisions that mitigate risks and optimize outcomes, reducing the likelihood of costly errors or missteps.

6. Continuous Monitoring and Adaptation:
AI facilitates continuous monitoring of project metrics and performance indicators, enabling product managers to track progress in real-time and adapt their strategies as needed. By staying vigilant and responsive to changes in the project environment, product managers can mitigate risks proactively and ensure project success.

7. Collaborative Risk Management:
AI promotes collaborative risk management by providing stakeholders with access to predictive insights and data-driven analyses. By fostering open communication and collaboration among cross-functional teams, product managers can leverage collective expertise to identify, assess, and address risks effectively, ensuring that everyone is aligned on risk mitigation strategies.

8. Iterative Improvement and Learning:
AI-powered risk mitigation is an iterative process that allows product managers to learn from past experiences and continuously improve risk management practices. By analyzing the effectiveness of risk mitigation strategies and adapting them based on feedback and insights, product managers can refine their approach over time, increasing their ability to navigate uncertainty successfully.

AI's predictive analytics capabilities empower product managers to address uncertainty and mitigate risks effectively by providing proactive insights, enabling data-driven decision-making, and fostering continuous learning and improvement. By leveraging AI-powered risk mitigation strategies, product managers can navigate the complexities of product development with confidence and ensure project success in the face of uncertainty.

Ethical Considerations in Predictive Analytics

Ethical considerations in predictive analytics are of utmost importance as product managers leverage AI-driven technologies to inform decision-making processes. Here's a detailed exploration of the ethical considerations that product managers must navigate:

1. Fairness and Bias Mitigation:

Predictive analytics algorithms must be designed and implemented to ensure fairness and mitigate bias. Product managers must proactively identify and address biases in training data, algorithmic decision-making, and model outputs to prevent discriminatory outcomes. Fairness-aware AI techniques, such as fairness constraints and bias detection algorithms, can help product managers mitigate bias and promote equitable outcomes.

2. Transparency and Explainability:

Transparency and explainability are essential components of ethical predictive analytics. Product managers must ensure that AI models and algorithms are transparent and interpretable, allowing stakeholders to understand how predictions are generated and why specific decisions are made. Explainable AI techniques, such as model interpretation methods and algorithmic transparency frameworks, enable product managers to provide clear explanations for AI-driven decisions and promote trust and accountability.

3. Accountability and Responsibility:

Product managers bear responsibility for the ethical use of predictive analytics within their products. They must establish accountability mechanisms to ensure that AI-driven decision-making processes are transparent, auditable, and accountable to stakeholders. Implementing governance frameworks, ethical guidelines, and oversight mechanisms can help product managers uphold ethical standards and ensure compliance with legal and regulatory requirements.

4. Privacy and Data Protection:

Predictive analytics often relies on vast amounts of personal data, raising concerns about privacy and data protection. Product managers must prioritize user privacy and data protection by implementing robust data governance practices, anonymizing sensitive information, and obtaining informed consent from users for data collection and processing activities. Adhering to privacy regulations, such as GDPR and CCPA, is essential to safeguarding user privacy rights and maintaining trust.

5. Security and Confidentiality:
Security and confidentiality are critical considerations in predictive analytics to protect sensitive information from unauthorized access or disclosure. Product managers must implement robust cybersecurity measures, encryption protocols, and access controls to safeguard data integrity and confidentiality. By prioritizing data security, product managers can mitigate the risk of data breaches and ensure the confidentiality of user information.

6. Equity and Social Impact:
Predictive analytics has the potential to exacerbate existing inequalities and disparities if not implemented thoughtfully. Product managers must consider the broader societal impact of AI-driven decision-making and strive to promote equity, diversity, and inclusion. They should evaluate the potential social consequences of predictive analytics applications and take proactive measures to mitigate unintended negative impacts on vulnerable populations.

7. Continuous Monitoring and Ethical Review:
Ethical considerations in predictive analytics require ongoing monitoring and ethical review throughout the product development lifecycle. Product managers should establish processes for ethical risk assessment, impact evaluation, and ethical review of AI applications to ensure that ethical principles are upheld and any ethical concerns are addressed promptly. By integrating ethical considerations into the product development process, product managers can promote responsible and ethical AI adoption.

Ethical considerations in predictive analytics are multifaceted and require careful attention from product managers. By prioritizing fairness, transparency, accountability, privacy, security, equity, and continuous monitoring, product managers can ensure that AI-driven predictive analytics applications are developed and deployed ethically and responsibly, thereby earning user trust and contributing positively to society.

This section illuminates the transformative impact of AI-powered predictive analytics on decision-making within the product development lifecycle. As product managers navigate these new horizons, they harness the power of foresight, ensuring that decisions are not merely reactive but proactive, aligning products with market trends, user needs, and strategic goals. In the confluence of AI and predictive analytics, decision-making becomes a dynamic, data-driven journey that propels product development into a future of informed, strategic, and user-centric innovation.

3. HUMAN-CENTRIC DESIGN IN THE AI ERA

In the age of Artificial Intelligence (AI), the essence of product design extends beyond functionality to an intricate dance between human intuition and machine intelligence. This chapter delves into the pivotal role of User Experience (UX) and User Interface (UI) design in shaping AI-powered products, emphasizing the importance of human-centric design principles to create seamless, intuitive, and meaningful interactions.

Evolving Landscape of UX/UI in AI Products

The integration of AI into products fundamentally reshapes the landscape of user experience (UX) and user interface (UI) design, ushering in an era where interfaces must seamlessly harmonize with intelligent systems. This transformation goes beyond the traditional paradigm of static screens and linear interactions, evolving into dynamic, adaptive experiences that respond intelligently to user behavior and leverage AI to provide personalized, predictive, and context-aware interactions.

1. Dynamic Adaptation to User Behavior:
AI-powered UX/UI designs are capable of dynamically adapting to user behavior in real time. By continuously analyzing user interactions, preferences, and feedback, intelligent systems can tailor the user experience to meet individual needs and expectations. This dynamic adaptation ensures that interfaces evolve with users, optimizing engagement and satisfaction.

2. Personalization and Context Awareness:

AI enables highly personalized and context-aware user experiences by leveraging data insights and predictive analytics. Interfaces can anticipate user needs, preferences, and intent, delivering tailored content, recommendations, and interactions based on individual user profiles and situational context. This level of personalization enhances user engagement and fosters deeper connections with the product.

3. Predictive Interaction Design:

With AI, UX/UI designers can incorporate predictive interaction design principles into their interfaces. By analyzing historical user data and behavioral patterns, intelligent systems can anticipate user actions and proactively surface relevant content, features, or functionalities before users explicitly request them. This predictive approach streamlines user workflows, reduces friction, and enhances overall usability.

4. Natural Language and Voice Interfaces:

AI-driven UX/UI designs increasingly incorporate natural language processing (NLP) and voice interfaces to enable more intuitive and conversational interactions. Users can interact with products using natural language commands, voice queries, or chatbots, eliminating the need for traditional graphical user interfaces (GUIs) and facilitating hands-free operation. This shift towards voice-driven interfaces enhances accessibility and convenience for users across diverse contexts.

5. Adaptive Visual Interfaces:

AI enables the creation of adaptive visual interfaces that adjust their layout, content, and styling based on user preferences, device characteristics, and environmental conditions. Interfaces can dynamically resize, reposition, or prioritize content elements to optimize readability, accessibility, and visual hierarchy across different screen sizes, resolutions, and viewing contexts. This adaptive approach ensures a consistent and optimized user experience across various devices and platforms.

6. Emotionally Intelligent Design:
AI-powered UX/UI designs have the potential to exhibit emotionally intelligent behaviors, such as empathy, recognition, and responsiveness to user emotions and moods. By analyzing facial expressions, voice tone, or user sentiment, interfaces can adapt their tone, messaging, or visual elements to resonate with users' emotional states and foster deeper emotional connections. This emotionally intelligent design approach enhances user satisfaction and loyalty.

7. Continuous Learning and Improvement:
AI-driven UX/UI designs embrace a philosophy of continuous learning and improvement, leveraging feedback loops and iterative optimization techniques to enhance usability and performance over time. Intelligent systems can analyze user interactions, A/B test design variations, and incorporate user feedback to iteratively refine the interface and address usability issues or pain points. This iterative approach ensures that interfaces evolve iteratively to meet changing user needs and preferences.

The evolving landscape of UX/UI in AI products represents a paradigm shift towards dynamic, adaptive, and personalized experiences. By harnessing the power of AI to understand user behavior, predict user intent, and adapt to individual preferences, UX/UI designers can create interfaces that delight users, streamline interactions, and foster deeper engagement with the product.

Bridging the Gap between Humans and Machines

Bridging the gap between humans and machines is at the core of human-centric design in the AI era. This approach seeks to create interfaces that facilitate intuitive interactions, ensuring that users can effectively harness the power of AI without being overwhelmed by its complexity. Achieving this goal requires UX/UI designers to possess a deep understanding of AI algorithms, as well as the ability to translate these complex functionalities into user-friendly interfaces that empower users.

1. Understanding AI Algorithms:
UX/UI designers must have a comprehensive understanding of the underlying AI algorithms powering the system. This includes familiarity with machine learning models, natural language processing techniques, computer vision algorithms, and other AI technologies. By understanding how these algorithms work and their capabilities, designers can better conceptualize and design interfaces that leverage AI effectively.

2. Translating Complexity into Simplicity:
One of the key challenges in designing AI-powered interfaces is simplifying complex functionalities for users. UX/UI designers need to distill the intricate workings of AI algorithms into intuitive and understandable concepts that users can grasp easily. This involves using familiar metaphors, visual representations, and language that resonate with users' mental models and prior knowledge.

3. Accessible AI Capabilities:
Human-centric design aims to make AI capabilities accessible to users of all levels of technical proficiency. Designers should prioritize accessibility features, such as clear and concise explanations of AI functionalities, tooltips, and guided tours to help users navigate complex features. Additionally,

incorporating features like voice commands, gesture-based interactions, and natural language interfaces can enhance accessibility for users with diverse needs and preferences.

4. Transparency and Trust:
Transparency is essential in building trust between users and AI-powered systems. UX/UI designers should strive to make AI-driven processes transparent by providing visibility into how decisions are made and why certain recommendations or actions are taken. This transparency can be achieved through informative notifications, explanations of algorithmic logic, and visualizations of data inputs and outputs.

5. Seamless Integration into Workflow:
Effective human-centric design ensures that AI capabilities are seamlessly integrated into the user's workflow, enhancing productivity and efficiency. Interfaces should be designed with the user's tasks and goals in mind, with AI functionalities positioned where they can provide the most value without disrupting the user's workflow. This requires careful consideration of information hierarchy, task flow, and interaction patterns.

6. Iterative User Testing and Feedback:
Human-centric design is an iterative process that relies on continuous user testing and feedback. UX/UI designers should conduct usability testing sessions with real users to gather insights into how well the interface supports their needs and how effectively they can interact with AI features. This feedback should inform iterative design improvements aimed at enhancing usability, clarity, and effectiveness.

7. Empowering Users:
Ultimately, the human-centric design aims to empower users to leverage AI capabilities to accomplish their goals more effectively. Interfaces should be designed to provide users with a sense of agency and control over AI-driven features,

allowing them to customize settings, adjust preferences, and intervene when necessary. By empowering users, designers can foster a sense of ownership and mastery over AI-powered systems.

Human-centric design in the AI era is about creating interfaces that bridge the gap between humans and machines, making AI capabilities accessible, transparent, and seamlessly integrated into the user's workflow. By prioritizing simplicity, accessibility, transparency, and empowerment, UX/UI designers can design interfaces that empower users to harness the full potential of AI in their daily tasks and activities.

Ethical Considerations in AI-Driven Design

Ethical considerations in AI-driven design are paramount as artificial intelligence becomes increasingly integrated into product development. Designers bear a significant responsibility in addressing ethical issues related to bias, privacy, transparency, and accountability. By adopting a human-centric approach, designers can ensure that AI-powered products prioritize user trust, fairness, and responsible data use.

1. Addressing Bias and Fairness:
AI algorithms are susceptible to bias, which can result in unfair outcomes, discrimination, and inequities. Designers must proactively identify and mitigate bias in AI systems by ensuring diverse representation in training data, evaluating algorithmic fairness, and implementing bias detection and mitigation techniques. By prioritizing fairness, designers can build AI systems that treat all users fairly and equitably.

2. Protecting User Privacy:
Privacy concerns are paramount in AI-driven design, especially given the vast amounts of personal data often

involved. Designers should implement robust privacy protections, such as data anonymization, encryption, and access controls, to safeguard user data from unauthorized access or misuse. Transparent privacy policies and user consent mechanisms are essential for building trust and ensuring that users have control over their personal information.

3. Ensuring Transparency and Explainability:
Transparency is crucial in AI-driven design to ensure that users understand how AI systems work and why certain decisions are made. Designers should strive to make AI algorithms transparent and explainable by providing clear explanations of algorithmic logic, highlighting data sources and inputs, and visualizing decision-making processes. Transparency fosters trust and empowers users to make informed decisions about how they interact with AI-powered products.

4. Promoting User Empowerment and Autonomy:
Designers should prioritize user empowerment and autonomy by providing users with control over their interactions with AI systems. This includes allowing users to customize settings, adjust preferences, and opt out of AI-driven features if desired. Empowering users to make informed choices about their use of AI-powered products enhances trust and fosters a sense of agency.

5. Responsible Data Use and Governance:
Designers must adhere to responsible data use practices and governance frameworks to ensure that AI-powered products respect user privacy and comply with legal and regulatory requirements. This includes implementing data minimization strategies, obtaining explicit user consent for data collection and processing, and establishing clear policies for data retention and deletion. By prioritizing responsible data use, designers can mitigate risks and build trust with users.

6. Ethical Decision-Making Frameworks:
Designers should adopt ethical decision-making frameworks to guide their design process and address ethical dilemmas effectively. These frameworks may include principles such as fairness, accountability, transparency, and user-centricity, which help designers evaluate the ethical implications of their design decisions and prioritize ethical considerations throughout the product development lifecycle.

7. Continuous Monitoring and Evaluation:
Ethical considerations should be integrated into all stages of the design process, from ideation to deployment and beyond. Designers should continuously monitor and evaluate the ethical implications of AI-powered products, soliciting feedback from users, stakeholders, and experts, and iterating on design solutions to address emerging ethical concerns. By adopting a proactive and iterative approach to ethical design, designers can ensure that AI-powered products prioritize user welfare and societal values.

Ethical considerations are integral to AI-driven design, and designers play a crucial role in addressing ethical issues related to bias, privacy, transparency, and accountability. By prioritizing fairness, privacy, transparency, user empowerment, responsible data use, ethical decision-making frameworks, and continuous monitoring and evaluation, designers can build AI-powered products that prioritize user trust, fairness, and responsible use of data.

Context-Aware Design for Personalization

Context-aware design for personalization harnesses the power of AI to create dynamic, adaptive user experiences tailored to individual preferences, behaviors, and contexts. This approach goes beyond traditional one-size-fits-all interfaces, allowing products to anticipate user needs and deliver relevant content, features, and interactions in real-time. UX/UI designers play a pivotal role in leveraging machine learning algorithms and data-driven insights to design interfaces that seamlessly integrate personalized experiences into the user's workflow.

1. Understanding User Context:
Context-aware design begins with a deep understanding of user contexts, including factors such as location, time, device, and past interactions. UX/UI designers analyze user data, behavioral patterns, and contextual cues to infer user intent and anticipate their needs in different situations. By understanding user contexts, designers can tailor interfaces to deliver timely and relevant content and functionality.

2. Leveraging Machine Learning Algorithms:
Machine learning algorithms play a crucial role in context-aware design by enabling personalized recommendations, predictive insights, and adaptive interfaces. Designers leverage algorithms such as collaborative filtering, content-based filtering, and reinforcement learning to analyze user data, learn from past interactions, and predict future preferences. These algorithms power features such as personalized recommendations, adaptive layouts, and context-aware notifications, enhancing the user experience.

3. Dynamic Adaptation and Personalization:
Context-aware design enables interfaces to dynamically adapt to changes in user contexts and preferences in real time. UX/UI designers create interfaces that respond to contextual cues, such as location, time of day, and user behavior, by adjusting content, layout, and functionality accordingly. This dynamic adaptation ensures that users receive personalized experiences tailored to their current context, enhancing engagement and satisfaction.

4. Balancing Personalization and Privacy:

One of the key challenges in context-aware design is finding the balance between personalization and privacy. While personalized experiences can enhance user engagement, they also raise concerns about data privacy and user consent. UX/UI designers must implement privacy-preserving design principles, such as data anonymization, user opt-in mechanisms, and transparent data practices, to ensure that users retain control over their personal information while still benefiting from personalized experiences.

5. User-Centric Design Principles:

Context-aware design is rooted in user-centric design principles, focusing on delivering value to users based on their needs, preferences, and contexts. UX/UI designers prioritize usability, accessibility, and simplicity while designing personalized interfaces, ensuring that interfaces remain intuitive and easy to use across different contexts and devices. By placing the user at the center of the design process, designers create interfaces that enhance user satisfaction and loyalty.

6. Iterative Design and Optimization:

Context-aware design is an iterative process that involves continuous refinement and optimization based on user feedback and data insights. UX/UI designers conduct user testing, A/B testing, and usability studies to gather feedback on personalized interfaces and identify areas for improvement. By iterating on design solutions and incorporating user feedback, designers optimize personalized experiences to better meet user needs and preferences over time.

Context-aware design for personalization leverages AI and machine learning algorithms to create dynamic, adaptive user experiences tailored to individual user contexts and preferences. UX/UI designers play a crucial role in understanding user contexts, leveraging machine learning algorithms, balancing personalization and privacy, applying user-centric design principles, and iteratively optimizing personalized interfaces to enhance user satisfaction and engagement.

Conversational Interfaces and Natural Language Processing

Conversational interfaces and Natural Language Processing (NLP) represent a paradigm shift in user interaction, enabling users to engage with products and services through natural language conversations. This transformative technology leverages AI algorithms to understand, interpret, and respond to user queries, commands, and requests in a human-like manner. UX/UI designers play a pivotal role in designing conversational interfaces that facilitate seamless and intuitive interactions between users and intelligent systems.

1. Understanding User Intent:
Designing effective conversational interfaces begins with a deep understanding of user intent. UX/UI designers analyze user needs, goals, and expectations to identify the types of conversations users are likely to have with the system. By understanding user intent, designers can craft conversational flows and dialogue structures that guide users toward successful interactions and outcomes.

2. Crafting Natural Language Interactions:
Natural Language Processing (NLP) technology enables conversational interfaces to understand and respond to user input in natural language. UX/UI designers must design interfaces that support a wide range of user utterances, variations, and language styles. This involves designing flexible dialogue structures, implementing robust language understanding algorithms, and providing contextual prompts and suggestions to guide users during conversations.

3. Seamless Integration with AI Capabilities:

Conversational interfaces often rely on AI-powered language processing capabilities to understand user input and generate appropriate responses. UX/UI designers must seamlessly integrate these AI capabilities into the interface, ensuring that users can interact with the system in a fluid and intuitive manner. This involves designing clear and concise prompts, providing informative feedback, and leveraging AI algorithms to generate contextually relevant responses.

4. Personalization and Context Awareness:

Personalization and context awareness play a crucial role in enhancing the effectiveness of conversational interfaces. UX/UI designers leverage user data, preferences, and contextual information to tailor interactions and responses to individual users. By personalizing the conversational experience, designers create more engaging and relevant interactions that resonate with users and meet their specific needs and preferences.

5. Designing Multi-Modal Interfaces:

Conversational interfaces often coexist with other interaction modalities, such as graphical user interfaces (GUIs) and voice interfaces. UX/UI designers must design multi-modal interfaces that seamlessly integrate conversational interactions with other interaction modes. This involves designing consistent user experiences across different modalities, providing alternative interaction pathways, and ensuring a cohesive and unified user experience.

6. Usability and Accessibility Considerations:

Usability and accessibility are paramount in the design of conversational interfaces. UX/UI designers must ensure that the interface is intuitive, easy to navigate, and accessible to users of all abilities. This involves designing clear and concise prompts, providing alternative input methods for users with disabilities, and adhering to accessibility standards and guidelines to ensure an inclusive user experience.

7. Iterative Design and Continuous Improvement:
Designing effective conversational interfaces is an iterative process that involves continuous refinement and improvement based on user feedback and data insights. UX/UI designers conduct user testing, usability studies, and A/B testing to gather feedback on the conversational experience and identify areas for optimization. By iterating on design solutions and incorporating user feedback, designers continuously improve the conversational interface to better meet user needs and preferences over time.

Designing conversational interfaces and leveraging Natural Language Processing (NLP) technology requires UX/UI designers to understand user intent, craft natural language interactions, seamlessly integrate AI capabilities, personalize the experience, design multi-modal interfaces, prioritize usability and accessibility, and engage in iterative design and continuous improvement. By embracing these principles and practices, designers can create conversational interfaces that deliver intuitive, engaging, and effective user experiences in the AI era.

Transparency in AI-Driven Interactions

Transparency in AI-driven interactions is essential for fostering trust and empowering users to make informed decisions. UX/UI designers play a critical role in ensuring that users understand how AI algorithms operate, the logic behind recommendations, and the implications of their actions within the system. By prioritizing transparency in design, designers can build trust and confidence in AI-powered products and services. Below are key considerations for incorporating transparency into AI-driven interactions:

1. Explainability of AI Algorithms:

UX/UI designers should strive to make AI algorithms understandable and transparent to users. This involves providing clear explanations of how AI algorithms work, the data they use, and the reasoning behind their recommendations or decisions. Designers can use user-friendly language, visual aids, and interactive elements to demystify complex AI concepts and make them accessible to users with varying levels of technical expertise.

2. Visualizing Data and Insights:

Visualizing data and insights can enhance transparency by making abstract concepts tangible and comprehensible to users. UX/UI designers can use data visualization techniques such as charts, graphs, and infographics to represent AI-generated insights, patterns, and trends. By presenting data in a visually engaging and interactive format, designers enable users to explore and understand the underlying information driving AI-driven interactions.

3. Providing Contextual Explanations:

Contextual explanations help users understand why AI-driven recommendations or decisions are being made and how they relate to their specific needs or goals. UX/UI designers can incorporate contextual explanations directly into the user interface, providing relevant information at the point of interaction. This enables users to make informed decisions and trust the recommendations provided by intelligent systems.

4. Offering Control and Customization Options:

Providing users with control and customization options enhances transparency by empowering them to influence AI-driven interactions according to their preferences and priorities. UX/UI designers can incorporate features such as settings menus, preference sliders, and customization tools that allow users to adjust the behavior of intelligent systems based on their individual needs and preferences. By offering control over AI-driven interactions, designers give users a sense of agency and ownership over their experiences.

5. Highlighting Data Sources and Privacy Policies:
Transparency around data sources and privacy policies is essential for building trust in AI-powered products and services. UX/UI designers should clearly communicate the sources of data used by AI algorithms, as well as the measures taken to protect user privacy and data security. This may include providing links to privacy policies, displaying data usage notifications, and offering options for users to manage their data preferences and permissions.

6. Educating Users about AI Technology:
Educating users about AI technology and its capabilities can help demystify AI-driven interactions and foster trust in intelligent systems. UX/UI designers can incorporate educational resources, tutorials, and tooltips that explain key AI concepts, such as machine learning, natural language processing, and predictive analytics. By increasing users' understanding of AI technology, designers empower them to engage more effectively with AI-driven interactions and make informed decisions.

7. Soliciting Feedback and Addressing Concerns:
UX/UI designers should actively solicit feedback from users and address any concerns or questions they may have about AI-driven interactions. This can be done through user surveys, feedback forms, and customer support channels. By listening to user feedback and responding promptly to concerns, designers demonstrate a commitment to transparency and accountability in the design of AI-powered products and services.

Transparency in AI-driven interactions is essential for building trust, empowering users, and ensuring responsible design practices. UX/UI designers can achieve transparency by explaining AI algorithms, visualizing data and insights, providing contextual explanations, offering control and customization options, highlighting data sources and privacy policies, educating users about AI technology, and soliciting feedback from users. By prioritizing transparency in design, designers can create AI-powered products and services that are user-friendly, trustworthy, and ethically responsible.

Accessibility and Inclusivity

Accessibility and inclusivity are paramount considerations in the design of AI-powered products, as they ensure that all users, regardless of ability, language, or cultural background, can fully engage with and benefit from the technology. UX/UI designers play a pivotal role in ensuring that AI interfaces are accessible and inclusive by adopting human-centric design principles and incorporating features that accommodate diverse user needs. Below are key considerations for promoting accessibility and inclusivity in AI-powered products:

1. Universal Design Principles:
UX/UI designers should adhere to universal design principles, which prioritize the creation of products that are usable by people with diverse abilities and characteristics. This involves designing interfaces that are intuitive, flexible, and easy to navigate, regardless of users' physical or cognitive capabilities. By adopting universal design principles, designers can create AI interfaces that are accessible to a broad range of users.

2. Accessible Interaction Modalities:
AI interfaces should support multiple interaction modalities to accommodate users with different abilities and preferences. This includes providing alternative input methods such as voice commands, keyboard shortcuts, and gesture-based

controls, in addition to traditional mouse and touch inputs. By offering accessible interaction modalities, designers ensure that users can interact with AI interfaces in a way that suits their individual needs and preferences.

3. Adaptive Content and Presentation:

AI interfaces should be designed to adapt to users' preferences and accessibility settings, such as font size, color contrast, and language preferences. UX/UI designers can implement features that allow users to customize the appearance and presentation of content, ensuring that it remains readable and understandable for all users. By offering adaptive content and presentation options, designers enhance the accessibility of AI interfaces for users with diverse needs.

4. Multilingual Support:

AI interfaces should support multiple languages to accommodate users from different linguistic backgrounds. UX/UI designers can incorporate features such as language selection menus, translation tools, and multilingual content to ensure that users can interact with AI interfaces in their preferred language. By providing multilingual support, designers promote inclusivity and ensure that AI-powered products are accessible to users worldwide.

5. Cultural Sensitivity and Localization:

AI interfaces should be culturally sensitive and localized to accommodate users from diverse cultural backgrounds. UX/UI designers should consider cultural norms, customs, and preferences when designing interfaces, avoiding culturally insensitive imagery, language, or symbols. By incorporating cultural sensitivity and localization into design practices, designers ensure that AI interfaces resonate with users from different cultural contexts.

6. Accessibility Standards Compliance:
AI interfaces should adhere to accessibility standards and guidelines, such as the Web Content Accessibility Guidelines (WCAG), to ensure compliance with legal and regulatory requirements. UX/UI designers should conduct accessibility audits and usability testing to identify and address potential barriers to access for users with disabilities. By following accessibility standards, designers ensure that AI-powered products are usable by all users, including those with disabilities.

7. Inclusive User Testing and Feedback:
UX/UI designers should conduct inclusive user testing and solicit feedback from users with diverse abilities, backgrounds, and perspectives. This involves actively involving users with disabilities, language barriers, or cultural differences in the design process to ensure that AI interfaces meet their needs and preferences. By incorporating inclusive user testing and feedback, designers can identify and address accessibility and inclusivity issues early in the design process.

Promoting accessibility and inclusivity in AI-powered products is essential for ensuring that all users can fully engage with and benefit from the technology. UX/UI designers can achieve this by adhering to universal design principles, supporting accessible interaction modalities, offering adaptive content and presentation options, providing multilingual support, incorporating cultural sensitivity and localization, complying with accessibility standards, and conducting inclusive user testing and feedback. By prioritizing accessibility and inclusivity in design practices, designers can create AI interfaces that are usable, inclusive, and empowering for all users.

Iterative Design in AI Products

Iterative design is a fundamental approach to developing AI products, recognizing that the dynamic nature of AI technologies requires constant refinement and adaptation to meet evolving user needs and technological advancements. UX/UI designers play a crucial role in this process, working collaboratively with AI developers to iteratively design, test, and refine interfaces based on user feedback, emerging trends, and improvements in AI algorithms. Below are key aspects of iterative design in AI products:

1. User-Centered Design Process:
Iterative design in AI products begins with a user-centered approach, where UX/UI designers prioritize understanding user needs, preferences, and pain points. By conducting user research, usability testing, and gathering feedback, designers gain valuable insights into how users interact with AI interfaces and what improvements are needed to enhance the user experience.

2. Agile Methodologies:
Agile methodologies, such as Scrum or Kanban, are commonly adopted in iterative design processes for AI products. These methodologies emphasize flexibility, collaboration, and responsiveness to change, allowing cross-functional teams to work iteratively and incrementally to deliver value to users. UX/UI designers collaborate closely with AI developers, product managers, and other stakeholders to prioritize features, iterate on designs, and adapt to evolving requirements.

3. Prototyping and User Testing:
Prototyping is a crucial component of iterative design in AI products, allowing designers to quickly visualize and test different design concepts. UX/UI designers create prototypes of AI interfaces and conduct usability testing with real users

to gather feedback, identify usability issues, and validate design decisions. Rapid prototyping and user testing enable designers to iterate on designs iteratively, refining interfaces based on user feedback and data-driven insights.

4. Continuous Improvement:
Iterative design in AI products is characterized by a cycle of continuous improvement, where designs are refined based on user feedback, performance metrics, and advancements in AI technology. UX/UI designers collaborate with AI developers to monitor user interactions, analyze usage data, and identify opportunities for optimization and enhancement. By continuously iterating on designs, designers ensure that AI products remain adaptive, responsive, and aligned with user needs and expectations.

5. Feedback Loops with AI Integration:
AI technologies, such as machine learning algorithms, can be integrated into the iterative design process to automate feedback loops and improve design decisions. UX/UI designers leverage AI-driven analytics tools to analyze user behavior, predict user preferences, and identify patterns in user interactions. By incorporating AI into the feedback loop, designers can gain valuable insights into user needs and preferences, enabling them to make data-driven design decisions and iterate on designs more effectively.

6. Cross-Functional Collaboration:
Iterative design in AI products requires close collaboration between UX/UI designers, AI developers, product managers, and other stakeholders. Cross-functional teams work together to define requirements, prioritize features, and iterate on designs iteratively. Regular communication, feedback sessions, and collaborative workshops facilitate alignment and ensure that design decisions are informed by a deep understanding of user needs and technical constraints.

7. Adaptation to Technological Advancements:
Iterative design in AI products involves adapting to technological advancements and innovations in AI algorithms and capabilities. UX/UI designers stay informed about the latest developments in AI technology, experimenting with new features, techniques, and design patterns to leverage the full potential of AI in enhancing the user experience. By staying agile and adaptable, designers can incorporate emerging technologies into their designs and iterate on interfaces to deliver innovative and cutting-edge AI products.

Iterative design is essential for developing AI products that are adaptive, responsive, and aligned with user needs. UX/UI designers play a central role in this process, working collaboratively with AI developers and other stakeholders to iterate on designs, gather feedback, and continuously improve the user experience. By embracing an iterative approach, designers ensure that AI products evolve iteratively, remain responsive to user needs, and deliver value to users in an ever-changing landscape.

Future Trends in Human-Centric AI Design

Anticipating future trends in human-centric AI design requires UX/UI designers to embrace a forward-thinking mindset and stay abreast of emerging technologies, user behaviors, and societal trends. Here are several potential future trends in human-centric AI design:

1. Augmented Reality (AR) Experiences:
AR technologies are poised to revolutionize the way users interact with AI-driven interfaces. UX/UI designers will need to explore innovative ways to integrate AR elements into products, creating immersive and interactive experiences that blend digital and physical environments seamlessly. Designing intuitive AR interfaces that enhance user

engagement and provide valuable contextual information will be a key focus for designers.

2. Conversational AI and Voice Interfaces:
Voice interfaces and conversational AI are becoming increasingly prevalent in everyday devices and applications. UX/UI designers will need to design conversational interfaces that are natural, intuitive, and responsive to user commands. Creating voice-driven experiences that mimic human conversation and adapt to user preferences will be essential for enhancing usability and user satisfaction.

3. Gesture and Motion-Based Interactions:
Gesture and motion-based interactions offer new possibilities for user engagement and interaction with AI-powered interfaces. UX/UI designers will explore innovative ways to leverage gestures, facial expressions, and body movements to control and interact with digital interfaces. Designing intuitive and ergonomic gesture-based interfaces that enhance usability and accessibility will be a focus for designers.

4. Personalized and Adaptive Interfaces:
AI-driven personalization will continue to shape the design of interfaces, providing users with tailored experiences based on their preferences, behavior, and context. UX/UI designers will need to create interfaces that dynamically adapt to individual user needs, offering personalized content, recommendations, and interactions in real time. Designing adaptive interfaces that anticipate user intent and provide relevant information proactively will be critical for enhancing user engagement and satisfaction.

5. Ethical and Inclusive Design Practices:
As AI becomes more integrated into everyday products and services, ethical and inclusive design practices will become increasingly important. UX/UI designers will need to consider

the ethical implications of AI algorithms, ensuring transparency, fairness, and accountability in design decisions. Designing interfaces that prioritize user privacy, security, and accessibility will be essential for building trust and fostering user adoption of AI-driven technologies.

6. Emotionally Intelligent Interfaces:
Emotionally intelligent interfaces will become more prevalent, leveraging AI algorithms to recognize and respond to user emotions. UX/UI designers will need to design interfaces that are empathetic, supportive, and capable of understanding and adapting to user emotions. Creating emotionally intelligent interfaces that can provide personalized support, feedback, and encouragement will be key for enhancing user satisfaction and engagement.

7. Human-AI Collaboration:
Human-AI collaboration will become increasingly common, with AI systems augmenting human capabilities in various tasks and workflows. UX/UI designers will need to design interfaces that facilitate seamless collaboration between humans and intelligent systems, ensuring that AI enhances, rather than replaces, human creativity, intuition, and decision-making. Designing interfaces that empower users to interact with AI as a trusted collaborator and assistant will be essential for fostering productive and effective human-AI collaboration.

Future trends in human-centric AI design will be characterized by innovation, personalization, and ethical considerations. UX/UI designers will play a pivotal role in shaping the future of AI interfaces, embracing emerging technologies, and designing experiences that prioritize user needs, preferences, and well-being. By staying adaptable, empathetic, and forward-thinking, designers can create AI-driven interfaces that enhance human experiences and empower users in an increasingly intelligent world.

This section explores the intricate dance between UX/UI design and AI, highlighting the essential role designers play in shaping interfaces that not only harness the power of intelligent systems but also prioritize the user experience. As we navigate the AI era, human-centric design principles become the guiding light, ensuring that the fusion of human intuition and machine intelligence results in products that are not just functional but deeply resonant with the diverse needs and expectations of users.

ETHICAL CONSIDERATIONS IN AI-DRIVEN DESIGN

In the age of Artificial Intelligence (AI), the marriage of technology and human-centric design brings forth a plethora of opportunities and challenges. This chapter delves into the critical realm of ethical considerations in AI-driven design, exploring how designers play a pivotal role in ensuring that AI-powered products prioritize transparency, fairness, user autonomy, and societal well-being.

The Ethical Imperative in AI Design

The ethical imperative in AI design encompasses a range of considerations that designers must address to ensure responsible and socially beneficial outcomes. Here are several key aspects of the ethical imperative in AI design:

1. Fairness and Bias Mitigation:
Designers must strive to create AI systems that are fair and unbiased, treating all users equitably regardless of their demographic characteristics. This involves identifying and mitigating biases in data and algorithms that could lead to discriminatory outcomes. Designers should implement techniques such as bias detection, fairness testing, and

algorithmic transparency to promote fairness in AI-powered products.

2. Inclusivity and Accessibility:

AI design should prioritize inclusivity and accessibility to ensure that products are usable by people of all abilities and backgrounds. Designers should consider diverse user needs, including those with disabilities, and incorporate accessibility features such as screen readers, keyboard navigation, and alternative input methods. By designing with inclusivity in mind, designers can create products that are accessible to everyone.

3. User Privacy and Data Protection:

Protecting user privacy and data security is paramount in AI design. Designers should implement robust privacy controls and data protection measures to safeguard user information from unauthorized access or misuse. This includes obtaining explicit user consent for data collection and processing, implementing encryption and anonymization techniques, and adhering to relevant privacy regulations such as GDPR and CCPA.

4. Transparency and Explainability:

AI systems should be transparent and explainable to users, enabling them to understand how algorithms make decisions and why certain recommendations are provided. Designers should design interfaces that provide clear explanations of AI-driven functionalities, including the data sources used, the reasoning behind recommendations, and any potential limitations or biases. Transparent design fosters trust and accountability, empowering users to make informed decisions.

5. Accountability and Responsibility:

Designers have a responsibility to ensure that AI systems are accountable for their actions and outcomes. This involves establishing clear lines of accountability within the design process and providing mechanisms for users to report issues or concerns. Designers should also consider the potential ethical implications of AI-driven decisions and be prepared to address them responsibly.

6. Ethical Decision-Making Frameworks:
Designers can benefit from adopting ethical decision-making frameworks to guide their design process. These frameworks provide a structured approach for identifying ethical issues, evaluating potential impacts, and making informed decisions that prioritize ethical considerations. By integrating ethical principles into the design process, designers can create products that align with societal values and ethical standards.

7. Continuous Ethical Reflection and Improvement:
Ethical considerations should be an ongoing focus throughout the design lifecycle, with designers engaging in continuous ethical reflection and improvement. This involves regularly reviewing and reassessing the ethical implications of AI-powered products, soliciting feedback from stakeholders, and making iterative improvements to address emerging ethical challenges. By fostering a culture of ethical awareness and reflection, designers can ensure that AI products evolve in a responsible and socially beneficial manner.

The ethical imperative in AI design requires designers to consider a range of ethical considerations throughout the design process, from fairness and inclusivity to privacy and accountability. By prioritizing ethical principles and adopting responsible design practices, designers can create AI-powered products that enhance user experiences while upholding societal values and ethical standards.

Addressing Bias and Fairness

Addressing bias and ensuring fairness in AI design is crucial to creating ethical and equitable products. Here's a detailed exploration of how designers can tackle this complex issue:

1. Understanding Bias in AI:
Bias in AI refers to the systematic and unfair favoritism or discrimination towards certain individuals or groups. Bias can manifest in various forms, including racial, gender, socioeconomic, and cultural biases. Designers must recognize that bias can be unintentionally embedded in AI systems through biased data, flawed algorithms, or biased decision-making processes.

2. Scrubbing Training Data:
One of the primary sources of bias in AI systems is biased training data. Designers should carefully scrutinize training datasets to identify and remove biases. This may involve cleaning the data to ensure it is representative of the target population and free from stereotypes or discriminatory patterns. Additionally, designers should augment datasets with diverse examples to mitigate underrepresentation and ensure balanced training.

3. Testing for Bias:
Designers should implement rigorous testing procedures to detect and measure bias in AI algorithms. This involves evaluating the system's performance across different demographic groups to identify disparities in outcomes. Various statistical techniques, such as demographic parity, equalized odds, and disparate impact analysis, can be employed to assess bias and ensure fairness in decision-making.

4. Mitigating Bias in Algorithms:
Once bias is identified, designers must take proactive measures to mitigate its impact. This may involve adjusting algorithmic parameters, modifying decision rules, or implementing bias-correction techniques to reduce disparate treatment or outcomes. Additionally, designers can introduce fairness constraints or regularization methods during model training to promote fairness and equity.

5. Ensuring Diversity in Design Teams:
Diversity within design teams is essential for mitigating bias and promoting inclusivity in AI design. Designers from diverse backgrounds bring unique perspectives and experiences to the table, helping to uncover and address blind spots in the design process. By fostering a culture of diversity and inclusion, design teams can create AI systems that are more sensitive to the needs and preferences of diverse user groups.

6. Implementing Ethical Guidelines and Standards:
Designers should adhere to established ethical guidelines and standards for AI design, such as the IEEE Ethically Aligned Design, the ACM Code of Ethics, or the principles outlined in the Universal Guidelines for AI. These guidelines provide a framework for identifying and addressing ethical issues, including bias and fairness, in AI systems. By following ethical best practices, designers can ensure that their AI products uphold principles of fairness, transparency, and accountability.

7. Continuous Monitoring and Evaluation:
Bias mitigation is an ongoing process that requires continuous monitoring and evaluation of AI systems in real-world contexts. Designers should implement mechanisms for monitoring system performance, collecting feedback from users, and conducting regular audits to identify and address any emerging biases or disparities. By maintaining vigilance

and proactively addressing bias, designers can ensure that their AI products remain fair, equitable, and inclusive over time.

Addressing bias and ensuring fairness in AI design requires a multifaceted approach that involves scrubbing training data, testing for bias, mitigating bias in algorithms, fostering diversity within design teams, adhering to ethical guidelines, and implementing continuous monitoring and evaluation. By prioritizing fairness and equity in the design process, designers can create AI systems that reflect the values of inclusivity, diversity, and social responsibility.

Transparency and Explainability

Transparency and explainability are crucial aspects of ethical AI design, ensuring that users understand how AI algorithms operate and why certain decisions are made. Here's a detailed exploration of how designers can achieve transparency and explainability in AI systems:

1. Clear Documentation and Communication:
Designers should provide clear documentation and communication about how AI algorithms work, including their objectives, inputs, decision-making processes, and limitations. This documentation should be accessible to users in easily understandable language, avoiding technical jargon or complexity that may obscure understanding

2. Visualizations and Explanations:
Visualizations can be powerful tools for explaining complex AI algorithms to users. Designers can use charts, diagrams, or interactive visualizations to illustrate how data flows through the system, how decisions are made, and what factors influence outcomes. Additionally, designers can provide textual explanations alongside visualizations to further clarify key concepts.

3. Interpretability Techniques:
Designers can employ interpretability techniques to make AI models more transparent and understandable. This may involve using techniques such as feature importance analysis, partial dependence plots, or local interpretable model-agnostic explanations (LIME) to highlight the factors driving model predictions and clarify how inputs are mapped to outputs.

4. User Control and Feedback:
Empowering users with control over AI-driven features and providing mechanisms for feedback can enhance transparency and trust. Designers should enable users to adjust settings, customize preferences, and provide feedback on algorithmic decisions. By involving users in the decision-making process, designers can foster transparency and accountability in AI systems.

5. Ethical Design Principles:
Designers should adhere to ethical design principles that prioritize transparency, fairness, and user autonomy. This involves designing AI systems with the user's best interests in mind, respecting their rights to privacy and informed consent, and minimizing the risk of unintended consequences or harm. By aligning design practices with ethical principles, designers can build trust and confidence in AI technologies.

6. Robust Testing and Validation:
Designers should conduct robust testing and validation of AI algorithms to ensure that they operate as intended and produce reliable results. This involves evaluating the performance of AI systems across diverse scenarios, datasets, and user groups to identify potential biases, errors, or unintended behaviors. Transparent reporting of testing methodologies and outcomes can help users understand the reliability and limitations of AI systems.

7. Continuous Improvement and Accountability:

Designers should prioritize continuous improvement and accountability in AI design, iterating on designs based on user feedback, emerging best practices, and evolving ethical standards. This involves monitoring the performance of AI systems over time, addressing any issues or concerns that arise, and maintaining transparency about changes made to the system. By fostering a culture of accountability, designers can demonstrate their commitment to transparency and ethical AI design.

Achieving transparency and explainability in AI design requires clear documentation, visualizations, interpretability techniques, user control and feedback mechanisms, adherence to ethical design principles, robust testing and validation, and a commitment to continuous improvement and accountability. By prioritizing transparency, designers can build trust and confidence in AI systems, empowering users to make informed decisions and fostering responsible use of AI technologies.

User Autonomy and Control

User autonomy and control are foundational principles in AI design, ensuring that users have agency over their interactions with AI-driven systems. Here's an in-depth exploration of how designers can uphold user autonomy and provide meaningful control:

1. Clear Settings and Preferences:

Designers should offer clear settings and preferences that allow users to customize their interactions with AI features. This may include options to enable or disable AI-driven functionalities, adjust preferences related to personalization or recommendations, and configure privacy settings. Clear, intuitive interfaces should guide users through these settings to ensure ease of use and understanding.

2. Granular Controls and Customization:
Providing granular controls and customization options empowers users to tailor their experiences according to their preferences and needs. Designers should offer a range of options for adjusting AI-driven features, such as fine-tuning recommendations, setting notification preferences, or specifying data-sharing preferences. By allowing users to customize their interactions, designers respect individual preferences and foster a sense of ownership over the user experience.

3. Opt-In and Opt-Out Mechanisms:
Transparency and choice are essential aspects of user autonomy. Designers should implement clear opt-in and opt-out mechanisms that give users control over whether they engage with AI-driven features or functionalities. This may involve presenting users with explicit choices during onboarding or within the product settings, clearly outlining the implications of their decisions, and respecting their preferences without imposing defaults.

4. Educational Resources and Explanations:
To support informed decision-making, designers should provide educational resources and explanations about AI-driven features and their implications. This may include tooltips, tutorials, or contextual help prompts that explain how AI algorithms work, what data is used, and how user choices impact their experiences. By offering transparent information, designers empower users to make informed decisions aligned with their preferences and values.

5. Feedback Mechanisms:
Enabling feedback mechanisms allows users to express their preferences, provide input on AI-driven features, and report

issues or concerns. Designers should establish accessible channels for users to submit feedback, such as feedback forms, in-app surveys, or direct contact options. Responsive feedback loops demonstrate a commitment to listening to user input and adapting AI-driven functionalities based on their needs and preferences.

6. Privacy and Data Control:
Central to user autonomy is control over personal data and privacy. Designers should prioritize data privacy by implementing robust data protection measures, obtaining explicit consent for data collection and processing, and providing users with options for managing their data. Transparent privacy policies and settings that enable users to control data sharing and visibility enhance user trust and confidence in the technology.

7. Respect for User Choices:
Ultimately, respecting user choices is paramount in upholding user autonomy. Designers should honor user preferences and decisions regarding their interactions with AI-driven features, avoiding intrusive or coercive practices that undermine user agency. By prioritizing user autonomy, designers cultivate trust, loyalty, and satisfaction among users, fostering positive experiences and long-term engagement with the product.

Upholding user autonomy and providing meaningful control in AI design involves offering clear settings and preferences, granular customization options, opt-in and opt-out mechanisms, educational resources and explanations, feedback mechanisms, privacy and data control measures, and a fundamental respect for user choices. By prioritizing user autonomy, designers empower users to shape their experiences, fostering trust, satisfaction, and engagement with AI-driven systems..

Privacy by Design

Privacy by Design is a fundamental concept in AI design, emphasizing the proactive integration of privacy considerations throughout the development process. Here's a comprehensive exploration of how designers can implement Privacy by Design principles in AI systems:

1. Data Minimization:
Designers should prioritize data minimization, collecting only the minimum amount of user data necessary to achieve the intended purpose. This involves identifying the specific data points required for AI functionality and avoiding unnecessary data collection. By minimizing data collection, designers reduce the risk of privacy breaches and ensure that user privacy is preserved.

2. Anonymization and Pseudonymization:
Anonymizing and pseudonymizing user data help protect user privacy by dissociating personal identifiers from individual records. Designers should implement robust anonymization techniques to prevent the identification of individual users from data sets. Pseudonymization involves replacing identifiable information with pseudonyms, further enhancing user privacy while still allowing for data analysis and processing.

3. Data Encryption and Security:
Ensuring the security of user data is essential in protecting privacy. Designers should implement strong encryption protocols to secure data both in transit and at rest. This involves using encryption algorithms to encode sensitive information, such as user credentials or personal data, and implementing secure storage mechanisms to prevent unauthorized access or data breaches.

4. User Consent and Control:

Transparency and user control are central to Privacy by Design. Designers should obtain explicit user consent for data collection and processing activities, clearly communicating the purposes and scope of data usage. Additionally, designers should provide users with granular control over their data, including options to review, edit, or delete their information, as well as settings to manage data-sharing preferences.

5. Privacy Impact Assessments (PIAs):

Conducting Privacy Impact Assessments (PIAs) helps identify and mitigate potential privacy risks throughout the design process. Designers should systematically assess the impact of AI features on user privacy, considering factors such as data sensitivity, data retention periods, and potential privacy vulnerabilities. PIAs enable designers to proactively address privacy concerns and implement appropriate safeguards.

6. Privacy-Enhancing Technologies (PETs):

Leveraging Privacy-Enhancing Technologies (PETs) strengthens user privacy within AI systems. Designers can integrate PETs such as differential privacy, federated learning, or homomorphic encryption to enhance data protection and minimize privacy risks. These technologies enable AI functionality while preserving user anonymity and confidentiality, aligning with Privacy by Design principles.

7. Transparent Data Practices:

Transparency fosters trust and accountability in AI systems. Designers should adopt transparent data practices, clearly articulating how user data is collected, processed, and utilized within the AI system. This includes providing accessible privacy policies, data usage notices, and user-friendly interfaces that enable users to understand and control their privacy settings.

8. Continuous Monitoring and Compliance:

Privacy is an ongoing concern that requires continuous monitoring and compliance efforts. Designers should implement mechanisms for monitoring data usage, detecting potential privacy incidents, and responding promptly to mitigate risks. Regular audits and compliance checks ensure that AI systems adhere to privacy regulations and industry best practices.

Privacy by Design entails minimizing data collection, anonymizing and pseudonymizing user data, encrypting and securing data, obtaining user consent and control, conducting Privacy Impact Assessments, leveraging Privacy-Enhancing Technologies, adopting transparent data practices, and ensuring continuous monitoring and compliance. By embedding privacy considerations into the very fabric of AI design, designers can uphold user privacy, trust, and confidence in AI systems.

Inclusivity and Accessibility

Inclusivity and accessibility are foundational principles in AI design, aiming to ensure that AI-powered products are usable and beneficial for all users, regardless of their abilities, languages, or cultural backgrounds. Here's a detailed exploration of how designers can prioritize inclusivity and accessibility in AI design:

1. User-Centered Design:

Designers should adopt a user-centered approach, placing the needs and preferences of diverse user groups at the forefront of the design process. This involves conducting thorough user research to understand the unique challenges and requirements of users with different abilities, languages, and cultural contexts.

2. Accessibility Standards and Guidelines:

Familiarity with accessibility standards and guidelines, such as the Web Content Accessibility Guidelines (WCAG), is essential for designing inclusive AI interfaces. Designers should ensure that AI-powered products comply with accessibility standards, making them perceivable, operable, understandable, and robust for users with disabilities.

3. Adaptive Interfaces:

Designers should create adaptive interfaces that accommodate diverse user needs and preferences. This may involve offering customizable settings, such as font size adjustments, color contrast options, and alternative input methods, to cater to users with different abilities and preferences.

4. Multilingual Support:

AI interfaces should support multiple languages to accommodate users from diverse linguistic backgrounds. Designers should provide robust localization capabilities, including translations, cultural adaptations, and support for non-Latin scripts, to ensure that AI-powered products are accessible to users worldwide.

5. Cultural Sensitivity:

Cultural sensitivity is paramount in AI design to avoid inadvertently excluding or offending users from different cultural backgrounds. Designers should consider cultural norms, values, and preferences when designing AI interfaces, ensuring that content and imagery resonate with diverse audiences respectfully and inclusively.

6. Inclusive Design Practices:

Inclusive design practices involve involving users with diverse abilities and backgrounds in the design process. Designers should engage in co-design sessions, usability testing, and feedback sessions with representative users to identify and address accessibility barriers and ensure that AI products are inclusive by design.

7. Assistive Technologies Compatibility:
AI interfaces should be compatible with assistive technologies commonly used by individuals with disabilities, such as screen readers, magnification software, and alternative input devices. Designers should test AI products with assistive technologies to verify compatibility and address any accessibility issues that may arise.

8. Continuous Improvement and Iteration:
Designing inclusive AI products is an iterative process that requires continuous improvement and iteration. Designers should solicit feedback from users with diverse abilities and backgrounds, monitor accessibility metrics, and prioritize accessibility enhancements in subsequent design iterations to ensure ongoing inclusivity.

By prioritizing inclusivity and accessibility in AI design, designers can create products that are usable, equitable, and beneficial for all users, fostering a more inclusive digital landscape.

Ethical Decision-Making in AI Interfaces

Incorporating ethical decision-making into AI interfaces is essential as conversational and interactive AI systems become more prevalent. Designers play a crucial role in embedding ethical frameworks within these systems to ensure that they operate in alignment with societal values. Here's a detailed exploration of how designers can integrate ethical decision-making into AI interfaces:

1. Defining Ethical Guidelines:
Designers should establish clear ethical guidelines for AI interfaces, outlining principles and values that guide decision-

making. These guidelines should address key ethical considerations such as fairness, transparency, privacy, accountability, and respect for user autonomy. By defining ethical parameters upfront, designers provide a framework for ethical decision-making throughout the development process.

2. Transparent Decision-Making Processes:
AI interfaces should provide users with insights into how ethical considerations are integrated into the decision-making process. Designers should strive to make decision-making processes transparent and understandable, allowing users to have visibility into how AI algorithms operate and the factors that influence their decisions. Transparency fosters trust and empowers users to make informed choices.

3. Fairness and Bias Mitigation:
Designers must actively work to identify and mitigate biases within AI algorithms to ensure fair and equitable outcomes. This involves scrutinizing training data, testing for bias, and implementing measures to address any disparities in the system's responses across diverse user groups. Designers should prioritize fairness in algorithmic decision-making to prevent discriminatory outcomes.

4. Privacy Protection:
Protecting user privacy is paramount in ethical AI design. Designers should implement robust privacy measures to safeguard user data and ensure that AI interfaces comply with privacy regulations and best practices. This may involve anonymizing user data, minimizing data collection, providing clear privacy notices, and offering users control over their personal information.

5. User Autonomy and Control:
Respecting user autonomy is essential in ethical AI design. Designers should provide users with meaningful controls

over AI-driven features and functionalities, allowing them to opt in or out of certain functionalities and customize their preferences. Empowering users to make informed choices enhances trust and fosters a sense of control over their interactions with AI interfaces.

6. Continual Ethical Review:
Ethical considerations should be an ongoing focus throughout the development lifecycle of AI interfaces. Designers should conduct regular ethical reviews and assessments to evaluate the impact of AI systems on users and society, identify potential ethical risks or issues, and implement corrective measures as needed. Continual ethical review ensures that AI interfaces evolve responsibly over time.

7. Collaborative Ethical Stewardship:
Ethical decision-making in AI interfaces requires collaboration across multidisciplinary teams, including designers, developers, ethicists, legal experts, and stakeholders. Designers act as ethical stewards, guiding the technology to align with societal values and ethical principles. By fostering a culture of ethical awareness and responsibility, designers contribute to the development of AI interfaces that benefit society as a whole.

By embedding ethical decision-making frameworks within AI interfaces, designers uphold ethical principles and values, promoting fairness, transparency, privacy, and user autonomy in the design and implementation of AI-powered systems.

Mitigating Unintended Consequences

Mitigating unintended consequences is crucial in AI design to ensure that AI products contribute positively to user experiences and societal well-being. Here's a detailed exploration of how designers can anticipate and address unintended consequences:

1. Thorough Impact Assessments:
Designers should conduct comprehensive impact assessments to identify potential risks and unintended consequences associated with AI design. This involves considering the broader implications of AI-powered systems on users, communities, and society as a whole. By systematically evaluating the potential impacts of AI products, designers can proactively address any foreseeable issues.

2. Risk Identification and Analysis:
Designers must identify and analyze potential risks and unintended consequences associated with AI design. This includes risks related to bias, discrimination, privacy violations, security vulnerabilities, and negative societal impacts. By conducting thorough risk assessments, designers can identify areas of concern and prioritize mitigation strategies accordingly.

3. Safeguards and Preventive Measures:
Designers should implement safeguards and preventive measures to mitigate potential risks and unintended consequences. This may involve incorporating checks and balances into AI algorithms to prevent biases or discriminatory outcomes, enhancing data security measures to protect user privacy, and implementing transparency mechanisms to ensure accountability. By proactively implementing preventive measures, designers can reduce the likelihood of unintended consequences.

4. User Testing and Feedback:
User testing and feedback play a crucial role in identifying and addressing unintended consequences in AI design. Designers should engage in iterative user testing to assess how users interact with AI products and identify any

unforeseen issues or negative outcomes. By soliciting feedback from diverse user groups, designers can gain insights into potential unintended consequences and iteratively improve the design to address them.

5. Ethical Considerations:
Ethical considerations should guide decision-making throughout the AI design process to mitigate unintended consequences. Designers should prioritize fairness, transparency, privacy, and user autonomy in AI design, ensuring that ethical principles are embedded into the design and implementation of AI-powered systems. By adhering to ethical guidelines, designers can minimize the risk of unintended negative impacts on users and society.

6. Continuous Monitoring and Evaluation:
Designers should continuously monitor and evaluate the performance and impact of AI products to identify and address any unintended consequences that may arise over time. This involves collecting and analyzing feedback from users, monitoring system behavior, and staying informed about emerging issues and concerns related to AI design. By maintaining vigilance and responsiveness, designers can effectively mitigate unintended consequences throughout the product lifecycle.

7. Collaborative Approach:
Mitigating unintended consequences requires collaboration across multidisciplinary teams, including designers, developers, ethicists, legal experts, and stakeholders. By fostering a culture of collaboration and knowledge sharing, designers can leverage diverse perspectives and expertise to anticipate and address potential risks and unintended consequences effectively.

By adopting a proactive approach to identifying and mitigating unintended consequences, designers can ensure that AI products are designed and implemented responsibly, contributing positively to user experiences and societal well-being.

Collaborative Ethical Design Practices

Collaborative ethical design practices are essential for ensuring that AI products prioritize inclusivity and accessibility. Here's an in-depth exploration of how cross-disciplinary teams can collaborate to integrate ethical considerations into AI design:

1. Multidisciplinary Teams:
Collaborative ethical design practices involve assembling multidisciplinary teams that bring together diverse expertise, including designers, developers, ethicists, social scientists, legal experts, and stakeholders. Each team member contributes unique perspectives and insights, enriching the ethical decision-making process.

2. Ethical Awareness and Education:
Designers must actively engage in ongoing dialogues within their teams and organizations to raise awareness about ethical considerations in AI design. This involves providing education and training on ethical principles, frameworks, and best practices to ensure that all team members have a foundational understanding of ethical issues related to AI.

3. Ethical Impact Assessments:
Collaborative teams should conduct ethical impact assessments to evaluate the potential implications of AI products on users, communities, and society as a whole. Ethicists and social scientists play a critical role in guiding these assessments, identifying potential risks, and proposing mitigation strategies to address ethical concerns.

4. Transparency and Accountability:
Transparency and accountability are essential components of collaborative ethical design practices. Designers, ethicists, and legal experts collaborate to ensure that AI systems are transparently designed and implemented, with clear explanations of how algorithms operate, the logic behind decision-making processes, and the implications of user interactions.

5. User-Centered Design:
Ethical design practices prioritize user-centered design, ensuring that AI products are inclusive and accessible to diverse user groups. Social scientists and user experience researchers collaborate with designers to conduct user research, gather feedback, and incorporate diverse perspectives into the design process to address the needs of all users.

6. Ethical Decision-Making Frameworks:
Collaborative teams develop and implement ethical decision-making frameworks that guide design choices and prioritize ethical principles such as fairness, transparency, privacy, and user autonomy. Ethicists and legal experts contribute to the development of these frameworks, ensuring that they align with legal and regulatory requirements and ethical standards.

7. Continuous Evaluation and Improvement:
Ethical design practices involve continuous evaluation and improvement of AI products to address emerging ethical issues and concerns. Cross-disciplinary teams collaborate to monitor user feedback, assess the impact of AI products on users and society, and iteratively refine design choices to ensure ethical integrity throughout the product lifecycle.

8. External Engagement and Stakeholder Dialogue:
Collaborative teams engage in external dialogue with stakeholders, including users, advocacy groups, regulators, and policymakers, to solicit feedback, address concerns, and

incorporate diverse perspectives into the design process. This external engagement ensures that AI products reflect the values and preferences of the broader community.

By embracing collaborative ethical design practices, multidisciplinary teams can ensure that AI products are designed and implemented in a manner that prioritizes inclusivity, accessibility, and ethical integrity, ultimately enhancing user experiences and societal well-being.

The Future of Ethical AI Design

The future of ethical AI design holds several key trends and challenges as technology advances. Here's a detailed exploration of what lies ahead:

1. Advanced AI Capabilities:
As AI technologies evolve, designers will face ethical challenges related to advanced capabilities such as deep learning, reinforcement learning, and autonomous decision-making. Designers must grapple with questions of accountability, transparency, and control as AI systems become more autonomous and self-learning.

2. Ethical Governance Frameworks:
The future of ethical AI design will involve the development and implementation of robust governance frameworks that guide the responsible use of AI technologies. These frameworks will outline principles, standards, and best practices for ethical AI design and deployment, providing a roadmap for designers to navigate complex ethical dilemmas.

3. Human-AI Collaboration:
Ethical AI design will increasingly focus on facilitating collaboration between humans and AI systems. Designers will need to create interfaces and interactions that empower users to understand, interact with, and control AI

147

technologies effectively. This human-centric approach ensures that AI systems augment human capabilities rather than replace them.

4. Explainable AI (XAI):
Explainable AI (XAI) will play a crucial role in ethical AI design, enabling designers to create transparent and understandable AI systems. Designers will need to develop techniques for explaining the inner workings of AI algorithms and decisions in a way that is accessible and meaningful to users, fostering trust and accountability.

5. Bias Mitigation and Fairness:
Addressing bias and ensuring fairness in AI systems will continue to be a priority for ethical AI design. Designers will need to implement techniques for detecting, mitigating, and preventing biases in AI algorithms and data sets, ensuring that AI systems produce equitable outcomes for all users.

6. Privacy-Preserving AI:
With growing concerns about data privacy, ethical AI design will emphasize the development of privacy-preserving AI technologies. Designers will need to implement privacy-enhancing techniques such as federated learning, differential privacy, and encrypted computation to protect user data while still enabling AI functionality.

7. Cross-Disciplinary Collaboration:
The future of ethical AI design will involve increased collaboration between designers, ethicists, social scientists, legal experts, and other stakeholders. Designers will need to work closely with multidisciplinary teams to address the complex ethical challenges associated with AI technologies and ensure that design choices reflect diverse perspectives and values.

8. Ethical Education and Training:
As AI becomes more prevalent in design practices, ethical education, and training will be essential for designers. Designers will need to develop a deep understanding of ethical principles, frameworks, and methodologies to navigate ethical dilemmas effectively and responsibly integrate ethical considerations into their design processes.

9. Global Standards and Regulation:
The future of ethical AI design will also be shaped by global standards and regulations. Designers will need to stay informed about evolving legal and regulatory requirements related to AI ethics and compliance, ensuring that their design practices align with international standards and best practices.

10. Continuous Learning and Adaptation:
Ethical AI design is a dynamic and evolving field, requiring designers to commit to continuous learning and adaptation. Designers will need to stay abreast of emerging technologies, ethical debates, and best practices, continuously refining their skills and approaches to meet the evolving challenges of AI design.

By embracing these trends and challenges, designers can pave the way for a future where AI technologies are ethically designed, responsibly deployed, and beneficial to society as a whole.

BALANCING AUTOMATION AND HUMAN TOUCH

In the ever-evolving landscape of AI-powered design, striking the right balance between automation and the human touch is a nuanced challenge. This chapter delves into the intricacies of human-centric design in the AI era, exploring how designers play a pivotal role in ensuring that automation enhances user experiences without compromising the essential elements of human interaction, empathy, and intuition.

The Duality of Automation and Human-Centric Design

The integration of AI into design processes introduces a duality between automation and human-centric design, presenting both opportunities and challenges for designers. Let's delve into the intricate balance between these two aspects:

1. Efficiency vs. Human Touch:
Automation offers efficiency by streamlining repetitive tasks, accelerating design iterations, and providing data-driven insights. However, relying too heavily on automation risks sacrificing the human touch that makes designs resonate with users emotionally. Designers must strike a balance between leveraging automation for efficiency and infusing designs with the creativity, empathy, and intuition that are hallmarks of human-centric design.

2. Data-Driven Insights vs. User Empathy:
AI-driven analytics and user research provide designers with valuable data-driven insights into user behavior, preferences, and trends. While these insights inform design decisions, designers must also cultivate empathy for users' needs, emotions, and experiences. Human-centric design requires designers to go beyond data and connect with users on a human level, understanding their aspirations, frustrations, and motivations.

3. Personalization vs. Privacy:
AI enables personalized experiences by tailoring content, recommendations, and interactions to individual users. However, personalization must be balanced with privacy considerations to respect users' autonomy and data rights.

Designers must implement privacy-preserving techniques and transparent communication to ensure that personalized experiences are built on trust and respect for user privacy.

4. Automation in Design Processes:
Automation plays a crucial role in optimizing design processes, from generating design variations to automating repetitive tasks such as layout design and image processing. By harnessing AI tools and algorithms, designers can expedite workflows, increase productivity, and focus on more creative and strategic aspects of design.

5. Human-Centered Design Principles:
Human-centered design principles remain essential in guiding design decisions and ensuring that designs meet users' needs and expectations. Designers must prioritize user research, usability testing, and iterative design approaches to create products and experiences that are intuitive, accessible, and meaningful to users.

6. Augmentation vs. Replacement:
AI augments rather than replaces human creativity and intuition in the design process. While automation streamlines certain tasks, such as data analysis and pattern recognition, human designers provide the critical thinking, emotional intelligence, and contextual understanding necessary to translate insights into compelling designs that resonate with users.

7. Iterative Collaboration:
Collaboration between designers and AI systems fosters an iterative process where human creativity and AI-driven insights complement each other. Designers refine and iterate designs based on AI-generated suggestions, user feedback, and their own creative instincts, continually refining the design until it achieves the desired balance of efficiency and human-centricity.

8. Ethical Considerations:

Ethical considerations underpin the interaction between automation and human-centric design. Designers must ensure that automated design processes adhere to ethical principles such as fairness, transparency, and user consent. Additionally, designers should critically evaluate the societal impact of automated design decisions and advocate for ethical AI practices within their organizations.

In navigating the duality of automation and human-centric design, designers must harness the power of AI to enhance efficiency and innovation while preserving the human touch that makes designs meaningful, empathetic, and inclusive. By striking the right balance between automation and human-centricity, designers can create products and experiences that enrich users' lives and contribute positively to society.

Augmenting Human Creativity with AI

Augmenting human creativity with AI represents a paradigm shift in the design process, where automation serves as a catalyst for innovation rather than a substitute for human ingenuity. Let's explore how AI augments human creativity in design:

1. Automating Routine Tasks:

AI streamlines repetitive tasks such as data analysis, image processing, and layout design, freeing designers from mundane chores and allowing them to focus on more creative aspects of the design process. By automating routine tasks, designers can allocate more time and mental energy to exploration, experimentation, and ideation.

2. Generating Design Variations:

AI algorithms can generate a multitude of design variations based on predefined parameters and constraints. Designers can leverage AI-powered tools to explore a vast array of design options rapidly, uncovering novel ideas and possibilities that may have been overlooked through manual exploration alone. This iterative process sparks creativity and encourages designers to think outside the box.

3. Enhancing Conceptualization:
AI tools assist designers in conceptualizing ideas by providing visualizations, simulations, and predictive insights. For example, generative design algorithms can produce complex geometries and structures that push the boundaries of traditional design paradigms. By visualizing concepts in a virtual environment, designers can iterate on designs more efficiently and refine their creative vision.

4. Inspiring Innovation:
AI-powered inspiration tools analyze vast datasets of design trends, historical references, and user preferences to inspire designers with fresh ideas and insights. These tools can uncover patterns, themes, and correlations that spark innovative thinking and inform the creative process. By exposing designers to diverse sources of inspiration, AI fosters a culture of innovation and experimentation.

5. Personalizing Creative Workflows:
AI tailors creative workflows to individual designers' preferences, habits, and working styles. For instance, AI-powered assistants can curate content, suggest design resources, and automate repetitive tasks based on designers' past behavior and feedback. By personalizing creative workflows, AI enhances designers' productivity and facilitates a more seamless and enjoyable design experience.

6. Cross-Disciplinary Collaboration:
AI facilitates collaboration between designers and other disciplines, such as data scientists, engineers, and domain experts. By integrating AI expertise into multidisciplinary teams, designers gain access to diverse perspectives,

knowledge, and skills that enrich the creative process. Collaborative environments foster cross-pollination of ideas and foster innovation at the intersection of different fields.

7. Exploring Novel Solutions:
AI enables designers to explore novel solutions to complex design problems by simulating scenarios, predicting outcomes, and optimizing designs based on data-driven insights. Designers can experiment with unconventional approaches and push the boundaries of traditional design conventions with the support of AI-powered tools and algorithms.

8. Iterative Feedback Loops:
AI facilitates iterative feedback loops where designers receive real-time feedback on their designs, enabling them to iterate rapidly and refine their creative concepts. By incorporating user feedback, performance metrics, and AI-generated suggestions, designers can iterate on designs iteratively, improving their quality and relevance over time.

In essence, augmenting human creativity with AI transforms the design process into a collaborative partnership between human designers and intelligent machines. By leveraging AI's capabilities to automate routine tasks, generate innovative ideas, and personalize creative workflows, designers can unleash their full creative potential and push the boundaries of design innovation.

Preserving Empathy in AI-Driven Interactions

Preserving empathy in AI-driven interactions is crucial to maintaining meaningful connections between users and intelligent systems. Here's a detailed exploration of how designers can ensure that AI interfaces retain empathy:

1. Understanding User Emotions and Needs:
Designers leverage AI-powered sentiment analysis and emotion recognition algorithms to understand users' emotional states and needs. By analyzing text, voice, and facial expressions, AI systems can detect subtle cues and tailor interactions accordingly. Designers use this insight to design interfaces that respond empathetically to users' emotions, providing support, encouragement, or reassurance as needed.

2. Empathetic Language and Tone:
AI interfaces use natural language processing (NLP) to communicate with users in a human-like manner. Designers craft dialogue scripts and conversational flows that convey empathy, warmth, and understanding. By using empathetic language and tone, AI systems can build rapport with users and create a more engaging and supportive interaction experience.

3. Personalization and Context Awareness:
AI interfaces personalize interactions based on users' preferences, behaviors, and contexts. Designers leverage user data and machine learning algorithms to anticipate users' needs and tailor responses accordingly. By adapting to individual preferences and situations, AI systems demonstrate empathy by acknowledging users' unique circumstances and providing relevant assistance.

4. Visual and Gestural Empathy:
Designers incorporate visual and gestural cues into AI interfaces to express empathy non-verbally. This may include using animations, illustrations, or avatar expressions to convey emotions such as empathy, concern, or understanding. By adding these visual elements, AI interfaces enhance the emotional resonance of interactions and create a more empathetic user experience.

5. Active Listening and Feedback:
AI interfaces demonstrate empathy by actively listening to users' input and providing thoughtful feedback. Designers implement features such as acknowledgment messages, progress indicators, and follow-up questions to signal that the system is attentive and responsive to users' needs. By demonstrating active listening and feedback, AI systems show that they value users' input and are committed to addressing their concerns.

6. Empathetic Error Handling:
Designers design error messages and error recovery flows with empathy in mind. AI interfaces communicate errors in a clear, non-judgmental manner and provide guidance on how users can resolve the issue. By empathetically acknowledging users' frustration or confusion, AI systems help users feel supported and reassured during challenging moments.

7. Ethical Considerations and User Well-being:
Designers prioritize ethical considerations in AI-driven interactions to ensure that user well-being is safeguarded. This may involve setting boundaries for data collection, respecting users' privacy preferences, and avoiding situations that may cause harm or discomfort. By prioritizing user well-being, AI interfaces demonstrate empathy and foster trust with users.

Preserving empathy in AI-driven interactions requires designers to understand users' emotions and needs, personalize interactions, incorporate visual and gestural cues, actively listen to feedback, handle errors empathetically, and prioritize ethical considerations. By infusing AI interfaces with empathetic elements, designers create more meaningful and supportive interaction experiences that foster trust and connection with users.

Customization vs. Standardization

The balance between customization and standardization is a critical consideration for designers as they integrate automation, particularly AI, into product experiences. Here's a detailed exploration of this challenge and how designers navigate it:

1. Understanding User Preferences:
Designers leverage AI to analyze user data and understand individual preferences, behaviors, and needs. By gathering insights from user interactions, AI systems can personalize experiences based on factors such as past behavior, demographic information, and stated preferences. This customization enhances user satisfaction by delivering content, features, and recommendations tailored to each user's unique preferences.

2. Personalization Algorithms:
AI algorithms power personalization by dynamically adjusting content, layout, and functionality to match user preferences. Designers develop algorithms that learn from user interactions and adapt the user experience in real-time. These algorithms can range from simple rules-based systems to sophisticated machine learning models that analyze large datasets to predict user preferences and behavior.

3. Balancing Flexibility and Consistency:
Designers strive to strike a balance between flexibility and consistency in AI-driven interfaces. While customization offers flexibility to meet individual needs, standardization ensures consistency in the overall user experience. Designers establish design patterns, style guides, and UI components that provide a consistent visual language and interaction model across different parts of the product. This standardization promotes usability and familiarity while allowing for customization within predefined parameters.

4. Modular Design and Component Libraries:
Designers adopt modular design principles and maintain component libraries to facilitate both customization and standardization. Modular design allows designers to create reusable UI components that can be assembled and customized to meet specific user needs. Component libraries ensure consistency by providing a standardized set of design elements, while still allowing for customization through variations and overrides.

5. User-Controlled Customization:
Designers empower users to control the level of customization in their experiences. AI-driven interfaces may include settings and preferences that allow users to adjust the level of personalization, such as choosing content preferences, setting notification preferences, or adjusting interface layouts. By giving users control over their customization options, designers ensure that users can tailor their experiences to suit their preferences without overwhelming them with choices.

6. Iterative Design and User Feedback:
Designers employ an iterative design process that incorporates user feedback to refine customization features. Through user testing, surveys, and analytics, designers gather insights into how users interact with personalized elements and identify areas for improvement. This iterative approach allows designers to fine-tune customization features to better align with user preferences and expectations over time.

7. Ethical Considerations:
Designers consider ethical implications when implementing customization features, particularly in areas such as privacy and data protection. Designers prioritize transparency and user consent, ensuring that users understand how their data is used to personalize their experiences and have the option

to opt out of personalized features if desired. By addressing ethical concerns, designers build trust and credibility with users, enhancing the overall user experience.

Designers navigate the balance between customization and standardization by leveraging AI to offer personalized experiences while maintaining consistency and usability. By adopting modular design principles, empowering users with control over customization options, and prioritizing ethical considerations, designers create AI-driven interfaces that cater to individual preferences without sacrificing the integrity of the user experience.

Redefining User Engagement

Redefining user engagement in the context of automation requires designers to reimagine how users interact with interfaces and the overall experience they have with products. Here's a detailed exploration of this concept and how designers address the challenge:

1. Understanding User Needs:
Designers start by deeply understanding user needs, preferences, and expectations. They conduct user research, gather feedback, and analyze user behavior data to gain insights into what motivates users to engage with products. This understanding serves as the foundation for designing engaging and relevant experiences.

2. Personalization and Context-Awareness:
Automation enables designers to create personalized and context-aware interactions that resonate with users. By leveraging data analytics and machine learning algorithms, designers can tailor content, recommendations, and interactions based on individual user preferences, behaviors, and situational context. This level of personalization enhances user engagement by delivering content and

experiences that are timely, relevant, and meaningful to users.

3. Interactive and Conversational Interfaces:
Designers incorporate interactive and conversational interfaces to facilitate engaging interactions with users. Chatbots, virtual assistants, and voice-enabled interfaces provide users with intuitive and conversational ways to interact with products. These interfaces simulate natural human conversation, making interactions more engaging and enjoyable for users.

4. Gamification and Reward Mechanisms:
Designers employ gamification and reward mechanisms to incentivize user engagement. By integrating elements such as points, badges, leaderboards, and challenges into the user experience, designers create a sense of achievement and progression that motivates users to interact with products more frequently and deeply. Gamification encourages users to explore different features, participate in activities, and return to the product regularly.

5. Multi-Channel Engagement:
Automation allows designers to engage users across multiple channels and touchpoints, creating seamless and consistent experiences. Designers design experiences that span websites, mobile apps, social media platforms, email, messaging apps, and other digital channels. This omnichannel approach ensures that users can engage with products wherever they are and whenever they prefer, enhancing convenience and accessibility.

6. Predictive and Proactive Engagement:
Automation enables designers to anticipate user needs and proactively engage users before they even realize they need assistance. By analyzing user behavior patterns and predictive analytics, designers can anticipate user intentions,

preferences, and potential pain points. They then design interfaces that provide timely recommendations, suggestions, or assistance, making interactions more efficient and effective for users.

7. Emotional Design and Brand Experience:
Designers focus on emotional design principles to evoke positive emotions and create memorable experiences for users. They pay attention to elements such as color, typography, imagery, and micro-interactions to create interfaces that resonate emotionally with users. By aligning the user experience with the brand's values and personality, designers create a cohesive and immersive brand experience that fosters user loyalty and engagement.

8. Iterative Design and Continuous Improvement:
Designers embrace an iterative design process that involves testing, learning, and refining interactions based on user feedback and data insights. They continuously monitor user engagement metrics, such as time spent on site, click-through rates, and conversion rates, to evaluate the effectiveness of interactions and identify areas for improvement. This iterative approach ensures that user engagement strategies evolve over time to meet changing user needs and preferences.

Designers redefine user engagement by leveraging automation to create personalized, interactive, and context-aware experiences that resonate with users on an emotional level. By incorporating elements such as personalization, conversational interfaces, gamification, and predictive engagement, designers foster meaningful connections with users and drive long-term engagement and loyalty.

Collaborative Human-AI Decision-Making

Collaborative human-AI decision-making represents a symbiotic relationship between human expertise and artificial intelligence (AI) capabilities, where both entities contribute to the decision-making process. Here's an in-depth exploration of this concept and how designers facilitate interfaces for such collaborative endeavors:

1. Transparency and Explainability:
Designers prioritize transparency and explainability in presenting AI-generated insights to humans. They ensure that users understand how AI algorithms arrive at their conclusions and recommendations. This transparency builds trust and confidence in AI-driven decision-making processes, empowering users to assess the validity and relevance of AI-generated insights.

2. User-Friendly Interfaces:
Designers create user-friendly interfaces that facilitate interactions between humans and AI systems. These interfaces are intuitive, easy to navigate, and visually appealing, ensuring a seamless and enjoyable user experience. Designers employ principles of user-centered design to understand user needs, preferences, and workflows, tailoring interfaces to meet the specific requirements of diverse user groups.

3. Interpretability of Results:
Designers ensure that AI-generated insights are presented in a format that is easily interpretable by humans. They use visualizations, charts, graphs, and natural language explanations to convey complex data and analytical results in a comprehensible manner. By simplifying technical jargon and presenting information in an accessible format, designers enable users to make sense of AI-generated insights and derive actionable conclusions.

4. Customizable Preferences:
Designers incorporate features that allow users to customize their preferences and parameters for AI-driven decision-

making. Users can adjust settings, criteria, and thresholds based on their domain expertise, preferences, and contextual requirements. This customization empowers users to tailor AI-generated insights to their specific needs and preferences, enhancing the relevance and utility of decision-making outputs.

5. Feedback Mechanisms:
Designers implement feedback mechanisms that enable users to provide input, corrections, and feedback on AI-generated insights. Users can flag inaccuracies, provide additional context, or suggest alternative approaches based on their domain knowledge and experience. This feedback loop facilitates continuous improvement and refinement of AI algorithms, ensuring that decision-making processes evolve over time to reflect changing user needs and feedback.

6. Human Oversight and Intervention:
Designers incorporate mechanisms for human oversight and intervention in AI-driven decision-making processes. Humans have the final say in approving, modifying or rejecting AI-generated recommendations based on their judgment, intuition, and expertise. Designers design interfaces that enable humans to easily review, validate, and override AI-generated insights, ensuring that decisions align with organizational goals, ethical considerations, and user preferences.

7. Education and Training:
Designers provide educational resources and training materials to help users understand the capabilities and limitations of AI systems. Users receive guidance on how to interpret AI-generated insights, assess their reliability, and incorporate them into decision-making processes effectively. This education empowers users to become informed and competent collaborators in human-AI decision-making efforts.

8. Continuous Monitoring and Evaluation:
Designers implement mechanisms for continuous monitoring and evaluation of AI-driven decision-making processes. They track key performance indicators, user satisfaction metrics, and decision outcomes to assess the effectiveness and impact of AI-generated insights. This monitoring enables designers to identify areas for improvement, refine AI algorithms, and enhance the overall decision-making experience for users.

Collaborative human-AI decision-making involves designing interfaces that promote transparency, usability, and user empowerment. By prioritizing transparency, interpretability, customization, feedback, human oversight, education, and continuous monitoring, designers facilitate effective collaboration between humans and AI systems in decision-making processes.

Adaptive Learning and Iterative Design

Adaptive learning and iterative design represent a dynamic approach to human-centric design in the AI era. This methodology emphasizes continuous improvement and responsiveness to user feedback and changing circumstances. Here's a detailed exploration of how adaptive learning and iterative design are applied in human-centric design:

1. Continuous Feedback Loops:
Designers establish continuous feedback loops to gather insights from users throughout the product development lifecycle. They solicit feedback through various channels such as user testing, surveys, analytics data, and direct user interactions. This feedback provides valuable insights into user preferences, pain points, and emerging needs, guiding iterative design decisions.

2. Data-Driven Iteration:
Designers leverage data analytics and user research to inform iterative design decisions. They analyze quantitative and qualitative data to identify patterns, trends, and areas for improvement. This data-driven approach enables designers to make informed decisions based on empirical evidence, rather than subjective opinions or assumptions.

3. User-Centric Design Thinking:
Designers adopt a user-centric design thinking approach, prioritizing the needs, goals, and experiences of users. They empathize with users, seeking to understand their perspectives, behaviors, and motivations. Designers employ techniques such as user personas, journey mapping, and empathy mapping to gain deeper insights into user needs and preferences, informing iterative design iterations.

4. Agile Methodologies:
Designers embrace agile methodologies such as Scrum or Kanban to facilitate iterative design and development cycles. They break down the design process into small, manageable tasks or sprints, allowing for frequent iterations and adaptations based on user feedback. Agile methodologies promote collaboration, flexibility, and responsiveness, enabling designers to quickly iterate and refine designs in response to changing requirements.

5. Prototyping and Testing:
Designers create prototypes to quickly validate design concepts and gather feedback from users. They conduct usability testing sessions to observe how users interact with prototypes and identify usability issues or areas for improvement. Prototyping and testing enable designers to iterate rapidly, refining designs based on real user insights and preferences.

6. Collaborative Cross-Functional Teams:
Designers collaborate closely with cross-functional teams, including developers, product managers, and stakeholders, throughout the iterative design process. They foster a culture of collaboration and communication, ensuring that everyone is aligned with the design goals and user-centric principles. Collaborative teams facilitate knowledge sharing, creativity, and collective problem-solving, driving iterative design improvements.

7. Flexible Design Tools and Workflows:
Designers utilize flexible design tools and workflows that support iterative design processes. They leverage tools such as prototyping software, design systems, and version control systems to streamline collaboration and iteration. Flexible workflows allow designers to iterate rapidly, experiment with different design solutions, and incorporate feedback efficiently.

8. Continuous Learning and Adaptation:
Designers embrace a mindset of continuous learning and adaptation, recognizing that design solutions evolve over time. They stay updated on emerging design trends, technologies, and user behaviors, incorporating new insights into their iterative design approach. Continuous learning enables designers to evolve their skills, perspectives, and design methodologies, driving ongoing improvement in human-centric design practices.

Adaptive learning and iterative design involve a user-centric, data-driven, and collaborative approach to product design. By continuously gathering feedback, iterating based on user insights, and fostering collaboration across cross-functional teams, designers create products that are responsive, adaptive, and aligned with the evolving needs and preferences of users.

Ethical Considerations in Balancing Automation

Ethical considerations in balancing automation in design reflect the importance of ensuring that technology serves users responsibly while respecting their rights, privacy, and autonomy. Here's an in-depth exploration of the ethical dimensions involved:

1. User Privacy and Data Protection:
Designers must prioritize user privacy and data protection when implementing automated processes. They should ensure that automated systems collect only the necessary data for their intended purposes and handle user data securely and confidentially. Designers should also provide transparent information about data collection practices and obtain user consent for data processing activities.

2. Fairness and Bias Mitigation:
Automated processes should be designed to mitigate biases and ensure fairness in outcomes. Designers must carefully assess and address potential biases in AI algorithms, data sets, and decision-making processes to prevent discriminatory or unfair outcomes. They should implement measures such as bias detection, algorithmic auditing, and fairness testing to identify and mitigate biases in automated systems.

3. Transparency and Explainability:
Designers should strive to make automated processes transparent and explainable to users. Users should understand how automated systems work, the logic behind their decisions, and the potential implications of their actions. Designers should provide clear explanations and insights into automated processes, enabling users to make informed decisions and understand the basis for system recommendations or actions.

4. User Autonomy and Control:
Automated processes should respect user autonomy and provide users with meaningful control over their interactions with technology. Designers should offer users options to customize and adjust automated settings according to their preferences and needs. They should also enable users to opt in or out of automated features and provide mechanisms for users to override or intervene in automated decisions when necessary.

5. Accountability and Responsibility:
Designers bear responsibility for the ethical implications of automated processes and should be held accountable for their decisions and actions. They should proactively consider the potential ethical consequences of automation and take steps to mitigate risks and prevent harm. Designers should also advocate for ethical design practices within their organizations and collaborate with stakeholders to uphold ethical standards in automated systems.

6. Human-Centered Design Principles:
Ethical considerations in balancing automation should be guided by human-centered design principles that prioritize the needs, well-being, and dignity of users. Designers should ensure that automated processes enhance user experiences, empower users, and contribute positively to their lives. They should incorporate empathy, inclusivity, and accessibility into automated systems, ensuring that they serve diverse user populations ethically and responsibly.

7. Continuous Ethical Reflection and Improvement:
Designers should engage in continuous ethical reflection and improvement to address emerging ethical challenges and dilemmas in automation. They should stay informed about developments in AI ethics, participate in ethical discussions and debates, and actively seek feedback from users and stakeholders on the ethical implications of automated

processes. Designers should be open to revising and improving automated systems based on ethical considerations and evolving societal norms.

Ethical considerations in balancing automation in design require designers to prioritize user privacy, fairness, transparency, autonomy, accountability, and human-centered design principles. By upholding ethical standards and responsibly integrating automation into design processes, designers can ensure that technology serves users in a manner that is ethical, respectful, and beneficial.

Empowering Users Through Control

Empowering users through control is a fundamental aspect of human-centric design, especially in the context of AI-driven products. Here's an in-depth exploration of how designers can empower users through meaningful control:

1. Customization Options:
Designers should offer users a range of customization options to tailor AI-driven features according to their preferences and needs. This could include adjustable settings for personalization, recommendations, notifications, and other AI-driven functionalities. By providing customization options, users can personalize their experiences to align with their individual preferences and usage patterns.

2. Granular Control Settings:
Designers should implement granular control settings that allow users to fine-tune AI-driven features at a detailed level. For example, users should have the ability to specify preferences for content filtering, privacy settings, data sharing, and other aspects of AI-driven functionalities. Granular control settings empower users to manage their

interactions with AI systems according to their specific requirements and concerns.

3. Opt-Out Mechanisms:
Designers should provide users with clear and accessible opt-out mechanisms for AI-driven features. This allows users to choose whether they want to participate in AI-powered functionalities or prefer to disable them altogether. Opt-out mechanisms should be straightforward, transparent, and easy to use, ensuring that users can exercise their autonomy over their interactions with AI systems.

4. Transparency and Explanation:
Designers should ensure transparency and provide clear explanations about how AI-driven features work and the implications of user choices. This includes informing users about the data collected, the algorithms used, and the potential impact on their experiences. Transparent communication builds trust and helps users make informed decisions about whether to enable or disable AI-driven functionalities.

5. User Feedback and Iterative Improvement:
Designers should solicit user feedback and use it to iteratively improve control mechanisms for AI-driven features. This involves actively listening to user concerns, addressing issues and limitations, and refining control settings based on user preferences and suggestions. By involving users in the design process, designers can create control mechanisms that are intuitive, effective, and responsive to user needs.

6. Accessibility Considerations:
Designers should ensure that control mechanisms are accessible to all users, including those with disabilities or special needs. This may involve providing alternative input methods, enhancing visual or auditory cues, and offering assistive technologies to support users with diverse abilities.

Accessibility considerations ensure that all users can fully participate in controlling their interactions with AI-powered products.

7. Education and Empowerment:
Designers should educate users about the benefits of control and empower them to make informed decisions about their interactions with AI systems. This includes providing educational resources, tutorials, and guidance on how to use control settings effectively. By empowering users with knowledge and understanding, designers enable them to take ownership of their experiences and confidently navigate AI-driven products.

Empowering users through control involves offering customization options, granular control settings, opt-out mechanisms, transparency, user feedback, accessibility considerations, and education. By incorporating these elements into AI-driven products, designers can empower users to manage their interactions with technology in a manner that aligns with their preferences, values, and needs.

The Future Harmony of Automation and Human Touch

The future harmony of automation and the human touch represents a vision where AI seamlessly complements and enhances human experiences, rather than replacing or overshadowing them. Here's a detailed exploration of how designers can navigate this evolving landscape to achieve this harmonious balance:

1. Augmented Creativity:
Designers envision a future where AI augments human creativity, serving as a powerful tool for ideation, exploration, and innovation. AI-driven tools can assist designers in generating ideas, exploring design variations, and uncovering insights from vast amounts of data. By leveraging AI in this

way, designers can push the boundaries of creativity and unlock new possibilities for design expression.

2. Enhanced Empathy:

Designers recognize the importance of empathy in human-centric design and aim to preserve and enhance this quality in AI-driven interactions. AI can be trained to recognize and respond to human emotions, preferences, and contexts, allowing for more empathetic and personalized user experiences. Designers strive to imbue AI interfaces with empathy, ensuring that users feel understood, supported, and valued.

3. Ethical Considerations:

Designers prioritize ethical considerations in the development of AI-driven products, ensuring that automation aligns with principles of fairness, transparency, and accountability. Ethical guidelines and frameworks guide designers in making decisions that uphold human values and respect user rights. By embedding ethical principles into AI design practices, designers foster trust and confidence in technology.

4. Collaborative Decision-Making:

Designers advocate for a collaborative approach to decision-making, where humans and AI work together to achieve optimal outcomes. AI can analyze vast amounts of data and generate insights, while humans provide context, intuition, and judgment. By facilitating collaborative decision-making processes, designers harness the strengths of both humans and machines, leading to more informed and effective outcomes.

5. User-Centered Design:

Designers remain committed to user-centered design principles, ensuring that human needs, preferences, and values drive the design process. AI is employed to enhance user experiences, streamline workflows, and anticipate user needs, but the ultimate goal is always to create products that resonate with and empower users. Designers prioritize usability, accessibility, and inclusivity, ensuring that AI-driven products are intuitive, engaging, and beneficial to all users.

6. Continuous Learning and Adaptation:
Designers embrace a mindset of continuous learning and adaptation, recognizing that the AI landscape is constantly evolving. They stay abreast of emerging technologies, trends, and best practices, incorporating new insights into their design processes. By remaining agile and responsive, designers can leverage the latest advancements in AI to create innovative and impactful user experiences.

7. Human-Centered Innovation:
Designers champion human-centered innovation, where technology serves as a catalyst for positive change in people's lives. AI is harnessed to address real-world challenges, enhance productivity, and promote well-being, while always keeping the human experience at the forefront. Designers strive to create solutions that empower individuals, foster connections, and enrich human experiences in meaningful ways.

The future harmony of automation and the human touch is characterized by augmented creativity, enhanced empathy, ethical considerations, collaborative decision-making, user-centered design, continuous learning and adaptation, and human-centered innovation. By navigating these principles, designers can pave the way for a future where AI enriches and enhances human experiences in profound and transformative ways.

4. AGILE METHODOLOGIES IN AI PRODUCT MANAGEMENT

ADAPTING AGILE FOR AI PROJECTS

In the dynamic intersection of Agile methodologies and Artificial Intelligence (AI) product management, a new paradigm emerges, demanding flexibility, collaboration, and adaptability. This chapter delves into the intricacies of adapting Agile methodologies for AI projects, exploring how product managers navigate the unique challenges posed by the iterative nature of AI development, the dynamic capabilities of intelligent systems, and the evolving needs of users.

The Agile Foundation

The Agile Foundation serves as the cornerstone of modern product management, offering a robust framework for iterative development, collaboration, and adaptability. In the context of AI product management, Agile methodologies provide a solid foundation that empowers product managers to navigate the complexities of AI projects effectively. Here's an in-depth exploration of how the Agile Foundation supports AI product management:

1. Iterative Development:
Agile methodologies advocate for iterative development cycles, where products are built incrementally through a series of short iterations or sprints. This approach aligns well with AI projects, which often involve experimentation, testing, and refinement of algorithms and models. Product managers leverage iterative development to gather feedback, validate

assumptions, and make course corrections based on real-world insights.

2. Collaboration and Cross-Functional Teams:
Agile promotes collaboration among cross-functional teams, including product managers, engineers, data scientists, designers, and other stakeholders. In AI product management, cross-functional collaboration is essential for bridging the gap between technical and non-technical domains. By fostering collaboration, Agile enables teams to leverage diverse perspectives, skills, and expertise to solve complex problems and deliver value to users.

3. Responsiveness to Change:
Agile methodologies emphasize adaptability and responsiveness to change, allowing teams to pivot quickly in response to evolving requirements, market dynamics, and user feedback. In the context of AI product management, where algorithms and models may need frequent updates and refinements, the ability to embrace change is crucial. Agile enables product managers to prioritize flexibility, enabling them to incorporate new insights and adjust strategies as needed.

4. Continuous Improvement:
Agile promotes a culture of continuous improvement, where teams reflect on their processes, outcomes, and learnings to identify opportunities for enhancement. This mindset of continuous improvement is particularly relevant in AI product management, where innovation and optimization are ongoing processes. Product managers leverage Agile principles to foster a culture of learning, experimentation, and adaptation, driving continuous innovation and growth.

5. Customer-Centric Approach:
Agile methodologies prioritize customer satisfaction and value delivery, encouraging teams to focus on meeting the

needs and expectations of users. In AI product management, this customer-centric approach is paramount, as the ultimate goal is to create AI-powered solutions that solve real-world problems and deliver tangible benefits to users. Product managers leverage Agile frameworks to prioritize user feedback, validate hypotheses, and iterate on product features to ensure maximum value and impact.

6. Risk Mitigation:
Agile methodologies incorporate risk mitigation strategies, such as early and frequent testing, incremental delivery, and stakeholder engagement. In AI product management, where projects may face uncertainties related to algorithm performance, data quality, or regulatory compliance, these risk mitigation techniques are invaluable. Product managers use Agile practices to identify and address potential risks early in the development process, minimizing the impact of unforeseen challenges.

7. Empowerment and Autonomy:
Agile empowers teams to make autonomous decisions, encouraging individuals to take ownership of their work and contribute to the overall success of the project. In AI product management, where innovation and creativity are key drivers, this empowerment is essential for fostering a culture of experimentation and exploration. Product managers leverage Agile principles to empower teams, enabling them to collaborate, innovate, and deliver high-quality AI solutions.

The Agile Foundation provides a robust framework for AI product management, enabling product managers to embrace iterative development, collaboration, responsiveness to change, continuous improvement, customer-centricity, risk mitigation, and empowerment. By leveraging Agile methodologies, product managers can navigate the complexities of AI projects with confidence, delivering innovative and impactful solutions that meet the needs of users and stakeholders.

Iterative Development in the AI Landscape

Iterative development lies at the core of Agile methodologies, emphasizing the incremental and iterative delivery of value to users. In the context of the AI landscape, where projects often involve complex algorithms, data processing, and machine learning models, iterative development becomes even more crucial. Here's a detailed exploration of how iterative development operates in the AI landscape:

1. Continuous Learning and Improvement:
Iterative development in the AI landscape is driven by a commitment to continuous learning and improvement. Product managers recognize that AI projects require ongoing experimentation, testing, and refinement to achieve optimal performance. By breaking down development tasks into manageable iterations, teams can focus on making incremental enhancements to algorithms, models, and functionalities.

2. Short, Focused Cycles:
Agile sprints provide a structured framework for iterative development, typically spanning one to four weeks. In the AI landscape, these sprints allow teams to focus on specific objectives, such as refining algorithms, collecting and analyzing data, or implementing new features. Short, focused cycles enable teams to maintain momentum, adapt to changing requirements, and deliver value to users quickly.

3. Experimentation and Validation:
Iterative development encourages experimentation and validation of hypotheses. AI projects often involve uncertainty, requiring teams to explore different approaches, algorithms, and parameters. By conducting experiments

177

within each iteration, teams can gather empirical evidence, validate assumptions, and make data-driven decisions about the direction of the project.

4. Feedback-Driven Iterations:

User feedback plays a crucial role in guiding iterative development in the AI landscape. Product managers prioritize collecting feedback from users, stakeholders, and domain experts at each stage of the development process. This feedback informs subsequent iterations, enabling teams to address user needs, preferences, and pain points effectively.

5. Refinement and Optimization:

Iterative development allows teams to focus on refining and optimizing AI algorithms and models. Through successive iterations, teams can fine-tune parameters, optimize performance metrics, and enhance the robustness and reliability of the AI system. This iterative approach to refinement ensures that the final product meets or exceeds user expectations.

6. Adaptability to Change:

Agile methodologies emphasize adaptability to change, allowing teams to pivot quickly in response to new information or evolving requirements. In the AI landscape, where projects may encounter challenges related to data quality, algorithm performance, or user behavior, this adaptability is essential. Iterative development enables teams to course-correct as needed, ensuring that the project remains aligned with its objectives.

7. Risk Management:

Iterative development mitigates risks by breaking down the project into smaller, manageable chunks. By focusing on delivering incremental value, teams can identify and address potential risks early in the development process. This proactive approach to risk management reduces the likelihood of project delays or failures and increases the overall likelihood of project success.

8. Cross-Functional Collaboration:
Iterative development fosters collaboration among cross-functional teams, including product managers, data scientists, engineers, designers, and other stakeholders. By working together in short, focused cycles, teams can leverage their diverse skills and expertise to solve complex problems and deliver high-quality AI solutions.

Iterative development serves as a linchpin in the AI landscape, enabling teams to continuously learn, experiment, validate, refine, and adapt their AI projects to meet user needs and achieve project objectives. By embracing iterative development within the framework of Agile methodologies, product managers can navigate the complexities of AI projects with confidence, delivering innovative and impactful solutions that drive value for users and stakeholders alike.

Collaborative Cross-Functional Teams

Collaborative cross-functional teams are the backbone of Agile methodologies, and their importance becomes even more pronounced with the integration of AI into product development. Here's an in-depth exploration of how collaborative cross-functional teams operate in the context of AI-powered product development:

1. Diverse Expertise:
Collaborative cross-functional teams bring together individuals with diverse expertise, including product management, data science, engineering, design, and domain knowledge. Each team member contributes unique insights and skills to the project, enriching the development process and enhancing the overall quality of the product.

2. Shared Vision and Goals:
Effective collaboration hinges on a shared vision and goals. Product managers play a central role in aligning team members around a common purpose, ensuring that everyone understands the objectives of the project and their role in achieving them. By fostering a shared sense of ownership and accountability, product managers create a cohesive team dynamic that drives progress and innovation.

3. Iterative Development:
Cross-functional teams collaborate iteratively, working in short, focused cycles to deliver incremental value to users. Agile methodologies provide a framework for iterative development, allowing teams to break down complex projects into manageable tasks and prioritize their efforts based on user feedback and evolving requirements.

4. Communication and Transparency:
Effective communication and transparency are essential for successful collaboration. Cross-functional teams engage in regular meetings, stand-ups, and workshops to share progress, discuss challenges, and align on priorities. Product managers facilitate open and honest communication, creating a safe space for team members to express ideas, ask questions, and provide feedback.

5. Problem-Solving and Innovation:
Collaborative cross-functional teams excel at problem-solving and innovation. By leveraging the diverse perspectives and expertise of team members, teams can identify creative solutions to complex challenges, explore new ideas, and push the boundaries of what's possible. Product managers encourage experimentation and iteration, empowering team members to take calculated risks and learn from failure.

6. User-Centric Design:

Cross-functional teams prioritize user-centric design, placing the needs and preferences of users at the forefront of the development process. Designers collaborate closely with data scientists, engineers, and product managers to ensure that AI-powered products are intuitive, accessible, and delightful to use. User feedback drives iteration and refinement, resulting in products that resonate with their intended audience.

7. Agile Principles and Practices:

Collaborative cross-functional teams adhere to Agile principles and practices, such as continuous improvement, self-organization, and adaptability. Teams embrace change as a natural part of the development process, remaining flexible and responsive to evolving requirements and market dynamics. Agile ceremonies, such as sprint planning, retrospectives, and reviews, provide structure and guidance for collaborative teamwork.

8. Continuous Learning and Growth:

Collaboration within cross-functional teams fosters continuous learning and growth. Team members have the opportunity to expand their skill sets, learn from each other's expertise, and contribute to projects that have a meaningful impact. Product managers support professional development and create opportunities for knowledge sharing and mentorship within the team.

Collaborative cross-functional teams are the engine driving innovation and success in AI-powered product development. By bringing together individuals with diverse backgrounds and skills, fostering a shared vision and goals, and embracing Agile principles and practices, these teams create products that meet user needs, exceed expectations, and drive value for the organization.

Embracing Change in AI Models

Embracing change in AI models is fundamental to the success of Agile methodologies in the AI landscape. Here's an in-depth exploration of how Agile principles facilitate this process and the role of product managers in fostering a culture of adaptability and continuous improvement:

1. Continuous Learning and Improvement:
Agile methodologies emphasize continuous learning and improvement, which aligns seamlessly with the iterative nature of AI development. Product managers encourage teams to embrace change as an opportunity for growth, learning, and refinement of AI models. By fostering a culture of experimentation and iteration, teams can adapt their approaches based on new insights and emerging best practices.

2. Flexibility and Adaptability:
Agile methodologies prioritize flexibility and adaptability, allowing teams to respond quickly to changing requirements and market dynamics. In the context of AI development, this means being open to revising model architectures, adjusting training data, or incorporating new algorithms as the project progresses. Product managers empower teams to make informed decisions and pivot when necessary to stay aligned with project goals and user needs.

3. Iterative Development and Feedback Loops:
Agile methodologies rely on iterative development and frequent feedback loops to drive progress and validate assumptions. In the context of AI models, this means breaking down complex tasks into smaller, manageable chunks and continuously refining models based on user feedback and real-world data. Product managers facilitate regular reviews

and retrospectives to gather feedback, identify areas for improvement, and adjust project plans accordingly.

4. Collaboration and Cross-Functional Teams:
Agile methodologies promote collaboration and communication within cross-functional teams, enabling diverse perspectives and expertise to contribute to AI model development. Product managers foster a collaborative environment where data scientists, engineers, designers, and domain experts work together to solve problems, share knowledge, and drive innovation. This collaborative approach ensures that teams can adapt to changes in AI models effectively and leverage the full potential of their collective expertise.

5. Risk Management and Contingency Planning:
Agile methodologies emphasize risk management and contingency planning to mitigate potential disruptions and uncertainties. Product managers work with teams to identify potential risks associated with changes in AI models, develop contingency plans, and establish clear criteria for evaluating the impact of changes on project timelines and objectives. This proactive approach helps teams navigate uncertainty and maintain project momentum in the face of change.

6. Transparency and Communication:
Agile methodologies promote transparency and communication, ensuring that stakeholders are informed and involved throughout the development process. Product managers communicate openly about changes in AI models, their potential implications, and the rationale behind decision-making. By fostering transparency and trust, product managers help teams navigate change more effectively and maintain stakeholder confidence.

7. Embracing Uncertainty and Ambiguity:
Agile methodologies encourage teams to embrace uncertainty and ambiguity as natural aspects of the development process. In the context of AI development, this means acknowledging that models may evolve unpredictably as new data becomes available or algorithms are refined. Product managers create a supportive environment where teams feel empowered to experiment, take calculated risks, and learn from both successes and failures.

Agile methodologies provide a robust framework for embracing change in AI models by promoting continuous learning, flexibility, collaboration, and transparency. Product managers play a central role in fostering a culture of adaptability and continuous improvement, enabling teams to navigate changes in AI development effectively and deliver value to stakeholders.

Continuous User Feedback Loops

Continuous user feedback loops are a cornerstone of Agile methodologies, facilitating the iterative refinement of AI products based on real-world user experiences and preferences. Here's a detailed exploration of how product managers leverage continuous feedback loops to enhance AI development:

1. Establishing Feedback Mechanisms:
Product managers begin by establishing various feedback mechanisms to gather insights from users throughout the AI development lifecycle. This may include user surveys, interviews, usability testing, user analytics, and feedback forms integrated directly into the product interface. These mechanisms ensure that product managers have access to a diverse range of qualitative and quantitative feedback sources.

2. Iterative Refinement of AI Algorithms:

User feedback serves as invaluable input for refining AI algorithms and models. Product managers analyze user interactions, preferences, and pain points to identify opportunities for improvement. This may involve adjusting algorithm parameters, fine-tuning machine learning models, or incorporating new data sources to enhance algorithmic accuracy and performance. By iterating on AI algorithms based on real-world user feedback, product managers ensure that the technology continues to evolve in alignment with user needs.

3. Improving User Experiences:

Continuous user feedback enables product managers to identify areas where the user experience can be enhanced. This could involve streamlining workflows, simplifying user interfaces, or adding new features that address user pain points or unmet needs. By incorporating user feedback into the design and development process, product managers ensure that AI products are intuitive, user-friendly, and capable of delivering meaningful value to users.

4. Aligning Features with User Needs:

User feedback guides product managers in prioritizing features and functionalities based on user needs and preferences. Through continuous feedback loops, product managers gain insights into which features resonate most with users and which may require further refinement or optimization. This user-centric approach ensures that AI products remain aligned with the evolving needs and expectations of their target audience.

5. Monitoring Performance Metrics:

In addition to qualitative feedback, product managers also track performance metrics related to user engagement, retention, and satisfaction. By monitoring these metrics over time, product managers can assess the impact of changes to

AI algorithms or product features and make data-driven decisions to optimize product performance. This data-driven approach ensures that product managers can iterate on AI products based on empirical evidence of their effectiveness in meeting user needs.

6. Adapting to Changing User Preferences:
User preferences and behaviors may evolve over time, necessitating ongoing adjustments to AI products. Product managers use continuous feedback loops to stay attuned to changing user preferences and market trends, ensuring that AI products remain relevant and competitive in dynamic environments. This adaptability allows product managers to proactively address emerging user needs and maintain a competitive edge in the marketplace.

7. Cultivating a Culture of Continuous Improvement:
Continuous feedback loops foster a culture of continuous improvement within product development teams. By soliciting and acting upon user feedback on a regular basis, product managers instill a mindset of responsiveness and agility, encouraging team members to iterate on AI products iteratively and relentlessly pursue opportunities for enhancement and innovation.

Continuous user feedback loops are integral to Agile AI development, enabling product managers to iteratively refine AI algorithms, improve user experiences, align features with user needs, and adapt to changing user preferences. By leveraging continuous feedback, product managers ensure that AI products remain user-centric, adaptive, and competitive in dynamic markets.

Adapting Sprint Planning for AI

Adapting sprint planning for AI projects within an Agile framework requires careful consideration of the unique characteristics of AI development, including the iterative nature of model training and refinement. Here's an in-depth exploration of how sprint planning can be tailored to suit the needs of AI projects:

1. Understanding AI Model Development Cycles:
Product managers collaborate closely with data scientists to gain a deep understanding of the AI model development lifecycle. This involves recognizing that AI models undergo iterative cycles of training, validation, testing, and refinement, each of which may span multiple sprints.

2. Aligning Sprints with Model Iterations:
Sprint planning for AI projects involves aligning sprint timelines with the iterative cycles of model development. Product managers work with data scientists to determine the duration and scope of each sprint based on the specific tasks and milestones associated with model training, evaluation, and optimization.

3. Defining Sprint Goals and Deliverables:
During sprint planning sessions, product managers and data scientists collaborate to define clear goals and deliverables for each sprint. These may include tasks such as data collection, preprocessing, feature engineering, model training, hyperparameter tuning, and performance evaluation.

4. Prioritizing Backlog Items:
Product managers maintain a prioritized backlog of AI-related tasks and user stories based on factors such as business value, technical feasibility, and user impact. During sprint planning, backlog items are reviewed, and the highest priority tasks are selected for inclusion in the upcoming sprint.

5. Balancing Feature Development and Model Improvement:
Sprint planning involves striking a balance between feature development and model improvement activities. Product

managers prioritize tasks that contribute to both enhancing the AI model's performance and delivering new features or functionalities to users.

6. Flexibility and Adaptability:
Agile AI teams embrace flexibility and adaptability in sprint planning to accommodate the dynamic nature of AI development. Product managers remain responsive to changes in project requirements, emerging insights from data analysis, and feedback from stakeholders, adjusting sprint plans as needed to maximize value delivery.

7. Continuous Evaluation and Iteration:
Sprint planning is an iterative process in itself, with product managers and data scientists continuously evaluating the effectiveness of sprint outcomes and refining plans for subsequent sprints. This continuous evaluation and iteration ensure that sprint planning remains aligned with evolving project goals and priorities.

8. Communication and Collaboration:
Effective communication and collaboration are essential during sprint planning sessions. Product managers facilitate discussions between cross-functional team members, ensuring that everyone has a clear understanding of sprint goals, priorities, and dependencies.

9. Monitoring Progress and Adapting as Needed:
Throughout the sprint, product managers monitor progress closely, tracking key metrics related to AI model performance, feature development, and user feedback. This allows them to identify any deviations from the plan and make timely adjustments to keep the project on track.

10. Retrospective and Continuous Improvement:
At the end of each sprint, the team conducts a retrospective to reflect on what went well, what could be improved, and

how processes can be optimized for future sprints. This continuous improvement mindset ensures that sprint planning practices evolve over time to better suit the needs of AI projects.

Adapting sprint planning for AI projects requires a nuanced approach that takes into account the iterative nature of model development, the need for flexibility and adaptability, and the importance of communication and collaboration across cross-functional teams. By aligning sprint planning with the unique characteristics of AI development, product managers can ensure that each sprint contributes to the ongoing improvement of AI models and the overall success of the project.

Balancing Predictability and Flexibility

Balancing predictability and flexibility is a nuanced endeavor for product managers, particularly in the context of Agile methodologies and AI projects. Here's an in-depth exploration of how product managers can navigate this delicate balance:

1. Establishing a Roadmap:
Product managers begin by creating a roadmap that outlines the overall vision, goals, and key milestones for the AI project. This roadmap serves as a guiding framework, providing a sense of direction and helping stakeholders understand the long-term trajectory of the project.

2. Defining Iterative Goals:
Within the overarching roadmap, product managers define iterative goals for each sprint or development cycle. These goals are focused, achievable objectives that contribute to the realization of broader project objectives while allowing for flexibility in implementation.

3. Embracing Unpredictability:
Product managers acknowledge the inherent unpredictability of AI development, characterized by factors such as uncertain data quality, evolving user needs, and the dynamic nature of AI algorithms. Instead of rigidly adhering to predetermined plans, they embrace uncertainty and remain open to adjusting course as new insights emerge.

4. Adapting Plans Based on Insights:
Agile product managers continuously monitor project progress and gather insights from user feedback, data analysis, and team collaboration. They use these insights to adapt plans in real-time, making course corrections, reprioritizing tasks, and seizing opportunities for improvement.

5. Maintaining Stakeholder Alignment:
Throughout the project lifecycle, product managers maintain open lines of communication with stakeholders, keeping them informed about changes in plans and seeking input on key decisions. This transparency fosters trust and ensures that stakeholders remain aligned with the project's goals and direction.

6. Flexibility in Resource Allocation:
Agile product managers maintain flexibility in resource allocation, recognizing that the needs of AI projects may evolve over time. They allocate resources dynamically based on changing priorities, emerging requirements, and the evolving capabilities of the team.

7. Iterative Roadmap Refinement:
The project roadmap is not set in stone but evolves iteratively based on feedback, insights, and the evolving landscape of AI technology. Product managers regularly review and refine the roadmap, adjusting timelines, milestones, and objectives to reflect the latest developments and priorities.

8. Managing Expectations:
Product managers play a crucial role in managing stakeholders' expectations regarding project predictability and flexibility. They communicate openly about the inherent uncertainties of AI development, setting realistic expectations and emphasizing the importance of adaptability in achieving project success.

9. Cultivating an Agile Mindset:
Above all, product managers cultivate an agile mindset within the team, fostering a culture of continuous learning, adaptation, and resilience. They encourage team members to embrace change, experiment with new approaches, and view setbacks as opportunities for growth.
10. Measuring Success:
Success in balancing predictability and flexibility is measured not only by the achievement of predefined milestones but also by the team's ability to adapt and respond effectively to changing circumstances. Product managers track key performance indicators (KPIs) related to project progress, stakeholder satisfaction, and the delivery of value to users.

Balancing predictability and flexibility in AI projects requires product managers to strike a delicate balance between maintaining a roadmap and embracing uncertainty. By fostering a culture of adaptability, transparency, and stakeholder alignment, product managers can navigate the complexities of AI development while delivering value to users and stakeholders.

Rapid Prototyping and Testing

Rapid prototyping and testing are foundational practices within Agile methodologies, and when coupled with AI, they offer a powerful approach to iteratively develop and refine intelligent systems. Here's a detailed exploration of how product managers leverage Agile principles for rapid prototyping and testing in AI projects:

1. Iterative Development Cycles:
Agile methodologies advocate for iterative development cycles, typically organized into sprints. Product managers break down AI project requirements into smaller, manageable tasks or user stories that can be completed within a single sprint. This iterative approach enables continuous progress and frequent feedback loops.

2. Quick Development of AI Functionalities:
Leveraging Agile frameworks, product managers prioritize the rapid development of AI functionalities. They focus on delivering minimum viable products (MVPs) or prototypes that demonstrate core AI capabilities early in the development process. This allows teams to gather feedback from users and stakeholders at an early stage.

3. User-Centric Prototyping:
Agile encourages a user-centric approach to prototyping, where product managers prioritize features based on user needs and feedback. In AI projects, this involves prototyping intelligent functionalities that address specific user pain points or deliver unique value propositions. User feedback guides the refinement of AI models and algorithms.

4. Cross-Functional Collaboration:
Agile promotes cross-functional collaboration, bringing together team members with diverse expertise to work towards common project goals. Product managers collaborate closely with data scientists, engineers, designers, and domain experts to ensure that AI prototypes are technically feasible, user-friendly, and aligned with business objectives.

5. Agile Testing Practices:

Agile emphasizes the importance of testing throughout the development lifecycle. Product managers coordinate with QA engineers and data scientists to establish automated testing frameworks for AI models and algorithms. Continuous integration and continuous deployment (CI/CD) pipelines enable rapid testing and validation of AI functionalities.

6. User Validation and Feedback:

Agile product managers prioritize user validation and feedback during the prototyping phase. They conduct usability tests, user interviews, and A/B testing to gather insights into how users interact with AI prototypes. Feedback from users informs iterative improvements to AI models, algorithms, and user interfaces.

7. Real-Time Data Analysis:

In AI projects, rapid prototyping involves collecting and analyzing real-time data to evaluate the performance of intelligent systems. Product managers leverage data analytics tools and techniques to monitor key metrics, such as accuracy, latency, and user engagement. This data-driven approach guides decision-making and prioritization of features.

8. Refinement Based on Feedback:

Agile encourages teams to embrace change and iterate based on feedback. Product managers use insights gathered from user testing and data analysis to refine AI prototypes iteratively. They prioritize features with the highest impact on user experience and business outcomes, ensuring that each iteration adds tangible value.

9. Balancing Speed and Quality:

While Agile promotes rapid prototyping, product managers must strike a balance between speed and quality. They prioritize the delivery of functional prototypes while ensuring that AI models meet performance standards, adhere to best practices, and comply with regulatory requirements.

10. Continuous Improvement:
Rapid prototyping and testing are not one-time activities but ongoing processes in Agile AI development. Product managers foster a culture of continuous improvement, encouraging teams to learn from each iteration, experiment with new ideas, and strive for incremental enhancements over time.

Rapid prototyping and testing in Agile AI development enable product managers to iteratively create, validate, and refine intelligent systems. By prioritizing user feedback, cross-functional collaboration, and data-driven decision-making, product managers deliver AI prototypes that meet user needs and drive business value.

Ensuring Transparency in AI Development

Ensuring transparency in AI development is essential for building trust, managing expectations, and facilitating effective collaboration within Agile teams. Here's a detailed exploration of how product managers ensure transparency throughout the AI development process:

1. Clear Communication of Goals and Objectives:
Product managers begin by clearly articulating the goals and objectives of the AI project to all stakeholders, including non-technical team members and external partners. They explain the intended outcomes of implementing AI solutions and how they align with broader business strategies.

2. Educating Non-Technical Stakeholders:
Product managers take on the role of educators, helping non-technical stakeholders understand the basics of AI technologies, their capabilities, and their limitations. They

conduct workshops, presentations, and training sessions to demystify AI concepts and terminology.

3. Documentation of AI Algorithms and Decisions:
Product managers ensure that AI algorithms, models, and decision-making processes are well-documented in accessible language. They create documentation that outlines how AI systems work, the data they use, the logic behind their decisions, and any potential biases or limitations.

4. Transparent AI Development Practices:
Agile promotes transparency in development practices, and product managers uphold this principle in AI projects. They ensure that all team members have visibility into the AI development process, including data collection, model training, testing procedures, and performance evaluation.

5. Regular Progress Updates:
Product managers provide regular progress updates to stakeholders, highlighting key milestones, achievements, and challenges encountered during AI development. They communicate openly about project timelines, resource allocation, and any adjustments made to the development roadmap.

6. Openness to Feedback and Questions:
Product managers foster an environment where team members feel comfortable asking questions and providing feedback on AI-related matters. They encourage open dialogue and collaboration, inviting input from diverse perspectives to improve transparency and decision-making.

7. Ethical Considerations and Risk Management:
Transparency extends to ethical considerations and risk management in AI development. Product managers discuss ethical implications, such as bias, fairness, and privacy, openly with the team and stakeholders. They proactively

address potential risks and develop mitigation strategies to ensure responsible AI deployment.

8. Real-Time Monitoring and Reporting:
Product managers implement tools and processes for real-time monitoring and reporting of AI systems' performance and behavior. They track key metrics, such as accuracy, reliability, and user satisfaction, and share this information transparently with stakeholders to foster trust and accountability.

9. Feedback Loops for Continuous Improvement:
Transparency also encompasses feedback loops for continuous improvement. Product managers gather feedback from users, team members, and external reviewers to identify areas for enhancement and refinement in AI systems. They prioritize transparency in how feedback is collected, analyzed, and acted upon.

10. Compliance and Regulatory Compliance:
Product managers ensure that AI development processes comply with relevant regulations, industry standards, and ethical guidelines. They communicate transparently about compliance requirements and work closely with legal and compliance teams to address any concerns or issues.

By prioritizing transparency in AI development, product managers create an environment of trust, collaboration, and accountability. They empower stakeholders to understand and engage with AI technologies effectively, fostering successful outcomes in Agile AI projects.

Scaling Agile for AI Enterprise Solutions

Scaling Agile for AI enterprise solutions involves adapting Agile methodologies to accommodate the unique challenges and complexities of large-scale AI development projects.

Here's a comprehensive exploration of how product managers can scale Agile effectively for AI enterprise solutions:

1. Selecting the Right Scaling Framework:
Product managers evaluate various scaling frameworks, such as SAFe, LeSS, Nexus, or Scrum@Scale, to determine the best fit for their organization's needs. Each framework offers different approaches to scaling Agile practices and aligning multiple Agile teams working on AI projects.

2. Establishing Agile Release Trains (ARTs):
In SAFe, product managers organize Agile teams into Agile Release Trains (ARTs), which serve as the primary organizing construct for large-scale development efforts. Each ART consists of multiple Agile teams working together to deliver value in synchronized increments.

3. Coordinating Across Multiple Teams:
Product managers facilitate coordination and collaboration across multiple Agile teams involved in AI development. They establish mechanisms for cross-team communication, such as regular sync meetings, joint planning sessions, and shared project management tools.

4. Aligning with Business Objectives:
Product managers ensure that AI development efforts are aligned with overarching business objectives and strategic goals. They work closely with business stakeholders to prioritize initiatives, allocate resources, and track progress toward key milestones.

5. Adapting Agile Ceremonies for Scale:
Product managers adapt Agile ceremonies, such as sprint planning, daily stand-ups, sprint reviews, and retrospectives, to accommodate the scale of AI enterprise solutions. They

may introduce additional layers of planning and coordination to ensure alignment across multiple teams.

6. Facilitating Cross-Functional Collaboration:
Product managers foster cross-functional collaboration between Agile teams, AI specialists, data scientists, domain experts, and business stakeholders. They create opportunities for knowledge sharing, skill development, and problem-solving across organizational boundaries.

7. Managing Dependencies and Risks:
Product managers identify and manage dependencies between Agile teams and external stakeholders to minimize delays and risks in AI development. They proactively address inter-team dependencies, resource constraints, and technical challenges to maintain project momentum.

8. Implementing DevOps Practices:
Product managers advocate for the adoption of DevOps practices to streamline the integration, deployment, and delivery of AI solutions. They promote automation, continuous integration, and continuous delivery (CI/CD) pipelines to accelerate time-to-market and improve product quality.

9. Measuring and Monitoring Progress:
Product managers establish key performance indicators (KPIs) and metrics to measure the progress and success of AI enterprise solutions. They track metrics related to team productivity, product quality, customer satisfaction, and business value delivery to inform decision-making and course corrections.

10. Driving Continuous Improvement:
Product managers foster a culture of continuous improvement within AI development teams and across the organization. They encourage feedback, experimentation,

and learning from both successes and failures to drive innovation and adaptability in large-scale Agile environments.

By effectively scaling Agile for AI enterprise solutions, product managers enable organizations to deliver value efficiently, adapt to change effectively and drive innovation in AI development initiatives. They play a central role in orchestrating collaboration, alignment, and delivery excellence across the enterprise to achieve strategic objectives and business outcomes.

This section navigates the fusion of Agile methodologies and AI product management, presenting a landscape where adaptability, collaboration, and iterative development form the pillars of successful AI projects. Product managers emerge as orchestrators, leveraging Agile principles to navigate the unique challenges posed by the dynamic, learning nature of AI systems, ensuring that products remain responsive to user needs and market dynamics.

ITERATIVE DEVELOPMENT IN THE AGE OF MACHINE LEARNING

In the fast-evolving realm of AI product management, the fusion of Agile methodologies and the iterative nature of Machine Learning (ML) presents a dynamic landscape. This chapter delves into the intricacies of adapting Agile for AI projects, specifically focusing on the nuances of iterative development in the age of machine learning. It explores how product managers navigate the challenges and leverage the strengths of Agile to harness the continuous learning and evolving capabilities of ML systems.

Unveiling the Iterative Essence of Machine Learning

Unveiling the iterative essence of machine learning (ML) involves understanding and leveraging the continuous cycle of training, testing, and refinement inherent in ML algorithms. Here's a detailed exploration of how product managers can embrace Agile methodologies to amplify this iterative essence in ML development:

1. Training Data Acquisition and Preparation:
Product managers collaborate with data scientists and domain experts to collect and preprocess training data. They ensure that datasets are representative, diverse, and properly labeled to facilitate effective model training.

2. Model Training and Evaluation:
In the ML development lifecycle, product managers oversee the iterative process of model training and evaluation. They work closely with data scientists to experiment with different algorithms, hyperparameters, and training methodologies to optimize model performance.

3. Iterative Experimentation and Prototyping:
Agile methodologies empower product managers to foster a culture of experimentation and prototyping in ML development. They encourage data scientists to iterate rapidly, testing hypotheses, and refining models based on real-world feedback and performance metrics.

4. Continuous Model Improvement:
Product managers facilitate the ongoing improvement of ML models through iterative cycles of feedback and refinement. They establish feedback loops with end-users, stakeholders, and subject matter experts to gather insights and identify opportunities for enhancement.

5. Adaptive Model Deployment:
Agile principles guide product managers in the adaptive deployment of ML models, allowing for incremental releases and continuous integration. They prioritize features based on user needs and market demands, deploying models in stages and iterating based on user feedback.

6. Real-Time Monitoring and Feedback:
Product managers implement mechanisms for real-time monitoring and feedback to track model performance in production environments. They leverage metrics such as accuracy, precision, recall, and user engagement to assess model effectiveness and identify areas for improvement.

7. Cross-Functional Collaboration:
Agile practices promote cross-functional collaboration between product managers, data scientists, engineers, designers, and business stakeholders. Product managers facilitate communication and alignment across teams, ensuring that everyone is aligned with project goals and priorities.

8. Agile Rituals Adapted for ML:
Product managers adapt Agile rituals, such as sprint planning, daily stand-ups, sprint reviews, and retrospectives, to accommodate the unique requirements of ML development. They foster a culture of transparency, accountability, and continuous improvement within ML teams.

9. Risk Management and Mitigation:
Product managers proactively identify and mitigate risks associated with ML development, including data biases, model drift, and ethical considerations. They implement strategies to address potential challenges and ensure that ML projects progress smoothly.

10. Embracing Uncertainty and Iteration:
Agile methodologies encourage product managers to embrace uncertainty and iteration in ML development. They understand that ML projects involve inherent uncertainties, and they adapt plans and priorities based on emerging insights and changing requirements.

By unveiling the iterative essence of machine learning and embracing Agile methodologies, product managers empower ML development teams to deliver high-quality models that meet user needs, drive business value, and adapt to evolving market dynamics. They foster a culture of innovation, collaboration, and continuous improvement, driving success in ML projects and initiatives.

Agile Sprints and ML Model Refinement

Agile sprints serve as the foundation for iterative development in the realm of machine learning (ML), where the focus is on refining and improving ML models over time. Here's a detailed exploration of how product managers collaborate with data scientists to structure sprints that facilitate ML model refinement:

1. Sprint Planning for Model Training:
Product managers work closely with data scientists during sprint planning sessions to outline tasks and objectives related to model training and refinement. They prioritize the backlog based on the current state of ML models, user feedback, and business requirements.

2. Defining Training Objectives and Milestones:
Within each sprint, product managers and data scientists define specific training objectives and milestones to be achieved. These objectives may include improving model accuracy, optimizing hyperparameters, addressing data biases, or enhancing model interpretability.

3. Data Acquisition and Preprocessing Tasks:

Sprint backlogs often include tasks related to data acquisition, preprocessing, and augmentation. Product managers ensure that data scientists have access to relevant datasets and tools needed to prepare training data for model training.

4. Model Training and Evaluation Iterations:

The core of each sprint involves iterative cycles of model training, evaluation, and refinement. Data scientists experiment with different algorithms, feature engineering techniques, and model architectures to improve performance metrics such as accuracy, precision, and recall.

5. Experimentation and Hypothesis Testing:

Agile sprints provide a structured framework for experimentation and hypothesis testing in ML model development. Data scientists conduct A/B tests, cross-validation experiments, and sensitivity analyses to validate hypotheses and make data-driven decisions.

6. Validation and Cross-Validation Processes:

Within each sprint, product managers oversee validation and cross-validation processes to assess model generalization and robustness. They ensure that models perform well on unseen data and are not overfitting to the training dataset.

7. Feedback Incorporation and Model Iteration:

Sprint reviews and retrospectives serve as opportunities to incorporate feedback from stakeholders, end-users, and validation results into the model refinement process. Product managers facilitate discussions on areas for improvement and prioritize tasks for the next sprint.

8. Incremental Model Deployment:
Agile sprints enable incremental model deployment, allowing product managers to release updated versions of ML models in a phased manner. They coordinate with engineering teams to deploy models to production environments and monitor their performance in real-world settings.

9. Monitoring and Iterative Improvement:
Post-deployment monitoring is an integral part of each sprint, allowing product managers to track model performance and user engagement metrics. They analyze feedback loops and iterate on models based on observed behavior, ensuring continuous improvement over time.

10. Adaptation to Changing Requirements:
Agile sprints provide flexibility for product managers to adapt to changing requirements and priorities. They iterate on sprint plans based on emerging insights, market trends, and user needs, ensuring that ML model refinement efforts remain aligned with business goals.

By structuring Agile sprints to accommodate the iterative cycles of ML model refinement, product managers empower data scientists to make incremental improvements, drive innovation, and deliver ML solutions that meet evolving user expectations and business objectives.

Continuous Integration of Data

Continuous integration of data is a fundamental aspect of machine learning (ML) development, and Agile methodologies provide a conducive environment for this iterative process. Here's a detailed exploration of how Agile facilitates the continuous integration of data into ML models:

1. Data Pipeline Design and Automation:
Agile teams collaborate to design and automate data pipelines that facilitate the seamless integration of new data into ML models. Product managers work with data engineers and scientists to define data sources, ingestion methods, preprocessing steps, and data storage solutions.

2. Incremental Data Acquisition:
Agile sprints enable product managers to prioritize tasks related to data acquisition and ingestion based on evolving project requirements. They ensure that data sources are continuously monitored and updated to capture new information, such as user interactions, sensor readings, or market trends.

3. Real-time Data Ingestion and Processing:
Agile development practices support the real-time ingestion and processing of streaming data streams. Product managers collaborate with data engineering teams to implement solutions that enable near-instantaneous updates to ML models based on incoming data feeds.

4. Dynamic Feature Engineering:
Agile teams iterate on feature engineering processes to extract meaningful insights from newly integrated data. Data scientists experiment with different feature combinations, transformations, and selections to enhance model performance and adapt to changing data distributions.

5. Model Re-training and Validation:
Continuous data integration triggers automatic re-training and validation of ML models within Agile development cycles. Product managers coordinate with data scientists to schedule model updates based on predefined criteria, such as data drift detection or performance degradation thresholds.

6. Feedback Loop Integration:

Agile sprints provide opportunities to incorporate feedback loops from model predictions into the data integration process. Product managers analyze model outputs, user feedback, and business metrics to identify areas for improvement and prioritize data integration tasks accordingly.

7. Version Control and Rollback Mechanisms:

Agile teams implement version control and rollback mechanisms to manage changes to data pipelines and ML models. Product managers ensure that changes are tracked, tested, and deployed in a controlled manner to mitigate the risk of introducing errors or biases into production systems.

8. Automated Testing and Quality Assurance:

Agile practices emphasize automated testing and quality assurance processes to validate data integrity, model performance, and system reliability. Product managers collaborate with QA teams to develop test suites that verify the correctness and robustness of data integration workflows.

9. Cross-functional Collaboration:

Agile encourages cross-functional collaboration between product managers, data scientists, engineers, and stakeholders to ensure that data integration efforts align with business objectives and user needs. Regular meetings, stand-ups, and retrospectives foster communication and alignment across teams.

10. Continuous Improvement and Optimization:

Agile principles promote a culture of continuous improvement and optimization in data integration processes. Product managers lead retrospective sessions to identify bottlenecks, inefficiencies, and opportunities for optimization, driving iterative enhancements to data pipelines and ML models.

By embracing Agile methodologies, product managers enable teams to leverage the iterative nature of ML development and continuously integrate new data into models. This approach ensures that ML algorithms remain adaptive, accurate, and effective in addressing evolving business challenges and user requirements.

Feedback Loops with Users and Models

Establishing robust feedback loops with both users and models is essential for driving iterative development in machine learning (ML) projects within an Agile framework. Here's an in-depth exploration of how Agile facilitates feedback loops with users and models:

1. User Feedback Integration:
Agile methodologies emphasize the importance of user feedback in shaping product development. Product managers actively solicit feedback from users through various channels such as surveys, interviews, usability tests, and user analytics. They ensure that user feedback is systematically collected, analyzed, and prioritized to inform iterative improvements to the product.

2. Model Performance Evaluation:
Concurrently, Agile teams continuously evaluate the performance of ML models deployed in production. They monitor key metrics such as accuracy, precision, recall, and F1-score to assess the effectiveness of models in real-world scenarios. Product managers collaborate closely with data scientists and engineers to track model performance metrics and identify areas for optimization.

3. Feedback Loop Closure:
Agile teams close the feedback loop by translating user insights and model performance metrics into actionable tasks for iteration. Product managers facilitate cross-functional

discussions to prioritize and implement changes based on the feedback received. This iterative process ensures that both user needs and model performance are addressed in tandem.

4. Iterative Model Refinement:
Based on user feedback and performance metrics, Agile teams iterate on ML models to improve their accuracy, robustness, and relevance. Data scientists experiment with different algorithms, features, and hyperparameters to optimize model performance iteratively. Product managers coordinate model refinement efforts to align with sprint goals and user feedback priorities.

5. Real-time Model Updates:
Agile practices enable teams to deploy real-time updates to ML models based on continuous feedback from users and model performance evaluations. Product managers work with DevOps teams to implement automated deployment pipelines that ensure seamless integration of model updates into production environments.

6. A/B Testing and Experimentation:
Agile teams leverage A/B testing and experimentation to validate the effectiveness of proposed changes to the product or ML models. Product managers design experiments to compare the performance of different variants and gather statistically significant results. This data-driven approach guides decision-making and informs further iterations.

7. User-Centric Design Iterations:
Informed by user feedback, Agile teams iteratively enhance the user experience by refining interface designs, feature prioritization, and usability aspects. Product managers collaborate with UX/UI designers to incorporate user-centric design principles into product iterations, ensuring that the

product evolves in alignment with user preferences and expectations.

8. Continuous Monitoring and Optimization:
Agile teams establish monitoring systems to track user engagement, satisfaction, and behavior over time. Product managers utilize analytics tools and dashboards to gain insights into user interactions and model performance in real-time. This continuous monitoring enables the proactive identification of issues and opportunities for optimization.

9. Stakeholder Engagement and Communication:
Agile methodologies promote transparent communication and collaboration with stakeholders throughout the feedback loop process. Product managers facilitate regular meetings, demos, and reviews to share progress, gather feedback, and align stakeholders' expectations with project goals.

10. Iterative Learning and Adaptation:
By incorporating feedback loops into every stage of the development process, Agile teams foster a culture of iterative learning and adaptation. Product managers encourage team members to reflect on feedback, iterate on solutions and continuously improve both the product and the underlying ML models.

Agile methodologies provide a structured framework for establishing and closing feedback loops with users and models, enabling iterative development and continuous improvement in ML projects. By embracing user-centric design principles and data-driven decision-making, Agile teams can create ML-powered products that are both effective and user-friendly.

Dynamic Prioritization of Features

Dynamic prioritization of features is a cornerstone of Agile methodology, particularly in the context of machine learning (ML) development. This approach recognizes the dynamic and iterative nature of ML projects, where requirements, user needs, and market conditions may evolve rapidly. Here's a more detailed exploration of dynamic prioritization in the context of ML development:

1. Continuous Assessment and Reprioritization: Agile teams, including product managers and cross-functional members, engage in continuous assessment and reprioritization of features throughout the ML development lifecycle. This involves regularly reviewing the project backlog, considering feedback from stakeholders, and re-evaluating the importance of each feature based on changing circumstances.

2. User-Centric Focus: Dynamic prioritization ensures that the features being developed align closely with the needs and expectations of end-users. Product managers gather feedback from users through various channels, such as user testing, surveys, and analytics data. This feedback informs the prioritization process, ensuring that the most valuable features are addressed first.

3. Market Dynamics Consideration: Agile teams monitor market dynamics, industry trends, and competitive landscape to adapt their feature prioritization strategy accordingly. This may involve responding to emerging market opportunities, addressing competitive threats, or pivoting based on shifts in consumer preferences or regulatory changes.

4. Iterative Learning and Adaptation: ML development involves a significant degree of experimentation and learning. Agile teams embrace this iterative process by prioritizing

features that enable rapid experimentation, hypothesis testing, and model iteration. Features that facilitate data collection, model training, and performance evaluation often receive high priority to support the learning cycle.

5. Risk Management: Dynamic prioritization allows teams to proactively manage risks by addressing critical features early in the development process. By identifying and mitigating potential risks through prioritization, teams can minimize project delays, budget overruns, or unexpected technical challenges that may arise during ML development.

6. Collaborative Decision-Making: Prioritization decisions are made collaboratively within Agile teams, drawing on the diverse perspectives and expertise of team members. Product managers facilitate discussions to ensure alignment with strategic goals, while also considering technical feasibility, resource constraints, and other factors that may impact prioritization decisions.

7. Flexibility and Adaptability: Agile methodologies emphasize flexibility and adaptability in response to changing requirements or new information. Dynamic prioritization allows teams to adjust their plans quickly in light of new insights, shifting priorities, or evolving project constraints, ensuring that the development process remains responsive to changing circumstances.

Dynamic prioritization of features in ML development under Agile methodologies enables teams to remain agile, responsive and focused on delivering value to users and stakeholders. By continuously reassessing and reprioritizing features based on user needs, market dynamics, and iterative learning, Agile teams can effectively navigate the complexities of ML projects and drive successful outcomes.

Rapid Prototyping and Experimentation

Rapid prototyping and experimentation represent fundamental practices in both Agile and machine learning (ML) development, offering a synergistic approach to innovation and product refinement. Here's a detailed exploration of how product managers leverage Agile frameworks to facilitate rapid prototyping and experimentation in the context of ML:

1. Agile Principles: Agile methodologies advocate for iterative and incremental development, emphasizing collaboration, flexibility, and customer feedback. These principles align closely with the iterative nature of ML development, making Agile frameworks well-suited for rapid prototyping and experimentation.

2. Cross-Functional Collaboration: Agile teams, comprising product managers, developers, data scientists, and other stakeholders, collaborate closely to rapidly prototype ML features. By bringing together diverse skill sets and perspectives, teams can iterate quickly, address technical challenges, and refine prototypes based on feedback from different disciplines.

3. Incremental Delivery: Agile encourages the delivery of working software in short, iterative cycles known as sprints. Product managers prioritize ML features based on user value and technical feasibility, enabling teams to deliver incremental improvements with each sprint. This incremental approach allows for early validation of ML models and features, reducing the risk of costly rework later in the development process.

4. User-Centric Design: Rapid prototyping enables product managers to gather early feedback from users through usability testing, alpha/beta releases, and other feedback

channels. By involving users in the prototyping process, product managers can validate assumptions, identify usability issues, and refine ML features to better meet user needs and expectations.

5. Experimentation Frameworks: Agile teams leverage experimentation frameworks such as A/B testing, multivariate testing, and bandit algorithms to systematically evaluate the performance of ML models and features. These frameworks enable teams to test hypotheses, measure the impact of changes, and make data-driven decisions about feature adoption and optimization.

6. Technical Infrastructure: Agile teams invest in robust technical infrastructure and tooling to support rapid prototyping and experimentation. This may include cloud-based ML platforms, development frameworks, version control systems, and continuous integration/continuous deployment (CI/CD) pipelines. These tools streamline the prototyping process, automate testing, and accelerate feature delivery.

7. Feedback Loops: Agile emphasizes the importance of continuous feedback loops to inform decision-making and drive improvement. Product managers establish feedback mechanisms to collect insights from users, stakeholders, and performance metrics. This feedback informs the iterative refinement of ML features, ensuring that the product evolves in response to changing requirements and market dynamics.

8. Risk Mitigation: Rapid prototyping and experimentation help mitigate risks associated with ML development, such as model performance issues, scalability challenges, and data quality issues. By identifying and addressing risks early in the development process, Agile teams can minimize project delays and ensure the successful delivery of ML-powered products.

Rapid prototyping and experimentation play a vital role in Agile ML development, enabling product managers to validate assumptions, gather user feedback, and iterate on ML features quickly. By embracing Agile principles and leveraging experimentation frameworks, teams can accelerate innovation, reduce time-to-market, and deliver ML-powered products that meet user needs and drive business value.

Flexibility in Response to Model Uncertainties

Flexibility in response to model uncertainties is a critical aspect of Agile methodology when applied to machine learning (ML) development. Here's a detailed exploration of how product managers foster flexibility to address uncertainties in ML models within an Agile framework:

1. Dynamic Planning: Agile methodologies prioritize adaptability and responsiveness to change. Product managers work closely with cross-functional teams to continuously reassess project plans, priorities, and resource allocations based on emerging uncertainties in ML models. This dynamic planning approach ensures that teams can quickly pivot and adjust course as needed to address evolving challenges.

2. Iterative Development: Agile promotes iterative development, allowing teams to break down complex ML projects into manageable increments. This iterative approach enables product managers to address uncertainties incrementally, focusing on validating assumptions, testing hypotheses, and refining ML models through successive iterations. By iterating rapidly, teams can explore different approaches, gather feedback, and course-correct as necessary to mitigate uncertainties.

3. Experimentation and Prototyping: Agile encourages experimentation and prototyping as a means to explore

214

uncertainties in ML models. Product managers facilitate rapid prototyping of ML features, allowing teams to test different algorithms, parameters, and data sources to identify the most effective solutions. By embracing a culture of experimentation, teams can uncover insights, validate assumptions, and refine ML models in an agile manner.

4. Continuous Learning: Agile fosters a culture of continuous learning and improvement. Product managers encourage teams to treat uncertainties as learning opportunities, fostering curiosity, creativity, and collaboration in exploring potential solutions. By embracing a growth mindset and leveraging lessons learned from past experiences, teams can iterate more effectively and develop resilient ML models capable of adapting to changing conditions.

5. Risk Management: Agile emphasizes proactive risk management to anticipate and mitigate uncertainties in ML development. Product managers work with teams to identify potential risks, develop contingency plans, and establish risk mitigation strategies early in the project lifecycle. By systematically addressing risks and uncertainties, teams can minimize their impact on project timelines and outcomes.

6. Transparent Communication: Agile promotes transparent communication and collaboration among team members, stakeholders, and external partners. Product managers foster open dialogue about uncertainties in ML models, encouraging team members to share insights, raise concerns, and propose solutions collaboratively. By fostering a culture of transparency and trust, teams can leverage collective expertise to address uncertainties more effectively.

7. Agile Rituals: Agile rituals such as daily stand-up meetings, sprint planning sessions, and retrospective meetings provide opportunities for teams to discuss uncertainties and adapt their approach accordingly. Product managers facilitate these

rituals to ensure that teams have the support and guidance they need to navigate uncertainties collaboratively and make informed decisions.

8. Feedback Loops: Agile emphasizes the importance of feedback loops to validate assumptions and course-correct as needed. Product managers establish feedback mechanisms to gather insights from users, stakeholders, and performance metrics, enabling teams to monitor model performance, identify anomalies, and adjust their approach in real-time. By leveraging feedback loops, teams can iteratively refine ML models and improve their effectiveness over time.

Flexibility in response to model uncertainties is essential for Agile ML development. By fostering a dynamic, iterative, and collaborative environment, product managers enable teams to navigate uncertainties with confidence, embrace opportunities for learning and improvement, and deliver resilient ML-powered solutions that meet the evolving needs of users and stakeholders.

Continuous Learning Culture

Continuous learning culture is a fundamental aspect of Agile methodologies, and when applied to ML-driven projects, it becomes even more crucial. Here's an in-depth exploration of how product managers foster a continuous learning culture within Agile ML projects:

1. Embracing Curiosity and Exploration: Product managers encourage teams to embrace a mindset of curiosity and exploration. They emphasize the importance of asking questions, challenging assumptions, and seeking out new learning opportunities. By fostering a culture of curiosity, teams are motivated to explore new ideas, experiment with different approaches, and push the boundaries of what is possible with ML technology.

2. Learning from Failure: Agile ML projects recognize that failure is an inherent part of the learning process. Product managers create a safe environment where teams feel empowered to take risks, experiment with new ideas, and learn from their failures. Instead of viewing failure as a setback, teams are encouraged to see it as an opportunity for growth and improvement. By embracing a culture of learning from failure, teams become more resilient, adaptable, and innovative in their approach to ML development.

3. Knowledge Sharing and Collaboration: Agile methodologies emphasize the importance of knowledge sharing and collaboration among team members. Product managers facilitate opportunities for cross-functional teams to share insights, best practices, and lessons learned from past experiences. By fostering a culture of collaboration, teams can leverage collective expertise to solve complex problems, accelerate learning, and drive innovation in ML-driven projects.

4. Continuous Improvement: Agile ML projects prioritize continuous improvement as a core value. Product managers encourage teams to reflect on their processes, identify areas for improvement, and implement changes iteratively. By fostering a culture of continuous improvement, teams can optimize their workflows, streamline their processes, and enhance their effectiveness in delivering ML-powered solutions.

5. Experimentation and Innovation: Agile methodologies promote experimentation and innovation as drivers of learning and growth. Product managers create opportunities for teams to experiment with new tools, techniques, and technologies in ML development. By fostering a culture of experimentation, teams can push the boundaries of ML capabilities, discover new insights, and unlock innovative solutions to complex problems.

6. Investing in Learning Resources: Product managers recognize the importance of investing in learning resources to support the continuous development of team members. They provide access to training programs, workshops, conferences, and online resources focused on ML, data science, and related topics. By empowering team members to expand their knowledge and skills, product managers ensure that teams remain at the forefront of ML innovation.

7. Celebrating Successes: Agile ML projects celebrate successes and milestones as a way to reinforce a culture of continuous learning and achievement. Product managers acknowledge and recognize the contributions of team members, highlight successful outcomes, and share lessons learned from successful projects. By celebrating successes, teams are motivated to continue learning, experimenting, and innovating in their ML development efforts.

A continuous learning culture is essential for Agile ML projects to thrive. By fostering curiosity, embracing failure, promoting collaboration, prioritizing continuous improvement, encouraging experimentation, investing in learning resources, and celebrating successes, product managers create an environment where teams can continually learn, adapt, and innovate in the dynamic landscape of ML-driven projects.

Addressing Ethical Considerations Iteratively

Addressing ethical considerations iteratively in ML-driven projects is essential for ensuring responsible and ethical AI development. Here's a detailed exploration of how product managers incorporate ethical considerations into each sprint of the iterative development process:

1. Establishing Ethical Guidelines: At the outset of the project, product managers work with cross-functional teams to establish clear ethical guidelines that govern the

development and deployment of ML algorithms. These guidelines outline principles related to fairness, bias mitigation, privacy protection, transparency, and accountability. By establishing ethical guidelines upfront, teams have a framework to guide their decision-making throughout the development process.

2. Integrating Ethical Reviews into Sprint Planning: In each sprint planning session, product managers allocate time to discuss and review ethical considerations related to the features or functionalities being developed. This may involve analyzing how ML algorithms may impact different user groups, identifying potential biases or fairness issues, and assessing the implications for user privacy. By integrating ethical reviews into sprint planning, teams proactively address ethical concerns at every stage of the development cycle.

3. Collaborating with Ethics Experts: Product managers collaborate with ethics experts, data ethicists, or ethic committees to ensure that ethical considerations are adequately addressed in ML-driven projects. These experts provide insights, guidance, and recommendations on how to mitigate ethical risks and ensure that the development process aligns with ethical best practices. By involving ethics experts, teams benefit from specialized knowledge and perspectives that enhance the ethical robustness of their AI solutions.

4. Implementing Ethical Impact Assessments: As part of the iterative development process, product managers implement ethical impact assessments to evaluate the potential ethical implications of ML algorithms. This involves conducting thorough analyses of how algorithms may affect different stakeholders, including users, communities, and society at large. Ethical impact assessments help teams identify and mitigate potential risks before they manifest in the final

product, ensuring that ethical considerations are prioritized throughout the development lifecycle.

5. Iterative Feedback and Adaptation: Throughout the development process, product managers gather feedback from stakeholders, including users, regulators, and advocacy groups, regarding ethical concerns or implications. This feedback loop allows teams to iteratively adapt and refine their approach to address emerging ethical issues. By incorporating feedback into each sprint, teams can proactively respond to ethical challenges and evolve their strategies to better align with ethical principles.

6. Transparency and Accountability: Product managers prioritize transparency and accountability in addressing ethical considerations. They ensure that stakeholders are kept informed about the ethical decisions and trade-offs made during the development process. Additionally, product managers establish mechanisms for accountability, such as documentation of ethical decisions, regular reporting on ethical compliance, and mechanisms for reporting and addressing ethical concerns raised by stakeholders.

7. Continuous Learning and Improvement: Ethical considerations in ML-driven projects are dynamic and evolve over time. Product managers foster a culture of continuous learning and improvement, encouraging teams to stay updated on emerging ethical issues, best practices, and regulatory requirements. By investing in ongoing education and training, teams can enhance their ethical awareness and responsiveness, ensuring that their AI solutions remain ethical and socially responsible in an ever-changing landscape.

Addressing ethical considerations iteratively in ML-driven projects requires a proactive and systematic approach. By establishing ethical guidelines, integrating ethical reviews into sprint planning, collaborating with ethics experts, implementing ethical impact assessments, gathering iterative feedback, prioritizing transparency and accountability, and fostering a culture of continuous learning and improvement, product managers ensure that ethical considerations are ingrained into every aspect of the development process, leading to responsible and ethical AI outcomes.

Scaling Agile Iterative Development for ML Enterprises

Scaling Agile iterative development for ML enterprises requires careful consideration of the unique challenges and complexities inherent in large-scale ML projects. Here's a detailed exploration of how product managers can effectively scale Agile principles for ML enterprises:

1. Adopting Scalable Agile Frameworks: Product managers leverage scalable Agile frameworks, such as SAFe (Scaled Agile Framework) or LeSS (Large Scale Scrum), to align the principles of Agile with the needs of large-scale ML projects. These frameworks provide structured approaches for scaling Agile practices across multiple teams, departments, and organizational levels. By adopting scalable Agile frameworks, product managers ensure that iterative development processes remain consistent and effective across the enterprise.

2. Establishing Cross-Functional Teams: In large-scale ML enterprises, product managers assemble cross-functional teams comprised of individuals with diverse expertise, including data scientists, engineers, domain experts, and business stakeholders. These cross-functional teams collaborate closely to drive innovation, address complex challenges, and deliver value to the organization. By establishing cross-functional teams, product managers ensure that Agile principles are applied holistically and that

teams have the necessary skills and resources to execute ML projects effectively.

3. Defining Clear Roles and Responsibilities: Product managers define clear roles and responsibilities within the Agile framework to ensure accountability and alignment across the enterprise. This involves clarifying the roles of product owners, scrum masters, development teams, and other stakeholders involved in the ML development process. By defining clear roles and responsibilities, product managers create a shared understanding of each team member's contributions and expectations, facilitating efficient collaboration and communication.

4. Implementing Agile Governance Structures: To facilitate the scaling of Agile practices, product managers implement Agile governance structures that provide oversight, guidance, and support throughout the ML development process. This may include establishing governance boards, steering committees, or Agile Centers of Excellence (CoEs) tasked with defining standards, best practices, and guidelines for Agile implementation. By implementing Agile governance structures, product managers ensure consistency, quality, and compliance across all ML projects within the enterprise.

5. Promoting Collaboration and Knowledge Sharing: Product managers foster a culture of collaboration and knowledge sharing across teams and departments involved in ML development. This involves organizing regular forums, workshops, and cross-functional meetings where teams can share insights, best practices, and lessons learned from their Agile experiences. By promoting collaboration and knowledge sharing, product managers facilitate continuous improvement and innovation within the enterprise, driving greater efficiency and effectiveness in ML development efforts.

6. Emphasizing Continuous Improvement: Scaling Agile iterative development for ML enterprises requires a commitment to continuous improvement and adaptation. Product managers encourage teams to regularly reflect on their processes, identify areas for improvement, and experiment with new approaches to enhance productivity and quality. By emphasizing continuous improvement, product managers create a culture of agility and resilience that enables the enterprise to respond effectively to changing market dynamics, technological advancements, and customer needs.

7. Investing in Agile Training and Coaching: To support the scaling of Agile practices, product managers invest in Agile training and coaching programs to equip teams with the knowledge, skills, and mindset needed to succeed in large-scale ML projects. This may involve providing Agile certification courses, organizing workshops, and hiring Agile coaches or consultants to provide guidance and support. By investing in Agile training and coaching, product managers empower teams to embrace Agile principles and practices, driving greater collaboration, innovation, and success in ML development initiatives.

Scaling Agile iterative development for ML enterprises requires a strategic and systematic approach that addresses the unique challenges and complexities of large-scale ML projects. By adopting scalable Agile frameworks, establishing cross-functional teams, defining clear roles and responsibilities, implementing Agile governance structures, promoting collaboration and knowledge sharing, emphasizing continuous improvement, and investing in Agile training and coaching, product managers can effectively scale Agile practices to drive innovation, agility, and success in ML development efforts across the enterprise.

REAL-TIME FEEDBACK LOOPS WITH AI INTEGRATION

Real-time feedback loops with AI integration represent a crucial aspect of modern product management, where Agile methodologies and Artificial Intelligence (AI) intersect to drive iterative and user-centric development processes. Here's a detailed exploration of how real-time feedback loops are established and leveraged within the context of AI-integrated Agile product management:

1. Establishing Real-Time Feedback Mechanisms: Product managers leverage AI capabilities to establish real-time feedback mechanisms within Agile development processes. These mechanisms may include AI-powered analytics tools, monitoring systems, or chatbots that continuously collect and analyze data related to user interactions, system performance, and market trends. By integrating AI into feedback mechanisms, product managers ensure that teams have access to timely and relevant insights to inform decision-making and drive product improvements.

2. Enabling Continuous Refinement: Real-time feedback loops enable continuous refinement of products throughout the development lifecycle. Product managers use AI-driven analytics to monitor user behavior, identify pain points, and uncover opportunities for optimization. Teams can then iterate on product features, user interfaces, and functionalities in response to real-time feedback, ensuring that the product evolves iteratively to meet changing user needs and preferences.

3. Facilitating Adaptive Development: Agile methodologies emphasize adaptability and responsiveness to change, and real-time feedback loops with AI integration enable teams to embrace these principles more effectively. By continuously collecting and analyzing data from AI systems, product

managers gain insights into emerging trends, user preferences, and market dynamics. Teams can then adapt their development strategies, priorities, and feature roadmaps in real-time to capitalize on opportunities and address challenges as they arise.

4. Driving User-Centric Innovation: Real-time feedback loops empower product managers to drive user-centric innovation by leveraging AI insights to inform product decisions. By understanding how users interact with the product, what features they find valuable, and where they encounter obstacles, product managers can prioritize enhancements that deliver the most significant impact. AI-integrated feedback mechanisms enable teams to iterate rapidly on product iterations, ensuring that each release aligns closely with user needs and expectations.

5. Enhancing Data-Driven Decision-Making: Real-time feedback loops with AI integration enable data-driven decision-making at every stage of the product development process. Product managers leverage AI analytics to generate actionable insights, identify trends, and forecast future outcomes based on real-time data streams. These insights inform strategic decisions related to feature prioritization, resource allocation, and product roadmap planning, enabling teams to make informed choices that drive product success.

6. Promoting Collaborative Learning and Improvement: Real-time feedback loops foster a culture of collaborative learning and improvement within Agile teams. By sharing AI-generated insights across cross-functional teams, product managers facilitate knowledge sharing, brainstorming, and collective problem-solving. Teams can learn from each other's experiences, experiment with new ideas, and iterate on solutions collaboratively, driving continuous improvement and innovation across the organization.

7. Ensuring Scalability and Resilience: Real-time feedback loops with AI integration enhance the scalability and resilience of Agile development processes. AI-powered monitoring and analytics systems can handle large volumes of data in real-time, enabling teams to scale their operations seamlessly as the product grows. Additionally, AI algorithms can detect anomalies, identify patterns, and predict future trends, helping teams anticipate and mitigate potential risks proactively.

Real-time feedback loops with AI integration represent a powerful enabler of Agile product management, driving continuous refinement, adaptive development, user-centric innovation, data-driven decision-making, collaborative learning, scalability, and resilience. By harnessing the capabilities of AI to establish real-time feedback mechanisms within Agile development processes, product managers can unlock new opportunities for product success and competitive advantage in today's rapidly evolving digital landscape.

The Symbiosis of Agile and AI

The symbiosis of Agile methodologies and Artificial Intelligence (AI) represents a harmonious integration of two powerful paradigms in modern product management. Here's a detailed exploration of how Agile and AI converge to create a symbiotic relationship that enhances adaptability, responsiveness, and innovation:

1. Adaptability and Flexibility: Agile methodologies are known for their emphasis on adaptability and flexibility, allowing teams to respond quickly to changes in requirements, market conditions, and user feedback. Similarly, AI systems possess the ability to adapt and learn from data, adjusting their behavior and predictions over time. When Agile and AI are combined, product managers can leverage the adaptability of

Agile methodologies to iterate rapidly on product features and development strategies, while AI algorithms continuously learn from real-time data to improve their performance and accuracy.

2. Real-Time Feedback Loops: Real-time feedback loops, a core tenet of Agile development, take on new dimensions when integrated with AI capabilities. AI algorithms can analyze vast amounts of data in real time, providing product teams with valuable insights into user behavior, system performance, and market trends. By incorporating AI-driven analytics into Agile processes, product managers can establish real-time feedback loops that enable continuous refinement and optimization of product features based on evolving user needs and preferences.

3. Predictive Analytics and Forecasting: AI's predictive analytics capabilities complement Agile methodologies by providing product teams with predictive insights and forecasting capabilities. AI algorithms can analyze historical data to identify patterns, trends, and potential future outcomes, helping product managers make informed decisions about feature prioritization, resource allocation, and product roadmap planning. By leveraging AI-driven predictive analytics within Agile development processes, product teams can anticipate market trends, identify opportunities, and mitigate risks more effectively, enhancing the overall success of the product.

4. Enhanced Automation and Efficiency: Agile and AI synergize to enhance automation and efficiency in product development processes. Agile methodologies emphasize the automation of repetitive tasks, such as testing, deployment, and integration, to streamline development workflows and increase productivity. AI technologies, such as machine learning and natural language processing, can further automate tasks, such as data analysis, content generation,

and customer support, freeing up valuable time for product teams to focus on high-impact activities. By integrating AI-driven automation into Agile processes, product managers can optimize resource allocation, reduce time-to-market, and improve overall efficiency.

5. Continuous Learning and Improvement: Both Agile methodologies and AI promote a culture of continuous learning and improvement within product teams. Agile encourages iterative development cycles, where teams learn from each iteration and incorporate feedback to improve subsequent releases. Similarly, AI systems learn from data and feedback to continuously improve their performance and accuracy over time. When Agile and AI are combined, product teams benefit from a synergistic approach to learning and improvement, where Agile methodologies drive iterative development cycles, while AI algorithms learn from real-time data to enhance their capabilities and insights.

6. Innovation and Creativity: The symbiosis of Agile and AI fosters a culture of innovation and creativity within product teams. Agile methodologies provide a framework for experimentation, iteration, and collaboration, encouraging teams to explore new ideas and approaches. AI technologies, such as deep learning and generative models, can inspire creativity by generating novel solutions, insights, and recommendations. By embracing the symbiosis of Agile and AI, product managers can unleash the full creative potential of their teams, driving innovation and differentiation in the marketplace.

The symbiosis of Agile methodologies and Artificial Intelligence represents a powerful fusion of adaptive development processes and intelligent learning systems. By integrating Agile and AI, product managers can leverage the strengths of both paradigms to enhance adaptability, responsiveness, efficiency, innovation, and continuous improvement in product development.

Integrating AI into Agile Feedback Loops

Integrating artificial intelligence (AI) into Agile feedback loops represents a strategic approach to maximizing the benefits of both methodologies. Here's a detailed exploration of this integration:

1. Understanding Agile Feedback Loops: Agile methodologies rely on iterative development cycles, where feedback loops play a crucial role. Feedback loops involve collecting insights from stakeholders, end-users, and team members at various stages of development. This feedback informs decision-making, drives improvements, and ensures that the product aligns with user needs and expectations.

2. The Role of AI in Feedback Loops: AI technologies, such as machine learning algorithms and natural language processing, can analyze vast amounts of data to extract valuable insights. These insights can include user behavior patterns, sentiment analysis from customer feedback, performance metrics, and predictive analytics. By incorporating AI-generated insights into feedback loops, product teams gain a deeper understanding of user preferences, market trends, and areas for optimization.

3. Enhancing Agility with AI Insights: Integrating AI insights into Agile feedback loops enhances the agility of product development in several ways:
- Real-time Data Analysis: AI algorithms can analyze data in real time, providing up-to-date insights that inform decision-making during sprint planning, backlog grooming, and daily stand-ups.
- Predictive Analytics: AI-powered predictive models forecast future trends, allowing teams to anticipate user

needs, identify potential issues, and proactively adjust their development roadmap.

- Personalized Recommendations: AI can generate personalized recommendations for product features, content, or user experiences based on individual preferences and behavior patterns.

Automated Testing and Quality Assurance: AI-driven testing tools can automate the identification of bugs, performance issues, and usability concerns, enabling faster resolution and continuous improvement.

4. Implementing AI-Driven Feedback Loops: To integrate AI into Agile feedback loops effectively, product teams should:
- Define Clear Objectives: Clearly define the goals and objectives of incorporating AI insights into the feedback loop, ensuring alignment with overall product strategy and user needs.
- Select Relevant AI Technologies: Choose AI technologies and tools that align with the specific requirements of the project, such as natural language processing for analyzing customer feedback or machine learning for predictive analytics.
- Establish Data Pipelines: Set up robust data pipelines to collect, preprocess, and analyze relevant data sources, ensuring the accuracy and reliability of AI-generated insights.
- Iterative Implementation: Adopt an iterative approach to integrating AI insights into feedback loops, allowing for continuous refinement and optimization based on user feedback and evolving project requirements.
- Collaborative Culture: Foster a collaborative culture where cross-functional teams actively engage with AI-generated insights, share feedback, and collaborate on implementing recommendations.

5. Measuring Impact and Iterating: Continuously measure the impact of AI-driven feedback loops on product development

outcomes, such as speed of delivery, user satisfaction, and business metrics. Use this feedback to iterate and refine the integration process, optimizing the value derived from AI insights over time.

User Feedback and AI-Driven Insights

User feedback and AI-driven insights represent two valuable sources of information that product managers can leverage to enhance product development and user experiences. Let's delve into a detailed exploration of this topic:

1. Traditional User Feedback: User feedback encompasses direct inputs, comments, and observations provided by users through various channels such as surveys, interviews, support tickets, reviews, and usability tests. This feedback provides valuable qualitative insights into user preferences, pain points, feature requests, and overall satisfaction with the product. Product managers collect, analyze, and prioritize user feedback to inform decision-making and drive iterative improvements to the product.

2. AI-Driven Insights: AI algorithms analyze vast amounts of data to extract meaningful patterns, trends, and predictions. These insights can include user behavior analysis, sentiment analysis of customer feedback, product usage metrics, and predictive analytics. AI-driven insights enable product managers to gain deeper insights into user preferences, identify emerging trends, predict user behavior, and optimize product performance. Examples of AI-driven insights include personalized recommendations, churn prediction, anomaly detection, and demand forecasting.

3. Establishing Real-time Feedback Loops: Product managers establish real-time feedback loops that integrate both traditional user feedback and AI-driven insights. These feedback loops facilitate continuous learning and adaptation,

ensuring that the product evolves in response to changing user needs and market dynamics. By leveraging AI-driven insights alongside traditional user feedback, product managers gain a more comprehensive understanding of user behavior and preferences.

4. Benefits of Dual-Source Feedback:
- Comprehensive Understanding: Combining traditional user feedback with AI-driven insights provides a more comprehensive understanding of user experiences and preferences.
- Data-Driven Decision-Making: AI-driven insights augment traditional user feedback by providing data-driven recommendations and predictions, enabling more informed decision-making.
- Proactive Identification of Issues: AI algorithms can proactively identify patterns or anomalies in user behavior that may not be immediately apparent through traditional feedback channels, allowing product managers to address issues before they escalate.
- Personalization and Optimization: AI-driven insights enable product personalization and optimization based on individual user preferences, enhancing user satisfaction and engagement.

5. Implementation Considerations:
- Data Integration: Ensure seamless integration of data sources to collect both traditional user feedback and AI-driven insights.
- Analytics Capabilities: Invest in robust analytics capabilities to analyze and derive insights from diverse data sources, including both structured and unstructured data.
- Cross-functional Collaboration: Foster collaboration between data scientists, UX/UI designers, engineers, and product managers to interpret insights and translate them into actionable product improvements.

- Iterative Improvement: Continuously iterate on feedback collection processes, AI algorithms, and product features based on insights derived from both user feedback and AI-driven analytics.

Integrating traditional user feedback with AI-driven insights in real-time feedback loops empowers product managers to make data-driven decisions, enhance user experiences, and drive product innovation. By leveraging the strengths of both sources of feedback, product teams can create more user-centric, adaptive, and successful products in today's competitive landscape.

Agile Sprints and AI Model Enhancement

Agile sprints and AI model enhancement represent a powerful convergence of iterative development methodologies and advanced machine learning techniques. Let's delve into a detailed exploration of this topic:

1. Agile Sprints: Agile methodology is characterized by iterative development cycles known as sprints. Sprints typically last from one to four weeks, during which cross-functional teams collaborate to deliver a set of predefined features or user stories. Agile promotes flexibility, adaptability, and continuous improvement, allowing teams to respond quickly to changing requirements and feedback.

2. AI Model Enhancement: AI model enhancement involves the iterative refinement and improvement of machine learning models. Machine learning models rely on data-driven algorithms to learn patterns, make predictions, and optimize performance. Enhancing AI models typically involves tasks such as data preprocessing, model training, hyperparameter tuning, and performance evaluation. Continuous refinement is essential to ensure that AI models remain accurate, robust, and relevant in dynamic environments.

3. Synchronization of Sprints and Model Enhancement: Product managers collaborate closely with data scientists to synchronize Agile sprints with AI model enhancement cycles. This involves aligning sprint goals and timelines with the iterative training and improvement cycles of AI models. By structuring sprints to accommodate tasks related to data collection, preprocessing, model training, and evaluation, product managers ensure that each sprint contributes to both user-facing features and the continuous refinement of underlying AI capabilities.

4. Integration Points: Agile sprints and AI model enhancement intersect at several integration points throughout the development process:
- Sprint Planning: Product managers collaborate with data scientists during sprint planning to prioritize tasks related to AI model enhancement alongside user-facing features. This ensures that development efforts are balanced between short-term user needs and long-term AI model improvement.
- Daily Stand-ups: Daily stand-up meetings provide opportunities for cross-functional teams to synchronize their efforts and address any challenges or dependencies related to AI model enhancement tasks.
- Sprint Reviews and Retrospectives: Sprint Reviews and retrospectives allow teams to reflect on the outcomes of AI model enhancement tasks and identify opportunities for improvement in future sprints.
- Continuous Integration and Deployment: Continuous integration and deployment pipelines enable seamless integration of AI model enhancements into the product, ensuring that improvements are delivered to users as soon as they are ready.

5. Benefits of Synchronization:
- Efficient Resource Allocation: Synchronizing Agile sprints with AI model enhancement cycles allows for efficient allocation of resources and effort across development tasks.
- Iterative Improvement: Continuous integration of AI model enhancements ensures that the product evolves alongside advancements in machine learning technology and changing user needs.
- Faster Time-to-Market: By embedding AI model enhancement tasks within Agile sprints, product managers can accelerate the delivery of improved AI capabilities to users.
- Enhanced Product Quality: Regular refinement of AI models leads to improved accuracy, reliability, and performance, enhancing the overall quality of the product.

The synchronization of Agile sprints and AI model enhancement cycles enables product managers to balance short-term user needs with long-term AI model improvement, resulting in more efficient, adaptive, and successful product development processes. By fostering collaboration between cross-functional teams and embracing an iterative approach, organizations can harness the full potential of Agile methodologies and advanced machine learning techniques to drive innovation and deliver value to users.

Continuous Integration of AI Recommendations

Continuous integration of AI recommendations is a pivotal practice that leverages Agile methodologies to incorporate real-time insights from intelligent systems into the development process. Let's delve into a detailed exploration of this topic:

1. Agile Methodologies: Agile methodologies emphasize iterative development, collaboration, and responsiveness to change. Agile frameworks such as Scrum and Kanban provide structured approaches to software development, enabling teams to adapt quickly to evolving requirements and feedback.

2. AI Recommendations: AI-driven recommendations are insights generated by intelligent systems based on data analysis, machine learning algorithms, and predictive analytics. These recommendations inform decision-making processes, optimize performance, and enhance user experiences across various domains, including product development, marketing, and customer service.

3. Collaborative Approach: Product managers, developers, data scientists, and other stakeholders collaborate to integrate AI recommendations seamlessly into the development process. Cross-functional teams work together to identify opportunities for AI-driven optimizations and implement them within the context of Agile workflows.

4. Real-time Adjustments: Agile methodologies enable teams to make real-time adjustments based on AI recommendations. Product managers prioritize tasks related to AI integration during sprint planning sessions, ensuring that development efforts align with the most pressing recommendations from intelligent systems.

5. Iterative Integration: Continuous integration of AI recommendations occurs throughout the development lifecycle. During each sprint, teams incorporate AI-driven insights into feature development, testing, and deployment processes. This iterative integration allows for rapid experimentation, validation, and refinement of AI-driven optimizations.

6. Feedback Loops: Agile frameworks facilitate feedback loops between AI systems and development teams. Teams monitor the performance of AI-driven features in production environments and gather feedback from users to validate the effectiveness of recommendations. This feedback informs subsequent iterations and ensures that AI-driven enhancements align with user needs and expectations.

7. Automation: Automation tools and pipelines streamline the integration of AI recommendations into development workflows. Continuous integration and deployment (CI/CD) pipelines automate the testing, deployment, and monitoring of AI-driven features, enabling teams to deliver updates to users quickly and efficiently.

8. Benefits of Continuous Integration:
- Agility: Continuous integration of AI recommendations enables teams to respond quickly to changing conditions and user feedback.
- Innovation: By incorporating AI-driven insights into development processes, teams can unlock new opportunities for innovation and optimization.
- Efficiency: Agile methodologies streamline the integration process, allowing teams to deliver AI-driven features with minimal overhead and delays.
- User Satisfaction: By continuously improving products based on AI recommendations, teams can enhance user satisfaction and retention over time.

The continuous integration of AI recommendations within Agile development processes empowers teams to innovate, adapt, and deliver value to users more effectively. By fostering collaboration, embracing feedback, and leveraging automation, organizations can harness the full potential of AI-driven insights to drive product excellence and customer satisfaction.

Dynamic Prioritization Informed by AI

Dynamic prioritization informed by AI is a critical practice that enhances the agility and responsiveness of Agile development processes. Let's delve into a detailed exploration of this topic:

1. Real-time Feedback from AI Systems: AI systems continuously generate insights based on data analysis, machine learning algorithms, and predictive analytics. These insights inform decision-making processes and provide valuable guidance for product development teams.

2. Adaptive Prioritization: Product managers and development teams adaptively prioritize features and tasks based on the real-time feedback provided by AI systems. Rather than relying solely on static backlog prioritization, teams dynamically adjust their priorities to address the most pressing needs identified by intelligent systems.

3. Cross-functional Collaboration: Dynamic prioritization involves collaboration between product managers, developers, data scientists, and other stakeholders. Cross-functional teams work together to understand the insights generated by AI systems and translate them into actionable priorities for development efforts.

4. Impactful Insights: AI systems provide insights into various aspects of product performance, user behavior, market trends, and more. Product managers leverage these insights to identify opportunities for improvement, address pain points, and capitalize on emerging trends.

5. Iterative Refinement: Dynamic prioritization is an iterative process that evolves over time based on continuous feedback and learning. Product managers regularly reassess

priorities in light of new insights and adjust development efforts accordingly.

6. Balancing Stakeholder Needs: Product managers balance the needs and priorities of various stakeholders, including customers, internal teams, and business objectives. AI-driven insights help prioritize features that deliver the most value to users while also aligning with strategic goals.

7. Maximizing Impact: By prioritizing features based on AI-driven insights, teams maximize the impact of their development efforts. Features that address critical pain points, capitalize on market opportunities, or drive user engagement are prioritized to deliver the greatest value to the organization.

8. Automation and Optimization: Automation tools and algorithms can further optimize the dynamic prioritization process. AI-powered recommendation engines can analyze vast amounts of data and suggest prioritization strategies based on predefined criteria, enabling teams to make data-driven decisions more efficiently.

9. Continuous Improvement: Dynamic prioritization is an ongoing process of continuous improvement. Product managers and development teams regularly review and refine their prioritization strategies based on feedback, performance metrics, and changing market dynamics.

10. Benefits of Dynamic Prioritization Informed by AI:
- Agility: Teams can respond quickly to changing conditions and user feedback, ensuring that development efforts remain aligned with evolving needs.
- *Efficiency: By focusing on features with the highest potential impact, teams optimize resource allocation and maximize productivity.

- Innovation: AI-driven insights uncover new opportunities for innovation and optimization, driving continuous improvement and competitive advantage.
- User Satisfaction: Prioritizing features based on user needs and preferences enhances user satisfaction and retention, ultimately contributing to business success.

Dynamic prioritization informed by AI empowers Agile teams to make data-driven decisions, adapt quickly to changing conditions, and deliver value to users more effectively. By leveraging AI-driven insights, organizations can optimize their development efforts, drive innovation, and achieve greater success in today's competitive landscape.

Agile Flexibility for AI Anomalies

Dealing with anomalies or unexpected behaviors in AI models is a common challenge faced by development teams, and Agile methodologies offer a flexible approach to address these issues effectively. Let's delve deeper into how Agile flexibility can mitigate the impact of AI anomalies:

1. Real-time Monitoring and Feedback: Agile frameworks emphasize real-time monitoring and feedback loops, enabling teams to detect anomalies as soon as they occur. Continuous integration and deployment pipelines facilitate the rapid detection of issues, allowing teams to respond promptly.

2. Cross-functional Collaboration: Agile teams are composed of cross-functional members with diverse expertise. When anomalies arise in AI models, teams collaborate across disciplines to understand the root cause and devise appropriate solutions. This collaborative approach ensures that anomalies are addressed comprehensively and effectively.

3. Iterative Problem-solving: Agile methodologies promote an iterative problem-solving approach. Instead of waiting for a perfect solution, teams address anomalies incrementally, implementing quick fixes and improvements as needed. This iterative process allows teams to adapt their strategies based on ongoing feedback and learning.

4. Flexible Prioritization: Agile frameworks enable teams to adjust their priorities dynamically in response to anomalies. If an anomaly poses a significant risk or impedes progress, teams can reprioritize tasks and allocate resources accordingly. This flexibility ensures that critical issues are addressed promptly without disrupting the overall development process.

5. Adaptive Planning: Agile planning is adaptive and responsive to change. When anomalies occur in AI models, teams adjust their plans and timelines to accommodate the necessary troubleshooting and resolution activities. This adaptive planning approach minimizes delays and ensures that development efforts remain on track.

6. Continuous Improvement: Agile methodologies promote a culture of continuous improvement. Rather than viewing anomalies as failures, teams treat them as learning opportunities. Through retrospective meetings and post-mortems, teams reflect on their experiences, identify lessons learned, and implement process improvements to prevent similar issues in the future.

7. Risk Mitigation Strategies: Agile teams proactively implement risk mitigation strategies to address potential anomalies before they occur. This may include conducting thorough testing, implementing failover mechanisms, and establishing contingency plans to minimize the impact of anomalies on the product and its users.

8. Transparency and Communication: Agile frameworks emphasize transparency and open communication. When anomalies occur, teams communicate openly with stakeholders, keeping them informed of the situation and any remediation efforts underway. This transparency fosters trust and collaboration among team members and stakeholders.

9. Experimentation and Innovation: Agile methodologies encourage experimentation and innovation. When faced with anomalies, teams explore creative solutions and experiment with alternative approaches to address the issue. This experimentation mindset fosters a culture of innovation and enables teams to discover novel solutions to complex problems.

10. Continuous Learning: Agile teams embrace a mindset of continuous learning and adaptation. By documenting their experiences and sharing knowledge within the team, they build institutional knowledge that strengthens their ability to address future anomalies more effectively.

Agile flexibility enables development teams to respond proactively and effectively to anomalies in AI models. By leveraging real-time feedback, cross-functional collaboration, and iterative problem-solving, Agile teams can minimize the impact of anomalies and ensure that development efforts remain on course towards delivering high-quality, resilient products.

AI-Driven Insights for Iterative Design

The integration of AI-driven insights into the iterative design process brings a new dimension to product development, allowing for more informed and adaptive design decisions. Let's delve deeper into how AI-driven insights enhance iterative design:

1. Real-time Feedback Integration: AI systems continuously analyze user interactions, preferences, and behaviors, providing real-time insights into how users engage with the product. By integrating these insights into the design process, product managers and designers gain a deeper understanding of user needs and preferences, allowing them to make informed design decisions.

2. Data-driven Design Decisions: AI-driven insights provide designers with access to vast amounts of data about user behavior and preferences. By leveraging this data, designers can identify patterns, trends, and areas for improvement in the user experience. This data-driven approach ensures that design decisions are based on empirical evidence rather than assumptions or intuition.

3. Personalized User Experiences: AI systems can analyze user data to create personalized user experiences tailored to individual preferences and behaviors. Designers can use AI-driven insights to create dynamic, adaptive interfaces that adjust in real time based on user interactions. This personalization enhances user engagement and satisfaction, leading to higher retention and conversion rates.

4. Predictive Design Optimization: AI algorithms can predict user behavior and preferences based on historical data and trends. Designers can use these predictive insights to anticipate user needs and optimize design elements proactively. For example, predictive analytics can help identify potential usability issues before they occur, allowing designers to iterate on the design to improve usability and satisfaction.

5. Automated Design Recommendations: AI systems can generate design recommendations based on user data and design principles. Designers can use these automated recommendations as a starting point for design exploration,

speeding up the iterative design process and enabling rapid prototyping and testing. This automation frees up designers to focus on higher-level creative tasks while AI handles repetitive design tasks.

6. Iterative Testing and Validation: AI-driven insights facilitate iterative testing and validation of design changes. By continuously monitoring user interactions and feedback, AI systems can identify the effectiveness of design changes and provide recommendations for further optimization. This iterative testing process ensures that design changes are data-driven and aligned with user preferences.

7. Cross-functional Collaboration: AI-driven insights encourage cross-functional collaboration between product managers, designers, data scientists, and engineers. By sharing AI-generated insights across teams, stakeholders can collaborate more effectively to iterate on design solutions and drive continuous improvement in the user experience.

8. Ethical Considerations: It's essential to consider ethical implications when integrating AI-driven insights into the design process. Designers must ensure that AI recommendations align with ethical guidelines and do not perpetuate biases or discriminatory practices. By incorporating ethical considerations into the design process, designers can create products that are not only user-centric but also ethical and inclusive.

AI-driven insights enhance the iterative design process by providing real-time feedback, data-driven design decisions, personalized user experiences, predictive design optimization, automated design recommendations, iterative testing and validation, cross-functional collaboration, and ethical considerations. By leveraging AI-driven insights, designers can create products that are not only intuitive and engaging but also intelligent and adaptive, meeting the evolving needs and preferences of users.

Ethical Considerations in Real-time Feedback

Ethical considerations in real-time feedback loops are paramount, especially in the context of integrating AI-generated insights into Agile methodologies. Let's explore the nuances of these ethical considerations in more detail:

1. Bias Mitigation: AI algorithms can inadvertently perpetuate biases present in training data, leading to unfair or discriminatory outcomes. Product managers must implement measures to mitigate bias in real-time feedback loops, such as ensuring diverse and representative training data, regularly auditing AI models for bias, and implementing bias correction techniques.

2. Fairness and Equity: Real-time feedback loops should prioritize fairness and equity in the insights provided to stakeholders. Product managers must ensure that AI-generated insights do not favor certain groups over others and that all users have equal access to opportunities and resources. This requires a careful examination of the impact of AI recommendations on different demographic groups and the implementation of fairness-aware algorithms.

3. Privacy Protection: Real-time feedback may involve the processing of sensitive user data, raising concerns about privacy and data protection. Product managers must implement robust privacy safeguards to ensure that user data is handled securely and by relevant regulations (e.g., GDPR, CCPA). This may include anonymizing user data, implementing access controls, and obtaining explicit user consent for data processing.

4. Transparency and Accountability: Transparency is crucial in real-time feedback loops to maintain user trust and accountability. Product managers should ensure that AI-generated insights are transparently communicated to stakeholders, including how they were generated, their limitations, and potential biases. Additionally, mechanisms for accountability should be established to address any ethical issues or concerns that arise during the feedback process.

5. Inclusivity and Accessibility: Real-time feedback loops should be inclusive and accessible to all users, regardless of their abilities or backgrounds. Product managers must consider the diverse needs of users and ensure that AI-generated insights are accessible to everyone. This may involve providing alternative formats for feedback, such as text-based summaries or audio descriptions, and incorporating accessibility features into AI interfaces.

6. Continuous Monitoring and Evaluation: Ethical considerations in real-time feedback require ongoing monitoring and evaluation to identify and address potential ethical issues. Product managers should establish mechanisms for continuous monitoring of AI-generated insights, including regular audits, user feedback mechanisms, and ethical reviews. Any ethical concerns that arise should be promptly addressed and mitigated to ensure the ethical integrity of the feedback process.

Ethical considerations in real-time feedback loops involve mitigating bias, promoting fairness and equity, protecting user privacy, ensuring transparency and accountability, promoting inclusivity and accessibility, and continuously monitoring and evaluating the ethical implications of AI-generated insights. By prioritizing ethical considerations, product managers can ensure that real-time feedback loops align with ethical standards and contribute to positive user experiences and societal well-being.

Scalability of Real-time Feedback in AI Enterprises

Scalability is a fundamental concern when implementing real-time feedback loops in AI enterprises. Let's delve deeper into how product managers address the scalability of these feedback mechanisms:

1. Infrastructure Scalability: Real-time feedback systems must be built on scalable infrastructure that can handle increasing volumes of data and user interactions. Product managers work closely with IT and engineering teams to design and deploy scalable architectures, such as cloud-based solutions or distributed computing platforms, that can accommodate growing workloads and support real-time data processing and analysis.

2. Data Management: Managing large volumes of data is essential for scalable real-time feedback loops. Product managers establish robust data management practices, including data ingestion, storage, and processing pipelines, to ensure that data can be efficiently collected, stored, and analyzed in real time. This may involve leveraging big data technologies like Hadoop or Spark to handle massive datasets and stream processing frameworks like Kafka or Flink for real-time data processing.

3. Scalable Algorithms: The algorithms used to generate real-time feedback must also be scalable to accommodate the increasing complexity of AI models and the growing volume of data. Product managers collaborate with data scientists and machine learning engineers to develop and deploy scalable algorithms that can efficiently process large datasets and adapt to changing business requirements. This may involve using distributed machine learning frameworks like TensorFlow or PyTorch to train models in parallel across multiple nodes or leveraging online learning techniques to update models in real time as new data becomes available.

4. Distributed Decision-Making: In large enterprises, decision-making processes may be distributed across multiple teams or departments. Product managers implement scalable feedback mechanisms that enable decentralized decision-making while ensuring consistency and alignment with organizational goals. This may involve establishing clear governance structures, communication channels, and decision-making frameworks to facilitate collaboration and coordination across teams.

5. Monitoring and Maintenance: Scalable real-time feedback loops require ongoing monitoring and maintenance to ensure continued performance and reliability. Product managers implement monitoring and alerting systems to track key performance metrics and detect any issues or anomalies in real time. Additionally, regular maintenance and optimization efforts are conducted to address scalability bottlenecks, optimize resource utilization, and improve system efficiency over time.

6. Adaptability and Flexibility: Scalability is not just about handling increasing volumes of data or users; it's also about adapting to changing business requirements and technological advancements. Product managers design scalable feedback loops that are flexible and adaptable, allowing them to evolve and grow alongside the enterprise. This may involve modular architectures, microservices-based designs, and agile development practices that enable rapid iteration and experimentation.

Scalability in real-time feedback loops for AI enterprises requires scalable infrastructure, efficient data management practices, scalable algorithms, distributed decision-making processes, proactive monitoring and maintenance, and adaptability and flexibility to accommodate changing business needs and technological advancements. By addressing these scalability considerations, product managers can ensure that real-time feedback mechanisms can support the growth and evolution of AI enterprises effectively.

5. DATA-DRIVEN DECISION MAKING

LEVERAGING BIG DATA FOR PRODUCT INSIGHTS

In the era of digital transformation, data has become the lifeblood of informed decision-making. This chapter delves into the profound impact of data-driven decision-making in the realm of product management, exploring how the vast landscape of Big Data is harnessed to extract valuable insights, guide strategic choices, and foster innovation within the product development lifecycle.

The Power of Big Data in Product Management

The Power of Big Data in Product Management is a transformative force shaping how businesses understand, develop, and refine their products. Let's explore this topic in more detail:

1. Data Abundance: Big Data provides product managers with access to an unprecedented volume, variety, and velocity of data from various sources, including customer interactions, user behavior, market trends, social media, and IoT devices. This abundance of data offers valuable insights into customer preferences, market dynamics, and emerging trends, enabling product managers to make data-driven decisions at every stage of the product lifecycle.

2. Market Understanding: Big Data analytics allow product managers to gain a deep understanding of their target market, including customer demographics, preferences, and buying behavior. By analyzing large datasets, product managers can identify market trends, consumer sentiment, and competitive intelligence, helping them to identify

untapped opportunities, anticipate customer needs, and position their products more effectively in the market.

3. User-Centric Design: Big Data enables product managers to adopt a user-centric approach to product design and development. By analyzing user data, including feedback, usage patterns, and pain points, product managers can gain valuable insights into user behavior and preferences, allowing them to tailor products to meet the needs and expectations of their target audience. This data-driven approach helps to improve user satisfaction, retention, and loyalty.

4. Predictive Analytics: Big Data enables product managers to leverage predictive analytics to forecast future trends, demand, and customer behavior. By analyzing historical data and identifying patterns, product managers can make informed predictions about market dynamics, product performance, and customer preferences, allowing them to proactively address potential challenges and capitalize on emerging opportunities.

5. Agile Decision-Making: Big Data empowers product managers to make agile, data-driven decisions in real time. By leveraging advanced analytics and visualization tools, product managers can quickly analyze large datasets, extract actionable insights, and respond rapidly to changing market conditions, customer feedback, and competitive threats. This agility enables product managers to iterate and adapt their products more effectively, accelerating time-to-market and maximizing ROI.

6. Performance Optimization: Big Data analytics enable product managers to monitor and optimize product performance continuously. By tracking key performance indicators (KPIs) and conducting A/B testing, product managers can identify areas for improvement, refine product

features, and optimize pricing, packaging, and promotion strategies to maximize revenue and profitability.

7. Risk Mitigation: Big Data analytics help product managers identify and mitigate potential risks and challenges associated with product development and deployment. By analyzing data from multiple sources, including customer feedback, quality assurance testing, and supply chain operations, product managers can anticipate potential issues, address them proactively, and minimize the impact on product quality, customer satisfaction, and brand reputation.

The power of Big Data in product management lies in its ability to provide product managers with actionable insights, predictive analytics, and agile decision-making capabilities, enabling them to develop innovative, user-centric products that meet the evolving needs and expectations of their customers while maximizing business value and competitive advantage.

Data-Driven Insights for Market Understanding

Data-driven insights for Market Understanding revolutionize how product managers navigate the intricacies of the market landscape. Let's delve deeper into this topic:

1. Comprehensive Market Analysis: Big Data empowers product managers with access to a wealth of information sourced from diverse channels such as social media, online forums, customer feedback, sales data, and industry reports. By harnessing this data, product managers can conduct comprehensive market analyses to identify emerging trends, consumer preferences, and competitive dynamics. This deeper understanding enables them to make informed decisions about product positioning, pricing strategies, and feature prioritization.

2. Customer Segmentation: Big Data analytics allow product managers to segment the market based on various criteria such as demographics, psychographics, purchasing behavior, and geographic location. By clustering customers into distinct groups, product managers can tailor marketing messages, product offerings, and customer experiences to resonate with specific segments. This targeted approach enhances customer engagement, loyalty, and satisfaction while maximizing the effectiveness of marketing efforts.

3. Competitor Analysis: Big Data provides product managers with valuable insights into competitor strategies, product performance, and market positioning. By monitoring competitor activities, analyzing pricing trends, and benchmarking product features, product managers can identify competitive threats and opportunities. This competitive intelligence enables them to refine their own product strategies, differentiate their offerings, and capitalize on gaps in the market.

4. Predictive Modeling: Big Data enables product managers to leverage predictive modeling techniques to forecast market trends, demand fluctuations, and customer behavior. By analyzing historical data and identifying patterns, product managers can develop predictive models that anticipate future market conditions and consumer preferences. This foresight enables them to proactively adjust their product strategies, allocate resources effectively, and stay ahead of market shifts.

5. Real-time Monitoring: Big Data platforms facilitate real-time monitoring of market dynamics, allowing product managers to track key performance indicators (KPIs), sentiment analysis, and social media trends. By staying attuned to changes in the market landscape, product managers can quickly identify emerging opportunities or threats and adjust their strategies

accordingly. This agility enables them to capitalize on market trends, mitigate risks, and maintain a competitive edge.

6. Iterative Optimization: Big Data-driven market understanding fosters an iterative approach to product development and marketing. By continuously analyzing market data, gathering feedback from customers, and monitoring competitor activities, product managers can iteratively optimize their product offerings, marketing campaigns, and go-to-market strategies. This iterative process ensures that products remain relevant, competitive, and aligned with evolving market demands.

Data-driven insights for Market Understanding empower product managers to navigate the complexities of the market landscape with precision and agility. By leveraging Big Data analytics, product managers can gain deeper insights into market dynamics, customer preferences, and competitive strategies, enabling them to make informed decisions, anticipate market trends, and drive business success.

Personalization Paradigm

The Personalization Paradigm represents a transformative shift in how products and services are designed, delivered, and experienced. Let's delve deeper into this topic:

1. Understanding User Preferences: Big Data empowers product managers with granular insights into user preferences, behaviors, and interactions. By analyzing vast datasets encompassing user demographics, browsing history, purchase patterns, and social media activity, product managers can gain a comprehensive understanding of individual user preferences. This deep understanding allows them to tailor product features, content, and recommendations to resonate with each user's unique interests and needs.

2. Dynamic Content Personalization: Big Data-driven personalization enables product managers to deliver dynamic content experiences that adapt in real time based on user interactions and preferences. By leveraging algorithms and machine learning models, product managers can customize content recommendations, product recommendations, and user interfaces to reflect each user's preferences, browsing history, and context. This dynamic content personalization enhances user engagement, satisfaction, and loyalty by delivering relevant and timely content that resonates with individual users.

3. Contextualized Experiences: Big Data analytics enables product managers to contextualize user experiences by considering factors such as location, device type, time of day, and past interactions. By integrating contextual signals into product design and delivery, product managers can create seamless and personalized experiences that anticipate user needs and preferences. Whether it's adjusting the interface layout for mobile users, recommending nearby events based on location, or suggesting relevant products based on browsing history, contextualized experiences enhance user engagement and satisfaction.

4. Predictive Personalization: Big Data facilitates predictive modeling techniques that enable product managers to anticipate user preferences and behaviors. By analyzing historical data and identifying patterns, product managers can develop predictive models that forecast future user actions, preferences, and needs. These predictive models empower product managers to proactively personalize user experiences, content recommendations, and product offerings, maximizing user satisfaction and driving conversions.

5. Iterative Optimization: The Personalization Paradigm fosters an iterative approach to product development and

optimization. By continuously analyzing user data, gathering feedback, and monitoring user interactions, product managers can iteratively refine personalization strategies to ensure relevance and effectiveness. This iterative optimization process enables product managers to adapt to changing user preferences, market dynamics, and technological advancements, maintaining a competitive edge in the ever-evolving digital landscape.

6. Ethical Considerations: While personalization offers numerous benefits, product managers must also consider ethical implications such as privacy, transparency, and user consent. Ethical personalization practices prioritize user trust and respect user privacy rights by providing transparent disclosure about data collection and usage, offering opt-in/opt-out mechanisms, and implementing robust security measures to safeguard user data. By prioritizing ethical considerations, product managers can build trust with users and foster long-term relationships based on mutual respect and transparency.

The Personalization Paradigm represents a new frontier in product management, powered by Big Data analytics and machine learning. By leveraging data-driven insights to personalize user experiences, product managers can create compelling, relevant, and engaging products that resonate with individual users, driving user satisfaction, loyalty, and business success.

User Behavior Analytics

User Behavior Analytics (UBA) offers a comprehensive view of how users engage with products, providing invaluable insights that drive informed decision-making and product optimization. Let's delve deeper into this topic:

1. Data Collection and Aggregation: User Behavior Analytics begins with the collection and aggregation of data from various sources, including web and mobile applications, IoT devices, and customer relationship management (CRM) systems. This data encompasses a wide range of user interactions, such as page views, clicks, scroll depth, time spent on a page, form submissions, and transactions. By aggregating this data into a centralized repository, product managers can gain a holistic view of user behavior across different touchpoints and channels.

2. Behavioral Segmentation: Once the data is collected, product managers utilize behavioral segmentation techniques to categorize users based on common behaviors, preferences, and characteristics. This segmentation allows product managers to identify distinct user segments with unique needs, motivations, and pain points. By understanding these segments, product managers can tailor product features, messaging, and experiences to resonate with each user group effectively.

3. User Journey Mapping: User Behavior Analytics enables product managers to map out the user journey, from initial engagement to conversion and beyond. By visualizing the user journey, product managers can identify key touchpoints, drop-off points, and areas of friction that may impede the user experience. This insight allows product managers to optimize the user journey by streamlining processes, removing barriers, and providing personalized guidance at each stage of the journey.

4. Conversion Funnel Analysis: Conversion funnel analysis is a fundamental aspect of User Behavior Analytics, enabling product managers to track user progression through various stages of the conversion process, such as awareness, consideration, and purchase. By analyzing conversion funnels, product managers can identify bottlenecks, optimize

conversion rates, and improve overall conversion performance. This analysis provides actionable insights into areas where user engagement can be enhanced and conversion barriers can be addressed.

5. Predictive Analytics: User Behavior Analytics also encompasses predictive analytics techniques that enable product managers to forecast future user behaviors and trends based on historical data patterns. By leveraging machine learning algorithms, product managers can develop predictive models that anticipate user actions, preferences, and needs. These predictive models empower product managers to proactively personalize user experiences, recommend relevant products, and mitigate churn risk.

6. Continuous Optimization: User Behavior Analytics fosters a culture of continuous optimization, where product managers iteratively refine product features, user interfaces, and marketing strategies based on user feedback and data-driven insights. By monitoring user behavior in real-time and A/B testing proposed changes, product managers can identify opportunities for improvement and implement iterative changes that enhance the overall user experience.

7. Ethical Considerations: While User Behavior Analytics offers numerous benefits, product managers must also prioritize ethical considerations such as user privacy, consent, and data security. Ethical user behavior analytics practices involve obtaining explicit user consent for data collection and usage, anonymizing personally identifiable information, and implementing robust security measures to protect user data from unauthorized access or misuse. By prioritizing ethical considerations, product managers can build trust with users and maintain the integrity of their products and brands.

User Behavior Analytics empowers product managers with actionable insights into user behaviors, preferences, and trends, enabling them to optimize products, personalize experiences, and drive business success. By leveraging data-driven insights and predictive analytics techniques, product managers can make informed decisions that enhance the user experience and maximize engagement, retention, and conversion rates.

Predictive Analytics for Future Trends

Predictive Analytics holds immense potential for product managers, enabling them to anticipate future trends, mitigate risks, and capitalize on emerging opportunities. Let's delve deeper into how predictive analytics harnesses Big Data to forecast future trends:

1. Historical Data Analysis: Predictive analytics begins with the analysis of historical data, encompassing a wide range of variables such as user behavior, market trends, competitor activities, and external factors like economic indicators and social trends. By examining historical data patterns and correlations, predictive models identify trends and patterns that provide insights into future developments.

2. Machine Learning Algorithms: Predictive analytics leverages advanced machine learning algorithms to analyze historical data and identify predictive patterns. These algorithms encompass a variety of techniques, including regression analysis, time series analysis, decision trees, neural networks, and ensemble methods. By training predictive models on historical data, product managers can develop models that accurately forecast future trends and outcomes.

3. Feature Selection and Engineering: Predictive analytics involves feature selection and engineering, where product managers identify relevant variables and data attributes that are most predictive of future trends. This process may involve

transforming raw data into meaningful features, extracting key insights, and selecting the most relevant predictors to include in the predictive model. Feature selection ensures that predictive models focus on the most influential factors that drive future outcomes.

4. Forecasting Future Trends: Once predictive models are trained on historical data and validated for accuracy, they can be used to forecast future trends and outcomes. Predictive analytics enables product managers to anticipate shifts in user behavior, market dynamics, and industry trends, allowing them to proactively adjust strategies, allocate resources, and prioritize initiatives to capitalize on emerging opportunities or mitigate potential risks.

5. Scenario Planning and Sensitivity Analysis: Predictive analytics facilitates scenario planning and sensitivity analysis, allowing product managers to simulate different scenarios and assess the potential impact of various factors on future trends. By conducting sensitivity analysis, product managers can identify key drivers of future outcomes and evaluate how changes in these variables may affect business performance. This insight enables product managers to develop robust contingency plans and adaptive strategies that account for uncertainty and volatility in the market.

6. Real-time Monitoring and Adaptation: Predictive analytics enables real-time monitoring of key metrics and indicators, allowing product managers to track changes in trends and respond quickly to emerging developments. By integrating predictive models into decision-making processes, product managers can make data-driven decisions in real time, adapt strategies dynamically, and capitalize on opportunities as they arise.

7. Ethical Considerations: While predictive analytics offers valuable insights into future trends, product managers must

also consider ethical implications such as privacy, fairness, and transparency. Ethical predictive analytics practices involve ensuring data privacy and security, avoiding bias in predictive models, and transparently communicating the limitations and uncertainties associated with predictions. By prioritizing ethical considerations, product managers can build trust with stakeholders and ensure the responsible use of predictive analytics.

Predictive Analytics empowers product managers to anticipate future trends, make proactive decisions, and stay ahead of the curve in an increasingly dynamic and competitive landscape. By harnessing the power of Big Data and advanced machine learning techniques, product managers can develop predictive models that provide actionable insights into future developments, enabling them to drive innovation, optimize strategies, and achieve sustainable business growth.

Iterative Development and Continuous Improvement

Iterative development and continuous improvement are foundational principles in modern product management, driven by data-driven decision-making and fueled by insights from Big Data. Let's explore how these principles intersect and drive the iterative approach to product development:

1. Data-Driven Decision-Making: Iterative development begins with data-driven decision-making. Product managers leverage Big Data insights to inform each iteration of the product, using quantitative and qualitative data to understand user behavior, preferences, and pain points. By analyzing data from various sources such as user analytics, market research, and customer feedback, product managers gain valuable insights that shape the direction of product development.

2. User Feedback and Performance Metrics: User feedback and performance metrics play a crucial role in iterative development. Product managers collect feedback from users through surveys, interviews, usability testing, and customer support interactions. They also monitor key performance metrics such as user engagement, retention rates, conversion rates, and customer satisfaction scores to evaluate the effectiveness of product features and identify areas for improvement.

3. Refinement of Features: Based on user feedback and performance metrics, product managers prioritize and refine features in each iteration. They identify pain points, address usability issues, and enhance functionality to better meet user needs and preferences. This iterative refinement process ensures that the product evolves, becoming increasingly aligned with user expectations and market demands.

4. Agile Methodologies: Iterative development is often facilitated by Agile methodologies such as Scrum or Kanban. These methodologies emphasize incremental progress, regular feedback loops, and continuous improvement. Product managers work in cross-functional teams, collaboratively planning and executing iterations, conducting regular retrospectives to reflect on progress and identify areas for improvement.

5. Experimentation and A/B Testing**: Iterative development involves experimentation and A/B testing to validate assumptions and optimize features. Product managers design experiments to test hypotheses, comparing different versions of features or user interfaces to determine which performs better in terms of user engagement, conversion rates, or other key metrics. By analyzing the results of experiments, product managers iteratively refine features to maximize their effectiveness.

6. Adapting to Market Conditions: Iterative development enables product managers to adapt to changing market conditions and emerging trends. By monitoring market dynamics and competitor activities, product managers identify opportunities and threats, adjusting product strategies and priorities accordingly. This adaptive approach ensures that the product remains competitive and relevant in a dynamic marketplace.

7. Continuous Learning and Adaptation: Iterative development fosters a culture of continuous learning and adaptation within product teams. Product managers encourage experimentation, innovation, and knowledge sharing, empowering team members to contribute ideas and insights that drive iterative improvements. This culture of continuous learning enables product teams to stay agile, responsive, and innovative in the face of evolving challenges and opportunities.

Iterative development and continuous improvement are essential components of modern product management, driven by data-driven decision-making, user feedback, and Agile methodologies. By embracing an iterative approach, product managers can refine features, optimize user experiences, and adapt to changing market conditions, ultimately delivering products that meet the evolving needs and expectations of users.

Dynamic Pricing Strategies

Dynamic pricing strategies, empowered by Big Data analytics, revolutionize how product managers approach pricing in industries where prices fluctuate based on various factors such as demand, competition, and market conditions. Let's delve deeper into how product managers leverage data-driven insights to optimize dynamic pricing strategies:

1. Real-time Market Monitoring: Dynamic pricing requires real-time monitoring of market conditions. Product managers utilize Big Data analytics to gather and analyze vast amounts of data from multiple sources, including market trends, competitor pricing, consumer sentiment, and economic indicators. By continuously monitoring this data, product managers gain a comprehensive understanding of the market dynamics that influence pricing decisions.

2. Predictive Analytics: Predictive analytics play a crucial role in dynamic pricing strategies. Product managers employ advanced analytics techniques to forecast future demand, identify price elasticity, and anticipate changes in consumer behavior. By analyzing historical data and applying predictive models, product managers can predict how changes in pricing will impact sales volume, revenue, and profitability.

3. Segmentation and Personalization: Big Data enables product managers to implement dynamic pricing strategies that are tailored to specific customer segments or individual customers. By segmenting customers based on demographics, purchase history, and browsing behavior, product managers can offer personalized pricing incentives, discounts, or promotions to maximize conversion rates and customer loyalty.

4. Competitive Analysis: Understanding competitor pricing is essential for effective dynamic pricing strategies. Product managers use Big Data analytics to monitor competitors' pricing strategies, track price changes, and identify pricing gaps or opportunities. By benchmarking against competitors and analyzing competitive data, product managers can adjust pricing dynamically to maintain competitiveness and capture market share.

5. Optimization Algorithms: Dynamic pricing often involves complex optimization algorithms that balance multiple factors

such as demand, inventory levels, production costs, and pricing constraints. Product managers leverage Big Data analytics to develop and refine these optimization algorithms, ensuring that pricing decisions are data-driven, strategic, and aligned with business objectives.

6. A/B Testing and Experimentation: A key aspect of dynamic pricing is experimentation and A/B testing. Product managers design pricing experiments to test different pricing strategies, discounts, or pricing models and measure their impact on key performance metrics such as sales, revenue, and profit margin. By analyzing the results of these experiments, product managers iteratively refine pricing strategies to optimize performance.

7. Regulatory Compliance and Ethical Considerations: Dynamic pricing strategies must comply with regulatory requirements and ethical guidelines. Product managers use Big Data analytics to ensure that pricing decisions are transparent, fair, and compliant with laws and regulations governing pricing practices. By incorporating ethical considerations into pricing algorithms and decision-making processes, product managers mitigate the risk of backlash or legal issues.

Dynamic pricing strategies powered by Big Data analytics enable product managers to optimize pricing decisions in real-time, maximize revenue, and gain a competitive edge in dynamic markets. By leveraging data-driven insights, segmentation, predictive analytics, and optimization algorithms, product managers can implement dynamic pricing strategies that are strategic, personalized, and responsive to changing market conditions.

Risk Mitigation and Decision Support

Risk mitigation and decision support are essential components of effective product management, and Big Data plays a crucial role in providing insights and guidance in these areas. Let's explore how Big Data enables product managers to mitigate risks and make informed decisions:

1. Identifying and Assessing Risks: Big Data analytics enables product managers to identify potential risks by analyzing vast amounts of data from various sources. This includes historical data, market trends, competitor activities, customer feedback, and industry reports. By leveraging advanced analytics techniques, such as predictive modeling and anomaly detection, product managers can detect patterns, anomalies, and emerging risks that may impact the success of their products.

2. Predictive Analytics for Risk Forecasting: Predictive analytics allows product managers to forecast potential risks and their likelihood of occurrence. By analyzing historical data and applying predictive models, product managers can anticipate future challenges, such as supply chain disruptions, market downturns, regulatory changes, or competitive threats. This proactive approach enables product managers to implement preemptive measures to mitigate risks before they escalate.

3. Scenario Planning and Simulation: Big Data analytics facilitates scenario planning and simulation exercises to assess the potential impact of various risk scenarios on product performance and business outcomes. Product managers can simulate different scenarios, such as changes in market conditions, shifts in consumer behavior, or unexpected events, to evaluate their implications and develop contingency plans accordingly.

4. Data-driven Decision Making: Big Data provides product managers with the information needed to make data-driven decisions. By analyzing relevant data sets and key performance indicators (KPIs), product managers can evaluate different options, assess trade-offs, and prioritize actions based on their potential impact on product success. Data-driven decision-making ensures that product managers have a clear understanding of the risks and opportunities associated with each decision.

5. Real-time Monitoring and Alerting: Big Data enables real-time monitoring of key metrics and alerts product managers to potential issues or deviations from expected performance. By setting up automated monitoring systems and dashboards, product managers can track product performance in real-time and receive alerts when predefined thresholds are exceeded. This proactive approach allows product managers to respond swiftly to emerging risks and take corrective actions before they escalate.

6. Cross-functional Collaboration: Big Data fosters cross-functional collaboration by providing a common data platform for stakeholders across the organization. Product managers can collaborate with teams such as marketing, sales, operations, and finance to assess risks holistically and develop coordinated mitigation strategies. By sharing data-driven insights and aligning on risk management priorities, cross-functional teams can work together to address challenges and drive product success.

7. Continuous Improvement and Learning: Big Data enables product managers to continuously learn and improve by analyzing the outcomes of risk mitigation strategies and decision-making processes. By collecting feedback, measuring performance, and conducting post-mortem analyses, product managers can identify lessons learned,

refine their approaches, and enhance their risk management capabilities over time.

Big Data serves as a powerful tool for risk mitigation and decision support in product management. By leveraging data-driven insights, predictive analytics, scenario planning, real-time monitoring, cross-functional collaboration, and continuous improvement, product managers can proactively identify risks, make informed decisions, and navigate challenges with confidence, ultimately driving product success.

Operational Efficiency and Resource Allocation

Operational efficiency and resource allocation are crucial components of successful product management, and Big Data analytics plays a pivotal role in optimizing these aspects. Let's delve deeper into how Big Data aids in enhancing operational efficiency and resource allocation:

1. Identifying Bottlenecks: Big Data analytics enables product managers to identify bottlenecks in various operational processes. By analyzing large volumes of data from different sources such as production systems, supply chain logistics, and customer interactions, product managers can pinpoint areas where inefficiencies occur. This could include delays in production, issues in the supply chain, or bottlenecks in customer service. Identifying these bottlenecks allows product managers to take corrective actions to streamline processes and improve overall efficiency.

2. Streamlining Processes: Big Data analytics provides insights into how processes can be streamlined to improve efficiency. By analyzing data on workflows, production cycles, and resource utilization, product managers can identify opportunities for automation, standardization, and optimization. For example, data analysis may reveal

opportunities to automate repetitive tasks, standardize workflows across teams, or optimize production schedules to minimize idle time and maximize output.

3. Optimizing Resource Allocation: Big Data analytics helps product managers allocate resources effectively by providing insights into where resources are most needed and where they can yield the highest impact. This includes both human and financial resources. By analyzing data on project timelines, resource utilization, and performance metrics, product managers can ensure that resources are allocated to projects and initiatives that align with strategic objectives and have the potential to drive the greatest value for the organization.

4. Forecasting Demand and Supply: Big Data analytics enables product managers to forecast demand and supply more accurately. By analyzing historical data on sales, customer behavior, and market trends, product managers can predict future demand for products and services. This allows them to adjust production schedules, inventory levels, and supply chain logistics accordingly, ensuring that the right amount of resources is available at the right time to meet customer demand while minimizing excess inventory and associated costs.

5. Improving Decision-Making: Big Data analytics provides product managers with data-driven insights that can inform decision-making processes related to resource allocation. By analyzing data on project performance, ROI, and market trends, product managers can make informed decisions about where to allocate resources, which projects to prioritize, and which initiatives to invest in. This data-driven approach helps mitigate risks and ensures that resources are allocated in a way that maximizes return on investment.

6. Monitoring and Optimization: Big Data analytics enables product managers to continuously monitor and optimize resource allocation processes. By collecting real-time data on resource utilization, project progress, and performance metrics, product managers can identify areas for improvement and make adjustments as needed. This iterative approach ensures that resources are allocated efficiently and effectively over time, leading to improved operational efficiency and better business outcomes.

Big Data analytics empowers product managers to enhance operational efficiency and optimize resource allocation by identifying bottlenecks, streamlining processes, forecasting demand and supply, improving decision-making, and continuously monitoring and optimizing resource allocation processes. By leveraging data-driven insights, product managers can make informed decisions that drive productivity, reduce costs, and ultimately improve the competitiveness and profitability of their products.

Ethical Considerations in Big Data Utilization

Ethical considerations in the utilization of Big Data are paramount as product managers navigate the complex landscape of data-driven decision-making. Let's delve deeper into the key aspects of ethical considerations in Big Data utilization:

1. Privacy Protection: One of the primary ethical considerations in Big Data utilization is the protection of privacy. Product managers must ensure that personal and sensitive information collected from users is handled with the utmost care and in compliance with relevant privacy regulations such as GDPR (General Data Protection Regulation) or CCPA (California Consumer Privacy Act). This includes obtaining explicit consent from users before collecting their data, implementing robust data encryption

and security measures, and providing users with transparency and control over their data.

2. Transparency and Accountability: Transparency and accountability are essential principles in ethical data utilization. Product managers should be transparent about how data is collected, stored, and used, as well as the purposes for which it is being utilized. This includes providing clear and easily understandable privacy policies, terms of service, and data usage agreements. Additionally, product managers should establish mechanisms for accountability, such as data governance frameworks and internal auditing processes, to ensure that data is used responsibly and ethically.

3. Fairness and Bias Mitigation: Ensuring fairness and mitigating bias in data-driven decision-making is another critical ethical consideration. Product managers must be vigilant in identifying and addressing biases in data collection, algorithms, and decision-making processes to prevent discriminatory outcomes. This may involve implementing bias detection tools, conducting regular audits of algorithms, and incorporating diversity and inclusivity considerations into the design and development process.

4. Informed Consent and User Empowerment: Informed consent and user empowerment are fundamental principles in ethical data utilization. Product managers should obtain explicit consent from users before collecting their data and ensure that users are fully informed about how their data will be used. Additionally, product managers should empower users to control their own data by providing options for data access, correction, and deletion. This includes implementing user-friendly privacy settings, data management tools, and mechanisms for opting out of data collection and processing.

5. Social Responsibility: Product managers have a social responsibility to ensure that data-driven decisions benefit society as a whole. This includes considering the potential social and ethical implications of data utilization, such as its impact on vulnerable populations, societal inequalities, and democratic values. Product managers should strive to use data in ways that promote social good, uphold human rights, and contribute to the well-being of individuals and communities.

6. Continuous Monitoring and Improvement: Ethical considerations in Big Data utilization require ongoing monitoring and improvement. Product managers should continuously evaluate their data practices, algorithms, and decision-making processes to identify and address ethical issues as they arise. This may involve conducting regular ethical impact assessments, soliciting feedback from stakeholders, and adapting policies and procedures in response to emerging ethical challenges.

Ethical considerations in Big Data utilization are essential for product managers to build trust with users, comply with regulations, and align products with societal values. By prioritizing privacy protection, transparency, fairness, informed consent, social responsibility, and continuous improvement, product managers can ensure that their data-driven decisions are ethical, responsible, and beneficial to individuals and society as a whole.

Future Trends in Data-Driven Product Management

As the digital landscape continues to evolve at a rapid pace, the future of data-driven product management holds immense promise and potential. This chapter delves into the emerging trends that are poised to shape the trajectory of product management in the years to come, with a particular focus on the transformative role of Big Data.

1. Artificial Intelligence (AI) and Machine Learning: The integration of AI and machine learning technologies represents a seismic shift in the realm of data-driven product management. These advanced technologies can analyze vast datasets with unprecedented speed and accuracy, uncovering hidden patterns, insights, and correlations that would otherwise remain elusive. Product managers will increasingly rely on AI-powered tools and algorithms to automate repetitive tasks, predict user behavior, and optimize product features in real-time.

2. Advanced Analytics: Beyond traditional data analysis techniques, advanced analytics methodologies such as predictive analytics, prescriptive analytics, and natural language processing are poised to revolutionize data-driven decision-making in product management. These sophisticated techniques enable product managers to forecast future trends, identify emerging opportunities, and prescribe actionable insights that drive strategic innovation and competitive advantage.

3. IoT and Sensor Data: The proliferation of Internet of Things (IoT) devices and sensor technologies is generating an unprecedented volume of real-time data streams. Product managers are increasingly leveraging this wealth of sensor data to gain deeper insights into user behavior, product usage patterns, and environmental conditions. By harnessing IoT data, product managers can optimize product performance, enhance user experiences, and unlock new revenue streams through innovative product offerings.

4. Personalization and Hyper-Targeting: As consumer expectations continue to evolve, personalized experiences and hyper-targeted marketing strategies are becoming increasingly important for product managers. Big Data enables product managers to segment their target audience

273

with granular precision, allowing for the delivery of personalized product recommendations, tailored marketing messages, and customized user experiences that resonate on an individual level.

5. Ethical and Responsible Data Management: With the growing concerns surrounding data privacy, security, and ethical use, product managers must prioritize ethical and responsible data management practices. This includes ensuring transparency in data collection and usage, obtaining informed consent from users, and implementing robust data security measures to protect sensitive information. By adhering to ethical principles and regulatory guidelines, product managers can build trust with users and maintain the integrity of their data-driven initiatives.

6. Continuous Innovation and Adaptation: In an era of rapid technological advancement and shifting consumer preferences, product managers must embrace a culture of continuous innovation and adaptation. This entails staying abreast of emerging trends, experimenting with new technologies and methodologies, and iteratively refining product strategies based on real-time feedback and market insights. By fostering a culture of innovation, product managers can future-proof their products and position them for long-term success in an ever-changing landscape.

The future of data-driven product management holds tremendous promise for innovation, growth, and success. By embracing emerging technologies, adopting advanced analytics methodologies, prioritizing ethical data management practices, and fostering a culture of continuous innovation, product managers can leverage the power of Big Data to drive strategic decision-making, enhance user experiences, and unlock new opportunities for growth and differentiation.

ANALYTICS AND METRICS IN AI PRODUCT MANAGEMENT

In the realm of AI product management, data-driven decision-making is amplified by the integration of advanced analytics and metrics. This chapter delves into the intricacies of leveraging data analytics to derive meaningful metrics, guiding product managers in making informed decisions throughout the AI product lifecycle.

The Analytical Foundation

Data analytics stands as the cornerstone upon which the edifice of data-driven decision-making in AI product management is built. Within this pivotal section, we delve into the profound significance of cultivating a robust analytical framework, one that serves as the bedrock for extracting invaluable insights from the vast expanse of datasets. These insights, meticulously unearthed through sophisticated analytical techniques, empower product managers with the clarity and foresight necessary to deftly navigate the intricate labyrinth of AI development.

At its essence, the analytical foundation serves as the compass guiding product managers through the multifaceted landscape of AI innovation. It provides a structured approach to wrangling complex and disparate datasets, transforming raw information into actionable intelligence. By harnessing the power of advanced analytics, product managers are equipped to distill patterns, trends, and correlations latent within the data, unveiling hidden gems of knowledge that illuminate the path forward.

Moreover, the analytical framework serves as a crucible wherein data is refined into actionable insights, akin to alchemists transmuting base metals into gold. Through a meticulous process of data exploration, statistical analysis, and predictive modeling, product managers are endowed with the foresight to anticipate market trends, consumer behaviors, and emerging opportunities. Armed with this prescient understanding, they are empowered to make informed decisions that drive innovation and propel their AI products to unprecedented heights of success.

Indeed, in the dynamic realm of AI development, where uncertainty reigns supreme and change is the only constant, the analytical foundation emerges as a stalwart bulwark against the tempestuous tides of ambiguity. It instills confidence amidst the chaos, providing product managers with the clarity and conviction to chart a course toward excellence. In essence, the analytical foundation is not merely a tool or technique but rather a guiding philosophy—an ethos that imbues AI product management with precision, insight, and purpose.

Defining Key Metrics for AI Products

At the heart of data-driven decision-making lies the meticulous process of defining and measuring key metrics. Product managers, as custodians of AI product development, are entrusted with the crucial task of identifying and aligning these metrics with the overarching goals and objectives of their products. In this section, we embark on an immersive journey into the intricacies of metric selection, exploring how each chosen metric, whether pertaining to user engagement, model performance, or business impact, serves as a compass guiding decision-making across the entire product lifecycle.

The process of defining key metrics transcends mere numerical values; it represents a strategic alignment of quantitative measures with qualitative objectives. Each metric serves as a beacon illuminating the path towards product success, offering invaluable insights into the efficacy and performance of AI-driven solutions. From the initial stages of product conception to the final phases of deployment and beyond, these metrics serve as constant companions, providing product managers with a comprehensive view of their product's journey.

In the realm of user engagement metrics, product managers delve into the intricate nuances of user behavior, seeking to understand and optimize the user experience. Metrics such as active users, session duration, and retention rates offer valuable insights into user engagement patterns, enabling product managers to refine and iterate upon their products to better cater to user needs and preferences.

Meanwhile, in the realm of model performance metrics, product managers venture into the realm of algorithmic efficacy and accuracy. Metrics such as precision, recall, and F1 score serve as yardsticks for evaluating the performance of AI models, providing critical feedback on their ability to make accurate predictions and classifications. Through the iterative refinement of these metrics, product managers can fine-tune their models to achieve optimal performance and reliability.

Finally, in the realm of business impact metrics, product managers navigate the intersection of AI technology and organizational objectives. Metrics such as return on investment (ROI), customer lifetime value (CLV), and market share offer tangible insights into the tangible value that AI products bring to the business. By aligning these metrics with strategic business goals, product managers can demonstrate the tangible impact of AI initiatives and secure buy-in from key stakeholders.

In essence, the process of defining key metrics for AI products transcends mere numerical values; it represents a strategic alignment of quantitative measures with qualitative objectives. Through the careful selection and evaluation of these metrics, product managers can unlock the full potential of AI-driven solutions, driving innovation, and delivering tangible value to both users and businesses alike.

User-Centric Analytics

In the realm of AI product management, the pursuit of user-centricity stands as a guiding principle, driving innovation and shaping the trajectory of product development. At the heart of this ethos lies the pivotal role of user-centric analytics—a sophisticated framework that empowers product managers to unravel the intricacies of user interactions, preferences, and satisfaction levels. This section embarks on an immersive exploration of how user-centric analytics serve as a beacon of insight, illuminating the path toward informed decision-making and iterative product refinement.

User-centric analytics represent far more than a mere collection of data points; they encapsulate a holistic understanding of user behavior, preferences, and sentiments. Through a comprehensive suite of analytical tools and methodologies, product managers glean invaluable insights into the nuances of user interactions, shedding light on the underlying motivations and desires that drive user engagement.

From the moment a user interacts with an AI product to the culmination of their journey, user-centric analytics serve as a constant companion, providing real-time feedback and actionable intelligence. Through the meticulous analysis of user engagement metrics, such as click-through rates, time spent on a page, and conversion rates, product managers gain a nuanced understanding of user behaviors, identifying pain points and opportunities for improvement.

Moreover, user-centric analytics offer a window into the realm of user preferences, illuminating the features and functionalities that resonate most strongly with users. By examining patterns in user interactions and feedback, product managers can tailor their products to better align with user expectations, driving increased adoption and satisfaction.

Beyond mere observations, user-centric analytics serve as a catalyst for informed decision-making, guiding product development toward user-centric enhancements and optimizations. Armed with a deep understanding of user needs and preferences, product managers can prioritize feature development initiatives, allocate resources effectively, and iterate rapidly to deliver an unparalleled user experience.

In essence, user-centric analytics represent the cornerstone of AI product management, offering a powerful lens through which product managers can unlock the full potential of their products. By embracing a data-driven approach grounded in user-centricity, product managers can navigate the complexities of product development with confidence, driving innovation and delivering transformative value to users.

Performance Metrics for AI Models

Within the dynamic landscape of AI product management, the performance of AI models stands as a linchpin, in determining the efficacy and impact of AI-driven solutions. At the forefront of this endeavor lie performance metrics—a comprehensive suite of quantitative measures that enable product managers to assess the effectiveness and reliability of AI algorithms. In this section, we embark on a deep dive into the multifaceted world of performance metrics, including accuracy, precision, recall, and F1 score, elucidating how these metrics serve as guiding beacons, steering decisions about model enhancements, iterations, and overall product performance.

Performance metrics represent far more than mere numerical values; they encapsulate the essence of algorithmic efficacy and reliability, offering a comprehensive snapshot of a model's predictive capabilities. At the heart of this framework lie metrics such as accuracy, which quantifies the overall correctness of predictions made by the model. However, accuracy alone may not suffice in scenarios where class imbalances or skewed distributions exist within the dataset.

To address these nuances, product managers delve into metrics such as precision, recall, and F1 score, which offer a more nuanced perspective on model performance. Precision measures the proportion of true positive predictions among all positive predictions made by the model, providing insights into the model's ability to minimize false positives. Recall, on the other hand, quantifies the proportion of true positive predictions among all actual positive instances in the dataset, shedding light on the model's capacity to capture relevant instances.

The F1 score, a harmonic mean of precision and recall, offers a balanced assessment of a model's performance, taking into account both false positives and false negatives. This metric serves as a reliable gauge of a model's overall effectiveness, providing product managers with a holistic understanding of its predictive capabilities.

Armed with these performance metrics, product managers embark on a journey of continuous improvement and optimization, iteratively refining AI models to enhance their efficacy and reliability. By scrutinizing performance metrics through the lens of user needs and business objectives, product managers can identify areas for improvement, prioritize feature enhancements, and allocate resources effectively to drive iterative model refinement.

In essence, performance metrics represent a cornerstone of AI product management, offering invaluable insights into the effectiveness and reliability of AI models. Through a rigorous analysis of these metrics, product managers can navigate the complexities of AI development with confidence, driving innovation and delivering transformative value to users and businesses alike.

Real-time Monitoring and Alerting

In the ever-evolving landscape of AI, the imperative for real-time monitoring looms large. As stewards of AI product development, product managers deploy sophisticated analytics tools that facilitate the continuous surveillance of AI models and product performance. This section embarks on an in-depth exploration of how real-time analytics and alerting mechanisms serve as bulwarks, empowering swift decision-making in response to anomalies, errors, or performance degradation.

Real-time monitoring represents far more than a passive observation; it embodies a proactive stance toward safeguarding the integrity and efficacy of AI-driven solutions. At its essence, real-time monitoring involves the vigilant scrutiny of key performance indicators (KPIs), metrics, and system logs, enabling product managers to stay attuned to the pulse of their AI ecosystem.

Central to this endeavor are advanced analytics tools and platforms, which offer a myriad of functionalities designed to facilitate seamless data ingestion, processing, and visualization. These tools serve as the eyes and ears of AI product managers, providing real-time insights into the performance of AI models, user interactions, and system health.

Moreover, real-time alerting mechanisms act as a force multiplier, empowering product managers with the agility to respond swiftly to emergent issues or deviations from expected behavior. By establishing predefined thresholds and triggers, product managers can configure automated alerts that notify them of anomalies, errors, or performance degradation in real-time.

These alerts serve as early warning signals, prompting product managers to initiate remedial actions or investigations to mitigate potential risks or issues before they escalate. Whether it be a sudden drop in model accuracy, a surge in error rates, or an unexpected spike in user churn, real-time alerts empower product managers to intervene proactively, preserving the integrity and reliability of AI-driven solutions.

Furthermore, real-time monitoring and alerting foster a culture of continuous improvement and optimization within AI product development teams. By providing timely feedback and insights, these mechanisms facilitate iterative refinement and enhancement of AI models, enabling product managers to stay ahead of the curve and deliver unparalleled value to users and businesses alike.

In essence, real-time monitoring and alerting represent a linchpin of AI product management, offering a proactive approach towards ensuring the resilience and effectiveness of AI-driven solutions. Through the judicious deployment of advanced analytics tools and alerting mechanisms, product managers can navigate the complexities of AI development with confidence, driving innovation and delivering transformative value in real time.

A/B Testing in AI Product Development

Amidst the intricate tapestry of AI product development, A/B testing emerges as a potent instrument of experimentation and decision-making. In the pursuit of innovation and optimization, product managers wield the tools of A/B testing to meticulously compare and contrast different iterations of AI features or algorithms. This section embarks on an immersive exploration of how A/B testing serves as a guiding light, empowering product managers to make informed decisions and refine their products to deliver optimal user experiences.

At its core, A/B testing embodies a philosophy of experimentation—a systematic approach to uncovering insights and validating hypotheses through empirical observation. Product managers meticulously design A/B tests, crafting controlled experiments that expose users to different variants or versions of AI features, algorithms, or user interfaces.

Central to the A/B testing paradigm is the notion of randomization, wherein users are randomly assigned to different test groups, each exposed to a distinct variant or iteration of the product. By ensuring statistical rigor and control over external variables, product managers can isolate the impact of specific changes and discern their effects on user behavior and outcomes.

Moreover, A/B testing serves as a crucible wherein hypotheses are put to the test, enabling product managers to validate assumptions and make data-driven decisions. Through the careful analysis of key performance indicators (KPIs) and metrics, such as conversion rates, engagement metrics, or user satisfaction scores, product managers gain invaluable insights into the relative efficacy and user-friendliness of each iteration.

Furthermore, A/B testing fosters a culture of iterative refinement and continuous improvement within AI product development teams. Armed with empirical evidence and insights gleaned from A/B tests, product managers can iterate rapidly, fine-tuning their products to better align with user needs, preferences, and expectations.

In essence, A/B testing represents far more than a mere tool or technique; it embodies a philosophy—a commitment to evidence-based decision-making and relentless pursuit of excellence. Through the judicious application of A/B testing methodologies, product managers can navigate the complexities of AI product development with confidence, driving innovation and delivering unparalleled value to users and businesses alike.

Conversion Funnel Analytics

Exploring the Depths of Conversion Funnel Analytics: Illuminating the Path to Product Conversion Success

In the realm of AI product management, where user conversion stands as a pivotal objective, the comprehension of the conversion funnel emerges as an indispensable asset. Product managers harness the power of analytics to dissect and deconstruct user journeys, unraveling the intricate layers of the conversion funnel to pinpoint drop-off points and optimize pathways to conversion. This section embarks on an immersive exploration of how conversion funnel analytics serve as guiding beacons, informing decisions pertaining to user onboarding, feature adoption, and overall product conversion.

At its essence, the conversion funnel represents a conceptual framework that delineates the stages through which users traverse on their journey towards conversion—from initial awareness and engagement to eventual conversion and retention. Within this framework, product managers leverage analytics to track user interactions and behaviors at each stage of the funnel, illuminating the pathways and obstacles that shape the user experience.

Central to this endeavor are advanced analytics tools and methodologies that enable product managers to visualize and analyze user journeys with granularity and precision. Through the meticulous examination of key performance indicators (KPIs) and metrics, such as conversion rates, funnel drop-off rates, and time to conversion, product managers gain insights into the efficacy and efficiency of the conversion funnel.

Moreover, conversion funnel analytics serve as a catalyst for informed decision-making, guiding product managers in the optimization of user onboarding processes, feature adoption strategies, and overall product conversion pathways. By identifying friction points and barriers to conversion, product managers can implement targeted interventions and enhancements to streamline the user experience and maximize conversion rates.

Furthermore, conversion funnel analytics foster a culture of continuous improvement and iteration within AI product development teams. Armed with insights gleaned from analytics, product managers can iterate rapidly, testing and refining various hypotheses to optimize the conversion funnel and drive incremental improvements in product conversion metrics.

In essence, conversion funnel analytics represent a cornerstone of AI product management, offering invaluable insights into the intricacies of user behavior and conversion dynamics. Through the judicious application of analytics tools and methodologies, product managers can navigate the complexities of the conversion funnel with confidence, driving innovation and delivering transformative value to users and businesses alike.

Business Impact Metrics

Exploring the Multifaceted Realm of Business Impact Metrics: Anchoring AI Product Development in Strategic Value Creation

In the intricate tapestry of AI product management, where the pursuit of user-centric excellence intertwines with the imperative of technical prowess, business impact metrics stand as beacons of strategic insight and value creation. Product managers delve into a rich tapestry of metrics encompassing revenue generation, customer acquisition costs, and overall business return on investment (ROI), embarking on a journey to align AI product development with broader business imperatives. This section embarks on an immersive exploration of how these metrics serve as navigational compasses, guiding strategic decisions and propelling AI product development towards transformative business outcomes.

At the heart of business impact metrics lies a profound commitment to value creation—a recognition that the true measure of AI product success extends far beyond mere technical performance or user satisfaction. Product managers meticulously track and analyze a myriad of metrics, ranging from revenue growth and profitability to customer lifetime value and market share, to assess the tangible impact of AI initiatives on organizational performance.

Central to this endeavor are advanced analytics tools and methodologies that enable product managers to glean insights into the complex interplay between AI product adoption, user behavior, and business outcomes. Through the careful analysis of key performance indicators (KPIs) and metrics, product managers gain a holistic understanding of the economic value generated by AI products, informing strategic decisions and resource allocations.

Moreover, business impact metrics serve as a compass guiding product managers in the prioritization of feature development initiatives, resource allocation, and investment decisions. By aligning AI product development with broader business objectives, product managers can ensure that their initiatives deliver tangible value and contribute to the organization's bottom line.

Furthermore, business impact metrics foster a culture of accountability and transparency within AI product development teams. By quantifying the economic value generated by AI initiatives, these metrics provide a common language for stakeholders across the organization, facilitating alignment and collaboration towards shared business goals.

In essence, business impact metrics represent far more than mere numbers on a dashboard; they embody a philosophy—a commitment to driving meaningful business outcomes through AI innovation. Through the judicious application of analytics tools and methodologies, product managers can navigate the complexities of AI product development with confidence, driving innovation and delivering transformative value to users and businesses alike.

Explainability Metrics for Transparent AI

In the ever-evolving landscape of AI innovation, where the boundaries of complexity are continually pushed, the imperative for explainability metrics stands as a beacon of transparency and trust. Product managers navigate the intricate terrain of AI model development armed with a suite of metrics designed to gauge the interpretability and transparency of algorithms. This section embarks on an immersive exploration of how these metrics serve as guiding principles, informing decisions related to user trust, ethical considerations, and compliance with transparency standards.

At the heart of explainability metrics lies a profound commitment to transparency—a recognition that the black box nature of many AI algorithms can breed distrust and skepticism among users and stakeholders. Product managers meticulously evaluate the interpretability and explainability of AI models through a lens of transparency, seeking to demystify the decision-making processes underlying algorithmic outputs.

Central to this endeavor are advanced analytics tools and methodologies that enable product managers to quantify the degree of explainability inherent in AI algorithms. These tools provide insights into the inner workings of models, shedding light on the features, variables, and decision paths that contribute to algorithmic outputs.

Moreover, explainability metrics serve as a catalyst for informed decision-making, guiding product managers in the optimization of AI models to enhance transparency and interpretability. By identifying opaque or inscrutable aspects of algorithms, product managers can implement targeted interventions and enhancements to improve the explainability of models, thereby fostering user trust and confidence.

Furthermore, explainability metrics play a pivotal role in addressing ethical considerations and ensuring compliance with transparency standards. In an era where concerns about algorithmic bias and fairness are at the forefront, product managers leverage explainability metrics to assess the ethical implications of AI algorithms and mitigate potential risks of unintended consequences.

In essence, explainability metrics represent a cornerstone of AI product management, offering a pathway to transparency and trust in the midst of complexity. Through the judicious application of analytics tools and methodologies, product managers can navigate the nuanced terrain of AI model development with confidence, driving innovation and delivering transformative value while upholding the principles of transparency and ethical responsibility.

Iterative Analytics-Driven Development

Within the dynamic realm of AI development, the iterative process intertwines seamlessly with analytics-driven decision-making, forming a symbiotic relationship that fuels continuous improvement and innovation. Product managers, as stewards of AI product development, cultivate a culture of relentless iteration, leveraging analytics as their guiding compass to refine products iteratively based on user feedback, evolving market dynamics, and the performance of AI models. This section embarks on an immersive exploration of how iterative analytics-driven development serves as the cornerstone of adaptive and user-focused AI products.

At the heart of iterative analytics-driven development lies a profound commitment to continuous learning—a recognition that the journey towards AI product excellence is marked by perpetual refinement and adaptation. Product managers harness the power of analytics to gather insights from diverse sources, including user interactions, market trends, and AI model performance, using these insights to inform strategic decisions and prioritize iterative enhancements.

Central to this endeavor are advanced analytics tools and methodologies that enable product managers to monitor and analyze key performance indicators (KPIs) and metrics in real-time. These tools provide a comprehensive view of product performance, empowering product managers to identify areas for improvement and prioritize iterative enhancements to maximize user satisfaction and product value.

Moreover, iterative analytics-driven development fosters a culture of agility and responsiveness within AI product development teams. By embracing a mindset of experimentation and adaptation, product managers can quickly iterate on product features and functionalities, responding swiftly to changing user needs, market dynamics, and technological advancements.

Furthermore, iterative analytics-driven development ensures that AI products remain adaptive and user-focused in the face of uncertainty and complexity. Through continuous iteration and refinement, product managers can optimize AI models, user experiences, and business processes to deliver unparalleled value to users and stakeholders.

In essence, iterative analytics-driven development represents a guiding philosophy—a commitment to harnessing the power of analytics to drive continuous improvement and innovation in AI product development. Through the judicious application of analytics tools and methodologies, product managers can navigate the complexities of AI development with confidence, delivering adaptive, user-focused products that exceed expectations and drive transformative impact.

Ethical Considerations in AI Analytics

In the ever-evolving realm of AI decision-making, where the power of analytics serves as a guiding light, ethical considerations emerge as a paramount concern. Product managers, as custodians of AI product development, must grapple with complex ethical dilemmas, ensuring fairness, mitigating bias, and safeguarding user privacy in analytics-driven decisions. This section embarks on a comprehensive exploration of the ethical imperatives that underpin AI analytics, illuminating the importance of building trust with users and aligning AI products with societal expectations.

At the heart of ethical considerations in AI analytics lies a profound commitment to fairness—a recognition that the algorithms and models powering AI systems have the potential to perpetuate or exacerbate societal inequalities. Product managers meticulously evaluate the fairness and equity of AI analytics processes, seeking to identify and mitigate biases that may inadvertently impact certain demographic groups or perpetuate discriminatory outcomes.

Central to this endeavor are advanced analytics tools and methodologies that enable product managers to assess the fairness of AI models and algorithms across various dimensions, including race, gender, ethnicity, and socioeconomic status. Through rigorous testing and validation, product managers can identify and address biases in data collection, feature engineering, and model training, ensuring that AI systems are designed and deployed in a manner that upholds principles of fairness and equity.

Moreover, ethical considerations extend beyond fairness to encompass the protection of user privacy and data rights. Product managers must navigate the delicate balance between data utility and user consent, implementing robust privacy-enhancing technologies and practices to safeguard sensitive information and mitigate the risk of data breaches or misuse.

Furthermore, ethical considerations in AI analytics serve as a cornerstone of trust-building and reputation management. By prioritizing fairness, transparency, and user-centricity in analytics-driven decisions, product managers can cultivate trust with users and stakeholders, fostering a sense of confidence and loyalty in AI products and services.

In essence, ethical considerations in AI analytics represent far more than a regulatory obligation; they embody a commitment to ethical integrity, social responsibility, and human dignity. Through the judicious application of ethics-aware analytics tools and methodologies, product managers can navigate the complex ethical landscape of AI decision-making with confidence, driving innovation and delivering transformative value while upholding the highest ethical standards.

Future Trends in Analytics-Driven AI Product Management

As we draw the curtains on this chapter, we cast our gaze toward the horizon of analytics-driven AI product management, envisioning a landscape ripe with emerging trends and transformative innovations. From advanced analytics techniques to the integration of AI in analytics platforms, these trends promise to revolutionize the capabilities of product managers, empowering them to leverage analytics for more sophisticated and nuanced decision-making. This section embarks on an exploration of these future trends, offering a glimpse into the evolving landscape of analytics-driven AI product management.

At the forefront of future trends in analytics-driven AI product management lie advanced analytics techniques, poised to unlock new realms of insight and foresight. From machine learning-driven predictive analytics to natural language processing-powered sentiment analysis, these techniques offer product managers a treasure trove of tools and methodologies to extract actionable intelligence from vast and complex datasets.

Moreover, augmented analytics emerges as a transformative force, reshaping the traditional paradigms of analytics-driven decision-making. By leveraging AI and machine learning algorithms to automate data preparation, insight generation, and model-building processes, augmented analytics platforms empower product managers to uncover hidden patterns, trends, and correlations with unprecedented speed and accuracy.

Furthermore, the integration of AI in analytics platforms heralds a new era of seamless integration and interoperability, bridging the gap between AI development and analytics-driven decision-making. With AI-powered analytics platforms, product managers can harness the full potential of AI technologies to drive actionable insights, optimize workflows, and unlock new opportunities for innovation and growth.

In essence, these emerging trends in analytics-driven AI product management represent a paradigm shift—a convergence of cutting-edge technologies and methodologies that promise to redefine the way product managers leverage analytics to drive business value. By embracing these trends and innovations, product managers can position themselves at the vanguard of analytics-driven AI product management, driving innovation, and delivering transformative impact in the years to come.

This illuminates the pivotal role of analytics and metrics in driving data-driven decision-making within the realm of AI product management. As product managers navigate the complexities of AI development, the integration of advanced analytics ensures that decisions are not only informed but also aligned with user needs, business objectives, and ethical considerations.

TURNING DATA INTO ACTIONABLE STRATEGIES

In the dynamic landscape of modern business, the ability to transform data into actionable strategies is a hallmark of effective decision-making. This chapter explores the crucial intersection of data-driven decision-making and strategic formulation, detailing how organizations can harness the power of data to inform, guide, and optimize their strategies.

The Strategic Imperative of Data

In the dynamic landscape of modern organizations, where data proliferates at an unprecedented rate, the strategic imperative of data emerges as a linchpin for success. This section delves into the foundational role of data, underscoring how its effective utilization becomes not just an asset but a cornerstone for developing informed and forward-thinking strategies.

At the heart of this strategic imperative lies a recognition of the transformative potential of data. In an era where information reigns supreme, organizations that can harness the power of data effectively gain a competitive edge. Data serves as a compass, guiding decision-makers through the complexities of the business landscape, illuminating opportunities, and mitigating risks.

Central to this endeavor is the concept of data-driven decision-making—a philosophy that places data at the center of organizational strategy and execution. By leveraging insights gleaned from data analysis, organizations can make informed decisions that drive growth, innovation, and competitive advantage.

Moreover, data serves as a catalyst for innovation and agility. By embracing a culture of experimentation and iteration, organizations can leverage data to test hypotheses, validate assumptions, and adapt strategies in real-time based on empirical evidence.

Furthermore, data serves as a unifying force, breaking down silos and fostering collaboration across departments and functions. By democratizing access to data and insights, organizations can empower employees at all levels to contribute meaningfully to decision-making processes, driving alignment and cohesion.

In essence, the strategic imperative of data represents a fundamental shift in the way organizations approach decision-making and strategy formulation. By recognizing the inherent value of data and embracing a data-driven mindset, organizations can unlock new opportunities for growth, innovation, and success in an increasingly complex and competitive business environment.

Strategic Alignment with Organizational Goals

At the core of effective data-driven decision-making lies a pivotal prerequisite: strategic alignment with organizational goals. This section delves into the intricate interplay between data and strategic objectives, elucidating how businesses can harness the power of data to gain deep insights into their overarching aspirations, thereby ensuring that every data-driven decision contributes meaningfully to the realization of strategic goals.

The journey towards strategic alignment commences with a holistic understanding of organizational objectives. By meticulously dissecting and distilling the core mission, vision, and strategic imperatives of the organization, decision-makers can establish a cohesive framework that serves as the guiding beacon for all data-driven endeavors.

Central to this endeavor is the strategic utilization of data as a catalyst for insight generation and informed decision-making. Through the judicious analysis of internal and external data sources, organizations can uncover patterns, trends, and correlations that provide invaluable insights into market dynamics, consumer behavior, and competitive landscapes.

Moreover, strategic alignment with organizational goals entails a relentless pursuit of relevance and applicability in data-driven decision-making. By scrutinizing data through the lens of strategic objectives, decision-makers can discern actionable insights and prioritize initiatives that directly contribute to the achievement of organizational goals.

Furthermore, strategic alignment fosters a culture of accountability and transparency, wherein data-driven decisions are subjected to rigorous scrutiny and evaluation against predefined performance metrics and key performance indicators (KPIs). By establishing clear benchmarks for success and measuring progress towards strategic objectives, organizations can ensure that their data-driven endeavors remain aligned with overarching goals.

In essence, strategic alignment with organizational goals represents a foundational pillar of effective data-driven decision-making. By integrating data into the strategic fabric of the organization and leveraging its insights to inform decision-making processes, organizations can navigate the complexities of the business landscape with confidence, driving innovation, and realizing their full potential for growth and success.

Identifying Key Performance Indicators (KPIs)

At the heart of transforming data into actionable strategies lies the critical process of identifying Key Performance Indicators (KPIs) – the compass that navigates organizations toward their goals. This section delves into the intricate process of selecting and defining KPIs, emphasizing their pivotal role in quantifying progress, measuring success, and guiding strategic initiatives.

The journey of identifying KPIs commences with a deep understanding of organizational objectives and priorities. By aligning KPIs with overarching goals, decision-makers can ensure that every data point measured is directly linked to the strategic imperatives of the organization.

Central to this endeavor is the strategic selection and definition of KPIs that encapsulate the essence of organizational success. Through a meticulous process of analysis and deliberation, decision-makers identify KPIs that are both meaningful and actionable, enabling them to track progress and make informed decisions in pursuit of strategic objectives.

Moreover, KPIs serve as the lighthouse that illuminates the path to success, providing organizations with clear benchmarks against which to measure progress and performance. By quantifying key aspects of business operations, such as revenue growth, customer satisfaction, or operational efficiency, KPIs offer decision-makers a tangible means of assessing the effectiveness of strategic initiatives and identifying areas for improvement.

Furthermore, KPIs play a vital role in fostering accountability and alignment across the organization. By establishing KPIs that are cascaded down through different levels of the organization, decision-makers can ensure that every individual and team is working towards common goals and objectives, driving cohesion and collaboration.

In essence, the identification of KPIs represents a foundational step in the journey towards data-driven decision-making. By selecting and defining KPIs that are closely aligned with organizational goals and priorities, decision-makers can leverage the power of data to drive strategic initiatives, achieve operational excellence, and realize their vision for success.

Analyzing Market Trends and Competitor Insights

At the core of strategic formulation lies a profound understanding of market trends and competitor landscapes— a dynamic process driven by data-driven insights. This section embarks on an immersive exploration of how organizations can leverage data to analyze market dynamics, unearth emerging trends, and glean invaluable insights into competitors' strategies, thereby shaping a strategic positioning that is agile and responsive to market realities.

The journey of market analysis and competitor insights commences with a comprehensive examination of market dynamics and trends. By harnessing the power of data analytics, organizations can uncover patterns, shifts, and disruptions within their respective industries, enabling them to anticipate market trends and capitalize on emerging opportunities.

Central to this endeavor is the strategic utilization of competitive intelligence—a multifaceted approach that entails gathering, analyzing, and interpreting data related to competitors' activities, strengths, and weaknesses. Through a meticulous analysis of competitor positioning, product offerings, pricing strategies, and customer engagements, organizations can gain valuable insights into the competitive landscape, informing strategic decisions and driving competitive advantage.

Moreover, market analysis and competitor insights serve as a catalyst for innovation and differentiation. By identifying unmet customer needs, emerging market segments, and gaps in competitors' offerings, organizations can develop tailored strategies and innovative solutions that resonate with target audiences and set them apart from competitors.

Furthermore, market analysis and competitor insights foster a culture of agility and adaptability within organizations. By continuously monitoring and analyzing market dynamics and competitor movements, organizations can adjust their strategies and tactics in real-time, responding swiftly to changing market conditions and emerging threats.

In essence, market analysis and competitor insights represent a cornerstone of strategic decision-making—a strategic imperative that empowers organizations to navigate the complexities of the business landscape with confidence and foresight. By leveraging data to gain deep insights into market trends and competitor strategies, organizations can position themselves for success, driving innovation, and realizing their vision for growth and prosperity.

Customer-Centric Strategy Development

In the realm of successful strategy formulation, customers reign supreme, serving as the North Star guiding organizations toward sustainable growth and competitive advantage. This section embarks on a comprehensive exploration of how organizations leverage data to gain profound insights into customer behaviors, preferences, and feedback, thereby fostering the development of customer-centric strategies that resonate deeply with target audiences.

At the heart of customer-centric strategy development lies a strategic imperative: the relentless pursuit of understanding and serving customers better. By harnessing the power of data analytics, organizations can uncover intricate patterns and trends within customer data, illuminating the motivations, desires, and pain points of their target audience.

Central to this endeavor is the strategic utilization of customer data to segment, profile, and personalize experiences for different customer segments. Through advanced analytics techniques such as predictive modeling, clustering analysis, and sentiment analysis, organizations can identify distinct customer segments, tailor products and services to meet their unique needs and deliver personalized experiences that foster loyalty and engagement.

Moreover, data-driven decision-making serves as a catalyst for innovation and differentiation in customer-centric strategy development. By mining customer feedback, social media interactions, and purchasing behaviors, organizations can uncover insights that drive product innovation, service enhancements, and marketing strategies that resonate with target audiences.

Furthermore, customer-centric strategy development fosters a culture of continuous improvement and iteration within organizations. By soliciting and incorporating customer feedback into strategic decision-making processes, organizations can adapt and refine their strategies in real-time, ensuring that they remain responsive to evolving customer needs and preferences.

In essence, customer-centric strategy development represents a strategic imperative—an unwavering commitment to understanding and serving customers better. By leveraging data to gain deep insights into customer behaviors and preferences, organizations can foster meaningful connections, drive loyalty, and unlock new opportunities for growth and success in an increasingly competitive marketplace.

Adaptive Strategies Through Iterative Learning

In the dynamic landscape of data-driven decision-making, the iterative process serves as a gateway to adaptive strategies that can pivot in real-time to meet changing market demands and user expectations. This section embarks on a deep dive into how continuous learning from data insights fosters an adaptive approach to strategy development, enabling organizations to refine and optimize their strategies based on evolving market conditions and user feedback.

At the heart of adaptive strategy development lies a commitment to continuous learning—an acknowledgment that the journey towards success is marked by ongoing experimentation, refinement, and adaptation. By leveraging data-driven insights, organizations can gain a nuanced understanding of market dynamics, user behaviors, and competitive landscapes, laying the foundation for strategic decisions that are agile and responsive to change.

Central to this endeavor is the iterative process of strategy refinement and optimization. Through a cyclical process of data collection, analysis, and action, organizations can gather insights from real-world outcomes, evaluate the effectiveness of their strategies, and make informed adjustments to better align with shifting market realities.

Moreover, iterative learning enables organizations to harness the power of feedback loops to drive continuous improvement. By soliciting and incorporating user feedback, organizations can identify areas for enhancement, iterate on product features, and tailor their offerings to better meet the needs and preferences of their target audience.

Furthermore, adaptive strategies foster a culture of agility and resilience within organizations. By embracing a mindset of experimentation and adaptation, organizations can navigate uncertainty and volatility with confidence, seizing opportunities and mitigating risks as they arise.

In essence, adaptive strategies through iterative learning represent a strategic imperative—a commitment to continuous improvement and innovation in the pursuit of organizational excellence. By leveraging data-driven insights to inform strategic decisions and embracing a culture of adaptation, organizations can thrive in an ever-changing business landscape, driving growth, and delivering value to customers and stakeholders alike.

Resource Allocation and Efficiency

Efficient resource allocation stands as a cornerstone of organizational success, enabling the effective execution of strategies and the maximization of impact across all facets of operations. This section embarks on a comprehensive exploration of how data-driven decision-making informs resource allocation strategies, empowering organizations to optimize the allocation of human, financial, and technological resources for maximum effectiveness and efficiency.

At the core of efficient resource allocation lies a strategic imperative: the judicious utilization of available resources to achieve organizational objectives. By harnessing the power of data analytics, organizations can gain deep insights into resource utilization patterns, identify inefficiencies, and uncover opportunities for optimization across various functional areas.

Central to this endeavor is the strategic allocation of human capital—organizations' most valuable asset. Through data-driven workforce planning and talent management strategies, organizations can ensure that the right people are in the right roles at the right time, maximizing productivity, and driving performance.

Moreover, data-driven decision-making enables organizations to optimize the allocation of financial resources, ensuring that investments are aligned with strategic priorities and deliver the greatest return on investment (ROI). By analyzing financial data and performance metrics, organizations can identify high-impact investment opportunities, mitigate risks, and allocate resources to initiatives that drive long-term value creation.

Furthermore, data-driven decision-making empowers organizations to optimize the allocation of technological resources, leveraging technology to streamline processes, automate tasks, and enhance operational efficiency. Through advanced analytics and predictive modeling, organizations can identify opportunities for technological innovation and investment, driving digital transformation and competitive advantage.

In essence, efficient resource allocation through data-driven decision-making represents a strategic imperative—a commitment to maximizing the impact of available resources and driving sustainable growth and success. By leveraging data analytics to inform resource allocation strategies, organizations can optimize their operations, drive innovation, and deliver value to customers and stakeholders alike.

Risk Mitigation and Contingency Planning

In the complex terrain of strategic decision-making, the ability to navigate uncertainties and mitigate risks stands as a critical imperative for organizational success. This section embarks on a detailed exploration of how data-driven decision-making empowers organizations to identify potential risks, assess their likelihood, and develop robust contingency plans, fostering resilience and adaptability within strategic frameworks.

At the heart of risk mitigation and contingency planning lies a strategic imperative: the proactive identification and management of potential threats to organizational objectives. By leveraging data analytics, organizations can gain insights into a myriad of factors that may pose risks to strategic initiatives, ranging from market volatility and regulatory changes to technological disruptions and competitive pressures.

Central to this endeavor is the strategic utilization of data to assess the likelihood and impact of identified risks. Through advanced analytics techniques such as predictive modeling and scenario analysis, organizations can quantify the probability of different risk scenarios occurring and evaluate their potential implications on strategic objectives, enabling informed decision-making and risk prioritization.

Moreover, data-driven decision-making enables organizations to develop robust contingency plans that serve as a safeguard against potential risks. By leveraging insights gleaned from data analytics, organizations can identify proactive measures and response strategies to mitigate risks, minimize their impact, and maintain continuity of operations in the face of adversity.

Furthermore, data-driven risk mitigation fosters a culture of resilience and adaptability within organizations. By embracing a mindset of continuous improvement and iteration, organizations can refine and optimize their contingency plans based on real-world outcomes and feedback, ensuring that they remain agile and responsive to evolving risk landscapes.

In essence, data-driven risk mitigation and contingency planning represent a strategic imperative—a commitment to proactively identify and manage risks to organizational objectives. By leveraging data analytics to inform risk assessment and decision-making processes, organizations can foster resilience, drive innovation, and navigate uncertainty with confidence, ensuring their ability to thrive in an ever-changing business landscape.

Aligning Data-Driven Tactics with Strategic Goals

In the intricate dance of organizational strategy, tactical execution serves as the engine that propels strategic aspirations into tangible outcomes. This section embarks on an in-depth exploration of the critical importance of aligning data-driven tactics with overarching strategic goals, highlighting how organizations leverage data insights to inform day-to-day decision-making and ensure that each tactical maneuver contributes synergistically to the larger strategic narrative.

At the heart of this symbiotic relationship lies a strategic imperative: the seamless integration of tactical precision with strategic vision. By harnessing the power of data analytics, organizations can gain granular insights into market dynamics, customer behaviors, and competitive landscapes, enabling them to develop tactical actions that are not only informed by data but also strategically aligned with organizational objectives.

Central to this endeavor is the strategic utilization of data to inform the selection, prioritization, and execution of tactical initiatives. Through advanced analytics techniques such as predictive modeling, trend analysis, and segmentation, organizations can identify opportunities for tactical interventions that are most likely to yield desired outcomes and drive progress towards strategic goals.

Moreover, data-driven decision-making empowers organizations to continuously monitor and evaluate the effectiveness of tactical actions in achieving strategic objectives. By leveraging real-time data insights, organizations can adjust and refine their tactics in response to evolving market conditions, customer feedback, and competitive dynamics, ensuring alignment with strategic priorities and maximizing the impact of tactical initiatives.

Furthermore, data-driven alignment of tactics with strategic goals fosters a culture of accountability and collaboration within organizations. By establishing clear metrics and KPIs to measure the success of tactical actions, organizations can foster transparency and alignment across teams and departments, driving cohesive execution and ensuring that everyone is working towards common strategic objectives.

In essence, aligning data-driven tactics with strategic goals represents a strategic imperative—a commitment to harnessing the power of data to drive informed decision-making and achieve organizational success. By leveraging data insights to inform tactical execution, organizations can navigate the complexities of the business landscape with precision and agility, driving innovation and realizing their vision for growth and prosperity.

Establishing a Culture of Data-Driven Decision-Making

In the dynamic landscape of modern organizations, the journey towards effective strategy formulation and execution begins with the cultivation of a culture that values and embraces data-driven decision-making as a fundamental pillar of organizational success. This section embarks on a comprehensive exploration of the organizational shifts necessary to foster a culture where data serves as the driving force behind strategic formulation and execution.

At the heart of this transformative journey lies a strategic imperative: the establishment of a culture that recognizes the inherent value of data as a strategic asset and empowers individuals at all levels of the organization to leverage data insights in their decision-making processes.

Central to this endeavor is the strategic alignment of organizational values, norms, and behaviors with the principles of data-driven decision-making. By fostering a shared understanding of the importance of data in driving business outcomes, organizations can create a fertile ground for the adoption and integration of data-driven practices into everyday operations.

Moreover, cultivating a culture of data-driven decision-making entails the development of organizational capabilities and infrastructure to support data-driven initiatives. This includes investments in data analytics tools, technologies, and talent development programs that equip employees with the skills and resources needed to leverage data effectively in their decision-making processes.

Furthermore, fostering a culture of data-driven decision-making requires a commitment to transparency and accountability. By establishing clear metrics and KPIs to measure the impact of data-driven initiatives, organizations can create a culture of accountability where individuals are held accountable for their decisions and actions based on data-driven insights.

In essence, establishing a culture of data-driven decision-making represents a strategic imperative—a commitment to harnessing the power of data to drive innovation, enhance performance, and achieve organizational success. By fostering a culture where data is valued, integrated, and leveraged in decision-making processes, organizations can unlock new opportunities for growth and competitiveness in an increasingly data-driven world.

Ethical Considerations in Data-Driven Strategy

In the ever-evolving realm of data-driven strategy, the ethical dimension emerges as a critical consideration, casting a spotlight on the responsible and principled use of data. This section embarks on an immersive exploration of the multifaceted ethical considerations that underpin data-driven decision-making, emphasizing the importance of ethical data practices, privacy safeguards, and transparency in ensuring alignment with societal expectations and legal standards.

At the heart of ethical considerations in data-driven strategy lies a profound commitment to integrity and responsibility—a recognition that the power wielded by data comes with inherent ethical responsibilities. As organizations leverage data to inform strategic decisions, it becomes imperative to navigate the ethical landscape with care and conscientiousness.

Central to this endeavor is the adoption of ethical data practices that prioritize the fair and responsible treatment of data. This includes adhering to principles of data minimization, purpose limitation, and data accuracy to ensure that data is collected, processed, and utilized in a manner that respects individual rights and privacy.

Moreover, ethical data practices extend to the implementation of robust privacy safeguards and data protection measures. By adopting privacy-enhancing technologies, implementing data encryption, and establishing stringent access controls, organizations can safeguard sensitive information and mitigate the risk of data breaches or misuse.

Furthermore, transparency emerges as a cornerstone of ethical data-driven strategy, fostering trust and accountability with stakeholders. By openly communicating data practices, policies, and procedures, organizations can demonstrate a commitment to transparency and build confidence in their data-driven decision-making processes.

In essence, ethical considerations in data-driven strategy represent far more than a regulatory obligation; they embody a commitment to ethical integrity, social responsibility, and human dignity. By upholding ethical data practices, implementing privacy safeguards, and fostering transparency, organizations can navigate the ethical landscape of data-driven strategy with confidence, ensuring that their strategic decisions align with societal expectations and legal standards while driving sustainable growth and value creation.

Future Trends in Data-Driven Strategy

As we draw the curtains on this chapter, we embark on a journey into the future of data-driven strategy, peering into a landscape illuminated by emerging trends and transformative innovations. This section delves into the dynamic realm of artificial intelligence, machine learning, and advanced analytics, exploring how these technologies will further revolutionize the capabilities of organizations in transforming data into increasingly sophisticated and nuanced actionable strategies.

At the forefront of future trends in data-driven strategy lies the transformative potential of artificial intelligence (AI) and machine learning (ML). As AI and ML technologies continue to evolve and mature, organizations are poised to unlock new realms of insight and foresight, empowering them to extract actionable intelligence from vast and complex datasets with unprecedented speed, accuracy, and efficiency.

Central to this evolution is the emergence of advanced analytics techniques, such as predictive modeling, prescriptive analytics, and cognitive computing, which enable organizations to move beyond descriptive analytics to anticipate future trends, identify opportunities, and mitigate risks before they materialize.

Moreover, the integration of AI and ML technologies into data-driven strategy holds the promise of automating decision-making processes, augmenting human intelligence, and driving innovation at scale. By leveraging AI-powered algorithms to analyze data, generate insights, and recommend strategic actions, organizations can achieve new levels of agility, innovation, and strategic foresight.

Furthermore, the democratization of data and analytics tools is poised to democratize decision-making processes, empowering individuals at all levels of the organization to leverage data insights in their day-to-day decision-making. Through intuitive and user-friendly analytics platforms, organizations can foster a culture of data-driven decision-making, driving innovation and agility from the ground up.

In essence, the future of data-driven strategy represents a convergence of cutting-edge technologies and forward-thinking methodologies, promising to reshape the way organizations approach strategic decision-making. By embracing emerging trends and innovations in AI, ML, and advanced analytics, organizations can position themselves at the vanguard of data-driven strategy, driving innovation, and realizing their vision for growth and success in an increasingly complex and competitive business landscape.

6. PERSONALIZATION & CUSTOMIZATION IN PRODUCT MANAGEMENT

AI'S CONTRIBUTION TO HYPER-PERSONALIZATION

In the era of heightened user expectations, personalization and customization have emerged as pivotal components of successful product management. This chapter delves into the transformative role of Artificial Intelligence (AI) in elevating personalization and customization to new heights, ushering in an era of hyper-personalized user experiences.

The Evolution of Personalization

Within the realm of product management, the evolution of personalization represents a captivating narrative that traces the trajectory from conventional methodologies to the era of AI-driven hyper-personalization. This section embarks on an immersive exploration of this evolutionary journey, spotlighting the paradigm shift from generic, one-size-fits-all approaches to tailored, individualized experiences that resonate deeply with users on a profound level.

At its inception, personalization in product management manifested through rudimentary segmentation and targeting strategies, where broad customer segments were identified based on demographic attributes or behavioral patterns. While effective to some extent, these conventional approaches were limited in their ability to deliver truly personalized experiences that catered to the unique needs and preferences of individual users.

However, with the advent of advanced data analytics techniques and AI-driven technologies, the landscape of personalization underwent a radical transformation. AI-powered algorithms empowered product managers to delve into the granular nuances of user behavior, preferences, and interactions, enabling them to craft hyper-personalized experiences that dynamically adapt and evolve in real-time based on individual user data.

Central to this evolution is the shift from static, rule-based personalization to dynamic, machine learning-driven personalization. By leveraging AI and machine learning algorithms, product managers can analyze vast volumes of data, identify intricate patterns and correlations, and anticipate user preferences with unprecedented accuracy and precision.

Moreover, the rise of AI-driven hyper-personalization has paved the way for a paradigm shift in customer expectations, as users increasingly demand personalized experiences that anticipate their needs and desires. In response, product managers must embrace a data-driven mindset and leverage AI technologies to deliver personalized experiences that delight and engage users at every touchpoint.

Furthermore, the evolution of personalization underscores the importance of ethical considerations and data privacy safeguards in product management practices. As organizations harness the power of AI to deliver hyper-personalized experiences, they must prioritize the ethical use of data, respect user privacy rights, and ensure transparency and accountability in their personalization strategies.

In essence, the evolution of personalization in product management represents a transformative journey—a journey fueled by innovation, driven by data, and guided by a relentless commitment to delivering meaningful and impactful user experiences. By embracing AI-driven hyper-personalization, product managers can unlock new opportunities for engagement, loyalty, and growth, ushering in a new era of personalized product experiences that resonate deeply with users and drive sustainable business success.

Understanding Hyper-Personalization

Within the realm of user experience, hyper-personalization emerges as a transformative paradigm that transcends surface-level customization, delving into the realms of intuition and anticipation. This section embarks on a deep dive into the concept of hyper-personalization, illuminating how AI harnesses granular user data, preferences, and behaviors to craft experiences that not only tailor but also anticipate individual needs, providing a level of personalization that feels intuitive, seamless, and profoundly impactful.

At its core, hyper-personalization represents a quantum leap beyond traditional customization approaches. While conventional customization endeavors to adapt experiences based on explicit user preferences or actions, hyper-personalization ventures into the realm of anticipatory intelligence, leveraging AI algorithms to analyze vast troves of data and discern subtle patterns and signals that reveal deeper insights into individual preferences, behaviors, and intents.

Central to this concept is the idea of context-aware personalization—a dynamic approach that takes into account not only explicit user inputs but also implicit cues and contextual factors to deliver experiences that are highly relevant and timely. By leveraging AI-driven algorithms, hyper-personalization anticipates user needs and preferences in real-time, seamlessly adapting content, recommendations, and interactions to match individual expectations and desires.

Moreover, hyper-personalization represents a paradigm shift in user experience design, where the focus shifts from reactive to proactive engagement. Rather than waiting for users to express their preferences or initiate interactions, hyper-personalized experiences anticipate user needs and desires, preemptively surfacing relevant content, recommendations, and actions to create frictionless and delightful experiences.

Furthermore, hyper-personalization holds the promise of forging deeper connections and fostering brand loyalty. By delivering experiences that feel intuitive, seamless, and deeply personalized, organizations can create emotional bonds with users, engendering a sense of trust, loyalty, and affinity that transcends transactional relationships.

In essence, hyper-personalization represents a convergence of data, AI, and design—a fusion of technology and empathy that unlocks new frontiers in user experience innovation. By embracing hyper-personalization, organizations can elevate their offerings beyond mere customization to deliver anticipatory experiences that resonate deeply with users, driving engagement, loyalty, and business success in an increasingly competitive digital landscape.

The Role of AI in Personalization

At the forefront of the hyper-personalization revolution stands Artificial Intelligence (AI) as the linchpin that propels personalization into uncharted territories of sophistication and relevance. This section embarks on an immersive exploration of the pivotal role played by AI, with its formidable capacity for machine learning, natural language processing, and predictive analytics, in transforming personalization from a static, rule-based system to a dynamic, self-learning model capable of adapting to users' evolving preferences in real-time.

At its essence, AI represents a paradigm shift in personalization—a departure from conventional approaches that rely on predetermined rules and static segmentation. Instead, AI-powered personalization harnesses the power of algorithms to analyze vast volumes of data, discern intricate patterns, and extract meaningful insights that inform personalized recommendations, content, and interactions.

Central to the transformative potential of AI in personalization is its capacity for machine learning—a branch of AI that enables systems to learn and improve from experience without being explicitly programmed. By leveraging machine learning algorithms, personalization systems can analyze user behaviors, interactions, and feedback to iteratively refine and optimize recommendations, adapting to users' evolving preferences with unparalleled accuracy and efficiency.

Moreover, AI-driven personalization extends beyond traditional boundaries to encompass natural language processing (NLP)—a subfield of AI that enables systems to understand, interpret, and generate human language. By integrating NLP capabilities into personalization systems, organizations can analyze textual data from various sources, such as customer reviews, social media posts, and support tickets, to derive deeper insights into user sentiments, preferences, and intents.

Furthermore, AI-powered personalization embraces the realm of predictive analytics—an analytical approach that leverages historical data to forecast future outcomes and behaviors. By employing predictive analytics algorithms, personalization systems can anticipate users' needs and desires, preemptively surfacing relevant content, recommendations, and actions to create seamless and intuitive user experiences.

In essence, the role of AI in personalization represents a transformative force—a convergence of advanced technologies and data-driven methodologies that redefines the user experience landscape. By harnessing the power of AI, organizations can unlock new frontiers in personalization, delivering tailored, anticipatory experiences that resonate deeply with users and drive engagement, loyalty, and business success in an increasingly competitive digital landscape.

Data-Driven User Insights

At the heart of hyper-personalization lies the transformative synergy between Artificial Intelligence (AI) and data-driven user insights—a dynamic partnership that propels personalization into uncharted realms of sophistication and relevance. This section embarks on an immersive exploration of AI's pivotal role in harnessing insights from vast datasets, delving into how AI analyzes user behaviors, interactions, and historical data to generate profound insights that serve as the bedrock for crafting highly personalized user experiences.

The cornerstone of AI's contribution to hyper-personalization lies in its formidable capacity to glean insights from vast and diverse datasets. Through advanced analytics techniques and machine learning algorithms, AI processes and interprets a myriad of data points, discerning intricate patterns, correlations, and trends that reveal invaluable insights into user behaviors, preferences, and intents.

Central to this transformative process is AI's ability to analyze user behaviors and interactions across multiple touchpoints and channels. By aggregating and synthesizing data from sources such as website visits, app interactions, social media engagements, and purchase history, AI constructs a comprehensive portrait of each user's digital footprint, enabling organizations to gain a holistic understanding of their preferences, habits, and needs.

Moreover, AI-driven user insights extend beyond surface-level observations to encompass nuanced contextual understanding. By leveraging natural language processing (NLP) and sentiment analysis techniques, AI interprets textual data from user reviews, feedback, and social media posts, deciphering underlying sentiments, emotions, and intentions to derive deeper insights into user preferences and sentiments.

Furthermore, AI empowers organizations to anticipate user needs and desires through predictive analytics—a sophisticated analytical approach that forecasts future behaviors and outcomes based on historical data. By employing predictive modeling and forecasting algorithms, AI predicts user preferences, trends, and behaviors, enabling organizations to proactively tailor experiences and recommendations to match individual user expectations.

In essence, the transformative power of data-driven user insights in hyper-personalization represents a convergence of advanced technologies and analytical methodologies—a fusion of AI and data science that unlocks new frontiers in user experience innovation. By harnessing the power of AI to analyze user behaviors, interactions, and historical data, organizations can uncover profound insights that inform personalized experiences, driving engagement, loyalty, and business success in an increasingly competitive digital landscape.

Predictive Analytics for Anticipatory Personalization

At the forefront of innovation in personalization stands Artificial Intelligence (AI) with its predictive analytics capabilities, propelling user experiences into the realm of anticipation and foresight. This section embarks on an immersive exploration of how AI models harness predictive analytics to forecast user preferences and behaviors, empowering product managers to proactively tailor experiences, recommend products, and surface content that aligns with users' future needs before they explicitly express them.

The cornerstone of anticipatory personalization lies in AI's predictive analytics capabilities—a sophisticated analytical approach that leverages historical data to forecast future behaviors and outcomes with remarkable accuracy. By employing predictive modeling, machine learning algorithms, and statistical techniques, AI models analyze patterns, trends, and correlations in user data to discern underlying signals and anticipate future preferences and behaviors.

Central to this transformative process is AI's ability to forecast user preferences and behaviors across various dimensions. By analyzing historical interactions, purchase patterns, and engagement metrics, AI models generate predictive insights that enable product managers to anticipate users' needs, desires, and intentions, shaping personalized experiences that resonate deeply with individual users.

Moreover, AI-driven predictive analytics empowers organizations to proactively tailor experiences, recommend products, and surface content based on anticipated user preferences and behaviors. By leveraging predictive insights, product managers can dynamically adapt content, offers, and recommendations in real-time, ensuring that users encounter relevant and timely information that meets their evolving needs and desires.

Furthermore, anticipatory personalization represents a paradigm shift in user experience design—a departure from reactive to proactive engagement strategies. Rather than waiting for users to express their preferences or initiate interactions, anticipatory personalization enables organizations to anticipate user needs and desires, preemptively delivering personalized experiences that delight and engage users at every touchpoint.

In essence, the dynamics of predictive analytics for anticipatory personalization herald a new era of user experience innovation—a fusion of AI and data-driven methodologies that unlocks new frontiers in personalized engagement and customer satisfaction. By harnessing the power of predictive analytics, organizations can anticipate user preferences and behaviors, shaping personalized experiences that foster loyalty, drive engagement, and propel business success in an increasingly competitive digital landscape.

Dynamic Content Personalization

In the ever-evolving landscape of user experience, the transition from static to dynamic content personalization marks a significant paradigm shift—a transformation fueled by the infusion of Artificial Intelligence (AI) into the fabric of user interaction. This section embarks on an immersive exploration of how AI revolutionizes content personalization, dynamically adjusting content, recommendations, and interfaces based on real-time user interactions to create adaptive and responsive experiences that evolve with each interaction, maximizing engagement and satisfaction.

At its core, dynamic content personalization represents a departure from traditional, one-size-fits-all approaches to content delivery. While static personalization endeavors to tailor content based on predefined rules or segmentation criteria, dynamic content personalization harnesses the power of AI algorithms to analyze real-time user interactions, preferences, and behaviors, dynamically adjusting content and recommendations to match individual user needs and interests.

Central to this transformative process is AI's capacity to process and interpret vast volumes of data in real-time, discerning patterns, trends, and signals that reveal insights into user preferences and intents. By leveraging machine learning algorithms, AI models dynamically adapt content, recommendations, and interfaces based on user engagement metrics, historical interactions, and contextual cues, ensuring that each user encounter is highly relevant and personalized.

Moreover, dynamic content personalization empowers organizations to create adaptive and responsive user experiences that evolve with each interaction. By dynamically adjusting content and recommendations in real-time, organizations can respond to user preferences, behaviors, and changing contexts, ensuring that users encounter the most relevant and engaging content at every touchpoint.

Furthermore, the infusion of AI into content personalization fosters innovation and experimentation, enabling organizations to continuously optimize and refine user experiences based on real-time insights and feedback. By leveraging AI-driven analytics, organizations can gain deeper insights into user preferences, engagement patterns, and content performance, informing iterative improvements and enhancements to content personalization strategies.

In essence, dynamic content personalization represents a transformative shift in user experience design—a convergence of AI and data-driven methodologies that unlocks new frontiers in engagement and satisfaction. By harnessing the power of AI to dynamically adapt content and recommendations based on real-time user interactions, organizations can create personalized experiences that resonate deeply with users, driving engagement, loyalty, and business success in an increasingly competitive digital landscape.

Hyper-Personalized Recommendations

In the realm of hyper-personalization, recommendation engines emerge as the cornerstone, powered by Artificial Intelligence (AI) algorithms that redefine the landscape of user experiences. This section embarks on an immersive journey into the heart of hyper-personalized recommendations, delving into how AI algorithms, leveraging collaborative filtering, content-based filtering, and reinforcement learning techniques, generate recommendations that transcend mere customization, spanning products, services, content, and features to create tailored journeys for each user.

At its core, hyper-personalized recommendations represent a paradigm shift—a departure from generic, one-size-fits-all recommendations to highly targeted and relevant suggestions that anticipate and cater to individual user preferences and needs. While traditional recommendation engines relied on simplistic rules or heuristics, AI-powered recommendation engines harness the power of advanced algorithms to analyze vast troves of data and discern intricate patterns and correlations, unlocking new levels of personalization and engagement.

Central to this transformative process is the utilization of collaborative filtering—a technique that leverages collective user behavior to generate recommendations. By analyzing user interactions, preferences, and feedback, collaborative filtering algorithms identify similarities and patterns among users, enabling them to recommend products, services, and content that align with individual tastes and interests.

Moreover, AI-powered recommendation engines leverage content-based filtering—a method that analyzes the intrinsic characteristics of items to generate recommendations. By examining attributes such as product descriptions, user reviews, and metadata, content-based filtering algorithms match users with items that closely match their preferences and profiles, ensuring that recommendations are highly relevant and tailored to individual tastes.

Furthermore, reinforcement learning techniques empower recommendation engines to adapt and evolve over time based on user feedback and interactions. By continuously learning from user behavior and adjusting recommendation strategies in real-time, reinforcement learning algorithms optimize recommendations to maximize user engagement and satisfaction, creating personalized experiences that foster loyalty and retention.

In essence, hyper-personalized recommendations represent the epitome of AI-driven personalization—a fusion of advanced technologies and data-driven methodologies that redefines the way users discover and engage with content, products, and services. By harnessing the power of AI algorithms, organizations can unlock new frontiers in recommendation engines, delivering tailored experiences that resonate deeply with users, driving engagement, loyalty, and business success in an increasingly competitive digital landscape.

Personalized User Interfaces

In the realm of user experience, the integration of Artificial Intelligence (AI) extends personalization beyond mere recommendations to the very fabric of user interfaces, ushering in a new era of tailored interactions that resonate deeply with individual users. This section embarks on an immersive exploration of how AI revolutionizes user interfaces, layouts, and designs, tailoring them based on individual preferences, accessibility needs, and interaction histories to create interfaces that feel intuitively crafted for each user, enhancing usability and engagement.

At its essence, personalized user interfaces represent a paradigm shift—a departure from static, one-size-fits-all designs to dynamic and adaptive interfaces that respond to the unique needs and preferences of individual users. While traditional user interfaces offered limited customization options, AI-driven interfaces harness the power of advanced algorithms to analyze user data and insights, dynamically adjusting layouts, designs, and features to match individual user profiles and preferences.

Central to this transformative process is AI's capacity to analyze user interactions and behavior patterns across multiple touchpoints and channels. By aggregating and synthesizing data from sources such as browsing history, clickstream data, and device preferences, AI models construct detailed user profiles that capture individual preferences, accessibility needs, and interaction histories, enabling organizations to tailor interfaces to match each user's unique profile.

Moreover, AI-powered personalized interfaces go beyond surface-level customization to encompass nuanced considerations such as accessibility needs and interaction preferences. By leveraging machine learning algorithms and

323

natural language processing techniques, AI models interpret user feedback, gestures, and interactions to infer underlying preferences and intents, ensuring that interfaces are designed to accommodate diverse user needs and enhance usability for all users.

Furthermore, personalized user interfaces foster engagement and satisfaction by creating seamless and intuitive user experiences that evolve with each interaction. By dynamically adjusting layouts, designs, and features based on real-time insights and feedback, AI-driven interfaces anticipate user needs and preferences, delivering tailored experiences that delight and engage users at every touchpoint.

In essence, personalized user interfaces represent a convergence of AI and user experience design—a fusion of technology and empathy that unlocks new frontiers in engagement, usability, and satisfaction. By harnessing the power of AI to tailor interfaces based on individual preferences and interaction histories, organizations can create intuitive and immersive user experiences that resonate deeply with users, driving engagement, loyalty, and business success in an increasingly competitive digital landscape.

Contextual Personalization Across Platforms

In the dynamic landscape of hyper-personalization, the concept transcends individual platforms to encompass a cohesive and consistent personalized experience across diverse channels and devices. This section delves into how Artificial Intelligence (AI) ensures a seamless journey for users, maintaining personalized interactions regardless of the platform—whether it be a website, mobile app, or any other touchpoint—enhancing the continuity of user experiences.

At its core, contextual personalization across platforms represents a paradigm shift—a departure from fragmented user experiences to a unified and cohesive journey that spans multiple touchpoints. While traditional personalization efforts focused on optimizing experiences within individual platforms, AI-driven contextual personalization endeavors to create a seamless and consistent experience that follows users across channels and devices.

Central to this transformative process is AI's capacity to analyze user data and preferences holistically, irrespective of the platform or device. By aggregating and synthesizing data from various sources, including browsing history, app usage patterns, and device preferences, AI models construct comprehensive user profiles that capture individual preferences, behaviors, and intents, enabling organizations to deliver personalized experiences that transcend platform boundaries.

Moreover, AI-powered contextual personalization ensures that users encounter consistent and relevant content, recommendations, and interactions across all platforms. By leveraging machine learning algorithms and predictive analytics, AI models anticipate user needs and preferences, dynamically adjusting content and recommendations based on contextual cues and user behaviors, ensuring that personalized interactions remain cohesive and seamless regardless of the platform.

Furthermore, contextual personalization fosters engagement and loyalty by creating a unified brand experience that resonates with users across all touchpoints. By maintaining consistency in messaging, branding, and user experience design, organizations can reinforce their brand identity and foster deeper connections with users, driving engagement, loyalty, and advocacy in an increasingly omnichannel world.

In essence, contextual personalization across platforms represents a convergence of AI and user experience design

—a fusion of technology and empathy that unlocks new frontiers in engagement and satisfaction. By harnessing the power of AI to deliver seamless and consistent experiences across channels and devices, organizations can create immersive and cohesive journeys that resonate deeply with users, driving engagement, loyalty, and business success in a digitally interconnected world.

Privacy and Trust in Hyper-Personalization

As the landscape of personalization evolves towards greater sophistication, the discourse surrounding privacy considerations takes center stage. This section delves into the intricate interplay between hyper-personalization and user privacy, emphasizing the imperative of striking a delicate balance. AI-driven personalization strategies must prioritize transparency, user control, and ethical data practices to build and maintain trust in an era where privacy concerns loom large.

At its core, the convergence of hyper-personalization and privacy considerations represents a nuanced and multifaceted challenge—a delicate dance between delivering tailored experiences and safeguarding user privacy. While hyper-personalization aims to enhance user engagement and satisfaction by delivering highly relevant and customized content, it must do so without compromising user privacy or infringing upon individual rights.

Central to this transformative discourse is the need for transparency and accountability in AI-driven personalization strategies. Organizations must adopt transparent practices that empower users to understand how their data is being collected, used, and shared for personalization purposes. By providing clear and accessible privacy policies, consent mechanisms, and opt-out options, organizations can foster trust and confidence among users, ensuring that

326

personalization efforts are conducted in an ethical and responsible manner.

Moreover, AI-driven personalization strategies must prioritize user control and consent, empowering individuals to exercise agency over their data and personalization preferences. By implementing granular controls and preferences settings, organizations can empower users to customize their personalization experience according to their preferences and comfort levels, thereby enhancing transparency, trust, and user autonomy.

Furthermore, ethical data practices play a pivotal role in building and maintaining trust in hyper-personalization initiatives. Organizations must adhere to principles of data minimization, anonymization, and security to protect user privacy and mitigate the risk of data breaches or misuse. By implementing robust data governance frameworks and compliance mechanisms, organizations can demonstrate their commitment to ethical data practices and safeguard user trust in an era where privacy concerns are paramount.

In essence, privacy and trust in hyper-personalization represent a critical intersection—an opportunity for organizations to demonstrate their commitment to user-centricity, transparency, and ethical stewardship of data. By prioritizing privacy considerations and adopting responsible personalization practices, organizations can foster trust and confidence among users, ensuring that hyper-personalization efforts are not only effective but also ethical and respectful of individual privacy rights.

Adaptive Learning for Continuous Personalization

At the heart of hyper-personalization lies the iterative and adaptive nature of Artificial Intelligence (AI), which facilitates continuous learning and refinement of personalization strategies. This section delves into how AI dynamically adjusts its personalization approaches based on user feedback, evolving preferences, and changing contexts, ensuring that hyper-personalization remains relevant and aligned with users' ever-shifting needs.

The essence of adaptive learning in AI-driven personalization represents a fundamental shift—a departure from static and rigid approaches to a dynamic and evolutionary framework that responds to real-time user interactions and feedback. While traditional personalization strategies relied on predefined rules or segmentation criteria, AI-driven adaptive learning harnesses the power of machine learning algorithms to analyze user data and behavior patterns, iteratively refining and optimizing personalization strategies based on insights gleaned from user feedback.

Central to this transformative process is AI's capacity to adapt and evolve in response to changing user preferences and contexts. By continuously monitoring user interactions, feedback, and engagement metrics, AI models dynamically adjust personalization strategies, ensuring that recommendations, content, and experiences remain relevant and impactful at each touchpoint of the user journey.

Moreover, adaptive learning enables AI to anticipate user needs and preferences, proactively surfacing relevant content and recommendations before users explicitly express them. By leveraging predictive analytics and reinforcement learning techniques, AI models identify emerging trends and patterns in user behavior, enabling organizations to deliver personalized experiences that resonate deeply with individual users, driving engagement and satisfaction.

Furthermore, adaptive learning fosters innovation and experimentation, empowering organizations to iterate and optimize personalization strategies based on real-time insights and feedback. By embracing a culture of continuous learning and improvement, organizations can stay ahead of evolving user expectations and preferences, ensuring that hyper-personalization remains a cornerstone of their user engagement strategy.

In essence, adaptive learning for iterative personalization represents a convergence of AI and user experience design —a fusion of technology and empathy that unlocks new frontiers in engagement and satisfaction. By harnessing the power of adaptive learning, organizations can create personalized experiences that evolve with users, driving engagement, loyalty, and business success in an increasingly competitive digital landscape.

Ethical Considerations in Hyper-Personalization

The journey through hyper-personalization in product management culminates with an examination of its ethical dimensions, as AI emerges as the catalyst for a transformative era in user experiences. This section delves into the profound ethical considerations surrounding hyper-personalization, highlighting the complexities of data usage, consent, and unintended biases that come to the forefront as AI gains unprecedented insights into users' lives. Emphasizing the importance of ethical frameworks to guide hyper-personalization strategies responsibly, this section seeks to navigate the delicate balance between innovation and ethical stewardship in the pursuit of user-centric innovation.

At its essence, the convergence of hyper-personalization and ethical considerations represents a pivotal juncture—an opportunity for product managers to reflect on the ethical implications of AI-driven personalization and customization. As AI algorithms delve deeper into users' preferences, behaviors, and identities, ethical considerations around data privacy, consent, and fairness become increasingly salient, necessitating a thoughtful and proactive approach to ethical decision-making.

Central to this discourse is the recognition of the potential risks and unintended consequences associated with hyper-personalization initiatives. While AI-driven personalization holds immense promise in enhancing user engagement and satisfaction, it also raises concerns about data exploitation, algorithmic bias, and user manipulation. Product managers must navigate these ethical complexities with vigilance and integrity, prioritizing transparency, fairness, and user empowerment in their personalization strategies.

Moreover, ethical frameworks serve as guiding principles to ensure that hyper-personalization initiatives uphold fundamental ethical values and principles. By adhering to principles of privacy by design, informed consent, and algorithmic transparency, product managers can mitigate the risk of unintended harms and build trust and confidence among users. Additionally, ongoing ethical oversight and accountability mechanisms are essential to monitor and evaluate the ethical implications of hyper-personalization strategies, fostering a culture of responsible innovation and ethical stewardship.

Furthermore, ethical considerations in hyper-personalization extend beyond individual user interactions to encompass broader societal implications. As AI-driven personalization reshapes the digital landscape, it has the potential to exacerbate existing inequalities, reinforce social biases, and perpetuate discrimination. Product managers must proactively address these systemic challenges, seeking to design inclusive and equitable personalization strategies that prioritize diversity, equity, and social justice.

In essence, ethical considerations in hyper-personalization represent a call to action—a reminder of the ethical responsibilities and moral imperatives inherent in the pursuit of user-centric innovation. By embracing ethical frameworks and principles, product managers can navigate the complexities of hyper-personalization with integrity and empathy, ensuring that AI-driven personalization serves as a force for good, enriching user experiences and fostering deeper connections with users in a manner that respects and upholds their rights and dignity.

CREATING TAILORED EXPERIENCES FOR USERS

In the rapidly evolving landscape of product management, personalization and customization have become integral strategies for creating meaningful user experiences. This chapter explores the art and science of tailoring products to individual preferences and needs, examining how product managers employ personalization and customization to forge deeper connections with users.

The Paradigm Shift to User-Centric Experiences

The journey towards user-centric product development unfolds with a profound paradigm shift—a departure from traditional, one-size-fits-all approaches to a new frontier of personalized and customized experiences. This section illuminates the transformative nature of this shift, driven by the intrinsic desire to meet individual user needs and expectations, heralding a new era of innovation and user empowerment in product development.

At its essence, the paradigm shift towards user-centric experiences represents a fundamental reorientation—a recognition that users are diverse, dynamic, and multidimensional beings, each with unique preferences, behaviors, and aspirations. While traditional product development approaches often adopted a homogeneous and standardized approach, user-centricity embraces the diversity and complexity of users, seeking to tailor experiences to match their individual needs and desires.

Central to this transformative journey is the acknowledgment that users are at the heart of product development—the ultimate arbiters of success and satisfaction. By shifting the focus from products to users, organizations can gain deeper insights into user needs, motivations, and pain points, enabling them to design products and experiences that resonate on a profound level, fostering loyalty, engagement, and advocacy among users.

Moreover, the paradigm shift towards user-centric experiences is driven by advancements in technology and data analytics, which empower organizations to personalize and customize experiences at scale. By leveraging AI, machine learning, and predictive analytics, organizations can analyze vast troves of user data to discern patterns, trends, and preferences, enabling them to deliver tailored experiences that anticipate and fulfill individual user needs and expectations.

Furthermore, the paradigm shift towards user-centric experiences reflects a broader cultural and societal shift—a recognition of the importance of empathy, inclusivity, and human-centered design in product development. By placing users at the center of the design process, organizations can co-create experiences that are not only functional and intuitive but also meaningful and impactful, enhancing the quality of life and enriching the human experience.

In essence, the paradigm shift towards user-centric experiences represents a renaissance—a rebirth of product development methodologies rooted in empathy, empowerment, and innovation. By embracing user-centricity as a guiding principle, organizations can unlock new opportunities for growth and differentiation, cultivating deeper connections with users and driving sustained success in an increasingly competitive and dynamic marketplace.

Defining Personalization and Customization

Embarking on a journey to understand tailored experiences necessitates a nuanced exploration of two fundamental concepts: personalization and customization. This section endeavors to delineate these concepts clearly, establishing personalization as the adaptation of a product based on user behavior and data, while customization involves users actively tailoring their experience to meet their preferences and needs. By grasping the subtle distinctions between these concepts, we lay the groundwork for a deeper understanding of the intricacies of tailored experiences and their implications for user engagement and satisfaction.

At its essence, personalization represents a dynamic and adaptive approach to user experiences—a process whereby products and services are tailored to align with individual user preferences, behaviors, and contexts. Personalization leverages insights gleaned from user data and behavior patterns to deliver relevant and contextually appropriate content, recommendations, and interactions, thereby enhancing user engagement and satisfaction.

In contrast, customization embodies a proactive and participatory approach to user experiences—a process whereby users actively engage with products or services to tailor their experience according to their preferences and needs. Customization empowers users to exert control over various aspects of their experience, allowing them to personalize settings, features, and functionalities to match their unique preferences and requirements.

Central to understanding these concepts is the recognition of the different roles played by users and technology in shaping tailored experiences. While personalization relies on algorithms and automation to analyze user data and adapt products or services accordingly, customization places users at the forefront, empowering them to make conscious choices and decisions to tailor their experience to their liking.

Moreover, the distinction between personalization and customization extends beyond technical implementation to encompass broader implications for user autonomy and empowerment. Personalization, although driven by user data, may raise concerns about privacy and data usage, as algorithms make inferences and decisions on behalf of users. On the other hand, customization places users in control, allowing them to exercise agency over their experience and shape it according to their preferences and values.

Furthermore, understanding the nuances between personalization and customization enables organizations to design tailored experiences that strike the right balance between relevance and user control. By leveraging personalization to deliver contextually relevant content and recommendations while providing opportunities for user customization, organizations can create seamless and engaging user experiences that cater to individual preferences and needs while respecting user autonomy and privacy.

In essence, defining personalization and customization sets the stage for a nuanced exploration of tailored experiences— a journey that encompasses both the art and science of delivering user-centric products and services that resonate deeply with users and foster meaningful and lasting connections. By embracing the distinctions between these concepts, organizations can unlock new opportunities for innovation and differentiation, driving engagement, loyalty, and satisfaction in an increasingly personalized and customized digital landscape.

The Human Touch in Digital Interactions

In an era where digital interactions permeate every aspect of our lives, preserving the human touch is indispensable. This section delves deep into the transformative role of personalization and customization, elucidating how these concepts imbue digital products with a sense of humanity, akin to the personalized service one might experience in a brick-and-mortar store. By empathetically understanding users on a personal level, product managers can cultivate meaningful connections and replicate the warmth and attentiveness of in-person interactions in the digital realm.

At its core, the integration of the human touch in digital interactions represents a paradigm shift—a departure from transactional exchanges to empathetic engagements that prioritize the individual needs and preferences of users. As digital products and services become increasingly ubiquitous, users crave experiences that resonate on a personal level, fostering a sense of connection and belonging in an otherwise impersonal digital landscape.

Central to this transformative journey is the recognition that behind every digital interaction lies a human being with unique desires, emotions, and aspirations. By leveraging personalization and customization, product managers can transcend the constraints of digital interfaces to forge genuine and meaningful connections with users, mirroring the warmth and attentiveness of face-to-face interactions.

Moreover, personalization and customization serve as catalysts for humanizing digital interactions, enabling product managers to tailor experiences to match individual user preferences and needs. Through personalized recommendations, curated content, and customizable features, digital products can adapt and evolve in real-time to meet the evolving expectations and desires of users, thereby fostering a sense of intimacy and familiarity in the digital realm.

Furthermore, the integration of the human touch in digital interactions entails a holistic approach that extends beyond technical implementation to encompass empathetic design principles and user-centered methodologies. By prioritizing user empathy, inclusivity, and accessibility, product managers can create digital experiences that resonate with users on an emotional level, transcending the limitations of technology to deliver moments of delight and connection.

In essence, the integration of the human touch in digital interactions represents a renaissance—a reimagining of the digital experience as a canvas for human connection and empathy. By infusing personalization and customization with a sense of humanity, product managers can create digital products and services that not only meet functional needs but also enrich the lives of users, fostering deeper connections and lasting relationships in an increasingly digital world.

Crafting Personalization Strategies

Embarking on the journey of successful personalization demands a meticulous approach grounded in robust strategies. This section ventures into the strategic considerations that underpin effective personalization, illuminating the multifaceted landscape where clear goals, data-driven insights, and continuous adaptation converge. Product managers are tasked with striking a delicate balance between tailoring experiences to individual needs and desires while respecting user privacy and preferences, thereby laying the groundwork for personalized experiences that resonate deeply with users and foster lasting connections.

At its core, crafting personalization strategies represents a strategic imperative—a concerted effort to align organizational objectives with user needs and expectations in pursuit of enhanced engagement and satisfaction. By setting clear goals and objectives, product managers can establish a roadmap for personalization initiatives that are not only impactful but also measurable and aligned with broader business objectives.

Central to this strategic framework is the reliance on data-driven insights to inform decision-making and optimize personalization strategies. By leveraging user data, behavioral analytics, and predictive modeling techniques, product managers can gain deep insights into user preferences, behaviors, and trends, enabling them to tailor experiences with precision and relevance.

Moreover, effective personalization strategies require a commitment to continuous adaptation and optimization—a recognition that user preferences and behaviors are dynamic and ever-evolving. Product managers must embrace a culture of experimentation and iteration, leveraging A/B testing, user feedback, and performance analytics to refine and optimize personalization strategies over time, ensuring that they remain aligned with user expectations and market dynamics.

Furthermore, successful personalization strategies necessitate a thoughtful approach to privacy and user consent. Product managers must prioritize transparency, user control, and ethical data practices to build and maintain trust with users, thereby fostering a relationship of mutual respect and reciprocity.

In essence, crafting personalization strategies represents a delicate balancing act—an intricate interplay between strategic foresight, data-driven insights, and ethical stewardship. By embracing a holistic approach that prioritizes user needs, respects user privacy, and drives continuous innovation, product managers can unlock the transformative potential of personalization, creating tailored experiences that resonate deeply with users and drive sustained success in an increasingly personalized digital landscape.

Leveraging User Data Responsibly

At the heart of personalization lies the bedrock of user data—a treasure trove of insights that fuels tailored experiences and drives engagement. Yet, with great data comes great responsibility. This section delves into the ethical considerations surrounding the collection, storage, and usage of user data, emphasizing the imperative of responsible data practices to build and maintain trust with users while harnessing their data to create personalized experiences that resonate deeply.

In the ever-evolving digital landscape, ethical considerations surrounding user data have become paramount. As custodians of user trust, product managers must prioritize transparency, consent, and security in all facets of data collection, storage, and usage.

Central to responsible data practices is the principle of transparency—an unwavering commitment to openness and honesty in communicating how user data is collected, processed, and utilized. By providing clear and accessible privacy policies, terms of service, and data usage agreements, product managers can empower users to make informed decisions about their data and build a relationship of trust and transparency.

Moreover, responsible data practices necessitate a robust framework for obtaining user consent—a recognition that users have the right to control how their data is collected, used, and shared. Product managers must implement clear and unambiguous consent mechanisms, ensuring that users are fully informed about the purposes and implications of data collection and have the ability to opt-in or opt-out based on their preferences.

Furthermore, safeguarding user data against unauthorized access, breaches, and misuse is paramount to ensuring data security and integrity. Product managers must implement stringent security measures, encryption protocols, and access controls to protect user data from cyber threats and vulnerabilities, thereby fostering a culture of trust and confidence in the security of personalization practices.

In essence, leveraging user data responsibly is not just a legal obligation but a moral imperative—a commitment to upholding ethical standards and principles in the pursuit of personalized experiences. By prioritizing transparency, consent, and security, product managers can navigate the ethical terrain of personalization with integrity and empathy, ensuring that user trust remains sacrosanct while harnessing the transformative power of data to create tailored experiences that enrich and enhance the lives of users.

User-Centric Customization

In the dynamic realm of digital interactions, customization stands as a beacon of empowerment—a gateway for users to exert control over their digital destinies. This section embarks on a deep dive into the intricacies of user-centric customization, shedding light on how product managers orchestrate personalized experiences that empower individuals to tailor interfaces, features, and content according to their unique preferences and desires. At its core, user-centric customization represents a paradigm shift—a departure from one-size-fits-all approaches to a bespoke journey where users are the architects of their digital interactions, imbuing each experience with a sense of ownership and agency.

The essence of user-centric customization lies in its ability to place users at the helm of their digital journey—empowering them to shape their experiences in alignment with their preferences, habits, and aspirations. Product managers play a pivotal role in facilitating this empowerment, offering users a diverse array of customization options and tools that cater to a spectrum of user needs and preferences.

At its core, user-centric customization encompasses various dimensions, spanning from visual preferences to functional features and content curation. Users can personalize interfaces by adjusting colors, layouts, and themes to reflect their aesthetic sensibilities. They can customize features and functionalities by toggling settings, preferences, and configurations to align with their workflow and usage patterns. Moreover, users can curate content by selecting preferences, interests, and filters to surface relevant and meaningful content that resonates with their tastes and interests.

The ultimate goal of user-centric customization is to foster a sense of ownership and identity in digital interactions—to transform users from passive consumers into active participants in the digital ecosystem. By offering users the tools and flexibility to tailor their experiences, product managers empower individuals to express their individuality, preferences, and values, thereby fostering deeper engagement, satisfaction, and loyalty.

Furthermore, user-centric customization represents a journey of continuous evolution and refinement—a recognition that user preferences and needs are dynamic and ever-changing. Product managers must embrace a culture of experimentation, iteration, and feedback, leveraging user insights and analytics to optimize customization options and experiences over time.

In essence, user-centric customization embodies the democratization of digital experiences—a movement towards empowerment, inclusivity, and self-expression in the digital realm. By embracing user-centricity as a guiding principle, product managers can unlock new avenues for innovation and differentiation, cultivating deeper connections with users and driving sustained success in an increasingly personalized and customized digital landscape.

Dynamic Content Personalization

In the ever-evolving landscape of digital interactions, dynamic content personalization emerges as a beacon of innovation—an evolution that propels personalized experiences to unprecedented heights. This section embarks on a profound exploration of how product managers harness the power of real-time data to orchestrate dynamic content personalization, revolutionizing the digital experience landscape by dynamically adjusting content, recommendations, and interfaces based on user interactions. The result is an immersive and adaptive user experience that evolves organically with each interaction, maximizing engagement, satisfaction, and user delight.

At its essence, dynamic content personalization represents a paradigm shift—a departure from static, one-size-fits-all approaches to a dynamic and responsive journey where content, recommendations, and interfaces adapt in real-time to match the unique preferences, behaviors, and contexts of individual users. Product managers serve as architects of this transformation, leveraging advanced algorithms, machine learning, and predictive analytics to analyze real-time data streams and dynamically adjust content and experiences accordingly.

Central to the concept of dynamic content personalization is its ability to offer users a tailored and contextualized experience that feels intuitive and seamless. By harnessing real-time data insights, product managers can deliver content and recommendations that resonate with users' interests, preferences, and intents, thereby enhancing relevance, engagement, and user satisfaction.

Moreover, dynamic content personalization encompasses various dimensions, spanning from personalized recommendations to adaptive interfaces and contextualized content delivery. Users encounter a curated journey where content is dynamically adjusted based on their browsing history, purchase behavior, demographics, and real-time interactions, ensuring that each interaction feels personalized and relevant.

The transformative power of dynamic content personalization lies in its ability to foster deeper connections and engagement with users. By offering a tailored and adaptive experience, product managers create opportunities for users to discover new content, products, and experiences that align with their interests and preferences, thereby fostering a sense of excitement, discovery, and fulfillment.

Furthermore, dynamic content personalization represents a journey of continuous refinement and optimization—a recognition that user preferences and behaviors are dynamic and ever-evolving. Product managers must embrace a culture of experimentation, iteration, and feedback, leveraging real-time analytics and user insights to optimize content personalization algorithms and experiences over time.

In essence, dynamic content personalization embodies the convergence of technology and empathy—a fusion that transcends the limitations of traditional personalization approaches to deliver experiences that feel intuitive, adaptive, and deeply resonant with users. By embracing the principles of dynamic content personalization, product managers can unlock new avenues for innovation and differentiation, driving engagement, satisfaction, and user loyalty in an increasingly dynamic and personalized digital landscape.

Personalized Recommendations

In the ever-expanding realm of personalized experiences, recommendation engines emerge as the linchpin—a pivotal force that propels tailored experiences to new heights. This section embarks on a profound exploration of how product managers harness the power of recommendation algorithms to orchestrate personalized recommendations, revolutionizing the digital experience landscape by offering tailored suggestions that span from products to content and features. The ultimate goal is to anticipate user preferences and elevate their journey through personalized suggestions that resonate deeply with their interests, needs, and desires.

At its core, personalized recommendations represent a paradigm shift—a departure from generic, one-size-fits-all approaches to a bespoke journey where users are guided through curated experiences that align with their unique preferences and contexts. Product managers serve as architects of this transformation, leveraging advanced recommendation algorithms, machine learning, and data analytics to analyze user behavior, preferences, and interactions and offer recommendations that are highly relevant and contextualized.

Central to the concept of personalized recommendations is its ability to offer users a curated and personalized journey that feels intuitive and seamless. By harnessing the power of recommendation algorithms, product managers can surface products, content, and features that resonate with users' interests, preferences, and intents, thereby enhancing engagement, satisfaction, and user delight.

Moreover, personalized recommendations encompass a diverse array of dimensions, spanning from product recommendations to content suggestions and feature discovery. Users encounter a curated journey where recommendations are dynamically adjusted based on their browsing history, purchase behavior, demographics, and real-time interactions, ensuring that each recommendation feels tailored and relevant to their needs and interests.

The transformative power of personalized recommendations lies in its ability to foster deeper connections and engagement with users. By offering tailored and contextually relevant recommendations, product managers create opportunities for users to discover new products, content, and experiences that align with their interests and preferences, thereby fostering a sense of excitement, exploration, and fulfillment.

Furthermore, personalized recommendations represent a journey of continuous refinement and optimization—a recognition that user preferences and behaviors are dynamic and ever-evolving. Product managers must embrace a culture of experimentation, iteration, and feedback, leveraging real-time analytics and user insights to optimize recommendation algorithms and experiences over time.

In essence, personalized recommendations embody the convergence of technology and empathy—a fusion that transcends the limitations of traditional recommendation approaches to deliver experiences that feel intuitive, adaptive, and deeply resonant with users. By embracing the principles of personalized recommendations, product managers can unlock new avenues for innovation and differentiation, driving engagement, satisfaction, and user loyalty in an increasingly personalized and tailored digital landscape.

Contextual Customization

In the ever-evolving landscape of personalized experiences, contextual customization emerges as a cornerstone—an innovative approach that considers the nuanced interplay between users' environments and circumstances. This section embarks on a profound exploration of how product managers orchestrate contextual customization, revolutionizing the digital experience landscape by tailoring experiences based on contextual cues such as location, device, or time of day. The ultimate goal is to ensure that the product adapts seamlessly to users' changing needs and scenarios, thereby enhancing relevance, usability, and user satisfaction.

At its essence, contextual customization represents a paradigm shift—a departure from static, one-size-fits-all approaches to a dynamic and responsive journey where experiences are tailored to match the unique environments and circumstances of individual users. Product managers serve as architects of this transformation, leveraging advanced algorithms, machine learning, and real-time data analytics to analyze contextual cues and dynamically adjust experiences accordingly.

Central to the concept of contextual customization is its ability to offer users a seamless and intuitive journey that feels relevant and timely. By harnessing contextual cues such as location, device type, time of day, and user preferences, product managers can personalize experiences in real-time to match users' current needs, preferences, and intents, thereby enhancing usability, engagement, and user satisfaction.

Moreover, contextual customization encompasses a diverse array of dimensions, spanning from personalized content delivery to adaptive interface designs and feature discovery. Users encounter a curated journey where experiences are dynamically adjusted based on their current context and circumstances, ensuring that each interaction feels tailored and relevant to their immediate needs and scenarios.

The transformative power of contextual customization lies in its ability to foster deeper connections and engagement with users. By offering experiences that are seamlessly aligned with users' environments and circumstances, product managers create opportunities for users to engage with the product in a more meaningful and relevant manner, thereby fostering a sense of trust, loyalty, and satisfaction.

Furthermore, contextual customization represents a journey of continuous refinement and optimization—a recognition that user contexts and circumstances are dynamic and ever-evolving. Product managers must embrace a culture of experimentation, iteration, and feedback, leveraging real-time analytics and user insights to optimize contextual customization strategies and experiences over time.

In essence, contextual customization embodies the convergence of technology and empathy—a fusion that transcends the limitations of traditional customization approaches to deliver experiences that feel intuitive, adaptive, and deeply resonant with users. By embracing the principles of contextual customization, product managers can unlock new avenues for innovation and differentiation, driving engagement, satisfaction, and user loyalty in an increasingly dynamic and personalized digital landscape.

Adaptive Learning for Continuous Improvement

In the dynamic landscape of personalized experiences, the journey towards excellence unfolds through continuous learning and refinement. This section embarks on a profound exploration of how product managers harness the power of adaptive learning techniques to drive continuous improvement in personalization and customization strategies. By incorporating user feedback and evolving preferences into the fabric of personalization algorithms, product managers navigate the iterative journey of adaptive learning, ensuring that tailored experiences remain relevant and resonant with users over time.

At its essence, adaptive learning represents a paradigm shift —a departure from static, one-size-fits-all approaches to a dynamic and responsive journey where experiences evolve organically in response to user feedback and evolving preferences. Product managers serve as stewards of this transformation, leveraging advanced machine learning algorithms, predictive analytics, and real-time data insights to analyze user interactions and dynamically adjust personalization strategies accordingly.

Central to the concept of adaptive learning is its ability to offer users a journey of continuous improvement—a journey where personalized experiences evolve and refine over time to match the changing needs, preferences, and behaviors of individual users. By incorporating user feedback, behavioral data, and performance metrics into the iterative cycle of learning and refinement, product managers ensure that personalization strategies remain relevant, effective, and impactful in meeting user expectations and driving engagement.

Moreover, adaptive learning encompasses a diverse array of techniques and methodologies, spanning from collaborative filtering to reinforcement learning and deep neural networks. Product managers leverage these techniques to extract meaningful insights from user interactions, identify patterns and trends, and iteratively refine personalization algorithms to enhance accuracy, relevance, and effectiveness.

The transformative power of adaptive learning lies in its ability to foster deeper connections and engagement with users. By offering experiences that evolve and adapt in response to user feedback and preferences, product managers create opportunities for users to engage with the product in a more meaningful and relevant manner, thereby fostering a sense of trust, loyalty, and satisfaction.

Furthermore, adaptive learning represents a journey of continuous evolution and refinement—a recognition that personalization strategies must evolve and adapt in tandem with users' ever-changing needs and preferences. Product managers must embrace a culture of experimentation, iteration, and feedback, leveraging real-time analytics and user insights to optimize personalization strategies and experiences over time.

In essence, adaptive learning embodies the convergence of technology and empathy—a fusion that transcends the limitations of traditional personalization approaches to deliver experiences that feel intuitive, adaptive, and deeply resonant with users. By embracing the principles of adaptive learning, product managers can unlock new avenues for innovation and differentiation, driving engagement, satisfaction, and user loyalty in an increasingly dynamic and personalized digital landscape.

Striking the Balance

In the intricate dance of digital experiences, finding the perfect equilibrium between personalization and customization emerges as an ongoing challenge—a delicate tightrope walk where product managers must navigate the delicate balance between offering tailored experiences and avoiding the pitfalls of over-customization. This section embarks on a profound exploration of how product managers grapple with this delicate equilibrium, striving to create experiences that feel personalized and relevant without crossing the line into intrusiveness or overwhelm.

At its essence, striking the right balance between personalization and customization represents a delicate art—a nuanced interplay between understanding user preferences and behaviors and respecting their boundaries and privacy. Product managers serve as guardians of this delicate balance, leveraging advanced algorithms, user insights, and ethical considerations to craft experiences that resonate deeply with users while preserving their autonomy and agency.

Central to the challenge of striking the balance is the need to offer tailored experiences that feel intuitive, relevant, and seamless, without intruding into users' personal space or overwhelming them with excessive customization options. Product managers must tread carefully, offering customization features and personalization algorithms that enhance user experiences without detracting from their sense of control or privacy.

Moreover, striking the right balance between personalization and customization encompasses a diverse array of considerations, spanning from user preferences and privacy concerns to usability and accessibility considerations. Product managers must consider the diverse needs and preferences of their user base, offering a spectrum of customization options and personalization features that cater to a range of user preferences and comfort levels.

The transformative power of striking the balance lies in its ability to foster deeper connections and engagement with users. By offering experiences that are personalized and tailored to users' individual needs and preferences, product managers create opportunities for users to engage with the product in a more meaningful and relevant manner, thereby fostering a sense of trust, loyalty, and satisfaction.

Furthermore, striking the balance represents a journey of continuous refinement and optimization—a recognition that user preferences and behaviors are dynamic and ever-evolving. Product managers must embrace a culture of experimentation, iteration, and feedback, leveraging real-time analytics and user insights to fine-tune personalization strategies and experiences over time.

In essence, striking the right balance between personalization and customization embodies the convergence of technology and empathy—a fusion that transcends the limitations of one-size-fits-all approaches to deliver experiences that feel intuitive, adaptive, and deeply resonant with users. By embracing the principles of striking the balance, product managers can unlock new avenues for innovation and differentiation, driving engagement, satisfaction, and user loyalty in an increasingly personalized and tailored digital landscape.

Future Trends in Tailored Experiences

As we cast our gaze towards the horizon, the chapter concludes by delving into the emerging trends that are set to shape the landscape of personalization and customization in the days to come. From AI-driven hyper-personalization to the integration of augmented reality interfaces and the seamless fusion of voice and gesture controls, these advancements offer a tantalizing glimpse into the future of tailored experiences in product management.

At its core, this section serves as a portal to the future—a realm where personalization and customization transcend the boundaries of conventional standards to usher in a new era of user-centric innovation and engagement. Product managers, armed with a deep understanding of user preferences, data-driven strategies, and ethical considerations, emerge as architects of tailored experiences that resonate deeply with their audience, fostering profound and enduring connections.

Central to the exploration of future trends is the emergence of AI-driven hyper-personalization—a paradigm shift that leverages the power of artificial intelligence to craft experiences that are not only tailored but anticipate individual needs and preferences with uncanny accuracy. By harnessing advanced algorithms and machine learning techniques, product managers unlock the potential to create experiences that feel intuitive, seamless, and deeply resonant with users.

Moreover, the integration of augmented reality interfaces and the seamless fusion of voice and gesture controls offer new avenues for immersive and interactive experiences. Product managers leverage these advancements to break free from the constraints of traditional interfaces, offering users a dynamic and multi-sensory journey that transcends the limitations of conventional interaction paradigms.

The transformative power of future trends lies in their ability to foster deeper connections and engagement with users. By embracing the principles of personalization and customization, product managers create opportunities for users to engage with the product in a more meaningful and immersive manner, thereby fostering a sense of excitement, exploration, and fulfillment.

Furthermore, the exploration of future trends represents a journey of continuous innovation and evolution—a recognition that the landscape of tailored experiences is dynamic and ever-changing. Product managers must remain vigilant, embracing a culture of experimentation, iteration, and adaptation to stay ahead of the curve and capitalize on emerging opportunities.

In essence, the exploration of future trends in tailored experiences embodies the convergence of vision and innovation—a fusion that transcends the limitations of the present to unlock new horizons of possibility and potential. By embracing the principles of future trends, product managers can chart a course towards a future where personalization and customization redefine the boundaries of user-centric innovation, driving engagement, satisfaction, and user loyalty in an increasingly dynamic and immersive digital landscape.

PRIVACY CONCERNS AND USER CONSENT

In the era of personalized and customized experiences, the ethical dimensions of user privacy and consent take center stage. This chapter delves into the nuanced landscape where product managers must navigate the fine line between tailoring experiences and safeguarding user privacy. It explores the challenges, considerations, and strategies for addressing privacy concerns while obtaining user consent for personalized and customized interactions.

The Balancing Act

As personalization and customization take center stage in the realm of product management, the chapter lays the groundwork by recognizing the intricate balancing act demanded. At its core, this balancing act revolves around achieving a harmonious equilibrium between tailoring experiences to suit user preferences while also safeguarding their privacy—a delicate dance that underpins the essence of this exploration.

Central to this exploration is the recognition that personalization and customization hold immense potential to enhance user experiences, driving engagement, satisfaction, and loyalty. However, this potential must be harnessed responsibly, with due consideration for the ethical implications and privacy concerns inherent in collecting and utilizing user data.

Moreover, this balancing act encompasses a multifaceted array of considerations, spanning from user consent and data transparency to the implementation of robust security measures and adherence to regulatory frameworks such as GDPR and CCPA. Product managers must navigate these complexities with finesse, ensuring that personalization efforts are aligned with users' expectations and comfort levels.

Furthermore, achieving the right equilibrium between personalization and privacy is not a one-time endeavor but an ongoing journey of refinement and adaptation. Product managers must embrace a culture of continuous learning and improvement, leveraging user feedback, and emerging best practices to fine-tune personalization strategies and privacy safeguards over time.

The transformative power of this balancing act lies in its ability to foster trust, transparency, and mutual respect between users and product providers. By prioritizing user privacy and consent while also delivering tailored experiences that meet users' needs and preferences, product managers can cultivate a sense of trust and loyalty that forms the bedrock of enduring customer relationships.

In essence, the exploration of the balancing act between personalization and privacy embodies the convergence of innovation and responsibility—a fusion that transcends the limitations of conventional approaches to product management, driving engagement, satisfaction, and user loyalty in an increasingly personalized and privacy-conscious digital landscape. By embracing the principles of this delicate balancing act, product managers can chart a course towards a future where personalized experiences coexist harmoniously with user privacy, fostering deep and lasting connections with their audience.

The Essence of User Privacy

In our journey through tailored experiences, this section embarks on a deep dive into the foundational principle of user privacy. It elucidates the critical importance of safeguarding personal information, delineating the boundaries that define sensitive data and underscoring the imperative of protecting it from unauthorized access, usage, and disclosure. By unpacking the essence of user privacy, we lay a solid groundwork for addressing concerns and navigating ethical considerations within the realm of tailored experiences.

At the heart of this exploration lies a profound recognition of the sanctity of personal information—a recognition that individuals possess a fundamental right to control and protect their own data. In an era marked by unprecedented digital interconnectedness, understanding the essence of user privacy becomes paramount, serving as a guiding principle for product managers as they navigate the complexities of personalized experiences.

Central to this understanding is a clear delineation of what constitutes personal information—a spectrum that encompasses a wide range of data points, from basic identifiers such as names and email addresses to more nuanced insights into user behaviors, preferences, and demographics. By recognizing the breadth and depth of personal information, product managers gain insight into the potential risks and implications associated with its collection, storage, and usage.

Moreover, understanding the essence of user privacy extends beyond mere compliance with regulatory requirements—it embodies a broader commitment to ethical stewardship and respect for individual autonomy. Product managers must go beyond the letter of the law, proactively implementing robust privacy safeguards and transparency measures to ensure that user data is treated with the utmost care and respect.

Furthermore, this understanding serves as a foundational framework for addressing concerns and mitigating risks within the realm of tailored experiences. By adopting a user-centric approach that prioritizes privacy by design, product managers can cultivate trust and confidence among users, fostering a culture of transparency and accountability that underpins the ethical use of personal information.

In essence, the exploration of user privacy embodies a fundamental recognition of the rights and responsibilities inherent in the digital age—a recognition that individuals have the right to control and protect their own data, and that product managers have a corresponding obligation to safeguard it. By embracing the principles of user privacy, product managers can navigate the complexities of tailored experiences with integrity and empathy, fostering deep and lasting relationships built on trust and respect.

The Ethical Imperative

In our exploration of tailored experiences, this chapter delves into the ethical dimensions that underpin privacy considerations, transcending mere legal obligations to embrace a broader imperative rooted in transparency, fairness, and user well-being. By examining the ethical dimensions of respecting user privacy, we shine a spotlight on the responsibility of product managers to navigate the complexities of personalized and customized interactions with integrity and empathy.

At its core, this exploration embodies a recognition that privacy considerations extend far beyond compliance with regulatory frameworks—they represent a moral imperative grounded in principles of respect, autonomy, and fairness. In an era marked by increasing digital interconnectedness, understanding the ethical imperative of privacy becomes paramount, serving as a guiding beacon for product managers as they navigate the ethical landscape of tailored experiences.

Central to this ethical imperative is a commitment to transparency—a commitment to providing users with clear and accessible information about how their data is collected, used, and shared. Product managers must go beyond mere legal requirements, proactively communicating with users in plain language and empowering them to make informed choices about their privacy preferences.

Moreover, embracing the ethical imperative of privacy requires a commitment to fairness and non-discrimination. Product managers must ensure that personalization and customization efforts do not inadvertently perpetuate biases or reinforce stereotypes, but rather strive to create inclusive and equitable experiences for all users, regardless of their background or identity.

Furthermore, prioritizing user well-being lies at the heart of the ethical imperative of privacy. Product managers must consider the potential impact of their actions on users' mental, emotional, and physical well-being, striving to create experiences that enhance rather than diminish quality of life. This may involve implementing privacy-enhancing features, providing users with control over their data, and offering support resources for those who may be adversely affected by personalized interactions.

In essence, the exploration of the ethical imperative of privacy embodies a fundamental recognition of the moral responsibilities inherent in the digital age—a recognition that product managers have a duty to uphold principles of transparency, fairness, and user well-being in their pursuit of tailored experiences. By embracing the ethical imperative of privacy, product managers can cultivate trust, foster empathy, and build relationships built on integrity and respect, paving the way for a more ethical and responsible digital future.

Regulatory Landscape

In the dynamic arena of product management, the evolving regulatory landscape surrounding user data protection stands as a pivotal force shaping industry practices. This section embarks on a comprehensive exploration of the key privacy regulations and frameworks that wield influence, such as the General Data Protection Regulation (GDPR) and the California Consumer Privacy Act (CCPA). By offering a detailed overview of these regulatory pillars, we illuminate the implications they hold for product managers, underscoring the critical importance of navigating this landscape with diligence and foresight.

At the heart of this exploration lies a recognition that privacy regulations are not mere legal requirements, but rather essential guardrails that safeguard user rights and promote responsible data stewardship. By delving into the intricacies of GDPR, CCPA, and other pertinent regulations, product managers gain insight into the principles and obligations that govern the collection, processing, and storage of user data.

Central to this understanding is a recognition of the principles enshrined within these regulations, including transparency, consent, and user control. Product managers must ensure that their practices align with these foundational principles, implementing robust mechanisms for obtaining user consent, providing clear and accessible privacy notices, and offering users meaningful options for managing their data.

Moreover, navigating the regulatory landscape requires a proactive approach to compliance and risk management. Product managers must stay abreast of evolving regulatory requirements, adapting their practices and policies accordingly to ensure ongoing compliance. This may involve conducting privacy impact assessments, appointing data protection officers, and implementing privacy by design principles throughout the product development lifecycle.

Furthermore, compliance with privacy regulations is not merely a legal obligation but also a cornerstone of building user trust and confidence. By demonstrating a commitment to privacy and data protection, product managers can cultivate a culture of trust and transparency, fostering deep and meaningful relationships with users built on a foundation of integrity and respect.

In essence, the exploration of the regulatory landscape surrounding user data protection embodies a recognition of the pivotal role that privacy regulations play in shaping product management practices. By embracing the principles and obligations outlined within these regulations, product managers can navigate the complexities of the regulatory terrain with confidence and integrity, ensuring compliance while building user trust and confidence in an increasingly data-driven world.

Informed Consent

Within the intricate landscape of personalized experiences, securing informed consent stands as a cornerstone principle. This section embarks on a comprehensive exploration of the concept of informed consent, delving deep into its significance and implications for both users and product managers alike. By shedding light on the importance of transparency and user empowerment, we underscore the pivotal role that informed consent plays in fostering trust and integrity within the realm of personalized interactions.

At the heart of this exploration lies a profound recognition of the fundamental right of users to have agency and control over their personal data. Informed consent serves as a mechanism through which users are empowered to make informed decisions regarding the collection, processing, and utilization of their data for personalization and customization purposes. Product managers bear the responsibility of ensuring that users are fully aware of how their data will be used and the implications thereof.

Central to the concept of informed consent is transparency— a commitment to providing clear and accessible information about data practices and privacy policies. Product managers must communicate in plain language, avoiding jargon and legalese, to ensure that users understand the implications of providing consent. This may involve providing detailed privacy notices, offering granular options for data sharing and usage, and facilitating mechanisms for users to revoke or modify their consent preferences.

Moreover, obtaining informed consent is not merely a legal requirement but also an ethical imperative. Product managers must cultivate a culture of respect and integrity, honoring users' autonomy and privacy preferences at all times. This involves seeking affirmative consent from users before collecting or utilizing their data for personalization purposes and respecting their choices and boundaries throughout the user journey.

Furthermore, obtaining informed consent is an ongoing process rather than a one-time event. Product managers must regularly review and update their consent mechanisms in response to changing user expectations, regulatory requirements, and technological advancements. By fostering a dynamic and responsive approach to informed consent, product managers can build trust and confidence among users, fostering a culture of transparency and accountability.

In essence, the exploration of informed consent embodies a recognition of the intrinsic value of user agency and autonomy within the realm of personalized experiences. By prioritizing transparency, user empowerment, and ethical stewardship, product managers can navigate the complexities of informed consent with integrity and empathy, fostering deep and meaningful relationships with users built on a foundation of trust and respect.

Communicating Privacy Policies Clearly

Within the realm of privacy management, transparent communication serves as a linchpin for addressing user concerns and fostering trust. This chapter delves into the critical importance of clear and accessible communication of privacy policies by product managers, illuminating how these efforts play a pivotal role in empowering users to make informed decisions about their personal information. By prioritizing transparency and accessibility, product managers can cultivate trust and confidence among users, laying a solid foundation for ethical data practices and personalized experiences.

At the heart of this discussion lies a profound recognition of the significance of privacy policies as a conduit for transparent communication. Privacy policies serve as a roadmap, outlining how user data will be collected, processed, and utilized within the context of personalized experiences. Product managers must ensure that these policies are articulated clearly and concisely, avoiding technical jargon and legalese that may obscure understanding.

Central to the communication of privacy policies is the use of accessible language that resonates with users across diverse backgrounds and levels of digital literacy. Product managers must employ plain language and intuitive formatting to convey complex concepts in a manner that is easily comprehensible to all users. This may involve breaking down information into digestible sections, providing examples or illustrations to clarify key points, and offering supplementary resources for users seeking further clarification.

Moreover, clear communication of privacy policies serves as a foundation for building trust and confidence among users. By demonstrating a commitment to transparency and accountability, product managers can instill a sense of confidence in users, assuring them that their personal information will be handled with care and respect. This, in turn, fosters a positive user experience and cultivates long-term relationships based on mutual trust and understanding.

Furthermore, communicating privacy policies clearly is not a one-time endeavor but an ongoing process of engagement and refinement. Product managers must actively solicit feedback from users and iterate on their communication strategies in response to evolving needs and expectations. By fostering a culture of continuous improvement and responsiveness, product managers can ensure that their privacy policies remain relevant and effective in safeguarding user privacy and trust.

In essence, the communication of privacy policies embodies a commitment to transparency, integrity, and user empowerment within the realm of personalized experiences. By prioritizing clear and accessible communication, product managers can build bridges of trust and understanding with users, laying the groundwork for ethical data practices and meaningful interactions that enrich the user experience.

Granular User Controls

In the ever-evolving landscape of digital interactions, empowering users with granular controls stands as a proactive and ethical strategy to safeguard privacy and foster user autonomy. This section embarks on an in-depth exploration of how product managers can implement sophisticated features that grant users precise control over their personalization settings. By offering a range of options, from specifying preferences to opting in or out of tailored features, users can navigate their digital experiences with confidence and assert control over the data shared for personalization.

At the heart of this discussion lies a profound recognition of the importance of user empowerment in the digital age. Granular user controls serve as a mechanism through which users can tailor their interactions with digital platforms to align with their unique preferences and privacy considerations. Product managers must design features that allow users to fine-tune their personalization settings, providing granular options to enable or disable specific features, adjust data sharing preferences, and customize the depth of personalization experienced.

Central to the implementation of granular user controls is the principle of transparency and user-centric design. Product managers must ensure that these controls are intuitive, accessible, and comprehensible to users of all levels of digital literacy. Clear explanations and tooltips should accompany each control, guiding users through their options and clarifying the implications of their choices. By prioritizing user education and empowerment, product managers can foster trust and confidence in the personalization process.

Moreover, granular user controls serve as a tangible manifestation of product managers' commitment to privacy by design principles. By embedding privacy controls directly into the user interface and experience, product managers demonstrate a proactive approach to privacy protection, allowing users to make informed decisions about their data sharing preferences in real time. This not only enhances user trust but also promotes a culture of transparency and accountability within digital ecosystems.

Furthermore, the implementation of granular user controls is an iterative process that requires continuous monitoring and refinement. Product managers should solicit user feedback and analyze usage patterns to identify areas for improvement and optimization. By incorporating user input into the design and functionality of granular controls, product managers can ensure that these features remain relevant, effective, and user-friendly in meeting the evolving needs and expectations of their user base.

In essence, the implementation of granular user controls represents a commitment to user empowerment, privacy protection, and ethical data practices within the realm of digital interactions. By offering users precise control over their personalization settings, product managers can foster a culture of trust, respect, and transparency, enriching the user experience and building lasting relationships based on mutual understanding and collaboration.

Privacy by Design

In the rapidly evolving digital landscape, the concept of privacy by design emerges as a fundamental principle for product managers to uphold. This section embarks on a comprehensive exploration of privacy by design, highlighting its pivotal role in promoting user privacy and data protection from the very inception of product development. By integrating privacy features into the core architecture and processes of their products, product managers can proactively address privacy concerns and cultivate a culture of trust and transparency.

At the heart of this discussion lies a profound recognition of the importance of embedding privacy considerations into the DNA of digital products. Privacy by design represents a proactive approach to privacy protection, where product managers prioritize user privacy and data security throughout the entire product development lifecycle. From conception to implementation, privacy features are seamlessly integrated into the core architecture and functionalities of the product, ensuring that user privacy is upheld as a foundational principle.

Central to the concept of privacy by design is the principle of proactive anticipation of privacy risks and challenges. Product managers must conduct thorough privacy impact assessments at each stage of product development, identifying potential privacy vulnerabilities and implementing robust safeguards to mitigate risks. By adopting a proactive mindset, product managers can preemptively address privacy concerns before they escalate, fostering a culture of privacy-conscious innovation and development.

Moreover, privacy by design encompasses a holistic approach to privacy protection, where privacy considerations are woven into every aspect of the product lifecycle. From data collection and processing to user authentication and access control, product managers must prioritize privacy at every touchpoint, ensuring that user data is handled with care and respect. By embedding privacy features into the core architecture and processes of their products, product managers can demonstrate a commitment to ethical data practices and user-centric design.

Furthermore, privacy by design promotes transparency and accountability within digital ecosystems. Product managers must communicate openly with users about privacy practices and provide clear explanations of how their data will be used and protected. By fostering transparency and trust, product managers can empower users to make informed decisions about their privacy preferences and build long-lasting relationships based on mutual respect and understanding.

In essence, privacy by design embodies a commitment to user privacy and data protection from the very inception of product development. By integrating privacy features into the core architecture and processes of their products, product managers can foster a culture of privacy-conscious innovation, transparency, and trust, laying a solid foundation for ethical data practices and user-centric design in the digital age.

Anonymization and Aggregation Techniques

In the intricate landscape of digital interactions, safeguarding user privacy stands as a paramount concern for product managers. This section embarks on a detailed exploration of anonymization and aggregation techniques, shedding light on how these sophisticated methods enable the extraction of valuable insights while preserving individual identities. By striking a delicate balance between personalization and anonymity, product managers can effectively mitigate privacy concerns and foster a culture of trust and transparency within their digital ecosystems.

At the core of this discussion lies a profound recognition of the importance of balancing personalization with privacy protection. Anonymization and aggregation techniques serve as powerful tools for product managers to uphold user privacy while still harnessing the power of data-driven insights. These methods involve obscuring or combining individual-level data points to prevent the identification of specific individuals, thereby safeguarding their privacy while still allowing for valuable analysis and decision-making.

Central to the concept of anonymization is the principle of irreversibility—ensuring that anonymized data cannot be feasibly linked back to individual users. Product managers must employ robust anonymization techniques, such as data masking, tokenization, or differential privacy, to ensure the anonymity of user data while preserving its utility for analysis and modeling. By anonymizing sensitive information, product managers can protect user privacy without compromising the quality or integrity of the data.

Moreover, aggregation techniques involve combining individual data points into larger, aggregated datasets to conceal individual identities while still enabling analysis at a group level. Product managers can aggregate data by summarizing or averaging individual values, grouping users into cohorts or segments, or applying statistical methods to derive aggregate insights. By aggregating data, product managers can glean valuable trends and patterns while protecting the anonymity of individual users.

Furthermore, striking the right balance between personalization and anonymity is crucial for mitigating privacy concerns and fostering user trust. Product managers must carefully consider the level of granularity required for personalization while ensuring that individual identities remain sufficiently protected. By implementing transparent data handling practices and providing clear explanations of anonymization and aggregation methods, product managers can reassure users of their commitment to privacy protection.

In essence, anonymization and aggregation techniques represent a sophisticated approach to privacy preservation in the digital age. By employing these advanced methods, product managers can extract valuable insights from user data while upholding the principles of privacy and data protection. By striking a delicate balance between personalization and anonymity, product managers can foster a culture of trust, transparency, and ethical data practices within their digital ecosystems, laying a solid foundation for sustainable growth and innovation.

Regular Audits and Compliance Checks

In the dynamic landscape of digital privacy, maintaining ongoing compliance with regulatory standards emerges as a paramount responsibility for product managers. This section embarks on an exhaustive exploration of the significance of conducting regular audits and compliance checks to ensure adherence to privacy regulations. By delving into the importance of privacy assessments, staying informed about evolving regulations, and adapting product management strategies accordingly, product managers can foster a culture of continuous improvement in privacy practices, thereby fortifying user trust and confidence.

At the core of this discussion lies a profound recognition of the evolving nature of privacy regulations and the need for proactive measures to ensure compliance. Regular audits serve as a crucial mechanism for product managers to assess the effectiveness of their privacy practices and identify areas for improvement. By conducting comprehensive privacy assessments at regular intervals, product managers can proactively identify and address potential privacy risks and vulnerabilities, thereby mitigating compliance issues before they escalate.

Central to the concept of regular audits is the principle of ongoing vigilance and adaptability. Product managers must stay abreast of evolving privacy regulations and industry best practices, continuously updating their privacy policies and procedures to reflect the latest requirements. By remaining proactive and responsive to changes in the regulatory landscape, product managers can ensure that their products maintain compliance with applicable laws and standards, thereby safeguarding user privacy and trust.

Moreover, regular audits foster a culture of continuous improvement in privacy practices within organizations. By establishing a regular cadence of audits and compliance checks, product managers can instill a sense of accountability and responsibility for privacy throughout the organization. These audits provide opportunities for collaboration and knowledge sharing across teams, promoting a holistic approach to privacy management and risk mitigation.

Furthermore, regular audits serve as a proactive measure to enhance transparency and accountability in privacy practices. By documenting audit findings and remediation efforts, product managers can demonstrate their commitment to privacy compliance to stakeholders, regulators, and users alike. Transparent communication about privacy practices builds trust and confidence among users, fostering stronger relationships and promoting a culture of privacy-conscious innovation.

In essence, regular audits and compliance checks represent a cornerstone of effective privacy management in the digital age. By conducting comprehensive privacy assessments, staying informed about regulatory developments, and fostering a culture of continuous improvement, product managers can uphold the principles of privacy and data protection, thereby fostering trust, transparency, and accountability within their digital ecosystems.

User Education and Empowerment

In the ever-evolving landscape of digital privacy, educating and empowering users emerge as pivotal strategies for addressing privacy concerns and fostering a culture of trust and transparency. This section embarks on an exhaustive exploration of user education and empowerment, shedding light on various strategies product managers can employ to raise awareness about privacy practices and empower users to make informed decisions.

At the heart of this discussion lies a profound recognition of the importance of transparency and communication in building user trust. User education encompasses a range of strategies aimed at providing users with clear and accessible information about privacy practices and their rights. Product managers can leverage various channels, including clear documentation, interactive tutorials, and user-friendly interfaces, to guide users in understanding and managing their privacy settings effectively.

Central to the concept of user education is the principle of clarity and accessibility. Product managers must ensure that privacy policies and procedures are communicated in clear and understandable language, avoiding technical jargon and complexity. By providing users with accessible information about how their data is collected, used, and protected, product managers can empower them to make informed decisions about their privacy preferences.

Moreover, interactive tutorials and user-friendly interfaces serve as valuable tools for engaging users in privacy education. Product managers can develop interactive guides and walkthroughs that explain key privacy concepts and demonstrate how to navigate privacy settings effectively. By offering hands-on learning experiences, product managers can empower users to take control of their privacy and customize their digital experiences according to their preferences.

Furthermore, ongoing communication and engagement are essential for sustaining user education initiatives. Product managers can utilize email newsletters, in-app notifications, and social media updates to keep users informed about privacy updates, security enhancements, and best practices. By fostering a dialogue with users, product managers can demonstrate their commitment to transparency and accountability in privacy management.

In essence, user education and empowerment represent integral components of effective privacy management in the digital age. By providing users with clear and accessible information about privacy practices, leveraging interactive tutorials and user-friendly interfaces, and fostering ongoing communication and engagement, product managers can empower users to make informed decisions about their privacy, thereby fostering trust, transparency, and accountability within their digital ecosystems.

Building Trust Through Transparent Practices

As the chapter draws to a close, it underscores the fundamental importance of transparency in cultivating and nurturing trust between product managers and users within the realm of personalized and customized experiences. Transparent practices, ranging from clear communication to robust user controls and ethical data handling, serve as the bedrock upon which trust is built and maintained in the digital landscape.

At the heart of this conclusion lies a profound acknowledgment of the delicate balance between personalization and privacy, and the pivotal role of product managers as guardians of ethical and transparent practices. In an era where user expectations for tailored experiences are higher than ever, product managers must navigate this intricate terrain with integrity and responsibility, ensuring that personalized interactions are not only delightful for users but also respectful of their privacy rights and choices.

Central to the concept of transparency is the principle of clear and accessible communication. Product managers must provide users with comprehensive information about how their data is collected, used, and protected, employing language that is easy to understand and free from ambiguity. By fostering transparency in data practices, product managers can empower users to make informed decisions about their privacy and cultivate a sense of trust and confidence in their digital interactions.

Moreover, robust user controls serve as a cornerstone of transparency and user empowerment. Product managers must provide users with granular controls over their privacy settings, allowing them to customize their experiences according to their preferences and comfort levels. By offering users the ability to opt in or out of personalized features, manage their data preferences, and access clear explanations of privacy policies, product managers can foster a culture of trust and transparency within their digital ecosystems.

Furthermore, ethical data handling practices are essential for maintaining transparency and trust. Product managers must adhere to principles of fairness, accountability, and respect for user rights throughout the data lifecycle, from collection and storage to processing and sharing. By prioritizing user privacy and consent, product managers can demonstrate their commitment to ethical values and build lasting relationships of trust with their users.

In essence, the conclusion emphasizes the critical importance of transparency and ethical practices in building and maintaining trust within the realm of personalized experiences. As product managers navigate the complexities of personalization and customization, they must remain steadfast in their dedication to transparency, integrity, and user empowerment, thereby fostering a culture of trust and mutual respect in the digital landscape.

7. COLLABORATION AND COMMUNICATION IN AI-DRIVEN TEAMS

BUILDING CROSS-FUNCTIONAL TEAMS FOR AI PRODUCTS

As the development of AI products becomes increasingly interdisciplinary, the importance of effective collaboration and communication within cross-functional teams is paramount. This chapter explores the intricacies of building and managing teams that bring together diverse expertise to harness the full potential of AI. It delves into the strategies, challenges, and best practices for fostering a collaborative environment that propels AI product development forward.

The Evolution of Cross-functional Collaboration

As we embark on this chapter, we delve into the dynamic evolution of cross-functional collaboration within the realm of AI-driven teams. Our journey begins with a retrospective glance, acknowledging the historical trajectory that has led us to the current landscape of interdisciplinary cooperation in AI product development.

Traditionally, teams operated within siloed structures, with each discipline confined to its own realm of expertise. Engineers focused solely on technical aspects, while designers honed their craft in isolation, and marketers pursued strategies devoid of technical input. However, the advent of AI technologies has shattered these barriers, necessitating a paradigm shift towards collaborative frameworks that transcend disciplinary boundaries.

373

We witness the emergence of a new ethos—one defined by the recognition of the interconnectedness and interdependence of various disciplines. In today's AI-driven landscape, success hinges upon the seamless integration of diverse perspectives, skill sets, and methodologies. Engineers collaborate closely with designers to ensure that technical advancements are harmoniously aligned with user-centric design principles. Marketers leverage insights from data scientists to craft strategies that resonate with target audiences on a deeper level.

This evolution is not merely a matter of convenience; it is a strategic imperative driven by the inherent complexity of AI products. The intricate interplay between data science, engineering, design, and marketing demands a holistic approach that transcends traditional boundaries. Cross-functional collaboration is no longer a luxury but a necessity for unlocking the full potential of AI-driven innovation.

As we navigate through this chapter, we will explore the intricacies of cross-functional collaboration within AI-driven teams. We will delve into the challenges and opportunities that arise when individuals with diverse backgrounds come together to tackle complex problems. Moreover, we will uncover strategies for fostering a culture of collaboration, where mutual respect, open communication, and shared objectives form the bedrock of success.

In essence, the evolution of cross-functional collaboration within AI-driven teams represents a transformative journey—one that transcends disciplinary constraints and unleashes the collective genius of diverse minds. Together, let us embark on this exploration and discover the boundless possibilities that await us at the intersection of collaboration and innovation.

The Multifaceted Nature of AI Projects

Embarking on an AI project is akin to setting sail into a sea of complexity, where the waters are teeming with diverse challenges and opportunities. At the heart of these endeavors lies a multifaceted landscape that demands a convergence of disparate skill sets, each contributing a vital piece to the puzzle of innovation.

Central to the success of AI projects is the recognition of their inherently multidimensional nature. These projects transcend the boundaries of traditional disciplines, drawing upon a rich tapestry of expertise spanning data science, machine learning, software engineering, user experience design, and domain-specific knowledge.

In the realm of data science, practitioners grapple with the intricacies of data collection, cleaning, and analysis, harnessing the power of algorithms to extract meaningful insights from vast troves of information. Meanwhile, machine learning experts delve into the realm of predictive modeling, seeking to uncover patterns and relationships that drive intelligent decision-making.

Complementing these technical endeavors are the skills of software engineers, who translate algorithmic innovations into scalable, efficient systems capable of handling real-world data streams with ease. User experience designers play a pivotal role in ensuring that AI-powered solutions are not only functional but also intuitive and user-friendly, crafting interfaces that facilitate seamless interaction between humans and machines.

Furthermore, domain expertise brings invaluable context to AI projects, guiding the development of solutions that are tailored to the unique needs and challenges of specific industries or applications. Whether in healthcare, finance, retail, or beyond, domain experts provide invaluable insights that inform the design and implementation of AI systems.

Amidst this diverse array of skills and perspectives, cross-functional teams emerge as the linchpin of success in AI projects. By bringing together individuals with varied backgrounds and expertise, these teams are uniquely equipped to tackle the multifaceted challenges that characterize AI innovation. Collaboration becomes not merely a choice but a necessity, as each member contributes their unique insights and capabilities towards a shared vision of excellence.

Forming the Cross-Functional AI Team

Assembling a cross-functional AI team is akin to orchestrating a symphony, where each instrument contributes its unique timbre to create a harmonious whole. Within this ensemble, diversity reigns supreme, with a rich tapestry of skills and expertise converging to tackle the multifaceted challenges of AI innovation.

At the heart of the ensemble are the data scientists, the virtuosos of analysis and modeling who wield statistical tools and machine learning algorithms with finesse. These individuals possess a deep understanding of data structures, predictive modeling techniques, and statistical inference, allowing them to distill insights from complex datasets and unlock the hidden patterns that underlie intelligent decision-making.

Complementing the data scientists are the engineers, the architects of AI systems who translate algorithmic innovations into scalable, robust solutions. Armed with expertise in software development and system architecture, these individuals design and implement the infrastructure necessary to operationalize AI models in real-world settings, ensuring that they perform reliably and efficiently under diverse conditions.

No AI team would be complete without the UX/UI designers, the artists who sculpt the interface through which humans interact with intelligent systems. Drawing upon principles of user-centered design and human-computer interaction, these individuals craft intuitive, aesthetically pleasing interfaces that facilitate seamless communication between users and machines, enhancing both usability and satisfaction.

Domain experts bring invaluable context to the team, offering deep insights into the specific industry or application domain in which the AI solution will operate. Whether in healthcare, finance, retail, or beyond, these individuals provide critical domain knowledge that informs the design and implementation of AI systems, ensuring that they are tailored to meet the unique needs and challenges of their intended users.

Rounding out the ensemble are the communication specialists, the conduits through which the team's insights and innovations are shared with the world. These individuals possess exceptional written and verbal communication skills, distilling complex technical concepts into clear, compelling narratives that resonate with both internal stakeholders and external audiences.

In the crucible of collaboration, these diverse talents converge, each contributing their unique perspective and expertise towards a shared goal of excellence in AI innovation. By fostering an environment of open communication, mutual respect, and shared purpose, cross-functional AI teams harness the collective power of diversity to tackle the most pressing challenges of our time.

The Role of Leadership in Cross-Functional Teams

At the helm of every cross-functional AI team stands a leader, a conductor who orchestrates the collective efforts of diverse talents toward a common vision of excellence. Leadership in the context of AI projects transcends mere management—it embodies a deep understanding of the intricacies of interdisciplinary collaboration, a keen awareness of the evolving landscape of AI technologies, and a steadfast commitment to fostering an inclusive, innovative culture.

Effective leaders within cross-functional AI teams exhibit a multifaceted array of attributes that enable them to navigate the complexities of AI projects with grace and agility. Foremost among these attributes is vision—an unwavering clarity of purpose that inspires and guides team members toward ambitious yet attainable goals. Leaders articulate a compelling narrative that defines the mission of the team, aligns with organizational objectives, and imbues every member with a sense of purpose and direction.

In addition to vision, effective leaders demonstrate adeptness in communication—a mastery of both articulating their own ideas and actively listening to the perspectives of others. Through clear, transparent communication, leaders foster an environment of open dialogue where ideas are freely exchanged, feedback is constructively given and received, and diverse viewpoints are valued and respected.

Crucially, leadership in cross-functional AI teams requires a keen understanding of the unique dynamics that characterize interdisciplinary collaboration. Leaders recognize and celebrate the diversity of talents and perspectives within their team, leveraging each individual's strengths to maximize collective impact. They cultivate an ethos of mutual respect, trust, and empathy, fostering a culture where every team member feels valued, supported, and empowered to contribute their best work.

Moreover, effective leaders possess a profound technical acumen—a deep understanding of AI technologies and methodologies that enables them to provide informed guidance and direction to their team. Whether grappling with complex algorithmic challenges, navigating the intricacies of data architecture, or evaluating the feasibility of technical solutions, leaders leverage their expertise to make sound, data-driven decisions that propel the team toward success.

Beyond technical prowess, leadership in cross-functional AI teams demands resilience, adaptability, and a willingness to embrace ambiguity. Leaders navigate the inevitable setbacks and uncertainties of AI projects with grace and fortitude, rallying their team in the face of adversity and inspiring confidence in the path forward.

Establishing Clear Communication Channels

Within the intricate tapestry of cross-functional AI teams, effective communication serves as the vital conduit through which ideas are shared, insights are exchanged, and progress is propelled forward. This section embarks on a journey into the heart of communication within AI teams, exploring the critical importance of establishing clear channels that facilitate seamless information flow and foster collaboration across diverse disciplines.

At the nucleus of effective communication lies the recognition of diversity—not only in skills and expertise but also in communication styles and preferences. Leaders within AI teams understand that each team member brings a unique perspective and voice to the table, and thus, they embrace a culture of inclusivity that celebrates this diversity. By acknowledging and accommodating different communication styles—be it through written documentation, verbal discussions, visual presentations, or interactive workshops—leaders ensure that every team member feels empowered to communicate effectively and contribute meaningfully to the collective dialogue.

Central to the establishment of clear communication channels is the cultivation of transparency and accessibility. Leaders create an environment where information is shared openly, decisions are communicated promptly, and feedback is solicited and welcomed. Whether through regular team meetings, project management tools, or collaborative platforms, leaders ensure that critical information is disseminated in a timely and transparent manner, enabling team members to stay informed, aligned, and engaged.

Moreover, effective communication within AI teams extends beyond the boundaries of individual disciplines—it encompasses the seamless integration of diverse perspectives and expertise. Leaders foster cross-disciplinary collaboration by creating opportunities for interdisciplinary dialogue, encouraging knowledge sharing and cross-training initiatives, and facilitating collaborative problem-solving sessions. By breaking down silos and promoting a culture of interdisciplinary collaboration, leaders harness the collective intelligence of the team, unlocking innovative solutions to complex challenges.

Furthermore, establishing clear communication channels within AI teams entails the judicious use of technology and tools that facilitate collaboration and information sharing. From project management platforms and communication apps to version control systems and collaborative document repositories, leaders leverage a diverse array of tools to streamline communication processes, enhance productivity, and foster a culture of knowledge sharing and collaboration.

Breaking Down Silos

Silos, like impenetrable barriers, have long been recognized as formidable obstacles to effective collaboration within cross-functional teams. In this section, we embark on a journey to explore the nuanced strategies and transformative practices that facilitate the breakdown of silos, nurturing an environment where collaboration flourishes, and the flow of information becomes unimpeded.

At the heart of dismantling silos lies the cultivation of a shared sense of purpose—a collective mission that transcends individual disciplines and unites team members in pursuit of a common goal. Leaders within cross-functional teams articulate a compelling vision, one that resonates with the diverse talents and perspectives represented within the team, igniting a sense of collective purpose and shared ownership of the project's success.

Moreover, breaking down silos necessitates the creation of spaces and platforms for open dialogue and knowledge sharing. Leaders foster a culture of transparency and inclusivity, where team members are encouraged to voice their ideas, share their expertise, and collaborate on problem-solving initiatives. Whether through regular team meetings, cross-disciplinary workshops, or collaborative brainstorming sessions, leaders create opportunities for cross-pollination of ideas and the exchange of insights across diverse disciplines.

Furthermore, breaking down silos entails the cultivation of trust and mutual respect among team members. Leaders foster an environment where individuals feel valued, respected, and empowered to contribute their unique perspectives and insights. By fostering a culture of psychological safety, where team members feel comfortable expressing their ideas, challenging assumptions, and engaging in constructive debate, leaders create the conditions for collaboration to thrive and silos to crumble.

In addition, technology serves as a powerful enabler in breaking down silos within cross-functional teams. Leaders leverage collaboration tools, project management platforms, and communication apps to facilitate information sharing, streamline workflows, and foster real-time collaboration across geographies and time zones. Through the judicious use of technology, leaders create a digital ecosystem that transcends organizational boundaries, enabling seamless collaboration and knowledge sharing among team members.

Collaborative Ideation and Problem-Solving

In the realm of AI projects, where complexity reigns and innovation is paramount, the art of collaborative ideation and problem-solving emerges as a linchpin for success. In this section, we embark on a journey to unravel the dynamic methodologies and transformative practices that underpin collaborative ideation and problem-solving within cross-functional teams, igniting a symphony of creativity and innovation that transcends disciplinary boundaries.

At the core of collaborative ideation and problem-solving lies the recognition of diversity as a catalyst for innovation. Leaders within cross-functional teams cultivate an environment where diverse perspectives converge, fostering a rich tapestry of ideas and insights that fuel the creative process. Through structured brainstorming sessions, design thinking workshops, and hackathons, team members are encouraged to explore unconventional ideas, challenge existing paradigms, and push the boundaries of conventional thinking.

Moreover, collaborative ideation and problem-solving entail the cultivation of a culture of constructive critique and feedback. Team members engage in spirited debates, offering perspectives, and insights that enrich the creative process and refine solutions iteratively. Through the judicious use of techniques such as peer reviews, design critiques, and cross-disciplinary feedback loops, team members collectively elevate their ideas, transforming raw concepts into refined solutions that embody the collective wisdom of the team.

Furthermore, collaborative ideation and problem-solving embrace the principles of co-creation and co-design. Team members from diverse disciplines collaborate closely, leveraging their respective expertise and insights to co-create solutions that transcend individual perspectives. By engaging in co-design workshops, collaborative prototyping sessions, and cross-disciplinary design sprints, team members harness the power of collective intelligence, weaving together disparate threads of expertise into cohesive solutions that address complex challenges holistically.

In addition, technology serves as a powerful enabler in collaborative ideation and problem-solving within cross-functional teams. Leaders leverage collaborative tools, virtual whiteboards, and digital brainstorming platforms to facilitate real-time collaboration and idea sharing across geographies and time zones. Through the seamless integration of technology into the creative process, team members transcend physical barriers, fostering a culture of virtual collaboration that transcends organizational boundaries.

Agile Methodologies for AI Teams

In the ever-evolving landscape of AI development, where uncertainty is the norm and innovation is relentless, the adoption of Agile methodologies emerges as a beacon of guidance for cross-functional teams. This section embarks on a comprehensive exploration of how Agile principles serve as a compass for navigating the complexities of AI projects, empowering teams to embrace change, iterate rapidly, and deliver value with unparalleled efficiency and agility.

At the heart of Agile methodologies lies the ethos of iterative development, a fundamental principle that resonates deeply within the realm of AI teams. Rather than adhering to rigid, linear processes, Agile encourages teams to embrace flexibility and responsiveness, iterating through cycles of experimentation, learning, and adaptation. Through practices such as Scrum, Kanban, and Lean, AI teams embark on a journey of continuous improvement, refining their approaches, and solutions iteratively to meet the evolving needs of the project and stakeholders.

Furthermore, Agile methodologies champion the spirit of collaboration and cross-functional teamwork, fostering a culture where communication flows freely, and expertise is shared generously. In the context of AI teams, where diverse skill sets converge, Agile principles catalyze synergy, enabling data scientists, engineers, designers, and domain experts to collaborate seamlessly towards a common goal. Through practices such as daily stand-ups, sprint planning meetings, and retrospectives, Agile teams synchronize their efforts, aligning their actions with the overarching objectives of the project.

Moreover, Agile methodologies emphasize the importance of customer-centricity and responsiveness to feedback, principles that resonate deeply within the context of AI development. By prioritizing customer value and feedback, Agile teams ensure that their solutions remain aligned with user needs and preferences, delivering tangible value with each iteration. Through practices such as user story mapping, acceptance criteria definition, and user testing, Agile teams glean invaluable insights from end-users, refining their solutions iteratively to maximize customer satisfaction and impact.

In addition, Agile methodologies embrace the principles of adaptability and resilience, equipping AI teams with the tools and mindset to navigate uncertainty and change with confidence. By embracing the concept of "inspect and adapt," Agile teams continuously evaluate their approaches, pivot when necessary, and course-correct in response to emerging challenges and opportunities. Through practices such as backlog grooming, sprint reviews, and incremental delivery, Agile teams maintain a relentless focus on delivering value iteratively, adapting their strategies to the evolving realities of the project landscape.

Overcoming Interdisciplinary Challenges

Interdisciplinary collaboration within cross-functional AI teams heralds a new era of innovation, where diverse expertise converges to unlock the full potential of AI-driven solutions. Yet, amidst the promise of synergy lies a terrain fraught with challenges stemming from differences in language, methodologies, and expectations. This section embarks on a journey of exploration, delving into the common challenges encountered within cross-functional AI teams and proposing robust strategies for overcoming these hurdles, fostering an environment where mutual understanding and appreciation for diverse perspectives thrive.

One of the foremost challenges in interdisciplinary collaboration within AI teams lies in the divergence of language and terminology across disciplines. Engineers may speak in the language of algorithms and code, while data scientists navigate the realm of statistical models and machine learning algorithms. Designers, on the other hand, are fluent in the language of user experience and interface design. Bridging these linguistic divides requires proactive communication and a willingness to translate concepts and ideas across disciplines. Through initiatives such as cross-disciplinary workshops, knowledge-sharing sessions, and the establishment of a shared glossary of terms, AI teams can foster a common lexicon that facilitates seamless communication and understanding.

Furthermore, differences in methodologies and approaches can pose significant challenges to interdisciplinary collaboration within AI teams. Engineers may favor a structured, systematic approach to problem-solving, while data scientists thrive in the realm of experimentation and exploration. Designers, meanwhile, prioritize user-centric design thinking methodologies. Harmonizing these disparate methodologies requires a spirit of openness and adaptability, where team members are encouraged to embrace diverse approaches and leverage the strengths of each discipline. By adopting a hybrid approach that integrates elements of agile development, design thinking, and lean methodologies, AI teams can navigate the complexities of interdisciplinary collaboration with agility and resilience.

Moreover, interdisciplinary collaboration within AI teams can be hindered by divergent expectations and priorities. Engineers may prioritize technical feasibility and scalability, while data scientists focus on model accuracy and performance metrics. Designers, meanwhile, advocate for user empathy and aesthetic appeal. Aligning these divergent expectations requires a shared understanding of the project goals and a commitment to collective success. By fostering a culture of empathy, respect, and shared ownership, AI teams can transcend disciplinary boundaries, rallying around a common vision and purpose.

In addition, the distributed nature of interdisciplinary AI teams, often spanning different geographical locations and time zones, can further exacerbate collaboration challenges. Virtual collaboration tools, such as video conferencing, collaborative document editing platforms, and project management software, become indispensable allies in overcoming these logistical hurdles. By leveraging technology to facilitate seamless communication and collaboration, AI teams can bridge geographical divides and harness the collective intelligence of distributed talent pools.

Continuous Learning and Skill Development

In the dynamic landscape of AI, where technologies and methodologies evolve at breakneck speed, the imperative for continuous learning and skill development within cross-functional teams cannot be overstated. This section embarks on a journey of exploration, delving into the significance of ongoing skill enhancement, knowledge dissemination, and staying abreast of industry advancements to ensure that AI teams not only keep pace with the rapid evolution of technology but also pioneer innovation at the vanguard of the field.

At the heart of continuous learning within cross-functional AI teams lies a commitment to staying abreast of the latest advancements and trends in AI technologies and methodologies. Whether it's the emergence of novel machine learning algorithms, advancements in natural language processing, or breakthroughs in computer vision, AI teams must remain vigilant in their pursuit of knowledge. By actively engaging with industry publications, attending conferences and workshops, and participating in online forums and discussion groups, team members can cultivate a deep understanding of the ever-changing AI landscape, empowering them to anticipate trends, embrace innovation, and drive transformative change.

Moreover, continuous learning within cross-functional AI teams extends beyond technical proficiency to encompass interdisciplinary skills and competencies. Engineers may benefit from gaining insights into data science principles, while data scientists may find value in understanding software engineering practices. Designers, meanwhile, can enhance their skill set by delving into UX/UI design methodologies. By fostering a culture of cross-disciplinary learning and knowledge sharing, AI teams can leverage the collective expertise of diverse talent pools, enriching their capabilities and fostering innovation at the intersection of disciplines.

Furthermore, continuous learning within cross-functional AI teams necessitates a commitment to personal and professional development at both the individual and organizational levels. From structured training programs and workshops to mentorship initiatives and peer-to-peer learning opportunities, AI teams must provide avenues for team members to expand their skill sets, deepen their expertise, and pursue their professional aspirations. By investing in the growth and development of their talent, organizations cultivate a culture of excellence, empowerment, and continuous improvement, propelling AI teams towards greater heights of achievement and innovation.

In addition, continuous learning within cross-functional AI teams is intrinsically linked to the ethos of experimentation and exploration. From hackathons and innovation challenges to sandbox environments and proof-of-concept projects, AI teams must provide avenues for hands-on experimentation and learning-by-doing. By encouraging a culture of curiosity, creativity, and calculated risk-taking, organizations foster an environment where team members are empowered to push the boundaries of what's possible, driving innovation and discovery at the forefront of AI.

Case Studies in Successful Collaboration

As we venture into the heart of this chapter, we are greeted by a tapestry of real-world case studies that vividly illustrate the transformative power of collaboration within cross-functional AI teams. These case studies serve as beacons of inspiration, illuminating the path towards success by showcasing how diverse expertise, effective communication, and collaborative approaches converge to propel AI projects to new heights across a myriad of industries and contexts.

In the realm of healthcare, we encounter a case study that exemplifies the symbiotic relationship between data scientists, healthcare professionals, and software engineers in the development of AI-driven diagnostic tools. By leveraging their respective expertise and insights, this cross-functional team navigated the complexities of medical data, algorithm development, and regulatory compliance to deliver groundbreaking solutions that revolutionized patient care and clinical decision-making.

Turning our gaze towards the realm of finance, we uncover a case study that underscores the pivotal role of collaboration between data analysts, risk management experts, and UX/UI designers in the development of AI-powered financial platforms. Through seamless communication, iterative feedback loops, and a shared commitment to excellence, this cross-functional team navigated the intricacies of algorithmic trading, fraud detection, and customer experience optimization, driving tangible value for clients and stakeholders alike.

In the realm of e-commerce, we encounter a case study that highlights the synergy between data scientists, marketing strategists, and customer experience specialists in the development of AI-driven recommendation engines. By harnessing the power of machine learning algorithms, user behavior analytics, and personalized content delivery, this cross-functional team curated tailored shopping experiences that captivated consumers, boosted engagement, and fostered brand loyalty.

Future Trends in Cross-Functional Collaboration for AI Products

As we draw the curtains on this chapter, our gaze extends towards the horizon, where the future of cross-functional collaboration within the AI domain beckons with promise and possibility. In this final section, we embark on a journey of exploration, delving into the emerging trends, practices, and technologies that are poised to redefine the landscape of interdisciplinary teamwork, offering a tantalizing glimpse into the evolving nature of collaboration in the realm of AI.

At the forefront of these future trends is the integration of cutting-edge technologies such as augmented reality (AR) and virtual reality (VR) into collaborative workflows, enabling team members to engage in immersive, virtual environments that transcend geographical boundaries. Through the lens of AR and VR, cross-functional AI teams will navigate projects with unprecedented fluidity, seamlessly sharing ideas, visualizing data, and co-creating solutions in a digital realm that blurs the lines between physical and virtual spaces.

Furthermore, the rise of advanced collaboration platforms powered by artificial intelligence and natural language processing promises to revolutionize the way cross-functional teams communicate and collaborate. These AI-driven platforms will facilitate real-time collaboration, automate mundane tasks, and provide intelligent insights to enhance decision-making, empowering teams to work more efficiently and effectively towards their shared goals.

Additionally, the advent of blockchain technology holds the potential to transform the way cross-functional teams manage and share data securely. By leveraging blockchain-based systems, teams can ensure the integrity, transparency, and traceability of data throughout the collaboration process, mitigating the risks of data breaches and unauthorized access while fostering trust and accountability among team members.

COMMUNICATING COMPLEX AI CONCEPTS TO NON-TECHNICAL STAKEHOLDERS

In the intricate landscape of AI-driven projects, effective communication is a linchpin for success. This chapter explores the nuances of conveying complex AI concepts to non-technical stakeholders, illuminating the strategies, challenges, and best practices for facilitating clear and meaningful dialogue between technical and non-technical team members.

Bridging the Communication Gap

Our chapter unfurls with a critical gaze towards the communication fissure that frequently separates the realm of technical expertise from the domain of non-technical stakeholders within AI teams. We embark on this journey with a steadfast commitment to bridging this gap, recognizing its pivotal role in fostering alignment, transparency, and a unified understanding across the entire spectrum of the AI project lifecycle.

At its core, the communication gap stems from the disparity in language, knowledge, and perspective between technical experts, such as data scientists and engineers, and non-technical stakeholders, including business leaders, marketers, and end-users. This disconnect often manifests in misaligned expectations, misinterpretations of technical jargon, and a lack of clarity regarding project objectives, requirements, and constraints.

To address this challenge head-on, our chapter sets forth a comprehensive roadmap for building sturdy bridges of communication that span the divide between technical and non-technical realms. We advocate for the establishment of common ground, where technical concepts are demystified, and non-technical stakeholders are empowered to engage meaningfully in discussions about AI projects.

Furthermore, we champion the cultivation of a culture of openness, where transparent communication flows freely between all members of the AI team, regardless of their technical acumen. Through clear and concise dialogue, we strive to dismantle the barriers that impede collaboration and hinder progress, paving the way for shared understanding and collective action.

Moreover, our chapter explores innovative communication strategies and tools that facilitate cross-disciplinary dialogue and collaboration within AI teams. From visualization techniques that transform complex data into intuitive insights to storytelling frameworks that convey technical concepts in relatable narratives, we embrace a multifaceted approach to communication that speaks to the diverse needs and preferences of team members.

Understanding the Audience

Effective communication is not merely about conveying information—it's about forging meaningful connections that resonate with the hearts and minds of the audience. Our chapter sets sail on a transformative journey of audience understanding, recognizing that the key to successful communication lies in embracing the diverse backgrounds, interests, and perspectives of non-technical stakeholders within AI teams.

To embark on this journey, we first delve into the rich tapestry of our audience's backgrounds, recognizing that they hail from a myriad of disciplines, including business, marketing, sales, and customer support. Each member brings a unique set of experiences, knowledge, and priorities to the table, shaping their perspectives and expectations regarding AI projects.

Next, we venture into the labyrinth of our audience's interests, recognizing that they are driven by a myriad of motivations, ranging from business objectives and market trends to customer needs and user experiences. By unraveling the intricacies of their interests, we gain valuable insights into the topics, themes, and narratives that are most likely to capture their attention and engage their intellect.

Furthermore, we navigate the landscape of our audience's perspectives, acknowledging that they perceive AI projects through different lenses, shaped by their roles, responsibilities, and areas of expertise. Some may approach projects with a strategic mindset, focusing on long-term goals and business outcomes, while others may adopt a more tactical approach, honing in on specific features and functionalities.

Armed with a deep understanding of our audience's backgrounds, interests, and perspectives, we embark on the quest to tailor our communication strategies to resonate with their specific needs and knowledge levels. We craft narratives that speak directly to their pain points, aspirations, and objectives, ensuring that our messages are not only heard but also felt on a visceral level.

Moreover, we embrace a diverse array of communication channels and formats, recognizing that our audience may have varying preferences for receiving information. From interactive workshops and engaging presentations to concise reports and visual aids, we leverage a multifaceted approach to communication that caters to the diverse needs and preferences of our audience.

Translating Technical Jargon

In the vast realm of AI, technical jargon often looms like an insurmountable obstacle, casting a shadow of confusion and intimidation over non-technical stakeholders. Yet, within this labyrinth of complex terminology lies an opportunity to bridge the divide between technical experts and their counterparts, fostering a shared understanding that transcends disciplinary boundaries.

Our chapter embarks on a daring expedition into the heart of this labyrinth, armed with the twin pillars of clarity and accessibility. We recognize that the first step in translating technical jargon is to unravel its intricacies, dissecting complex concepts into digestible nuggets of knowledge that can be easily grasped by non-technical minds.

To achieve this feat, we employ a diverse array of communication techniques, ranging from analogies and metaphors to real-world examples and interactive demonstrations. By anchoring technical concepts in familiar contexts and everyday experiences, we provide non-technical stakeholders with a roadmap for navigating the labyrinth of AI terminology with confidence and ease.

Moreover, we embrace the power of storytelling as a transformative tool for translating technical jargon into accessible language. Through compelling narratives and engaging anecdotes, we breathe life into abstract concepts, weaving a tapestry of meaning that resonates with the hearts and minds of our audience.

Furthermore, we recognize the importance of context in shaping the interpretation of technical jargon. By tailoring our explanations to the specific needs and knowledge levels of our audience, we ensure that technical concepts are conveyed in a manner that is relevant, relatable, and actionable.

Visual Storytelling with Data

In the vast landscape of AI, where complexity often reigns supreme, visual storytelling emerges as a beacon of clarity, illuminating the path to understanding for both technical and non-technical audiences alike. Our chapter embarks on an immersive exploration of this transformative practice, delving into the art of visual storytelling with data as a means of demystifying complex AI concepts and fostering meaningful engagement.

At the heart of visual storytelling lies the profound ability to translate abstract ideas and intricate data into visual representations that resonate with human cognition. Through a strategic blend of visualizations, infographics, and data-driven narratives, we embark on a journey to unlock the power of imagery in conveying complex technical information.

Visualizations serve as our first port of call, offering a rich tapestry of charts, graphs, and diagrams that transform raw data into visual insights. From line graphs tracing the trajectory of machine learning algorithms to heat maps revealing patterns in data sets, visualizations provide a window into the hidden patterns and relationships that underpin AI concepts.

Infographics stand as our next frontier, offering a dynamic canvas upon which to weave a narrative tapestry of information. Through a carefully curated blend of images, icons, and text, infographics distill complex AI concepts into bite-sized visual nuggets that captivate the imagination and convey key insights with precision and clarity.

Data-driven narratives emerge as our final destination, offering a compelling storytelling framework that marries the power of data with the art of narrative. Through a captivating blend of storytelling techniques, we breathe life into AI concepts, crafting immersive narratives that transport audiences on a journey of discovery through the complexities of AI.

Analogies and Metaphors in Communication

In the vast expanse of AI discourse, where technical jargon often reigns supreme, analogies and metaphors emerge as invaluable instruments of communication, serving as bridges that span the gap between the intricate world of data science and the uncharted territories of non-technical minds. Our exploration of this transformative practice embarks on a journey to unravel the intricate tapestry of analogies and metaphors, illuminating their profound role in simplifying complex AI concepts and fostering meaningful understanding among diverse audiences.

Analogies and metaphors stand as beacons of clarity in the realm of technical discourse, offering relatable comparisons that resonate with human experience and cognition. By drawing parallels between abstract AI concepts and familiar real-world scenarios, analogies and metaphors breathe life into complex ideas, transforming them from enigmatic puzzles into accessible narratives that captivate the imagination and spark curiosity.

As we traverse the landscape of analogies and metaphors, we embark on a voyage of discovery, uncovering the myriad ways in which these linguistic devices can illuminate the complexities of AI for non-technical stakeholders. From comparing neural networks to interconnected highways bustling with traffic to likening machine learning algorithms to voracious learners devouring vast libraries of data, analogies and metaphors offer a rich tapestry of imagery that renders complex AI concepts tangible and relatable.

Moreover, analogies and metaphors serve as catalysts for engagement and comprehension, inviting audiences to embark on a journey of exploration and discovery. By anchoring abstract AI concepts within familiar frameworks, these linguistic devices empower non-technical stakeholders to navigate the complexities of AI with confidence and clarity, fostering meaningful dialogue and collaboration across diverse domains.

Interactive Workshops and Training Sessions

In the realm of AI education and collaboration, interactive workshops and training sessions emerge as dynamic arenas where non-technical stakeholders embark on immersive journeys of discovery and learning. These hands-on experiences serve as vibrant ecosystems teeming with opportunity, where the enigmatic complexities of AI are demystified through active engagement, real-world applications, and collaborative exploration.

The essence of interactive workshops lies in their ability to transcend traditional modes of education, offering participants a firsthand glimpse into the inner workings of AI processes through experiential learning and practical experimentation. By immersing themselves in interactive activities, non-technical stakeholders are afforded the opportunity to grapple with AI concepts in a tangible and accessible manner, bridging the gap between theory and practice with each interactive exercise.

397

Central to the success of interactive workshops is their capacity to foster deep engagement and meaningful interaction among participants. Through hands-on activities, group discussions, and collaborative problem-solving exercises, non-technical stakeholders are empowered to actively participate in the learning process, sharing insights, asking questions, and gaining practical experience that transcends mere theoretical understanding.

Moreover, interactive workshops serve as incubators of innovation and creativity, providing participants with the freedom to explore, experiment, and ideate in a supportive and collaborative environment. By encouraging curiosity and experimentation, these sessions ignite the spark of innovation within non-technical stakeholders, empowering them to harness the transformative potential of AI in their respective domains.

At the heart of interactive workshops lies the belief that knowledge is best cultivated through active participation and experiential learning. By providing non-technical stakeholders with the tools, resources, and guidance they need to navigate the complexities of AI, these sessions pave the way for a future where interdisciplinary collaboration thrives, and the boundaries between technical and non-technical domains blur in the pursuit of shared understanding and collective innovation.

Storytelling for Impactful Communication

In the realm of AI communication, storytelling emerges as a potent tool for transcending technical jargon and fostering meaningful connections with non-technical stakeholders. By weaving narratives that illuminate the journey, challenges, and triumphs of AI projects, storytellers imbue complex concepts with context, emotion, and resonance, transforming abstract ideas into compelling narratives that captivate, inspire, and inform.

At its core, storytelling is a deeply human art form that transcends boundaries of language and discipline, tapping into universal themes, emotions, and experiences that resonate with audiences on a profound level. By leveraging the narrative power of storytelling, communicators are able to distill the complexities of AI projects into relatable and memorable tales that engage the imagination, spark curiosity, and inspire action.

The essence of storytelling lies in its ability to add depth, texture, and meaning to the technical intricacies of AI, framing them within a broader narrative arc that unfolds over time. Through compelling stories, non-technical stakeholders are invited to embark on a journey of discovery, following the twists and turns of AI projects as they navigate challenges, overcome obstacles, and ultimately achieve success.

Moreover, storytelling serves as a vehicle for empathy and understanding, allowing non-technical stakeholders to connect with the human side of AI projects—the people behind the technology, their motivations, aspirations, and struggles. By highlighting the human dimension of AI, storytellers create empathy bridges that bridge the gap between technical expertise and real-world impact, fostering a deeper appreciation for the transformative potential of AI in society.

Central to the art of storytelling is the recognition that every AI project has its own unique narrative, shaped by the individuals involved, the challenges encountered, and the lessons learned along the way. By crafting narratives that authentically reflect the lived experiences of AI teams, storytellers are able to capture the essence of AI projects in a way that resonates with audiences and leaves a lasting impression.

In essence, storytelling serves as a bridge between the technical and non-technical realms of AI communication, offering a compelling and accessible medium through which complex concepts can be conveyed with clarity, impact, and resonance. By harnessing the narrative power of storytelling, communicators can illuminate the transformative potential of AI projects, inspiring curiosity, fostering understanding, and forging connections that transcend disciplinary boundaries.

Collaborative Decision-Making Processes

In the dynamic landscape of AI development, decision-making processes must be inclusive, transparent, and collaborative to harness the collective wisdom and expertise of diverse stakeholders. This section delves into the methodologies and practices that enable non-technical team members to actively participate in AI discussions, ensuring that decisions are informed by a broad spectrum of perspectives, insights, and considerations.

At the heart of inclusive decision-making processes lies the principle of empowerment, which entails giving non-technical stakeholders a voice and a seat at the table in AI discussions. By inviting their input, ideas, and feedback, organizations cultivate a culture of collaboration and inclusivity, where every team member feels valued, heard, and empowered to contribute to the project's success.

One approach to inclusive decision-making is to leverage collaborative methodologies that facilitate open dialogue, knowledge sharing, and consensus building among team members. Techniques such as brainstorming sessions, design thinking workshops, and affinity mapping exercises can be used to surface diverse viewpoints, explore alternative solutions, and arrive at decisions that reflect the collective wisdom of the team.

Moreover, inclusive decision-making processes involve transparent communication and information sharing, ensuring that non-technical stakeholders have access to the relevant data, insights, and context needed to make informed decisions. By providing visibility into the decision-making process, organizations foster trust, accountability, and alignment among team members, creating a shared understanding of the project's goals, priorities, and constraints.

In addition to collaborative methodologies, technology can also play a role in facilitating inclusive decision-making in AI projects. Collaboration tools, project management platforms, and online forums provide virtual spaces where team members can collaborate, share ideas, and co-create solutions in real time, regardless of their geographical location or time zone.

Furthermore, inclusive decision-making processes involve ongoing feedback loops and mechanisms for soliciting input from non-technical stakeholders throughout the project lifecycle. By actively seeking out and incorporating feedback from end users, customers, and other stakeholders, organizations ensure that decisions are grounded in real-world insights and aligned with the needs and expectations of the target audience.

In essence, inclusive decision-making processes in AI projects are characterized by openness, transparency, and collaboration, enabling non-technical stakeholders to actively contribute to discussions, shape outcomes, and drive meaningful impact. By embracing inclusive decision-making practices, organizations can leverage the collective intelligence of their teams to tackle complex challenges, innovate effectively, and achieve success in the fast-paced world of AI development.

Clear Documentation and Reporting

In the intricate landscape of AI projects, clear and comprehensive documentation serves as a vital communication tool that bridges the gap between technical complexities and non-technical stakeholders' understanding. This section delves into the significance of developing documentation and reports that not only elucidate intricate AI concepts but also provide actionable insights and promote transparency throughout the project lifecycle.

At its core, clear documentation aims to distill complex AI concepts into digestible insights that resonate with non-technical stakeholders. By articulating key findings, methodologies, and outcomes in a concise and understandable manner, documentation empowers stakeholders to grasp the essence of AI projects, make informed decisions, and contribute meaningfully to project discussions and initiatives.

Moreover, well-crafted documentation serves as a comprehensive reference point for non-technical stakeholders, offering insights into project goals, timelines, milestones, and progress. By providing a detailed overview of project objectives, documentation fosters alignment and clarity among team members, ensuring that everyone is on the same page and working towards common goals.

Furthermore, documentation plays a pivotal role in promoting transparency and accountability within AI projects. By documenting project decisions, rationale, and outcomes, organizations establish a transparent record of their activities, enabling stakeholders to track progress, understand decision-making processes, and hold teams accountable for their actions and results.

In addition to clarity and transparency, documentation also facilitates knowledge sharing and organizational learning. By documenting best practices, lessons learned, and key insights gained throughout the project lifecycle, organizations create a repository of valuable knowledge that can be leveraged to inform future initiatives, avoid pitfalls, and drive continuous improvement.

To ensure the effectiveness of documentation, it is essential to tailor communication strategies to the specific needs and preferences of non-technical stakeholders. This may involve using plain language, visual aids, and real-world examples to convey complex concepts in a relatable and accessible manner. Additionally, incorporating feedback mechanisms into documentation processes allows stakeholders to provide input, ask questions, and request clarification, ensuring that documentation remains relevant, accurate, and valuable.

Feedback Loops for Continuous Improvement

In the dynamic landscape of AI projects, feedback loops serve as invaluable tools for fostering continuous improvement in communication strategies. This section delves into the implementation of feedback mechanisms designed to solicit insights and perspectives from non-technical stakeholders, thereby facilitating iterative refinement and enhancement of communication practices to better meet the evolving needs of the team.

Feedback loops are instrumental in creating a culture of open dialogue and constructive criticism, enabling stakeholders to express their opinions, voice concerns, and provide suggestions for improving communication effectiveness. By actively seeking feedback from non-technical team members, organizations demonstrate a commitment to listening to diverse perspectives and valuing the input of every stakeholder in the communication process.

The establishment of feedback mechanisms involves the thoughtful design of channels and processes through which stakeholders can share their feedback on communication practices. This may include conducting regular surveys, organizing feedback sessions or workshops, setting up dedicated communication channels such as forums or discussion boards, or simply encouraging open communication through one-on-one conversations or email correspondence.

Moreover, feedback mechanisms should be designed to elicit specific insights on the clarity, relevance, and impact of communication strategies. Stakeholders may be asked to provide feedback on the comprehensibility of technical terminology, the effectiveness of visual aids or presentations, the relevance of information shared, and the overall impact of communication on their understanding and engagement with the project.

Iterative feedback enables communication strategies to evolve and adapt in response to changing project dynamics, stakeholder preferences, and organizational objectives. By incorporating feedback into regular communication planning and execution cycles, organizations can identify areas for improvement, address gaps or shortcomings, and refine communication practices to better align with the needs and expectations of non-technical stakeholders.

Furthermore, feedback loops foster a culture of continuous learning and improvement within the organization, encouraging team members to reflect on their communication approaches, experiment with new techniques or formats, and actively seek opportunities for growth and development. By embracing feedback as a catalyst for positive change, organizations demonstrate a commitment to excellence in communication and a dedication to delivering value to all stakeholders involved in AI projects.

Building a Collaborative Culture

In the realm of AI projects, fostering a collaborative culture within the organization is not just beneficial but essential for effective communication and project success. This section delves deeply into the organizational aspects of cultivating a culture where both technical and non-technical team members are encouraged to actively engage, collaborate, and contribute their insights towards the achievement of shared goals in AI projects.

At the heart of building a collaborative culture lies the recognition of the diverse expertise and perspectives that each team member brings to the table. Organizations must embrace the idea that collaboration is not limited to specific roles or departments but extends across the entire project ecosystem, encompassing individuals with varying skill sets, backgrounds, and areas of expertise.

One key aspect of fostering a collaborative culture is promoting transparency and openness in communication. Organizations should strive to create an environment where team members feel empowered to share their ideas, express their opinions, and raise concerns without fear of judgment or reprisal. This culture of openness encourages dialogue, fosters trust, and enables constructive exchanges of feedback and ideas among team members.

Moreover, building a collaborative culture involves breaking down organizational silos and barriers that may hinder communication and collaboration. Organizations should actively promote cross-functional collaboration by creating opportunities for team members from different departments or disciplines to come together, exchange knowledge, and work towards common objectives. This may involve organizing cross-functional workshops, collaborative problem-solving sessions, or interdepartmental projects that encourage collaboration and knowledge sharing.

Furthermore, leadership plays a crucial role in fostering a collaborative culture within the organization. Leaders should lead by example, demonstrating a commitment to collaboration, inclusivity, and open communication in their interactions with team members. By setting clear expectations, providing support and encouragement, and recognizing and rewarding collaborative efforts, leaders can create an environment where collaboration is valued and encouraged at all levels of the organization.

Additionally, organizations can leverage technology to facilitate collaboration and communication among team members, particularly in distributed or remote work environments. Collaboration tools such as project management software, video conferencing platforms, and collaborative document editing tools can help streamline communication, facilitate real-time collaboration, and ensure that team members stay connected and engaged regardless of their physical location.

Mitigating Misunderstandings and Addressing Concerns

In the intricate landscape of AI projects, communication challenges and concerns can occasionally arise, potentially hindering progress and collaboration. This section delves into proactive strategies aimed at mitigating misunderstandings, addressing concerns, and fostering an environment of open dialogue where non-technical stakeholders feel empowered to voice questions or reservations.

One proactive strategy for mitigating misunderstandings is to establish clear channels of communication from the outset of the project. Organizations should define communication protocols, including designated meeting times, platforms for discussions, and guidelines for sharing updates and information. By setting clear expectations and providing a structured framework for communication, teams can minimize the risk of miscommunication and ensure that everyone is on the same page regarding project objectives, timelines, and expectations.

Moreover, creating a culture of transparency and openness is essential for addressing concerns and fostering constructive dialogue. Organizations should encourage non-technical stakeholders to express any questions, uncertainties, or apprehensions they may have about the project, and provide avenues for them to voice their concerns in a supportive and non-judgmental environment. This may involve setting up regular feedback sessions, anonymous suggestion boxes, or one-on-one meetings with project leaders to address individual concerns.

In addition to proactive communication, organizations should be prepared to respond promptly and effectively to any concerns or misunderstandings that arise during the project lifecycle. This may involve appointing designated communication leads who are responsible for addressing inquiries and concerns from non-technical stakeholders, providing timely updates and clarifications, and facilitating discussions to resolve any issues that may arise.

Furthermore, organizations can leverage tools and techniques such as visualization, storytelling, and interactive demonstrations to help non-technical stakeholders better understand complex AI concepts and processes. By presenting information in a clear, accessible, and engaging manner, teams can alleviate concerns, demystify technical jargon, and foster a shared understanding of the project among all stakeholders.

Ultimately, by implementing proactive communication strategies, fostering a culture of transparency and openness, and leveraging effective tools and techniques for knowledge sharing and understanding, organizations can mitigate misunderstandings, address concerns, and promote collaborative dialogue in AI projects, ultimately driving success and innovation.

Future Trends in Communicating AI Concepts

As the landscape of AI continues to evolve, so too do the methods and strategies for communicating complex concepts to non-technical stakeholders. This chapter delves into the future trends shaping the communication of AI concepts, considering emerging technologies, tools, and methodologies that promise to enhance the efficiency and effectiveness of conveying intricate information to diverse audiences.

One significant trend on the horizon is the increasing integration of immersive technologies, such as augmented reality (AR) and virtual reality (VR), into communication practices. These immersive experiences have the potential to provide non-technical stakeholders with interactive and engaging opportunities to explore AI concepts in a three-dimensional environment, fostering deeper understanding and engagement.

Furthermore, advancements in natural language processing (NLP) and conversational AI present opportunities for more intuitive and conversational interactions with AI systems. Chatbots and virtual assistants equipped with NLP capabilities can serve as interactive guides, helping non-technical stakeholders navigate complex concepts and obtain relevant information in a conversational manner.

Moreover, the proliferation of data visualization tools and techniques continues to revolutionize how complex information is presented and understood. Interactive dashboards, infographics, and data-driven visualizations enable non-technical stakeholders to explore AI concepts through interactive and intuitive interfaces, facilitating deeper insights and understanding.

Additionally, the growing emphasis on storytelling and narrative-driven communication is expected to play a significant role in conveying AI concepts effectively. By framing AI projects within compelling narratives and real-world scenarios, organizations can make abstract concepts more relatable and engaging, fostering empathy and resonance among non-technical stakeholders.

Lastly, the rise of collaborative platforms and remote communication tools is transforming how teams collaborate and communicate in AI projects. Virtual collaboration spaces, project management tools, and asynchronous communication platforms enable geographically dispersed teams to collaborate seamlessly, fostering cross-functional communication and knowledge sharing.

OVERCOMING CHALLENGES IN REMOTE AI PRODUCT MANAGEMENT

The landscape of AI product management has undergone significant transformations, with remote work becoming a prevalent mode of operation. This chapter explores the unique challenges that remote work poses for AI-driven teams and provides insights into strategies, tools, and practices to foster effective collaboration and communication in a distributed environment.

The Remote Paradigm in AI Product Management

Remote work brings forth a new set of dynamics and considerations, reshaping the traditional landscape of AI product management. With team members scattered across different locations and time zones, fostering effective collaboration becomes both paramount and intricate. The chapter explores the various strategies and technologies that enable remote teams to collaborate seamlessly, emphasizing the importance of clear communication channels, robust project management tools, and virtual collaboration platforms.

Moreover, the chapter delves into the nuances of communication in a remote environment, acknowledging the need for deliberate efforts to maintain transparency, clarity, and engagement among team members. It explores innovative communication methodologies and practices designed to bridge the physical divide, ensuring that information flows freely and efficiently across remote teams.

Furthermore, the chapter delves into the unique challenges that remote work poses to team dynamics and culture. It addresses the importance of nurturing a sense of belonging and camaraderie among remote team members, despite the absence of face-to-face interactions. Strategies for fostering a positive remote work culture, promoting virtual team-building activities, and cultivating a supportive environment are discussed in detail.

Additionally, the chapter examines the role of leadership in navigating the remote work paradigm within AI product management teams. It underscores the importance of adaptive leadership styles, empathetic communication, and proactive engagement in fostering cohesion and motivation among remote team members.

Navigating Time Zone Differences

The section delves into the intricate challenge posed by time zone differences within globalized teams, recognizing their potential impact on synchronous collaboration. It explores a range of strategies aimed at navigating these disparities effectively, ensuring that team members across different geographic regions can collaborate seamlessly despite variations in local time.

The discussion begins by acknowledging the inherent complexities introduced by time zone differences, which can hinder real-time communication and coordination among team members. It underscores the importance of adopting a proactive approach to address these challenges, rather than viewing them as insurmountable obstacles.

One of the key strategies explored in the section is the promotion of asynchronous communication practices within the team. By embracing asynchronous communication channels such as email, messaging platforms, and project management tools, team members can exchange information and collaborate on tasks without the need for simultaneous availability. This allows individuals to work flexibly according to their own schedules, thereby mitigating the impact of time zone disparities.

Additionally, the section emphasizes the value of adopting flexible scheduling practices that accommodate the diverse time zones of team members. This may involve rotating meeting times to ensure equitable participation across different regions, as well as leveraging tools that facilitate easy scheduling and coordination, such as shared calendars and time zone converters.

Furthermore, the section explores the role of technology in facilitating seamless collaboration across time zones. It highlights the importance of leveraging communication and collaboration tools specifically designed to support globalized teams, such as video conferencing platforms with built-in time zone awareness features, collaborative document editing tools, and virtual whiteboards.

Moreover, the section delves into the cultural considerations inherent in navigating time zone differences, recognizing the need for sensitivity and understanding among team members from diverse cultural backgrounds. It emphasizes the importance of fostering a culture of respect, empathy, and inclusivity within the team, which can help mitigate potential challenges stemming from cultural differences in communication styles and work practices.

Ensuring Effective Virtual Communication

The section delves into the multifaceted challenges associated with virtual communication within remote AI teams, recognizing the importance of clarity, engagement, and connection in fostering collaboration and productivity. It explores a range of strategies aimed at ensuring effective virtual communication and maintaining a cohesive team dynamic despite physical distance.

The discussion begins by acknowledging the unique challenges posed by virtual communication, including potential issues related to clarity, engagement, and miscommunication. It emphasizes the need for proactive measures to address these challenges and create an environment conducive to effective collaboration and communication.

One of the key strategies explored in the section is the use of video conferencing technology to facilitate face-to-face interactions among team members. By leveraging video conferencing platforms, remote AI teams can conduct virtual meetings, brainstorming sessions, and collaborative discussions that closely mimic the experience of in-person communication. This helps to foster a sense of connection and engagement among team members, despite their physical separation.

Additionally, the section highlights the importance of utilizing collaborative platforms and tools to support virtual communication and collaboration. These platforms enable team members to share documents, collaborate on projects in real-time, and communicate asynchronously through messaging channels. By centralizing communication and project management within a unified digital environment, remote AI teams can streamline their workflows and maintain visibility into ongoing activities.

Furthermore, the section emphasizes the value of clear and concise documentation in supporting virtual communication within remote AI teams. Comprehensive documentation ensures that team members have access to relevant information, project updates, and decision-making processes, even when working asynchronously across different time zones. This helps to minimize misunderstandings and discrepancies and promotes alignment and transparency within the team.

Moreover, the section explores strategies for enhancing engagement and participation during virtual meetings and discussions. This may involve implementing techniques such as active listening, encouraging open dialogue and collaboration, and structuring meetings to maximize interactivity and involvement among team members.

Leveraging Collaborative Tools

The section delves into the diverse array of collaborative tools available to remote AI product management teams, recognizing their instrumental role in optimizing workflows, facilitating communication, and fostering seamless collaboration across distributed teams. It offers an in-depth exploration of various categories of collaborative tools, highlighting their functionalities, benefits, and implications for remote AI product management.

The discussion begins by acknowledging the significance of collaborative tools in overcoming the challenges associated with remote work and enabling effective collaboration among geographically dispersed team members. It emphasizes the pivotal role that these tools play in streamlining workflows, promoting transparency, and enhancing productivity within remote AI product management teams.

One category of collaborative tools explored in the section is project management platforms. These platforms, such as Asana, Trello, or Jira, provide comprehensive solutions for organizing tasks, tracking project progress, and facilitating team collaboration. They offer features such as task assignment, milestone tracking, and real-time updates, allowing remote AI product management teams to effectively manage projects and allocate resources in a distributed environment.

Another essential category of collaborative tools discussed is version control systems, such as Git or SVN. These systems enable teams to manage code repositories, track changes, and collaborate on software development projects effectively. By providing a centralized repository for codebase management and version tracking, version control systems facilitate collaboration among remote developers and ensure the integrity and consistency of code across distributed teams.

Additionally, the section explores the role of virtual whiteboards and visual collaboration tools in enhancing remote collaboration within AI product management teams. Tools like Miro or MURAL enable teams to brainstorm ideas, visualize concepts, and collaborate on designs in a virtual environment. They facilitate interactive workshops, design sprints, and ideation sessions, allowing remote team members to actively contribute to creative processes and decision-making.

Furthermore, the section discusses the importance of communication apps and video conferencing tools in facilitating real-time communication and collaboration among remote AI product management teams. Platforms such as Slack, Microsoft Teams, or Zoom provide channels for instant messaging, voice calls, and video conferences, enabling remote team members to communicate effectively, share updates, and collaborate on projects in real-time.

Maintaining Team Cohesion and Culture

The section delves into the complexities of preserving team cohesion and culture in remote AI environments, acknowledging the unique challenges that virtual work can pose to team dynamics and interpersonal connections. It offers a comprehensive examination of strategies and initiatives aimed at maintaining a strong sense of cohesion and reinforcing organizational culture within remote AI teams.

The discussion begins by recognizing the importance of regular team check-ins as a foundational element of maintaining cohesion in virtual environments. These check-ins, conducted via video conferencing platforms or team collaboration tools, serve as opportunities for team members to connect, share updates, and address any challenges or concerns they may be facing. By fostering open communication and facilitating meaningful interactions, regular team check-ins help to strengthen bonds and build trust among remote AI team members.

Furthermore, the section explores the role of virtual social activities in nurturing a sense of camaraderie and belonging within remote AI teams. From virtual coffee breaks and team lunches to online games and virtual happy hours, these activities provide opportunities for team members to socialize, bond, and forge personal connections outside of work-related tasks. By creating space for informal interactions and shared experiences, virtual social activities contribute to a positive team culture and foster a sense of community among remote AI team members.

Additionally, the section discusses initiatives aimed at reinforcing the team's shared values and goals in a remote setting. This may include virtual team-building exercises, workshops on organizational values, or collaborative projects that align with the team's mission and vision. By engaging remote AI team members in activities that highlight the organization's core principles and objectives, these initiatives help to foster a sense of purpose and commitment among team members, driving alignment and cohesion within the team.

Moreover, the section emphasizes the importance of leadership in cultivating a cohesive and inclusive culture within remote AI teams. Leaders play a critical role in setting the tone, modeling desired behaviors, and promoting a culture of collaboration, respect, and empathy. By demonstrating transparency, fostering open communication, and recognizing and celebrating team achievements, leaders can cultivate a positive and supportive environment that encourages engagement and fosters trust among remote AI team members.

Facilitating Remote Workshops and Brainstorming Sessions

This section provides a comprehensive examination of the strategies and tools available to facilitate workshops and brainstorming sessions in remote AI product development settings. It recognizes the importance of these collaborative activities in driving innovation, problem-solving, and decision-making, and explores how organizations can adapt and optimize them for remote work environments.

The discussion begins by acknowledging the need for virtual facilitation techniques that can effectively engage remote participants and foster productive collaboration. It explores various facilitation strategies, such as setting clear objectives and agendas, establishing ground rules for participation, and utilizing interactive activities and icebreakers to encourage engagement and creativity among remote team members. Additionally, the section discusses the role of skilled facilitators in guiding discussions, managing group dynamics, and ensuring that workshops and brainstorming sessions run smoothly and efficiently in a virtual context.

Furthermore, the section explores the use of digital whiteboarding tools as essential resources for facilitating remote workshops and brainstorming sessions. These tools enable participants to visualize ideas, concepts, and relationships in real-time, fostering collaboration and creativity in virtual environments. The discussion includes an overview of popular digital whiteboarding platforms, their features and functionalities, and best practices for incorporating them into remote collaborative sessions effectively.

Moreover, the section highlights the importance of interactive platforms and collaboration tools in enabling effective ideation and decision-making in remote settings. It explores the use of video conferencing platforms, collaborative document editors, and project management software to facilitate real-time communication, document sharing, and task coordination among remote team members. By leveraging these tools, organizations can create immersive and interactive virtual environments that replicate the collaborative energy of in-person workshops and brainstorming sessions.

Addressing Communication Overload and Burnout

This section delves into the complexities surrounding communication overload and burnout that remote work can exacerbate within AI teams. It acknowledges the heightened risk of these challenges due to the virtual nature of collaboration, which often blurs the boundaries between work and personal life. To counteract these issues, the section explores a range of strategies aimed at promoting well-being and sustainable productivity among remote team members.

Firstly, the section emphasizes the importance of establishing clear communication norms tailored to remote work environments. It discusses the implementation of guidelines for communication frequency, channel selection, and response expectations to prevent information overload and ensure that communication remains efficient and purposeful. Additionally, it highlights the significance of asynchronous communication methods, such as email and messaging platforms, in allowing team members to manage their communication flow and prioritize tasks effectively.

Furthermore, the section explores strategies for promoting work-life balance among remote team members to prevent burnout. It discusses the importance of setting boundaries between work and personal time, encouraging regular breaks and time off, and providing resources for managing stress and mental health. By fostering a culture that values well-being and recognizes the importance of downtime, organizations can mitigate the risk of burnout and support the long-term resilience of their remote teams.

Moreover, the section emphasizes the role of leadership in addressing communication overload and burnout within remote AI teams. It discusses the importance of leaders modeling healthy communication practices, actively monitoring team dynamics, and providing support and resources to team members experiencing burnout or excessive stress. Additionally, it highlights the value of regular check-ins and one-on-one meetings to maintain open lines of communication and identify potential issues before they escalate.

Building Trust and Accountability

Establishing trust and accountability lies at the core of successful collaboration within remote AI teams. This section delves into the multifaceted strategies aimed at cultivating trust and fostering a sense of accountability among team members, essential for maintaining cohesion and productivity in a virtual work environment.

Transparent communication emerges as a cornerstone in building trust within remote AI teams. The section underscores the importance of open and honest communication channels that facilitate the sharing of ideas, concerns, and progress updates. By encouraging transparency in communication, team members can develop a deeper understanding of each other's roles, expectations, and challenges, laying the groundwork for mutual trust and respect.

Consistent follow-ups play a pivotal role in reinforcing trust and accountability within remote AI teams. Regular check-ins, status updates, and progress reports serve as mechanisms for staying connected and informed about ongoing projects. By maintaining a cadence of communication, team members can demonstrate reliability and commitment to their responsibilities, fostering a culture of accountability and dependability.

Moreover, the section highlights the significance of focusing on deliverables as a means of building trust and accountability in remote AI teams. Setting clear goals, timelines, and expectations for deliverables empowers team members to take ownership of their tasks and demonstrate tangible progress toward shared objectives. Celebrating milestones and achievements further reinforces a sense of accountability and motivation among team members, driving collective success.

In addition to transparent communication and deliverable-focused approaches, establishing accountability mechanisms is essential for promoting trust within remote AI teams. The section explores the implementation of tools and processes for tracking progress, identifying bottlenecks, and resolving issues promptly. By holding each team member accountable for their contributions and outcomes, remote AI teams can foster a culture of responsibility and commitment to shared goals.

Adapting Agile Methodologies to Remote Work

Agile methodologies serve as a cornerstone in AI product management, promoting flexibility, collaboration, and iterative development. However, the transition to remote work necessitates adaptations to traditional Agile practices to ensure their effectiveness in virtual environments. This section delves into strategies for modifying Agile methodologies to suit remote collaboration, focusing on key principles such as frequent communication, adaptive planning, and iterative development.

Frequent communication emerges as a critical aspect of adapting Agile methodologies to remote work. The section emphasizes the need for robust communication channels that facilitate real-time interaction and collaboration among remote team members. Utilizing video conferencing, instant messaging platforms, and virtual stand-up meetings enables teams to maintain regular communication, address challenges promptly, and stay aligned on project goals and priorities despite physical distance.

Adaptive planning becomes essential in remote Agile environments to accommodate evolving project requirements and team dynamics. The section discusses the importance of agile planning sessions that allow remote teams to review and adjust project timelines, goals, and deliverables collaboratively. By embracing flexibility and responsiveness in planning, remote Agile teams can effectively navigate uncertainties and adapt to changing circumstances while ensuring project progress and alignment with stakeholder expectations.

Iterative development remains a fundamental aspect of Agile methodologies, even in remote settings. The section explores how remote teams can leverage iterative development cycles to break down complex projects into manageable increments, enabling continuous feedback and validation from stakeholders. By embracing an iterative approach to development, remote Agile teams can mitigate risks, identify and address issues early, and deliver value incrementally, enhancing project visibility and stakeholder satisfaction.

Fostering Continuous Learning and Skill Development

Maintaining a commitment to ongoing learning and skill enhancement is crucial for remote AI teams to thrive. Despite physical distance, these teams can cultivate a vibrant culture of learning through various strategic approaches. One such method involves organizing virtual training sessions, where team members can engage in interactive workshops, seminars, or courses tailored to their specific roles and interests. These sessions not only provide valuable learning opportunities but also foster a sense of community and collaboration among remote colleagues.

Additionally, establishing knowledge-sharing platforms is essential for promoting continuous learning within remote AI teams. These platforms serve as repositories of information where team members can access resources, best practices, case studies, and other relevant materials to enhance their knowledge and skills. Through active participation in these platforms, team members can contribute their expertise, ask questions, and engage in discussions, thereby enriching the collective knowledge of the team.

Moreover, implementing mentorship programs can further bolster the culture of learning within remote AI teams. Pairing less experienced team members with seasoned professionals allows for the exchange of insights, guidance, and feedback. Mentors can offer valuable advice, share their experiences, and provide support to mentees as they navigate their career paths and strive for professional growth. These mentorship relationships foster a collaborative environment where knowledge transfer occurs organically, ultimately benefiting both mentors and mentees.

By embracing these strategies, remote AI teams can ensure that distance does not impede their pursuit of continuous learning and skill development. Instead, they can leverage virtual platforms, knowledge-sharing initiatives, and mentorship programs to empower team members to stay informed, engaged, and adaptable in an ever-evolving industry landscape.

Mitigating Isolation and Promoting Inclusivity

Addressing the challenge of isolation in remote work environments is crucial for maintaining high team morale and fostering inclusivity among team members. To combat feelings of isolation, it's essential to implement a range of strategies aimed at creating a sense of camaraderie and belonging within the team.

One effective approach involves organizing virtual team-building activities that allow team members to bond and collaborate in a fun and engaging manner. These activities could include online games, virtual coffee breaks, or team challenges that encourage interaction and foster a sense of unity despite physical distance. By providing opportunities for socialization and team bonding, remote teams can strengthen relationships and mitigate feelings of isolation.

Furthermore, implementing inclusivity initiatives is essential for promoting a sense of belonging among all team members, regardless of their backgrounds or circumstances. This can involve creating diversity and inclusion programs, establishing affinity groups, or offering resources and support tailored to the unique needs of different individuals within the team. By actively promoting inclusivity, remote teams can ensure that every team member feels valued, respected, and supported in their professional environment.

In addition to team-building activities and inclusivity initiatives, establishing structured channels for open communication is crucial for mitigating isolation in remote work settings. Providing platforms for regular check-ins, team meetings, and one-on-one discussions enables team members to connect, share ideas, and address any concerns they may have. Open communication channels facilitate transparency, collaboration, and a sense of community within the team, helping to counteract feelings of isolation and promote a supportive work environment.

Ultimately, by prioritizing strategies such as virtual team-building activities, inclusivity initiatives, and open communication channels, remote teams can mitigate the challenges of isolation and promote a culture of inclusivity where every team member feels valued, connected, and empowered to contribute to the team's success.

Future Trends in Remote AI Product Management

Delving into the horizon of remote AI product management unveils a landscape teeming with potential and innovation. As we peer into the future, it becomes evident that a myriad of emerging technologies, virtual collaboration tools, and evolving methodologies are poised to revolutionize the way AI-driven teams operate remotely, offering a tantalizing glimpse into the future of distributed collaboration.

This exploration isn't merely speculative; it's grounded in the tangible advancements and trends shaping the industry. From the integration of cutting-edge AI algorithms to the adoption of immersive virtual reality interfaces, the evolution of technology is paving the way for unprecedented levels of connectivity and efficiency in remote work environments. Likewise, the proliferation of sophisticated virtual collaboration platforms, augmented by features like real-time collaboration, advanced analytics, and immersive virtual environments, is empowering remote teams to collaborate seamlessly across geographical boundaries.

Moreover, the evolution of methodologies in remote AI product management is reshaping the way teams approach project execution and collaboration. Agile frameworks tailored for remote work, such as Remote Agile and Agile at Scale, are gaining traction, enabling teams to adapt quickly to changing requirements and maintain productivity in distributed settings. Additionally, the rise of DevOps practices in AI development is streamlining the deployment and management of AI solutions, fostering a culture of continuous integration, delivery, and feedback.

However, realizing the full potential of these advancements requires more than just technological prowess; it demands a strategic approach encompassing tailored strategies, collaborative tools, and a culture of communication and inclusivity. By embracing these elements, remote AI teams can transcend the challenges posed by geographical dispersion and emerge stronger and more resilient in the evolving landscape of distributed product management. From cultivating a culture of transparency and open communication to nurturing a diverse and inclusive team environment, the key lies in fostering an ethos of collaboration and innovation that propels remote AI teams toward unparalleled success in the digital era.

8. SECURITY & TRUST IN AI PRODUCTS

ADDRESSING SECURITY CONCERNS IN AI

In an era where AI products are integral to various aspects of our lives, ensuring security and building trust are paramount. This chapter delves into the intricate landscape of security concerns in AI, exploring strategies, best practices, and frameworks to safeguard AI products. It addresses the challenges of securing AI systems, instilling trust in users, and fostering a culture of responsible and ethical AI development.

The Imperative of Security in AI Products

Security is not just a feature but an imperative in the realm of AI products. As we embark on this chapter, it's paramount to underscore the pivotal role security plays in every facet of AI product development and deployment. The consequences of security breaches in AI systems extend far beyond mere data loss or system downtime; they can have profound and widespread impacts on individuals, organizations, and society at large. From compromised personal information to manipulated algorithms leading to biased or discriminatory outcomes, the repercussions of security lapses in AI products are multifaceted and potentially catastrophic.

In today's hyperconnected world, where AI systems permeate various aspects of our lives, the stakes have never been higher. Malicious actors exploit vulnerabilities in AI algorithms and systems to perpetrate a wide range of cyber threats, including data breaches, identity theft, financial fraud, and even attacks on critical infrastructure. Moreover, the increasing interconnectedness of AI systems with the Internet of Things (IoT) and other emerging technologies amplifies the attack surface, rendering traditional security measures inadequate in the face of evolving threats.

Against this backdrop, the imperative for proactive security measures in AI products cannot be overstated. It's not enough to reactively patch vulnerabilities or implement rudimentary security protocols; rather, a holistic approach to security that permeates every stage of the AI product lifecycle is essential. This entails embedding security considerations into the design phase, conducting rigorous security testing and validation, implementing robust encryption and access controls, and continuously monitoring and updating AI systems to mitigate emerging threats.

Furthermore, addressing security concerns in AI products requires collaboration and cooperation across interdisciplinary teams, including data scientists, engineers, cybersecurity experts, legal professionals, and ethicists. By fostering a culture of security awareness and accountability within organizations, stakeholders can collectively work towards building resilient and trustworthy AI systems that safeguard user privacy, uphold ethical standards, and mitigate the risks of malicious exploitation.

Security is not merely a technical concern but a fundamental ethical and societal imperative in the development and deployment of AI products. By prioritizing security at every stage of the AI product lifecycle and fostering a collaborative approach to addressing security challenges, organizations can uphold trust and integrity in AI systems, thereby realizing their transformative potential while safeguarding against potential harms.

Identifying and Mitigating Cyber Threats

In the ever-evolving landscape of AI products, the specter of cyber threats looms large, casting a shadow over the integrity and security of these innovative technologies. From insidious data breaches to sophisticated adversarial attacks, the range of potential threats facing AI systems is vast and multifaceted. As we delve into this section, it becomes apparent that a comprehensive understanding of these threats and robust strategies for their identification and mitigation are imperative for safeguarding the integrity and functionality of AI products.

At the forefront of our discussion is the notion of proactive threat modeling—an essential practice for preemptively identifying and assessing potential vulnerabilities and attack vectors in AI systems. By systematically analyzing the various components, interfaces, and dependencies of AI products, organizations can anticipate and mitigate potential security risks before they manifest into full-fledged threats. This involves mapping out potential attack scenarios, identifying critical assets and entry points, and evaluating the effectiveness of existing security measures in mitigating these risks.

Furthermore, conducting rigorous vulnerability assessments is essential for uncovering and addressing weaknesses in AI systems that could be exploited by malicious actors. This entails subjecting AI algorithms, models, and infrastructure to comprehensive security testing, including penetration testing, code review, and fuzz testing, to identify vulnerabilities and weaknesses that may be leveraged to compromise the integrity or confidentiality of the system. By proactively identifying and addressing these vulnerabilities, organizations can fortify their defenses against potential cyber threats and minimize the likelihood of successful attacks.

Integral to the mitigation of cyber threats in AI products is the integration of security measures at every stage of the development lifecycle. From the initial design phase to deployment and maintenance, security considerations should be woven into the fabric of AI product development processes. This includes implementing robust encryption mechanisms to protect sensitive data, enforcing access controls to restrict unauthorized access to AI systems, and integrating anomaly detection and monitoring capabilities to detect and respond to suspicious activities in real-time.

Moreover, fostering a culture of security awareness and accountability within organizations is paramount for effectively mitigating cyber threats in AI products. This involves educating stakeholders about common security risks and best practices, promoting adherence to security policies and procedures, and empowering individuals to report and address security incidents promptly. By instilling a culture of vigilance and resilience, organizations can strengthen their defenses against cyber threats and ensure the continued integrity and functionality of their AI products.

The landscape of cyber threats facing AI products is complex and ever-evolving, requiring proactive measures and a multi-faceted approach to identification and mitigation. By embracing practices such as proactive threat modeling, rigorous vulnerability assessments, and the integration of security measures throughout the development lifecycle, organizations can fortify their defenses against potential threats and safeguard the integrity and security of their AI products in an increasingly hostile digital landscape.

Data Security and Privacy in AI Systems

In the intricate ecosystem of AI systems, data serves as the cornerstone upon which innovation thrives. However, with the increasing reliance on vast troves of sensitive data, the imperative of data security and privacy emerges as a paramount concern. This section embarks on a comprehensive exploration of the strategies and practices essential for safeguarding the integrity, confidentiality, and privacy of data within AI systems, delving into the intricacies of encryption, access controls, data anonymization, and regulatory compliance.

At the heart of our discussion lies the deployment of robust encryption methods to shield sensitive data from unauthorized access and interception. Encryption serves as a potent shield against potential cyber threats, rendering data indecipherable to malicious actors and ensuring its confidentiality throughout transmission and storage. From symmetric and asymmetric encryption algorithms to advanced cryptographic techniques like homomorphic encryption and secure multi-party computation, organizations must employ a diverse array of encryption methods tailored to the unique requirements and sensitivities of their data assets.

Furthermore, implementing stringent access controls is essential for regulating and restricting access to sensitive data within AI systems. By delineating access privileges based on user roles, responsibilities, and authentication credentials, organizations can mitigate the risk of unauthorized access and insider threats, thereby safeguarding the integrity and confidentiality of their data assets. Access control mechanisms encompass a spectrum of techniques, including role-based access control (RBAC), attribute-based access control (ABAC), and dynamic access control policies, each offering varying degrees of granularity and flexibility in enforcing data access restrictions.

Moreover, data anonymization emerges as a pivotal strategy for preserving privacy and confidentiality in AI systems, particularly when dealing with personally identifiable information (PII) and sensitive personal data. By obscuring or removing identifying information from datasets, organizations can minimize the risk of re-identification and unauthorized disclosure, while still retaining the utility and value of the data for analytical purposes. Techniques such as data masking, tokenization, and differential privacy offer effective means of anonymizing data while preserving its statistical properties and utility for AI-driven insights and decision-making.

In addition to technical safeguards, organizations must also navigate a complex landscape of privacy regulations and compliance requirements, including the General Data Protection Regulation (GDPR), the California Consumer Privacy Act (CCPA), and other jurisdiction-specific data protection laws. Compliance with these regulations necessitates adherence to stringent data handling practices, including obtaining explicit consent for data collection and processing, implementing robust data governance and accountability mechanisms, and maintaining comprehensive records of data processing activities. Moreover, organizations must adopt a proactive approach to ethical data handling, prioritizing principles of transparency, fairness, and accountability in their data practices to ensure the responsible and ethical deployment of AI systems.

Data security and privacy represent fundamental pillars of trust and integrity in AI systems, demanding a multifaceted approach encompassing encryption, access controls, data anonymization, and regulatory compliance. By embracing these strategies and practices, organizations can navigate the complexities of data security and privacy with confidence, safeguarding the confidentiality, integrity, and privacy of their data assets while unlocking the transformative potential of AI-driven innovation.

Adversarial Attacks and Defensive Mechanisms

In the intricate world of AI systems, adversarial attacks stand out as a particularly formidable challenge, representing a sophisticated form of cyber threat where malicious actors exploit vulnerabilities to subvert and manipulate the outputs of AI models. As we embark on this exploration, it becomes evident that understanding the landscape of adversarial attacks and implementing robust defensive mechanisms are paramount for safeguarding the integrity and reliability of AI systems.

Adversarial attacks encompass a diverse array of techniques aimed at deceiving AI models and inducing erroneous or malicious behavior. From carefully crafted input perturbations to targeted evasion and poisoning attacks, adversaries employ a variety of strategies to exploit vulnerabilities in AI algorithms and systems, often with far-reaching consequences for security, privacy, and trust. These attacks can manifest across a spectrum of applications, including image classification, natural language processing, and autonomous systems, posing significant challenges to the robustness and reliability of AI-driven decision-making processes.

To combat the threat posed by adversarial attacks, organizations must adopt a multi-faceted approach that integrates proactive defensive mechanisms throughout the AI development lifecycle. One key strategy involves fortifying AI models through robust training techniques designed to enhance resilience against adversarial manipulation. This entails augmenting training datasets with adversarial examples, perturbing inputs during training to expose models to potential attack scenarios, and leveraging techniques such as adversarial training and defensive distillation to enhance model robustness and generalization.

Moreover, implementing anomaly detection mechanisms can help detect and mitigate adversarial attacks in real-time by monitoring model outputs for deviations from expected behavior. By leveraging techniques such as statistical anomaly detection, anomaly-based intrusion detection systems, and outlier analysis, organizations can identify and flag suspicious activities indicative of adversarial manipulation, enabling timely intervention and response to potential threats.

Furthermore, adversarial attacks can be mitigated through the deployment of adversarial defenses specifically designed to thwart malicious manipulation attempts. These defenses encompass a spectrum of techniques, including gradient masking, feature squeezing, and input preprocessing, aimed at increasing the resilience of AI models to adversarial perturbations while maintaining performance and functionality. Additionally, deploying ensemble methods and model diversity techniques can help mitigate the impact of adversarial attacks by introducing variability and redundancy into AI systems, making them more robust and resilient to manipulation.

In addition to technical defenses, organizations must also cultivate a culture of security awareness and vigilance, empowering stakeholders to recognize and respond to potential adversarial threats effectively. This involves educating developers, data scientists, and end-users about common adversarial attack vectors and best practices for mitigating their impact, as well as fostering collaboration and information sharing within the AI security community to stay abreast of emerging threats and defensive strategies.

Adversarial attacks represent a pervasive and evolving threat to the integrity and reliability of AI systems, demanding proactive defensive measures and a comprehensive understanding of attack vectors and defensive mechanisms.

By integrating robust training techniques, anomaly detection mechanisms, and adversarial defenses into AI systems, organizations can fortify their defenses against malicious manipulation attempts and safeguard the trust and integrity of AI-driven decision-making processes in an increasingly hostile digital landscape.

Secure Model Deployment and Operation

Ensuring the secure deployment and operation of AI models is not merely a component but a cornerstone of holistic system security. As we delve into this critical aspect, it's essential to recognize the multifaceted nature of securing model deployment, which encompasses a spectrum of best practices ranging from containerization and access controls to continuous monitoring and secure DevOps pipelines. By adopting a comprehensive approach that addresses each of these facets, organizations can fortify their defenses and safeguard the integrity and reliability of AI systems throughout their lifecycle.

At the forefront of securing model deployment lies the practice of containerization—a technique that encapsulates AI models, dependencies, and runtime environments within isolated containers to ensure consistency, portability, and security. By containerizing AI models, organizations can mitigate the risk of dependency conflicts, streamline deployment workflows, and enforce fine-grained access controls, thereby reducing the attack surface and enhancing the resilience of deployed models against potential security threats.

Moreover, implementing robust access controls is essential for regulating and restricting access to deployed AI models, ensuring that only authorized users and systems can interact with sensitive resources. Access control mechanisms encompass a range of techniques, including role-based

434

access control (RBAC), attribute-based access control (ABAC), and identity and access management (IAM), each offering varying degrees of granularity and flexibility in enforcing access restrictions based on user roles, privileges, and authentication credentials.

Furthermore, continuous monitoring emerges as a critical practice for detecting and responding to security incidents in real-time, thereby minimizing the impact of potential threats on deployed AI models. By leveraging monitoring tools and techniques, organizations can monitor the performance, behavior, and usage patterns of deployed models, detect anomalies and security breaches, and trigger automated responses or alerts to mitigate potential risks promptly. Continuous monitoring enables organizations to maintain situational awareness and visibility into the security posture of deployed AI models, empowering them to proactively identify and address emerging threats before they escalate into full-blown security incidents.

Integral to the secure deployment and operation of AI models is the adoption of a secure DevOps pipeline—a methodology that integrates security considerations into every stage of the AI product lifecycle, from development and testing to deployment and maintenance. By incorporating security controls, automated security testing, and vulnerability scanning into CI/CD pipelines, organizations can ensure that security is woven into the fabric of the development process, enabling them to identify and remediate security vulnerabilities early and often. Moreover, embracing principles of DevSecOps promotes collaboration and communication between development, operations, and security teams, fostering a culture of shared responsibility and accountability for security across the organization.

Securing the deployment and operation of AI models requires a multifaceted approach that encompasses containerization, access controls, continuous monitoring, and secure DevOps practices. By adopting these best practices and integrating security into every aspect of the AI product lifecycle, organizations can fortify their defenses, mitigate security risks, and safeguard the integrity and reliability of deployed AI models in an increasingly dynamic and complex threat landscape.

Trustworthy AI: Building User Confidence

Establishing user trust is not merely an auxiliary concern but a fundamental pillar of successful AI deployment. This section embarks on a comprehensive exploration of the concept of trustworthy AI, where transparency, explainability, and accountability serve as the bedrock upon which user confidence is built. By delving into the intricacies of trustworthy AI, we uncover a myriad of strategies and best practices aimed at fostering transparency, engendering trust, and empowering users to make informed decisions about AI-driven products and services.

At the heart of trustworthy AI lies the principle of transparency—the practice of openly communicating how AI is used, its capabilities, limitations, and potential impact on users. Transparency enables users to understand the underlying mechanisms and algorithms driving AI systems, empowering them to make informed decisions about their usage and implications. By providing clear and accessible information about data sources, model training methodologies, and decision-making processes, organizations can instill confidence in users and cultivate a culture of transparency and openness in AI deployment.

Furthermore, ensuring the explainability of AI-driven decisions is essential for building user trust and confidence in AI systems. Explainability entails the ability to elucidate and justify the rationale behind AI-generated recommendations, predictions, and decisions in a clear, interpretable manner. By adopting explainable AI techniques such as model interpretability, feature importance analysis, and decision tree visualization, organizations can demystify the black-box nature of AI algorithms, enabling users to comprehend the factors influencing AI-driven outcomes and fostering trust in the reliability and fairness of AI systems.

Moreover, accountability emerges as a critical component of trustworthy AI, where organizations assume responsibility for the ethical and responsible deployment of AI systems and uphold principles of fairness, equity, and non-discrimination. By establishing mechanisms for user feedback, redress, and recourse, organizations can empower users to report concerns, provide input on AI performance, and seek resolution for issues related to bias, errors, or unintended consequences. Additionally, implementing robust governance frameworks, ethical guidelines, and oversight mechanisms can help ensure that AI systems adhere to ethical standards and regulatory requirements, thereby enhancing accountability and promoting responsible AI deployment.

In addition to transparency, explainability, and accountability, fostering a culture of user engagement and collaboration is essential for building user confidence in AI products. By soliciting user feedback, incorporating user preferences and preferences into AI models, and involving users in the design and development process, organizations can co-create AI solutions that meet user needs, preferences, and expectations. Furthermore, fostering open dialogue and communication channels between users and AI developers facilitates mutual understanding, trust, and collaboration, ultimately enhancing user confidence in AI-driven products and services.

Building user confidence in AI products requires a multifaceted approach that encompasses transparency, explainability, accountability, and user engagement. By embracing these principles and practices, organizations can foster trust, empower users, and ensure the ethical and responsible deployment of AI systems, thereby unlocking the full potential of AI-driven innovation while safeguarding user rights, privacy, and well-being in an increasingly AI-driven world.

Ethical Considerations in AI Security

In the realm of AI security, ethical considerations are not merely complementary but foundational, shaping the very fabric of security practices and policies. This section embarks on a comprehensive exploration of the ethical dimensions inherent in AI security, delving into issues of fairness, accountability, transparency, and responsible governance. By examining these ethical considerations through a critical lens, we uncover the complexities and challenges inherent in aligning security measures with ethical principles to ensure the responsible development and deployment of AI products.

At the forefront of ethical considerations in AI security lies the principle of fairness—the imperative to ensure that security measures do not inadvertently perpetuate or exacerbate biases, discrimination, or inequities. In the context of AI systems, fairness encompasses a range of considerations, including algorithmic bias, representation bias, and disparate impact, which can manifest in various forms, such as differential treatment of individuals based on protected characteristics or underrepresentation of certain demographic groups in training datasets. Addressing fairness concerns requires proactive measures to mitigate bias, promote diversity and inclusivity in data collection and model training, and incorporate fairness-aware techniques into security algorithms and decision-making processes.

Moreover, accountability emerges as a critical ethical consideration in AI security, where organizations assume responsibility for the consequences of their security practices and decisions. Accountability entails transparency and traceability in security processes, mechanisms for oversight and redress, and clear lines of responsibility and accountability for security incidents and breaches. By establishing robust governance frameworks, ethical guidelines, and accountability mechanisms, organizations can ensure that security measures align with ethical principles and regulatory requirements, thereby fostering trust and confidence in AI-driven security solutions.

Transparency represents another key ethical consideration in AI security, where organizations are expected to provide clear and accessible information about their security practices, policies, and technologies. Transparency enables users to understand how their data is being used, processed, and protected, empowering them to make informed decisions about their privacy and security. By adopting transparent security practices, such as clear communication about data collection and usage policies, open access to security audits and assessments, and transparent decision-making processes, organizations can build trust and credibility with users and stakeholders, thereby enhancing the ethical integrity of AI-driven security solutions.

Furthermore, ensuring the responsible governance of AI security practices is essential for upholding ethical standards and principles. Responsible governance entails the establishment of ethical guidelines, codes of conduct, and regulatory frameworks that govern the development, deployment, and use of AI-driven security solutions. By integrating ethical considerations into organizational policies and practices, fostering a culture of ethical awareness and accountability, and engaging stakeholders in ethical decision-making processes, organizations can mitigate ethical risks and ensure the responsible and ethical deployment of AI security solutions.

Ethical considerations are integral to AI security, shaping the design, development, and deployment of security measures and technologies. By addressing issues of fairness, accountability, transparency, and responsible governance, organizations can ensure that security practices align with ethical principles, promote trust and confidence in AI-driven security solutions, and uphold the rights, dignity, and well-being of individuals in an increasingly AI-driven world.

Regulatory Compliance and Standards

In the intricate terrain of AI security, compliance with regulations and adherence to standards are indispensable cornerstones for ensuring the integrity, privacy, and security of AI-driven systems and applications. This section embarks on a comprehensive exploration of the regulatory landscape and standards governing AI security, providing insights into key regulations, industry-specific requirements, and the role of compliance frameworks in shaping responsible AI development practices.

At the forefront of regulatory compliance in AI security lies a myriad of regulations and laws aimed at safeguarding user privacy, data protection, and ethical use of AI technologies. Chief among these is the General Data Protection Regulation (GDPR), which imposes stringent requirements for the collection, processing, and storage of personal data, including provisions for data minimization, purpose limitation, and user consent. Additionally, sector-specific regulations such as the Health Insurance Portability and Accountability Act (HIPAA) in healthcare and the Payment Card Industry Data Security Standard (PCI DSS) in finance impose industry-specific requirements for securing sensitive data and protecting against data breaches.

Moreover, international standards bodies and industry consortia play a pivotal role in establishing best practices and guidelines for AI security. Standards such as ISO/IEC 27001 for information security management systems, ISO/IEC 27701 for privacy information management, and NIST SP 800-53 for security and privacy controls provide organizations with a framework for implementing robust security measures and ensuring compliance with regulatory requirements. Additionally, industry-specific standards and frameworks, such as the HITRUST Common Security Framework in healthcare and the NIST Cybersecurity Framework in critical infrastructure, offer sector-specific guidance for addressing unique security challenges and compliance obligations.

In addition to regulatory compliance and standards, compliance frameworks play a crucial role in guiding AI security practices and fostering a culture of responsible AI development. These frameworks provide organizations with a structured approach to assessing, managing, and mitigating risks associated with AI deployment, enabling them to align security measures with regulatory requirements, industry best practices, and organizational objectives. By adopting compliance frameworks such as the GDPR Compliance Framework, the NIST Risk Management Framework, or the OWASP Application Security Verification Standard, organizations can streamline compliance efforts, enhance risk visibility, and demonstrate adherence to regulatory requirements and industry standards.

Furthermore, compliance with regulations and adherence to standards not only mitigate legal and regulatory risks but also enhance trust and credibility with stakeholders, including customers, partners, and regulatory authorities. By demonstrating a commitment to compliance and responsible AI development practices, organizations can differentiate themselves in the marketplace, build trust and confidence with users, and mitigate reputational risks associated with security breaches or non-compliance. Moreover, compliance with regulations and adherence to standards serve as a catalyst for innovation, driving organizations to adopt robust security measures, implement best practices, and leverage emerging technologies to enhance the security and resilience of AI-driven systems and applications.

Navigating the complex landscape of regulatory compliance and standards is essential for ensuring the security and integrity of AI-driven systems and applications. By understanding key regulations, industry-specific requirements, and compliance frameworks, organizations can develop a proactive approach to AI security, mitigate legal and regulatory risks, and foster a culture of responsible AI development that prioritizes user privacy, data protection, and ethical use of AI technologies.

Building a Security-Aware Culture

Creating a security-aware culture within AI teams is not merely about implementing technical safeguards; it's about fostering a collective mindset and ethos that prioritizes security as a fundamental organizational imperative. This section embarks on a comprehensive exploration of strategies for cultivating a security-aware culture within AI teams, delving into the pivotal role of education, training, ongoing awareness programs, and organizational norms in shaping attitudes, behaviors, and practices towards security.

At the heart of building a security-aware culture lies the recognition that security is everyone's responsibility. From data scientists and developers to project managers and executives, every team member plays a critical role in maintaining the integrity, confidentiality, and availability of AI systems and data. As such, organizations must invest in comprehensive education and training programs that equip team members with the knowledge, skills, and awareness needed to identify, mitigate, and respond to security threats effectively.

Education and training programs serve as foundational pillars for building a security-aware culture, providing team members with the requisite knowledge and understanding of security principles, best practices, and procedures. By offering specialized training on topics such as secure coding practices, threat modeling, incident response, and compliance requirements, organizations can empower team members to make informed decisions and take proactive measures to protect against security threats.

Moreover, ongoing awareness programs play a pivotal role in reinforcing security principles and fostering a culture of vigilance and accountability within AI teams. These programs encompass a variety of activities, including security briefings, newsletters, workshops, and simulated phishing exercises, designed to keep team members informed about emerging threats, security trends, and organizational policies. By promoting regular communication and engagement on security-related topics, organizations can reinforce the importance of security and instill a sense of collective responsibility for safeguarding AI systems and data.

Furthermore, fostering a security-aware culture requires establishing organizational norms and practices that prioritize security as a core value. This entails integrating security considerations into the fabric of daily operations, from project planning and development to deployment and maintenance. By implementing security-by-design principles, conducting security reviews and audits, and enforcing adherence to security policies and procedures, organizations can create a climate where security is embedded into every aspect of AI development and operation.

In addition to education, training, and awareness programs, leadership plays a pivotal role in shaping a security-aware culture within AI teams. Executives and managers must lead by example, demonstrating a commitment to security and providing the necessary resources and support to foster a culture of security excellence. By championing security initiatives, allocating budget and resources for security measures, and holding team members accountable for security outcomes, leaders can create an environment where security is valued, prioritized, and ingrained into the organizational DNA.

Building a security-aware culture within AI teams requires a multifaceted approach that encompasses education, training, ongoing awareness programs, organizational norms, and leadership commitment. By investing in these strategies, organizations can cultivate a workforce that is knowledgeable, vigilant, and proactive in safeguarding AI systems and data against evolving threats, thereby mitigating risks and ensuring the resilience and integrity of AI-driven technologies.

Collaborative Approaches to Security

In the dynamic landscape of cybersecurity, fostering collaboration among diverse stakeholders is not just advantageous—it's essential for fortifying the overall security posture of AI products and systems. This section embarks on an in-depth exploration of the significance of cross-functional collaboration between security experts, data scientists, product managers, legal teams, and other key stakeholders in mitigating security risks, enhancing threat detection capabilities, and fostering a culture of security excellence.

At the heart of collaborative approaches to security lies the recognition that effective security is a collective responsibility that transcends individual roles or departments. By bringing together multidisciplinary teams with diverse expertise, perspectives, and insights, organizations can leverage a wealth of knowledge and experience to address complex security challenges and develop robust, holistic solutions that mitigate risks across the entire AI product lifecycle.

One of the primary benefits of cross-functional collaboration in security is the ability to gain a comprehensive understanding of security risks and vulnerabilities from multiple vantage points. Security experts bring specialized knowledge of threat landscapes, attack vectors, and defensive strategies, while data scientists offer insights into the unique security considerations inherent in AI algorithms, models, and datasets. Product managers provide valuable input on user requirements, functionality, and usability, while legal teams offer guidance on regulatory compliance, risk management, and liability issues. By synthesizing these diverse perspectives, organizations can develop a more nuanced understanding of security risks and devise more effective strategies for mitigating them.

Moreover, collaborative approaches to security enable organizations to implement security measures that are tailored to the specific needs and characteristics of AI products and systems. By involving stakeholders from various disciplines in security planning and decision-making processes, organizations can ensure that security considerations are integrated into every stage of the AI product lifecycle—from design and development to deployment and maintenance. This holistic approach to security helps identify and address security vulnerabilities early in the development process, reducing the likelihood of security incidents and enhancing the resilience of AI products against emerging threats.

Furthermore, cross-functional collaboration facilitates effective communication and coordination among stakeholders, enabling timely responses to security incidents and emerging threats. By establishing clear lines of communication, escalation procedures, and incident response plans, organizations can ensure that security issues are promptly identified, escalated, and resolved in a coordinated manner. This proactive approach to security helps minimize the impact of security incidents on AI products and systems, mitigating potential damage to reputation, user trust, and organizational credibility.

In addition to enhancing security effectiveness, collaborative approaches also foster a culture of security awareness and accountability within organizations. By promoting cross-functional collaboration, organizations can instill a sense of shared responsibility for security among all stakeholders, empowering them to actively contribute to security initiatives, share knowledge and best practices, and advocate for security-related priorities. This culture of collective ownership and collaboration creates a strong foundation for building a resilient and secure environment for AI innovation, ensuring that security remains a top priority across the organization.

Collaborative approaches to security are essential for mitigating security risks, enhancing threat detection capabilities, and fostering a culture of security excellence within organizations. By bringing together diverse stakeholders with complementary expertise and perspectives, organizations can develop more comprehensive security strategies, implement tailored security measures, and respond more effectively to security incidents and emerging threats. This collaborative approach not only strengthens the overall security posture of AI products and systems but also promotes a culture of security awareness, accountability, and innovation that is essential for success in today's rapidly evolving threat landscape.

Incident Response and Continuous Improvement

Incident response and continuous improvement form the bedrock of effective AI security practices, serving as proactive measures to prepare for, mitigate, and learn from security incidents. This section embarks on an in-depth exploration of incident response planning and continuous improvement strategies, encompassing the full spectrum of incident handling—from identification and containment to eradication, recovery, and post-incident analysis.

At the core of incident response planning lies the development of comprehensive incident response plans (IRPs) tailored to the unique characteristics and requirements of AI systems and applications. These plans outline the procedures, roles, and responsibilities for responding to security incidents, ensuring a coordinated and effective response when incidents occur. Key components of IRPs include:

1. Identification: Establishing mechanisms for detecting and alerting on security incidents, such as intrusion detection systems, log monitoring, and anomaly detection techniques. Rapid identification of security incidents is essential for minimizing the impact and scope of potential breaches.

2. Containment: Implementing measures to contain and prevent the spread of security incidents, such as isolating affected systems, disabling compromised accounts, and implementing access controls to limit further damage. Containment efforts are aimed at preventing the escalation of security incidents and mitigating their impact on AI systems and data.

3. Eradication: Conducting thorough investigations to identify the root cause of security incidents, remediate vulnerabilities, and eliminate malicious activity from affected systems.

Eradication efforts aim to restore the integrity and functionality of AI systems while preventing recurrence of similar incidents in the future.

4. Recovery: Restoring affected systems and data to a secure and operational state following a security incident, including data restoration, system reconfiguration, and patching of vulnerabilities. Recovery efforts focus on minimizing downtime, restoring service availability, and ensuring business continuity in the aftermath of security incidents.

5. Lessons learned: Conduct post-incident analysis and documentation to identify lessons learned, root causes, and areas for improvement in incident response processes and procedures. Lessons learned from security incidents serve as valuable insights for refining incident response plans, enhancing security controls, and strengthening the overall security posture of AI systems.

Continuous improvement is essential for ensuring that AI products evolve to address emerging security challenges and threats. This involves leveraging insights gained from post-incident analysis, security assessments, threat intelligence, and industry best practices to iteratively enhance security measures and incident response capabilities. Key strategies for continuous improvement include:

1. Iterative refinement of incident response plans based on lessons learned from security incidents, security audits, and tabletop exercises. IRPs should be regularly reviewed, updated, and tested to ensure their effectiveness and relevance in addressing evolving security threats.

2. Integration of security incident data into risk management processes to identify trends, patterns, and recurring issues that may indicate systemic weaknesses or vulnerabilities in AI systems. By analyzing security incident data, organizations

can prioritize security investments and allocate resources to address the most critical risks.

3. Collaboration and information sharing with industry peers, security researchers, and government agencies to stay abreast of emerging threats, vulnerabilities, and best practices in AI security. By participating in information-sharing initiatives and industry forums, organizations can gain valuable insights into emerging security trends and potential threats, enabling them to proactively adapt and respond to changing threat landscapes.

4. Automation and orchestration of incident response processes to streamline response efforts, reduce manual intervention, and improve response times. By leveraging automation tools and technologies, organizations can accelerate incident detection, analysis, and remediation, enabling them to respond more effectively to security incidents and minimize their impact on AI systems and data.

Incident response and continuous improvement are essential components of effective AI security practices, enabling organizations to prepare for, mitigate, and learn from security incidents. By developing comprehensive incident response plans, leveraging insights from post-incident analysis, and continuously refining security measures and processes, organizations can strengthen the resilience and integrity of AI systems, enhance their ability to detect and respond to security threats and adapt to evolving security challenges in an increasingly dynamic and complex threat landscape.

Future Trends in AI Security

Exploring the future trends in AI security unveils a landscape shaped by emerging technologies, evolving threat landscapes, and dynamic regulatory frameworks. This section embarks on an extensive journey to forecast the trajectory of

AI security, analyzing key trends that are set to influence its future direction. By anticipating these trends, AI practitioners can strategically position themselves to navigate evolving risks and challenges, thereby ensuring the creation of secure, trustworthy, and ethically sound AI products.

Emerging technologies stand at the forefront of future trends in AI security, presenting both opportunities and challenges for safeguarding AI systems and data. As AI continues to advance, novel technologies such as federated learning, homomorphic encryption, and secure multi-party computation are poised to revolutionize the way data is collected, processed, and protected in AI-driven environments. These technologies offer innovative solutions for enhancing data privacy, confidentiality, and security, while also introducing new complexities and vulnerabilities that require careful consideration and mitigation.

Moreover, the evolving threat landscape presents a dynamic and multifaceted challenge for AI security practitioners, as adversaries increasingly leverage sophisticated techniques and strategies to exploit vulnerabilities in AI systems and applications. From adversarial attacks and data poisoning to supply chain vulnerabilities and insider threats, the range and complexity of security risks facing AI-driven environments continue to expand, necessitating proactive measures to detect, mitigate, and respond to emerging threats. By adopting threat intelligence, machine learning-based anomaly detection, and proactive security controls, AI practitioners can enhance their ability to anticipate, identify, and mitigate security threats in real-time, thereby minimizing the risk of security breaches and data compromises.

Furthermore, regulatory developments play a pivotal role in shaping the future of AI security, as policymakers seek to address emerging challenges and risks associated with AI technologies. From data protection regulations such as the

GDPR and CCPA to AI-specific regulations such as the EU's proposed Artificial Intelligence Act, regulatory frameworks are evolving to establish clear guidelines and standards for the responsible development, deployment, and use of AI systems. By staying abreast of regulatory developments and compliance requirements, AI practitioners can ensure that their security measures align with legal and ethical standards, thereby mitigating legal and reputational risks associated with non-compliance.

In addition to technological advancements, threat landscapes, and regulatory developments, the future of AI security hinges on the integration of robust security measures, the fostering of a culture of trustworthiness and ethical considerations, and the promotion of responsible AI practices. By embedding security-by-design principles into AI development processes, fostering transparency, explainability, and accountability in AI algorithms and decision-making processes, and promoting ethical AI practices that prioritize fairness, equity, and inclusivity, AI practitioners can contribute to the creation of AI products that are not only secure and trustworthy but also ethical and socially responsible.

The future of AI security is characterized by a convergence of emerging technologies, evolving threat landscapes, and dynamic regulatory frameworks, presenting both opportunities and challenges for AI practitioners. By anticipating future trends, integrating robust security measures, and promoting ethical AI practices, AI practitioners can proactively adapt to evolving risks and challenges, thereby ensuring the creation of AI products that are secure, trustworthy, and ethically sound in an increasingly complex and interconnected digital landscape.

ESTABLISHING TRUST WITH USERS

In the evolving landscape of AI products, establishing trust with users is a foundational element that underpins the success and adoption of innovative technologies. This chapter delves into the multifaceted dimensions of building trust, emphasizing the importance of transparency, user-centric design, ethical considerations, and proactive communication in fostering a relationship of trust between AI products and their users.

The Essence of Trust in AI Products

Understanding the essence of trust in AI products is paramount to their successful adoption and sustained use. This chapter embarks on a comprehensive exploration of trust as the cornerstone of user acceptance, engagement, and the establishment of enduring relationships with AI systems. By delving into the intrinsic significance of trust, we uncover its multifaceted dimensions and its profound impact on user perceptions, behaviors, and experiences with AI technologies.

At the heart of the discussion lies the recognition that trust forms the bedrock of user confidence and satisfaction in AI products. Trust is not merely a byproduct of functionality or performance; it is a fundamental attribute that underpins user perceptions of reliability, predictability, and ethical soundness in AI systems. Users are more likely to engage with and rely on AI products when they perceive them as trustworthy, consistent, and aligned with their expectations and values.

One of the key themes explored in this chapter is the role of trust in fostering user acceptance and engagement with AI systems. Trust enables users to overcome skepticism, uncertainty, and fear of the unknown, empowering them to embrace AI technologies with confidence and enthusiasm. Whether it's using AI-powered virtual assistants, autonomous vehicles, or recommendation systems, users are more inclined to engage with AI products when they trust that they will deliver reliable, accurate, and beneficial outcomes.

Moreover, trust plays a crucial role in establishing long-term relationships between users and AI systems. In an increasingly interconnected and digitized world, users are bombarded with a myriad of options for AI-driven products and services. However, it is trust that distinguishes one product from another, influencing user loyalty, advocacy, and retention over time. Users are more likely to remain loyal to AI products that consistently deliver on their promises, demonstrate ethical behavior, and prioritize user interests and well-being.

Furthermore, the various dimensions of trust are essential for building user confidence in AI products. These dimensions include reliability, transparency, explainability, fairness, and privacy. Reliability entails the consistent and accurate performance of AI systems across different contexts and scenarios. Transparency involves open and clear communication about how AI algorithms work, how decisions are made, and how user data is collected and used. Explainability entails the ability to provide understandable explanations for AI-generated recommendations, predictions, and decisions, fostering user trust and confidence in AI systems. Fairness involves ensuring that AI systems do not exhibit bias or discrimination against individuals or groups based on protected characteristics. Privacy involves protecting user data and ensuring that AI systems adhere to privacy regulations and ethical principles.

The essence of trust in AI products transcends mere functionality or performance; it is a fundamental attribute that shapes user perceptions, behaviors, and experiences with AI technologies. By establishing trust as the bedrock of user acceptance, engagement, and long-term relationships, AI practitioners can create AI products that are not only functional and efficient but also ethical, transparent, and trustworthy in the eyes of users.

Transparency as a Pillar of Trust

Transparency serves as a foundational pillar in fostering trust within the realm of AI products. This section embarks on a comprehensive exploration of transparency as an indispensable element in building and maintaining trust between users and AI systems. By delving into the multifaceted dimensions of transparency, from openly communicating the inner workings of AI algorithms to elucidating data usage and decision-making processes, this discussion elucidates how transparent practices empower users with knowledge and understanding, thereby bolstering confidence and fostering trust in AI products.

At the heart of transparency lies the principle of openness and clarity in communication, enabling users to gain insights into how AI algorithms operate, how decisions are made, and how their data is utilized. By demystifying the technology and providing users with visibility into the underlying mechanisms of AI systems, transparency fosters a sense of understanding and control, empowering users to make informed decisions and assessments about the reliability, fairness, and ethical soundness of AI products.

One of the key themes explored in this section is the role of transparency in mitigating user uncertainty and skepticism towards AI technologies. In an era marked by growing concerns over data privacy, algorithmic bias, and ethical implications of AI, transparency serves as a powerful antidote to mistrust and apprehension. By openly communicating about how AI algorithms work, the sources and quality of data used for training, and the criteria used for decision-making, organizations can alleviate user concerns and instill confidence in the reliability and integrity of AI systems.

Moreover, transparency plays a crucial role in empowering users with knowledge and agency, enabling them to understand and assess the implications of AI technologies on their lives, privacy, and well-being. By providing clear and accessible information about data collection, processing, and usage practices, organizations empower users to exercise informed consent and make meaningful choices about their engagement with AI products and services. Transparency enables users to understand the potential risks and benefits of AI technologies, enabling them to weigh the trade-offs and make decisions that align with their values and preferences.

Furthermore, transparency fosters accountability and responsibility in AI development and deployment practices, ensuring that organizations adhere to ethical standards and regulatory requirements. By adopting transparent practices, organizations demonstrate a commitment to ethical behavior, integrity, and user trust, thereby mitigating reputational risks and legal liabilities associated with non-compliance or unethical conduct. Transparency also facilitates external scrutiny and oversight, enabling stakeholders, regulators, and advocacy groups to assess the fairness, accountability, and ethical implications of AI systems and hold organizations accountable for their actions.

Transparency serves as a fundamental pillar of trust-building in AI products, enabling organizations to foster understanding, confidence, and accountability among users. By adopting transparent practices, organizations can demystify AI technologies, empower users with knowledge and agency, and demonstrate a commitment to ethical behavior and responsible AI development practices. Ultimately, transparency enables organizations to build enduring relationships with users based on trust, integrity, and mutual respect, thereby fostering a culture of transparency and openness in the AI ecosystem.

Explainability in AI Decision-Making

Explainability in AI decision-making is not just a desirable feature; it's a fundamental requirement for fostering user trust and confidence in AI systems. This section embarks on an extensive exploration of the critical role of explainability in AI decision-making, elucidating strategies and techniques for making AI algorithms and decisions more understandable and transparent to users. By delving into the nuances of explainability, from the use of interpretable models to the design of user-friendly interfaces, this discussion unveils how explainability empowers users with insights into how AI arrives at specific outcomes, thereby enhancing trust and facilitating informed decision-making.

At the core of explainability lies the principle of transparency and clarity in AI decision-making processes, enabling users to understand the rationale, logic, and factors that influence AI-generated outcomes. By providing users with insights into the inner workings of AI algorithms, explainability fosters a sense of trust, predictability, and control, empowering users to assess the reliability, fairness, and ethical soundness of AI-driven decisions.

One of the key themes explored in this section is the use of interpretable models as a foundational approach to achieving explainability in AI decision-making. Interpretable models, such as decision trees, linear regression, and rule-based systems, offer transparent and understandable representations of how AI algorithms process data and make predictions. By leveraging interpretable models, organizations can provide users with clear and intuitive explanations for AI-generated outcomes, thereby enhancing user understanding and confidence in AI systems.

Moreover, the section delves into the importance of contextual explanations in enhancing the interpretability of AI decisions. Contextual explanations provide users with insights into the factors and considerations that influence AI-generated outcomes within specific contexts or scenarios. By contextualizing explanations based on user preferences, goals, and constraints, organizations can tailor explanations to meet the diverse needs and expectations of users, thereby enhancing the relevance, clarity, and utility of explainability in AI decision-making.

Furthermore, the design of user-friendly interfaces plays a crucial role in facilitating explainability and enhancing user engagement with AI systems. User-friendly interfaces enable organizations to present explanations in a clear, intuitive, and visually appealing manner, making complex AI algorithms and decisions more accessible and understandable to users. By incorporating interactive visualizations, natural language explanations, and personalized recommendations, organizations can empower users to explore and interpret AI-generated outcomes in a manner that aligns with their cognitive abilities, preferences, and information needs.

Explainability is a critical aspect of user trust and confidence in AI decision-making, enabling organizations to enhance transparency, predictability, and control in AI systems. By adopting strategies for achieving explainability, such as leveraging interpretable models, providing contextual explanations, and designing user-friendly interfaces, organizations can empower users with insights into how AI arrives at specific outcomes, thereby fostering trust, facilitating informed decision-making, and promoting the responsible and ethical use of AI technologies. Ultimately, explainability enables organizations to build enduring relationships with users based on transparency, accountability, and mutual understanding in the AI ecosystem.

User-Centric Design for Trustworthiness

User-centric design serves as a cornerstone in the construction of trustworthy AI products, wielding significant influence in fostering user trust and confidence. This section undertakes an exhaustive examination of the critical role played by user-centric design in ensuring the trustworthiness of AI products. By emphasizing the need to prioritize the user's perspective, this discussion delves into the intricate interplay between intuitive interfaces, clear user journeys, and features that align with user expectations, all of which contribute to a positive user experience and enhance trust in the product.

At the heart of user-centric design lies the recognition that users are the ultimate arbiters of trust in AI products. By placing the user's needs, preferences, and expectations at the forefront of the design process, organizations can create AI products that resonate with users and instill confidence in their reliability, usability, and ethical soundness. User-centric design involves understanding user behaviors, motivations, and pain points through methods such as user research, usability testing, and persona development, and incorporating these insights into the design of AI products.

One of the key themes explored in this section is the importance of intuitive interfaces in fostering trust and confidence in AI products. Intuitive interfaces are designed to be easy to navigate, understand, and use, minimizing cognitive load and friction for users. By employing principles of simplicity, consistency, and familiarity, organizations can create interfaces that empower users to interact with AI products confidently and effortlessly, thereby enhancing their trust and satisfaction with the product.

Moreover, the section delves into the significance of clear user journeys in guiding users through the AI product experience. Clear user journeys map out the steps and interactions that users take to accomplish their goals within the product, providing a seamless and intuitive pathway to desired outcomes. By designing user journeys that are logical, coherent, and easy to follow, organizations can reduce user confusion, frustration, and mistrust, thereby fostering a positive and engaging user experience that inspires confidence and loyalty.

Furthermore, the section highlights the importance of aligning product features with user expectations to build trust and credibility. User expectations are shaped by prior experiences, cultural norms, and industry standards, and play a crucial role in shaping perceptions of trustworthiness in AI products. By incorporating features that meet or exceed user expectations, organizations can establish a sense of reliability, consistency, and authenticity, thereby enhancing user trust and loyalty over time.

User-centric design is a fundamental enabler of trustworthiness in AI products, facilitating positive user experiences and enhancing user trust and confidence in the product. By prioritizing intuitive interfaces, clear user journeys, and features that align with user expectations, organizations can create AI products that resonate with users and inspire trust, thereby fostering long-term relationships and driving success in the competitive AI marketplace. Ultimately, user-centric design empowers organizations to build AI products that not only meet user needs but also exceed user expectations, setting the stage for sustainable growth and innovation in the evolving landscape of AI technologies.

Ethical Considerations in AI Design

Ethical considerations are not just an afterthought in AI design; they are the very foundation upon which trustworthy AI is built. This section embarks on an in-depth exploration of the ethical dimensions inherent in AI design, illuminating key principles such as fairness, accountability, and the mitigation of bias. By delving into the proactive integration of ethical considerations into the design and development process, this discussion underscores the imperative of ensuring that AI products not only function effectively but also align with societal values and expectations, thereby fostering trust and promoting responsible AI innovation.

At the core of ethical considerations in AI design lies the principle of fairness, which entails ensuring that AI systems treat all individuals and groups equitably and without discrimination. Fairness involves identifying and mitigating biases that may be present in AI algorithms or datasets, such as biases related to race, gender, age, or socioeconomic status. By adopting techniques such as bias detection, bias mitigation, and fairness-aware AI algorithms, organizations can enhance the fairness and inclusivity of AI systems, thereby promoting trust and confidence among users.

Moreover, the section delves into the importance of accountability in AI design, which involves establishing mechanisms for transparency, oversight, and recourse in the event of AI-related harms or failures. Accountability entails clearly defining roles and responsibilities for all stakeholders involved in the design, development, and deployment of AI systems, as well as establishing mechanisms for auditing, monitoring, and remedying AI-related issues. By holding organizations accountable for the ethical implications of their AI products, accountability promotes transparency, integrity, and user trust in the AI ecosystem.

Furthermore, the section addresses the imperative of avoiding bias in AI design, which involves identifying and mitigating biases that may arise from the data used to train AI algorithms or the algorithms themselves. Bias can manifest in various forms, including algorithmic bias, data bias, and societal bias, and can have profound implications for the fairness, accuracy, and inclusivity of AI systems. By adopting strategies such as diverse dataset collection, bias-aware algorithm development, and ongoing bias monitoring, organizations can reduce the risk of bias in AI systems and promote trust and confidence among users.

In addition to fairness, accountability, and bias mitigation, the section explores other ethical considerations in AI design, such as privacy, transparency, and consent. Privacy involves protecting user data and respecting user privacy rights, while transparency involves openly communicating about how AI algorithms work, how decisions are made, and how user data is collected and used. Consent involves obtaining informed consent from users for the collection, processing, and use of their data for AI purposes, ensuring that users have control over their personal information and are empowered to make meaningful choices about their engagement with AI products.

Ethical considerations are integral to the design, development, and deployment of trustworthy AI. By prioritizing principles such as fairness, accountability, and the avoidance of bias, organizations can create AI products that align with societal values and expectations, thereby fostering trust, promoting user acceptance, and driving positive societal impact. Ultimately, ethical AI design is not just a moral imperative; it is also a strategic imperative that enables organizations to build enduring relationships with users, mitigate risks, and unlock the full potential of AI technologies in a responsible and sustainable manner.

User Feedback and Iterative Improvement

User feedback serves as a cornerstone in the iterative refinement of AI products, wielding significant influence in building and sustaining trust over time. This section embarks on an exhaustive exploration of the pivotal role played by user feedback in driving iterative improvement in AI products. By delving into the multifaceted dimensions of soliciting and incorporating user feedback, this discussion unveils how feedback loops facilitate the continuous enhancement of AI products, address user concerns, and foster a collaborative relationship between users and the AI system.

At the heart of user feedback lies the principle of user-centricity, which entails actively seeking and valuing the perspectives, insights, and experiences of users throughout the product lifecycle. By soliciting feedback from users at various touchpoints, organizations can gain valuable insights into user needs, preferences, pain points, and areas for improvement, thereby informing the iterative refinement of AI products and enhancing their relevance, usability, and effectiveness.

One of the key themes explored in this section is the importance of feedback loops in driving continuous improvement in AI products. Feedback loops enable organizations to collect, analyze, and act upon user feedback in a systematic and iterative manner, thereby closing the loop between user input and product enhancement. By establishing mechanisms for soliciting feedback through channels such as user surveys, feedback forms, user testing sessions, and customer support interactions, organizations can create a feedback-rich environment that empowers users to contribute to the evolution of AI products.

Moreover, the section delves into the significance of incorporating user feedback into the design and

462

development process to address user concerns and enhance product features. User feedback serves as a valuable source of input for prioritizing product enhancements, identifying usability issues, and validating new features and functionalities. By incorporating user feedback into product planning, design, and implementation, organizations can ensure that AI products align with user needs, preferences, and expectations, thereby enhancing user satisfaction and trust.

Furthermore, the section highlights the importance of fostering a collaborative relationship between users and the AI system through effective feedback mechanisms. Collaborative feedback processes involve engaging users as active participants in the co-creation and refinement of AI products, soliciting their input, and involving them in decision-making processes. By empowering users to contribute to the improvement of AI products, organizations can foster a sense of ownership, loyalty, and trust among users, thereby strengthening the long-term relationship between users and the AI system.

In addition to soliciting and incorporating user feedback, the section explores best practices for effectively managing and responding to feedback, such as establishing clear feedback channels, providing timely responses, and closing the feedback loop by communicating outcomes and actions taken in response to user input. By adopting a proactive approach to feedback management, organizations can demonstrate a commitment to listening to user concerns, addressing their needs, and continuously improving the quality and performance of AI products.

User feedback serves as a powerful tool for driving iterative improvement and building trust in AI products. By establishing feedback loops, incorporating user feedback into the design and development process, and fostering a collaborative relationship between users and the AI system, organizations can create AI products that meet user needs, exceed user expectations, and inspire confidence and loyalty over time. Ultimately, user feedback enables organizations to iterate, innovate, and evolve in response to changing user needs and market dynamics, thereby driving success and sustainability in the competitive landscape of AI technologies.

Building User Empowerment Through Control

Empowering users with a sense of control over their interactions with AI is not just a nicety; it's a fundamental element in building and sustaining trust. This section embarks on an exhaustive exploration of the concept of user empowerment, shedding light on how features such as customization, privacy settings, and opt-in/opt-out mechanisms empower users to shape their AI experience according to their preferences and needs. By delving into the multifaceted dimensions of user empowerment, this discussion unveils how giving users agency and control fosters a sense of trust, ownership, and accountability, thereby enhancing user satisfaction and confidence in AI products.

At the heart of user empowerment lies the principle of autonomy, which entails respecting and honoring users' right to make informed choices and decisions about their interactions with AI systems. By providing users with control over various aspects of their AI experience, organizations can empower users to tailor the product to suit their individual preferences, needs, and values, thereby enhancing their sense of ownership and agency.

One of the key themes explored in this section is the importance of customization in fostering user empowerment. Customization features enable users to personalize their AI experience by adjusting settings, preferences, and functionalities to align with their unique needs and preferences. By offering a range of customization options, such as personalized recommendations, configurable interfaces, and adaptive learning algorithms, organizations can empower users to create a personalized and tailored AI experience that reflects their individual preferences and interests.

Moreover, the section delves into the significance of privacy settings in empowering users to control the use and sharing of their personal data within AI systems. Privacy settings enable users to manage their privacy preferences, control the collection, storage, and use of their personal information, and dictate how their data is shared with third parties. By providing granular privacy controls and transparent data practices, organizations can empower users to make informed decisions about their privacy and data security, thereby fostering trust and confidence in the AI system.

Furthermore, the section highlights the importance of opt-in/opt-out mechanisms in giving users control over their participation in AI-powered features and services. Opt-in/opt-out mechanisms enable users to choose whether to participate in specific AI functionalities or services, such as personalized recommendations, targeted advertising, or data sharing agreements. By respecting users' preferences and allowing them to opt in or out of AI features and services, organizations can demonstrate a commitment to user autonomy and choice, thereby fostering trust and transparency in their AI offerings.

In addition to customization, privacy settings, and opt-in/opt-out mechanisms, the section explores other strategies for building user empowerment through control, such as transparent decision-making processes, clear communication about AI capabilities and limitations, and mechanisms for user feedback and redress. By adopting a user-centric approach to design and development, organizations can empower users to take an active role in shaping their AI experience, thereby fostering trust, loyalty, and engagement over time.

Building user empowerment through control is a critical component of fostering trust and confidence in AI products. By providing users with agency and control over their interactions with AI systems, organizations can enhance user satisfaction, promote transparency and accountability, and cultivate long-term relationships built on trust and mutual respect. Ultimately, user empowerment through control enables organizations to create AI products that meet user needs, exceed user expectations, and inspire confidence and loyalty in an increasingly digital and interconnected world.

Clear Communication of Security Measures

Clear communication of security measures is not just a formality; it's a critical aspect of fostering trust and confidence in AI products. This section embarks on a comprehensive exploration of the importance of transparently communicating the security measures implemented in AI products, shedding light on how providing detailed information about data protection, encryption protocols, and cybersecurity practices contributes to user confidence in the safety and integrity of the AI system. By delving into the multifaceted dimensions of clear communication, this discussion unveils how transparency empowers users to make informed decisions, mitigates uncertainty, and fosters trust in the security of AI products.

At the heart of clear communication lies the principle of transparency, which entails openly sharing information about the security measures, protocols, and practices implemented to safeguard user data and mitigate cybersecurity risks. By providing users with visibility into the security architecture and practices of the AI system, organizations can demonstrate a commitment to protecting user privacy, ensuring data integrity, and maintaining the confidentiality of sensitive information.

One of the key themes explored in this section is the importance of providing information about data protection measures in AI products. Data protection measures encompass a range of practices aimed at safeguarding user data from unauthorized access, manipulation, or disclosure. By clearly communicating how user data is collected, stored, processed, and protected within the AI system, organizations can reassure users about the security and confidentiality of their personal information, thereby fostering trust and confidence in the product.

Moreover, the section delves into the significance of encryption protocols in securing data transmission and storage within AI systems. Encryption protocols employ cryptographic techniques to encode sensitive data, rendering it unreadable to unauthorized parties. By communicating the use of encryption protocols and adherence to industry-standard encryption algorithms, organizations can reassure users about the security and integrity of their data, both in transit and at rest, thereby enhancing trust and confidence in the AI system.

Furthermore, the section highlights the importance of cybersecurity practices in mitigating risks and vulnerabilities in AI products. Cybersecurity practices encompass a range of measures aimed at identifying, preventing, and responding to security threats, such as malware, phishing attacks, and unauthorized access. By transparently communicating about cybersecurity practices, including vulnerability assessments, penetration testing, and incident response procedures, organizations can demonstrate a commitment to proactive risk management and user protection, thereby enhancing trust and confidence in the security of the AI system.

In addition to data protection, encryption protocols, and cybersecurity practices, the section explores other aspects of clear communication, such as privacy policies, terms of service, and security certifications. By providing users with easy access to comprehensive and understandable information about the security measures implemented in the AI system, organizations can empower users to make informed decisions about their engagement with the product, thereby fostering trust, transparency, and accountability in the AI ecosystem.

Clear communication of security measures is essential for fostering trust and confidence in AI products. By transparently sharing information about data protection, encryption protocols, cybersecurity practices, and other security measures, organizations can empower users to make informed decisions, mitigate uncertainty, and build trust in the safety and integrity of the AI system. Ultimately, clear communication enables organizations to demonstrate a commitment to user privacy, security, and trustworthiness, thereby fostering long-term relationships built on transparency, integrity, and mutual respect.

Proactive Communication in Times of Change

In periods of change or system updates, proactive communication becomes not just a necessity but a linchpin in maintaining trust and user satisfaction. This section embarks on an extensive examination of the pivotal role played by proactive communication, shedding light on how transparent and timely dissemination of information regarding changes in AI algorithms, updates, or potential disruptions contributes to user understanding, mitigates uncertainty, and reinforces the commitment to transparency. By delving into the multifaceted dimensions of proactive communication, this discussion unveils how proactive communication fosters a sense of trust, accountability, and partnership between users and AI system providers.

At the core of proactive communication lies the recognition that users value transparency and clarity during periods of change or uncertainty. By proactively communicating about changes in AI algorithms, updates, or potential disruptions, organizations can empower users with the information they need to understand the implications, prepare for any adjustments, and navigate the evolving landscape with confidence.

One of the key themes explored in this section is the importance of transparent and timely communication about changes in AI algorithms. AI algorithms are constantly evolving to adapt to changing data patterns, user behaviors, and business requirements. By proactively communicating about updates, improvements, or modifications to AI algorithms, organizations can provide users with insights into the rationale, impact, and expected outcomes of the changes, thereby fostering understanding and acceptance among users.

Moreover, the section delves into the significance of communicating updates or potential disruptions to AI systems in a timely manner. Timely communication enables users to stay informed about any changes or disruptions that may affect their interactions with the AI system, allowing them to adjust their expectations, workflows, or behaviors accordingly. By proactively notifying users about scheduled maintenance, downtime, or system updates, organizations can minimize disruptions, alleviate concerns, and maintain trust and confidence in the reliability and availability of the AI system.

Furthermore, the section highlights the importance of proactive communication in reinforcing the commitment to transparency and accountability. Proactive communication demonstrates a commitment to open and honest dialogue with users, acknowledging their concerns, addressing their questions, and soliciting their feedback. By engaging users in a transparent and collaborative communication process, organizations can build trust, foster loyalty, and strengthen the long-term relationship between users and the AI system.

In addition to transparent and timely communication, the section explores other strategies for proactively engaging users during times of change or uncertainty, such as providing educational resources, conducting user surveys, and offering support channels for user assistance. By proactively engaging users in the change management process, organizations can empower them to navigate transitions, adapt to new features or functionalities, and provide valuable insights and feedback for continuous improvement.

Proactive communication is essential for maintaining trust and user satisfaction during times of change or system updates. By proactively communicating about changes in AI algorithms, updates, or potential disruptions, organizations can foster understanding, mitigate uncertainty, and reinforce the commitment to transparency and accountability. Ultimately, proactive communication enables organizations to build enduring relationships with users based on trust, integrity, and mutual respect, thereby driving success and sustainability in the competitive landscape of AI technologies.

Trust Seals, Certifications, and Compliance

In the digital age, where concerns about data privacy and security are paramount, trust seals, certifications, and compliance with industry standards serve as beacons of assurance, providing users with external validation of an AI product's trustworthiness. This section embarks on a comprehensive exploration of the pivotal role played by trust seals, certifications, and compliance with privacy regulations in building and maintaining user trust. By delving into the multifaceted dimensions of certifications and compliance, this discussion unveils how showcasing adherence to recognized standards reinforces the ethical and secure practices of AI products, instilling confidence and peace of mind among users.

At the core of trust seals, certifications, and compliance lies the principle of accountability, which entails demonstrating a commitment to upholding industry best practices, standards, and regulations related to data privacy, security, and ethical conduct. By obtaining certifications and adhering to compliance requirements, organizations can provide users with tangible evidence of their dedication to safeguarding user data, mitigating risks, and maintaining the integrity and trustworthiness of the AI product.

One of the key themes explored in this section is the role of certifications in validating the trustworthiness of AI products. Certifications, such as ISO 27001 for information security management or SOC 2 for data privacy and security, serve as independent assessments of an organization's adherence to industry-standard practices and protocols. By obtaining certifications from reputable certification bodies, organizations can demonstrate their commitment to implementing robust security controls, safeguarding user data, and maintaining compliance with industry regulations, thereby enhancing user trust and confidence in the AI product.

Moreover, the section delves into the significance of compliance with privacy regulations, such as the General Data Protection Regulation (GDPR) or the California Consumer Privacy Act (CCPA), in building user trust. Privacy regulations establish legal requirements for the collection, processing, and protection of user data, aiming to safeguard user privacy rights and mitigate the risk of data misuse or exploitation. By ensuring compliance with privacy regulations, organizations can reassure users about the ethical handling of their personal information, foster transparency and accountability, and mitigate the risk of regulatory penalties or fines.

Furthermore, the section highlights the importance of showcasing adherence to recognized standards and certifications as a means of providing users with reassurance regarding the ethical and secure practices of the AI product. Trust seals and badges prominently displayed on the AI product's website or promotional materials signal to users that the organization has undergone rigorous assessments and met stringent criteria for trustworthiness and compliance. By leveraging trust seals and certifications as symbols of credibility and integrity, organizations can differentiate themselves in the marketplace, attract users, and foster long-term relationships built on trust and confidence.

In addition to certifications and compliance with privacy regulations, the section explores other strategies for building trust through external validation, such as third-party audits, independent reviews, and user testimonials. By soliciting feedback from independent auditors, security experts, or industry peers, organizations can gain valuable insights into areas for improvement, address any concerns or vulnerabilities, and enhance the overall trustworthiness and reliability of the AI product.

Trust seals, certifications, and compliance with industry standards play a pivotal role in building user trust and confidence in AI products. By obtaining certifications, adhering to privacy regulations, and showcasing adherence to recognized standards, organizations can provide users with tangible evidence of their commitment to ethical and secure practices, thereby instilling confidence and peace of mind among users. Ultimately, external validation serves as a powerful tool for building and maintaining trust in the competitive landscape of AI technologies, enabling organizations to differentiate themselves, attract users, and drive success and sustainability in the digital age.

Educating Users about AI

Educating users about AI technologies isn't just a proactive approach—it's a cornerstone in building trust and fostering meaningful engagement. This section delves into the multifaceted strategies and initiatives aimed at educating users about AI, going beyond simple user guides and tutorials to encompass a rich array of interactive content and immersive experiences designed to familiarize users with the capabilities, limitations, and ethical considerations surrounding AI. By prioritizing user education, organizations can empower users to make informed decisions, mitigate uncertainty, and engage confidently with AI products, thereby strengthening trust and fostering long-term relationships.

At the core of user education lies the recognition that informed users are empowered users. By providing users with comprehensive and accessible information about AI technologies, organizations can demystify complex concepts, dispel misconceptions, and promote a deeper understanding of how AI works, its potential applications, and its societal impact. By fostering a culture of curiosity, learning, and exploration, organizations can empower users to navigate the ever-changing landscape of AI technologies with confidence and competence.

One of the key themes explored in this section is the importance of interactive and experiential learning experiences in engaging users and deepening their understanding of AI. Rather than relying solely on traditional

473

user guides or tutorials, organizations can leverage interactive content such as online courses, webinars, workshops, and simulations to provide users with hands-on opportunities to explore AI concepts, experiment with AI tools, and gain practical skills and insights. By fostering active engagement and participation, organizations can create immersive learning experiences that resonate with users and enhance their understanding and appreciation of AI technologies.

Moreover, the section delves into the significance of addressing the ethical implications and societal impact of AI in user education initiatives. AI technologies raise complex ethical questions related to privacy, fairness, accountability, and transparency, which require careful consideration and discussion. By incorporating discussions about ethics, bias, and responsible AI practices into user education programs, organizations can empower users to critically evaluate the ethical implications of AI technologies, advocate for ethical AI development and deployment, and contribute to the creation of AI systems that align with societal values and expectations.

Furthermore, the section highlights the importance of tailoring user education initiatives to the diverse needs, preferences, and learning styles of users. Not all users have the same level of familiarity or comfort with AI technologies, and effective user education requires flexibility, accessibility, and inclusivity. By offering a variety of educational resources, formats, and delivery methods, organizations can accommodate diverse learning needs and preferences, ensuring that all users have access to the knowledge and skills they need to engage confidently with AI products.

In addition to interactive content and ethical discussions, the section explores other strategies for educating users about AI, such as user-friendly documentation, help centers, and community forums. By providing users with easily accessible resources and support channels for learning and assistance, organizations can empower users to overcome challenges, troubleshoot issues, and deepen their understanding of AI technologies in a supportive and collaborative environment.

User education is a foundational element in building trust and fostering meaningful engagement with AI products. By prioritizing interactive and experiential learning experiences, addressing ethical considerations, and accommodating diverse learning needs and preferences, organizations can empower users to navigate the complexities of AI technologies with confidence and competence. Ultimately, user education enables organizations to build enduring relationships with users based on trust, transparency, and mutual respect, thereby driving success and sustainability in the rapidly evolving landscape of AI technologies.

Handling Trust Challenges and Crisis Management

Navigating trust challenges and crisis management is a multifaceted endeavor that demands a proactive and strategic approach. This section embarks on a comprehensive exploration of the strategies and best practices for handling trust challenges, from addressing user concerns to transparently managing crises. By delving into the nuances of trust dynamics and crisis response, this discussion unveils how organizations can mitigate trust challenges, rebuild confidence, and emerge stronger from adversity.

At the heart of handling trust challenges lies the recognition that trust is fragile and can be easily eroded by a variety of factors, including breaches of privacy, security incidents, or ethical lapses. By acknowledging the potential vulnerabilities and risks associated with AI technologies, organizations can proactively anticipate trust challenges and develop robust strategies for mitigating and managing them effectively.

One of the key themes explored in this section is the importance of proactive communication in addressing user concerns and managing trust challenges. Swift and transparent communication can help mitigate the impact of trust challenges by providing users with timely updates, information, and reassurance. By acknowledging concerns, expressing empathy, and demonstrating a commitment to addressing issues transparently, organizations can build trust and confidence among users, even in the face of adversity.

Moreover, the section delves into the significance of proactive engagement and relationship-building in building resilience and trust. By fostering open and honest dialogue with users, soliciting feedback, and actively listening to concerns, organizations can strengthen relationships, build trust, and cultivate a sense of partnership and collaboration. By demonstrating a commitment to transparency, accountability, and continuous improvement, organizations can enhance their credibility and resilience in the eyes of users, thereby mitigating the impact of trust challenges and crises.

Furthermore, the section highlights the importance of effective crisis management strategies in responding to trust challenges and mitigating their impact. Crisis management involves a coordinated and systematic approach to identifying, assessing, and responding to crises, with a focus on minimizing harm, restoring trust, and preserving organizational reputation. By establishing clear protocols, escalation procedures, and communication channels for crisis response, organizations can effectively manage crises, mitigate their impact, and rebuild trust in the aftermath.

In addition to proactive communication and crisis management, the section explores other strategies for handling trust challenges, such as proactive monitoring and risk mitigation, continuous improvement, and learning from past experiences. By adopting a proactive and adaptive approach to trust management, organizations can identify potential vulnerabilities, address root causes, and strengthen their resilience and trustworthiness over time.

Handling trust challenges and crisis management is a critical competency for organizations operating in the dynamic and complex landscape of AI technologies. By prioritizing proactive communication, relationship-building, and crisis management strategies, organizations can effectively mitigate trust challenges, rebuild confidence, and emerge stronger from adversity. Ultimately, trust is not built in times of ease but in moments of challenge and uncertainty, and organizations that demonstrate integrity, transparency, and resilience in the face of adversity can earn the trust and loyalty of users over the long term.

Future Trends in Building Trust with AI Users

As we peer into the horizon, it's evident that the landscape of trust-building with AI users is poised for significant evolution. This conclusion embarks on an in-depth exploration of the future trends that will shape the dynamics of trust-building in AI, encompassing emerging technologies, evolving user expectations, and shifting ethical considerations. By anticipating these trends, AI practitioners can proactively adapt their strategies to meet the evolving needs and preferences of users, thereby fostering stronger and more resilient relationships built on trust and transparency.

At the forefront of future trends in trust-building with AI users is the continued advancement of emerging technologies. From advancements in natural language processing and computer vision to the proliferation of AI-powered chatbots and virtual assistants, these technological innovations hold immense potential to enhance user experiences and deepen engagement with AI products. By leveraging these technologies to deliver personalized, context-aware experiences that anticipate and respond to user needs, organizations can foster trust and confidence among users, thereby driving adoption and loyalty in an increasingly competitive landscape.

Moreover, the future of trust-building with AI users will be shaped by evolving user expectations and preferences. As users become increasingly discerning and demanding in their interactions with AI products, organizations will need to prioritize transparency, accountability, and user empowerment to build and maintain trust. By providing users with greater visibility into AI algorithms, decision-making processes, and data usage practices, organizations can empower users to make informed decisions and exercise greater control over their AI experiences, thereby fostering trust and confidence in the product.

Furthermore, the future of trust-building in AI will be characterized by heightened ethical considerations and societal expectations. As AI technologies become more pervasive and influential in various aspects of daily life, organizations will face growing pressure to ensure that their AI products are developed and deployed responsibly, ethically, and equitably. By embracing principles of fairness, accountability, and transparency in AI development and deployment, organizations can mitigate the risk of bias, discrimination, and unintended consequences, thereby fostering trust and confidence among users and stakeholders.

In addition to technological advancements, evolving user expectations, and ethical considerations, the future of trust-building in AI will be shaped by proactive communication and engagement strategies. Organizations that prioritize transparency, user-centric design, ethical considerations, and proactive communication will be better positioned to cultivate a relationship of trust with users that is essential for long-term success. By engaging users in meaningful dialogue, soliciting feedback, and addressing concerns in a timely and transparent manner, organizations can demonstrate their commitment to building trust and fostering mutually beneficial relationships with users.

The future of trust-building with AI users is characterized by a convergence of technological advancements, evolving user expectations, shifting ethical considerations, and proactive communication strategies. By embracing these trends and adapting their strategies accordingly, AI practitioners can cultivate a relationship of trust with users that is essential for driving adoption, loyalty, and long-term success in the ever-evolving landscape of AI technologies.

COMPLIANCE AND REGULATORY CONSIDERATIONS

In the ever-evolving landscape of AI products, adherence to compliance and regulatory standards is pivotal for ensuring security, user trust, and ethical practices. This chapter explores the complex terrain of compliance and regulatory considerations in the development and deployment of AI products. It delves into the frameworks, standards, and legal aspects that govern AI, emphasizing the importance of aligning AI practices with established guidelines to foster a secure and trustworthy environment.

The Regulatory Landscape of AI

The regulatory landscape of AI is a complex and multifaceted terrain, encompassing a diverse array of frameworks at international, national, and industry levels. This chapter initiates by offering a comprehensive overview of these regulatory frameworks, shedding light on the dynamic interplay between global, regional, and local regulations that shape the development and deployment of AI technologies. By exploring the intricacies of these regulations, AI practitioners gain valuable insights into the key considerations and challenges they must navigate to ensure compliance and ethical conduct in their AI endeavors.

At the international level, the regulatory landscape of AI is characterized by a patchwork of initiatives, guidelines, and frameworks proposed by intergovernmental organizations, industry consortia, and standard-setting bodies. Organizations such as the United Nations, the Organisation for Economic Co-operation and Development (OECD), and the International Organization for Standardization (ISO) have issued guidelines and recommendations aimed at promoting responsible AI development and deployment on a global scale. By examining these international frameworks, AI practitioners can gain a deeper understanding of the principles and best practices that underpin ethical AI governance and compliance.

Moreover, at the national level, governments around the world are increasingly enacting legislation and regulations to address the opportunities and challenges presented by AI technologies. Countries such as the United States, European Union, China, and Canada have introduced or proposed AI-specific laws and policies aimed at regulating various aspects of AI development, deployment, and use. These regulations cover a wide range of issues, including data privacy, algorithmic transparency, accountability, and liability. By navigating the nuances of national regulations, AI practitioners can ensure compliance with legal requirements and mitigate the risk of regulatory penalties or sanctions.

Furthermore, within specific industries and sectors, regulatory bodies and industry associations play a critical role in shaping the regulatory landscape of AI. Organizations such as the U.S. Food and Drug Administration (FDA), the European Medicines

Agency (EMA), and the Financial Stability Board (FSB) have issued guidance and regulations tailored to the unique challenges and considerations of their respective industries. By aligning with industry-specific regulations and standards, AI practitioners can address sector-specific requirements and ensure that their AI applications meet the highest standards of safety, reliability, and effectiveness.

In addition to understanding the diverse and evolving regulatory frameworks, AI practitioners must also stay abreast of emerging standards and best practices in AI governance and compliance. Standard-setting bodies such as the IEEE, the National Institute of Standards and Technology (NIST), and the Partnership on AI (PAI) are actively developing guidelines, frameworks, and tools to support responsible AI development and deployment. By leveraging these resources, AI practitioners can adopt industry best practices, benchmark their AI initiatives against recognized standards, and demonstrate a commitment to ethical conduct and compliance.

The regulatory landscape of AI is a dynamic and evolving ecosystem characterized by international, national, and industry-specific regulations, standards, and best practices. By understanding the complexities of this regulatory landscape and staying abreast of emerging standards, AI practitioners can navigate regulatory challenges, ensure compliance with legal requirements, and promote responsible AI development and deployment. Ultimately, by embracing regulatory compliance as a strategic imperative, AI practitioners can build trust, mitigate risk, and unlock the full potential of AI technologies to drive innovation and positive societal impact.

GDPR and Data Protection

Data protection stands as a cornerstone in the landscape of AI compliance, with the General Data Protection Regulation (GDPR) emerging as a pivotal reference point in this domain. This section embarks on a comprehensive exploration of the implications of GDPR for AI products, delving into the multifaceted dimensions of compliance and the strategies required to ensure alignment with GDPR requirements, thereby safeguarding user privacy and promoting ethical data practices.

At the heart of GDPR compliance lies a commitment to upholding the fundamental rights and freedoms of individuals concerning the processing of personal data. By adhering to GDPR principles such as transparency, fairness, and accountability, organizations can demonstrate their commitment to ethical data practices and build trust with users.

One of the key themes explored in this section is the principle of data minimization, which requires organizations to collect and process only the personal data that is necessary for a specific purpose. By minimizing the collection and use of personal data, organizations can reduce the risk of data breaches, mitigate privacy concerns, and enhance user trust. This principle is particularly relevant in the context of AI, where large volumes of data are often used to train and optimize AI models. By adopting data minimization strategies, such as anonymization, aggregation, and selective data sampling, organizations can ensure that their AI practices comply with GDPR requirements while still achieving their objectives.

Moreover, the section delves into the principle of purpose limitation, which requires organizations to clearly define the purposes for which personal data is collected and processed and to ensure that data is not used for incompatible purposes. In the context of AI, this principle underscores the importance of transparency and user consent in data processing activities. By providing users with clear and understandable information about how their data will be used in AI applications and obtaining their consent for such processing, organizations can ensure compliance with GDPR requirements and respect user privacy preferences.

Furthermore, the section highlights the right to explanation, which grants individuals the right to obtain meaningful information about the logic, significance, and consequences of automated decision-making processes that affect them. In the context of AI, this right requires organizations to provide users with explanations for the decisions made by AI systems that impact their rights and interests. By implementing transparent and interpretable AI models, organizations can empower users to understand and challenge automated decisions, thereby promoting accountability and fairness in AI applications.

In addition to data minimization, purpose limitation, and the right to explanation, the section explores other strategies for ensuring GDPR compliance in AI products, such as conducting data protection impact assessments, implementing privacy-enhancing technologies, and appointing data protection officers. By adopting a holistic approach to GDPR compliance, organizations can build user trust, mitigate regulatory risks, and promote responsible data practices in the development and deployment of AI technologies.

GDPR compliance is a critical aspect of AI governance, requiring organizations to uphold principles such as data minimization, purpose limitation, and the right to explanation to protect user privacy and promote ethical data practices. By understanding the implications of GDPR for AI products and implementing strategies to ensure compliance, organizations can build trust with users, mitigate regulatory risks, and unlock the full potential of AI technologies to drive innovation and positive societal impact.

CCPA and Consumer Privacy Rights

The California Consumer Privacy Act (CCPA) serves as a significant milestone in the realm of consumer privacy rights, reflecting a broader societal shift towards greater transparency, control, and accountability over personal data. This section embarks on an exhaustive exploration of the CCPA's implications for AI products, delving into its multifaceted dimensions and the strategies required for AI practitioners to navigate compliance while delivering personalized and effective user experiences.

At its core, the CCPA embodies a commitment to empowering consumers with greater control and transparency over their personal data. By granting consumers rights such as the right to know, the right to delete, and the right to opt-out of the sale of their personal information, the CCPA aims to provide individuals with greater autonomy and agency in their interactions with businesses. In the context of AI products, compliance with the CCPA requires organizations to implement robust data governance practices, transparency mechanisms, and user consent mechanisms to ensure that user privacy rights are respected and upheld.

One of the key themes explored in this section is the CCPA's impact on user rights and data transparency in AI products. The CCPA requires organizations to provide consumers with clear and understandable information about their data collection, processing, and sharing practices, as well as the purposes for which personal information is used. In the context of AI, this requirement underscores the importance of transparency and accountability in data-driven decision-making processes. By implementing mechanisms for data transparency, such as privacy notices, data access requests, and data subject rights portals, organizations can empower users to make informed decisions about their personal data and exercise greater control over its use.

Moreover, the section delves into the CCPA's obligation to inform users about data collection practices and the sale of personal information. Under the CCPA, organizations are required to provide consumers with notice of their data collection practices, including the categories of personal information collected, the purposes for which it is used, and the categories of third parties with whom it is shared. In the context of AI products, this requirement necessitates transparent and user-friendly privacy policies, consent mechanisms, and data disclosure practices to ensure that users are fully informed about how their data is being used and shared.

Furthermore, the section highlights the challenges and opportunities for AI practitioners in complying with the CCPA while delivering personalized and effective user experiences. The CCPA's requirements for data transparency, user consent, and data rights present complex technical and operational challenges for organizations that rely on AI technologies to deliver personalized services and experiences. By adopting privacy-by-design principles, implementing privacy-enhancing technologies, and integrating privacy controls into AI systems, organizations can strike a balance between compliance with the CCPA and the delivery of innovative and user-centric AI products.

In addition to compliance challenges, the section explores the opportunities for AI practitioners to leverage the CCPA as a catalyst for building trust and loyalty with users. By prioritizing transparency, accountability, and user control in their data practices, organizations can differentiate themselves in the marketplace, attract users who value privacy and data protection, and foster long-term relationships built on trust and respect.

The CCPA represents a landmark initiative in the realm of consumer privacy rights, shaping the regulatory landscape and influencing business practices in California and beyond. By understanding the implications of the CCPA for AI products and implementing strategies to ensure compliance while delivering personalized and effective user experiences, AI practitioners can navigate the complexities of data privacy regulation, build trust with users, and unlock the full potential of AI technologies to drive innovation and positive societal impact.

Industry-Specific Regulations

Industry-specific regulations play a crucial role in shaping the development, deployment, and use of AI applications across various sectors. This section embarks on an in-depth exploration of the diverse array of industry-specific considerations, ranging from healthcare regulations like the Health Insurance Portability and Accountability Act (HIPAA) to financial regulations such as the Financial Industry Regulatory Authority (FINRA) rules and automotive safety standards. By delving into the nuances of these regulations, AI practitioners gain valuable insights into the unique challenges and opportunities inherent in different industries and the strategies required to ensure compliance and mitigate sector-specific risks effectively.

In the healthcare sector, regulations such as HIPAA impose stringent requirements on the handling, storage, and transmission of protected health information (PHI). AI applications in healthcare must comply with HIPAA regulations to safeguard patient privacy and confidentiality.

This requires AI practitioners to implement robust security measures, access controls, and data encryption protocols to protect PHI from unauthorized access or disclosure. Moreover, AI systems must be designed to ensure the integrity and accuracy of medical data and maintain compliance with HIPAA's requirements for data access, auditability, and accountability.

Similarly, in the financial services industry, regulations such as those enforced by FINRA impose strict requirements on the use of AI in areas such as algorithmic trading, risk management, and customer communications. AI applications in finance must comply with FINRA regulations to ensure fairness, transparency, and accountability in algorithmic decision-making processes. This requires AI practitioners to implement rigorous testing, validation, and monitoring procedures to detect and mitigate potential biases, errors, or vulnerabilities in AI models. Moreover, AI systems must be designed to provide clear explanations for algorithmic decisions and maintain compliance with FINRA's requirements for record-keeping, reporting, and auditability.

In the automotive industry, safety standards such as those established by organizations like the National Highway Traffic Safety Administration (NHTSA) and the Society of Automotive Engineers (SAE) govern the development and deployment of AI-driven technologies in autonomous vehicles and advanced driver-assistance systems (ADAS). AI applications in automotive must comply with safety standards to ensure the reliability, robustness, and effectiveness of AI systems in real-world driving conditions. This requires AI practitioners to conduct rigorous testing, validation, and verification of AI algorithms to demonstrate compliance with safety standards and mitigate the risk of accidents, injuries, or fatalities.

Furthermore, beyond healthcare, finance, and automotive, other industries such as aerospace, energy, and manufacturing may have their own sector-specific regulations governing the use of AI applications. AI practitioners must be aware of and comply with these regulations to ensure the safety, reliability, and legal compliance of AI systems in diverse industry contexts.

Industry-specific regulations play a critical role in shaping the development, deployment, and use of AI applications across various sectors. By understanding the nuances of these regulations and tailoring AI practices to align with sector-specific requirements, AI practitioners can ensure compliance, mitigate industry-specific risks, and unlock the full potential of AI technologies to drive innovation and positive societal impact in diverse industry domains.

Explainability and Algorithmic Accountability

Explainability and algorithmic accountability are increasingly recognized as fundamental pillars of AI compliance and ethical AI development. This section embarks on a thorough exploration of these critical aspects, delving into the growing demand for transparent AI decision-making processes and the imperative for explainable AI models. By examining the evolving regulatory landscape and user expectations, AI practitioners gain valuable insights into the strategies required to incorporate explainability into AI products, thereby meeting regulatory expectations, fostering trust with users, and promoting ethical AI practices.

At the heart of the demand for explainability and algorithmic accountability lies a growing recognition of the need to understand and interpret the decisions made by AI systems. As AI technologies become increasingly pervasive and influential in various aspects of society, stakeholders are calling for greater transparency and accountability in AI decision-making processes. Users, regulators, and policymakers are demanding explanations for algorithmic decisions that impact individuals' rights, opportunities, and outcomes. By providing clear and understandable explanations for AI decisions, organizations can empower users to understand, trust, and challenge algorithmic outcomes, thereby promoting fairness, accountability, and ethical conduct in AI applications.

One of the key themes explored in this section is the imperative for explainable AI models. Explainable AI refers to the ability of AI systems to provide understandable explanations for their decisions, predictions, and recommendations. Explainable AI models are essential for ensuring transparency, accountability, and trustworthiness in AI applications, particularly in high-stakes domains such as healthcare, finance, and criminal justice. By adopting explainable AI techniques, such as interpretable machine learning algorithms, rule-based systems, and model-agnostic interpretability methods, organizations can provide users with insights into how AI arrives at specific decisions, thereby enabling them to assess, validate, and trust algorithmic outcomes.

Moreover, the section delves into the strategies for incorporating explainability into AI products to meet regulatory expectations and build user trust. Regulators and policymakers around the world are increasingly recognizing the importance of explainable AI in ensuring fairness, transparency, and accountability in AI applications. Regulations such as the European Union's General Data Protection Regulation (GDPR) and the California Consumer Privacy Act (CCPA) require organizations to provide users with meaningful information about the logic, significance, and consequences of automated decision-making processes that affect them. By implementing transparent and interpretable AI models, organizations can ensure compliance with regulatory requirements and address user expectations for transparency and accountability in AI decision-making.

Furthermore, the section highlights the challenges and opportunities for AI practitioners in incorporating explainability into AI products. While explainable AI techniques offer significant benefits in terms of transparency and accountability, they also present technical, operational, and legal challenges for organizations. Technical challenges include ensuring the interpretability, robustness, and performance of AI models, particularly in complex and high-dimensional data environments. Operational challenges include integrating explainable AI techniques into existing workflows, systems, and processes, and managing the trade-offs between explainability, accuracy, and performance. Legal challenges include navigating the regulatory landscape, addressing user rights to explanations, and mitigating the risk of legal liability or regulatory sanctions for algorithmic bias, discrimination, or unfairness.

In addition to addressing challenges, the section explores the opportunities for AI practitioners to leverage explainability as a strategic advantage in the marketplace. Organizations that prioritize explainable AI can differentiate themselves from competitors, attract users who value transparency and accountability, and build long-term relationships based on trust and confidence. By embracing explainability as a core principle of ethical AI development, organizations can enhance their credibility, reputation, and competitive positioning in the AI market.

Explainability and algorithmic accountability are emerging as critical aspects of AI compliance and ethical AI development. By understanding the demand for explainability, adopting transparent and interpretable AI models, and incorporating explainability into AI products, organizations can meet regulatory expectations, build user trust, and promote ethical AI practices. Ultimately, explainable AI is not only a regulatory requirement but also a strategic imperative for organizations seeking to harness the full potential of AI technologies to drive innovation, growth, and positive societal impact.

Fairness and Bias Mitigation

Fairness and bias mitigation are paramount considerations in the development and deployment of AI models, essential for ensuring ethical conduct and regulatory compliance. This section undertakes a comprehensive exploration of the multifaceted dimensions of fairness in AI, delving into regulatory expectations, guidelines, and best practices for bias mitigation. By examining the evolving landscape of fairness in AI, AI practitioners gain valuable insights into the strategies required to detect and mitigate biases effectively, thereby promoting fair and equitable outcomes in AI applications.

At the core of the discussion lies the recognition of the need to address biases that may inadvertently manifest in AI algorithms, leading to unfair or discriminatory outcomes. As AI technologies become increasingly pervasive in various domains, stakeholders are increasingly concerned about the potential for bias to perpetuate or exacerbate inequalities, prejudices, and injustices. From employment decisions to criminal justice sentencing, biases in AI algorithms have profound implications for individuals' rights, opportunities, and outcomes. By adopting a proactive approach to fairness and bias mitigation, organizations can mitigate the risk of bias-related harm, promote fairness, and uphold ethical standards in AI applications.

One of the key themes explored in this section is the regulatory expectations and guidelines for bias mitigation in AI. Regulators and policymakers around the world are increasingly recognizing the importance of fairness and equity in AI applications and issuing guidelines, frameworks, and directives to address biases and discrimination.

491

Regulations such as the General Data Protection Regulation (GDPR), the California Consumer Privacy Act (CCPA), and the Fair Credit Reporting Act (FCRA) require organizations to ensure that AI algorithms are fair, transparent, and accountable. By adhering to regulatory requirements and guidelines, organizations can demonstrate compliance with legal and ethical standards and mitigate the risk of legal liability or reputational harm.

Moreover, the section delves into the methods and techniques for detecting and mitigating biases in AI algorithms. Bias mitigation encompasses a range of approaches, including data preprocessing, algorithmic fairness constraints, and post-processing techniques. Data preprocessing involves identifying and removing biased or discriminatory patterns in training data, such as underrepresented or overrepresented groups. Algorithmic fairness constraints involve incorporating fairness criteria into the design and optimization of AI models to ensure equitable outcomes across different demographic groups. Post-processing techniques involve adjusting algorithmic outputs to mitigate biases and ensure fairness in decision-making processes. By adopting a combination of these approaches, organizations can detect and mitigate biases effectively, promote fairness, and enhance the credibility and trustworthiness of their AI applications.

Furthermore, the section highlights the challenges and opportunities for AI practitioners in addressing fairness and bias mitigation. While fairness and bias mitigation are essential goals, they also present technical, operational, and ethical challenges for organizations. Technical challenges include identifying and quantifying biases in AI algorithms, developing effective bias detection and mitigation techniques, and evaluating the impact of bias mitigation strategies on algorithmic performance and fairness. Operational challenges include integrating bias mitigation techniques into existing workflows, systems, and processes, and managing the trade-offs between fairness, accuracy, and performance. Ethical challenges include balancing competing interests and values, addressing the root causes of bias, and ensuring accountability and transparency in bias mitigation efforts.

In addition to addressing challenges, the section explores the opportunities for AI practitioners to leverage fairness and bias mitigation as a strategic advantage in the marketplace. Organizations that prioritize fairness and equity in their AI applications can differentiate themselves from competitors, attract users who value fairness and transparency, and build long-term relationships based on trust and confidence. By embracing fairness and bias mitigation as core principles of ethical AI development, organizations can enhance their credibility, reputation, and competitive positioning in the AI market.

Fairness and bias mitigation are critical considerations in AI development and deployment, essential for ensuring ethical conduct, regulatory compliance, and societal trust. By understanding the regulatory expectations, adopting bias mitigation techniques, and promoting fairness in AI applications, organizations can mitigate the risk of bias-related harm, promote fairness, and uphold ethical standards in AI development and deployment. Ultimately, fairness and bias mitigation are not only legal and ethical imperatives but also strategic imperatives for organizations seeking to harness the full potential of AI technologies to drive innovation, growth, and positive societal impact.

Security Standards and Cybersecurity Compliance

Security standards and cybersecurity compliance form the bedrock of robust cybersecurity practices, essential for safeguarding AI products against evolving cyber threats and vulnerabilities. This section embarks on an exhaustive exploration of the diverse array of established cybersecurity frameworks, including but not limited to ISO/IEC 27001, the NIST Cybersecurity Framework, and others. By examining these frameworks in detail, AI practitioners gain valuable insights into the strategies required to enhance the overall security posture of AI products, mitigate cyber threats, and ensure compliance with regulatory requirements and industry best practices.

At the heart of the discussion lies the recognition of the dynamic and complex nature of cybersecurity threats facing AI products. As AI technologies become increasingly integral to various aspects of business operations, they also become lucrative targets for cyber attackers seeking to exploit vulnerabilities, compromise data integrity, and disrupt critical services. From data breaches and ransomware attacks to insider threats and supply chain vulnerabilities, the threat landscape facing AI products is multifaceted and constantly evolving. By adopting a proactive approach to cybersecurity and adhering to established security standards, organizations can mitigate the risk of cyber threats, protect sensitive data, and maintain the trust and confidence of users and stakeholders.

One of the key themes explored in this section is the role of established cybersecurity frameworks in enhancing the overall security posture of AI products. These frameworks provide organizations with a structured and systematic approach to cybersecurity risk management, encompassing areas such as risk assessment, threat detection, incident response, and continuous improvement. By aligning their cybersecurity practices with established frameworks such as ISO/IEC 27001 and the NIST Cybersecurity Framework, organizations can establish a comprehensive and effective cybersecurity program that addresses the unique challenges and requirements of AI products.

Moreover, the section delves into the specific requirements and recommendations outlined in these cybersecurity frameworks for AI products. For example, ISO/IEC 27001 provides a set of internationally recognized standards for information security management systems (ISMS), covering areas such as risk assessment, access control, encryption, and incident response. Similarly, the NIST Cybersecurity Framework offers a flexible and scalable framework for managing cybersecurity risks, comprising five core functions: identify, protect, detect, respond, and recover. By leveraging the guidance provided by these frameworks, organizations can develop tailored cybersecurity policies, procedures, and controls that address the specific risks and vulnerabilities associated with AI products.

Furthermore, the section highlights the challenges and opportunities for AI practitioners in implementing cybersecurity standards and achieving compliance. While cybersecurity standards provide valuable guidance and best practices for securing AI products, they also present technical, operational, and organizational challenges for organizations. Technical challenges include identifying and prioritizing cybersecurity risks, implementing effective security controls, and integrating cybersecurity measures into AI systems and workflows. Operational challenges include aligning cybersecurity practices with business objectives, managing resource constraints, and fostering a culture of cybersecurity awareness and accountability. Organizational challenges include navigating the regulatory landscape, addressing compliance requirements, and building partnerships with cybersecurity experts and stakeholders.

In addition to addressing challenges, the section explores the opportunities for AI practitioners to leverage cybersecurity standards as a strategic advantage in the marketplace. Organizations that prioritize cybersecurity and achieve compliance with established standards can differentiate themselves from competitors, attract users who value security and privacy, and build long-term relationships based on trust and confidence. By embracing cybersecurity standards as a core principle of AI development and deployment, organizations can enhance their credibility, reputation, and competitive positioning in the AI market.

Security standards and cybersecurity compliance are foundational for safeguarding AI products against cyber threats and vulnerabilities. By understanding the role of established cybersecurity frameworks, addressing the challenges and opportunities of cybersecurity implementation, and prioritizing security in AI development and deployment, organizations can mitigate the risk of cyber threats, protect sensitive data, and maintain the trust and confidence of users and stakeholders. Ultimately, cybersecurity is not only a technical requirement but also a strategic imperative for organizations seeking to harness the full potential of AI technologies to drive innovation, growth, and positive societal impact.

Audits, Assessments, and Certification

Audits, assessments, and certifications represent proactive measures that organizations can take to demonstrate regulatory compliance and enhance the credibility of their AI products. This section embarks on a comprehensive exploration of the multifaceted role that independent audits, impact assessments, and certifications play in ensuring compliance with AI regulations and standards. By examining these processes in detail, AI practitioners gain valuable insights into the strategies required to navigate the complex regulatory landscape, mitigate compliance risks, and instill confidence in users and stakeholders.

At the core of the discussion lies the recognition of the importance of transparency, accountability, and third-party validation in demonstrating regulatory compliance and building trust with users and stakeholders. As regulatory requirements governing AI continue to evolve and become more stringent, organizations are increasingly turning to independent audits, impact assessments, and certifications to validate their compliance efforts and reassure users about the safety, reliability, and ethical conduct of their AI products. By subjecting their AI systems to external scrutiny and evaluation, organizations can identify and address compliance gaps, mitigate regulatory risks, and demonstrate their commitment to ethical AI practices.

One of the key themes explored in this section is the role of independent audits in assessing and validating compliance with AI regulations. Independent audits involve the systematic review and evaluation of an organization's AI systems, processes, and controls by an external auditor or certification body. These audits assess whether the organization's AI practices align with regulatory requirements, industry standards, and best practices, and identify areas for improvement or remediation. By undergoing independent audits, organizations can gain valuable insights into their compliance posture, address compliance deficiencies, and demonstrate their commitment to regulatory compliance and ethical conduct.

Moreover, the section delves into the significance of impact assessments in evaluating the ethical, social, and legal implications of AI systems. Impact assessments involve the systematic evaluation of the potential risks, benefits, and unintended consequences of AI applications on individuals, communities, and society as a whole. These assessments consider factors such as fairness, transparency, accountability, privacy, and human rights, and assess the potential impact of AI systems on vulnerable or marginalized populations. By conducting impact assessments, organizations can proactively identify and mitigate ethical risks, address stakeholder concerns, and promote responsible AI development and deployment.

Furthermore, the section explores the value of certifications in demonstrating compliance and fostering trust with users and stakeholders. Certifications provide organizations with independent validation of their compliance efforts and serve as a tangible proof of their commitment to regulatory compliance and ethical conduct. Certifications such as ISO 27001, SOC 2, and the AI Ethics Mark certify that an organization's AI systems meet specific standards for security, privacy, transparency, and accountability. By obtaining certifications, organizations can differentiate themselves in the marketplace, attract users who value security and trust, and build long-term relationships based on transparency and integrity.

In addition to discussing the benefits of audits, assessments, and certifications, the section also addresses the challenges and opportunities for organizations in pursuing these compliance measures. While audits, assessments, and certifications provide valuable validation of compliance efforts, they also present technical, operational, and financial challenges for organizations. Technical challenges include preparing for audits, gathering evidence, and addressing audit findings. Operational challenges include integrating compliance measures into existing workflows, systems, and processes, and managing the costs and resources associated with compliance efforts. Financial challenges include budget constraints, compliance costs, and the return on investment of compliance initiatives.

Audits, assessments, and certifications are proactive steps toward regulatory compliance and trust-building in AI. By understanding the role of independent audits, impact assessments, and certifications, addressing the challenges and opportunities of compliance measures, and prioritizing transparency and accountability in AI development and deployment, organizations can mitigate regulatory risks, build trust with users and stakeholders, and promote ethical AI practices. Ultimately, audits, assessments, and certifications are not only regulatory requirements but also strategic imperatives for organizations seeking to demonstrate their commitment to ethical conduct, regulatory compliance, and responsible AI innovation.

Privacy by Design and Default

Privacy by design and default principles represent essential elements in ensuring compliance with privacy regulations and fostering user trust in AI products. This section embarks on an in-depth exploration of the strategies and methodologies for integrating privacy considerations into the design and development of AI products from their inception. By examining these principles in detail, AI practitioners gain valuable insights into the proactive measures required to align with regulatory expectations, protect user privacy, and uphold ethical standards in AI development and deployment.

At the heart of the discussion lies the recognition of the importance of privacy as a fundamental right and the need to embed privacy protections into the fabric of AI systems. As privacy regulations such as the General Data Protection Regulation (GDPR) and the California Consumer Privacy Act (CCPA) impose stringent requirements for data protection and privacy, organizations must adopt a proactive approach to privacy by design and default. By integrating privacy considerations into every stage of the AI product lifecycle, from design and development to deployment and beyond, organizations can mitigate privacy risks, enhance user trust, and demonstrate their commitment to privacy and data protection.

One of the key themes explored in this section is the proactive adoption of privacy-enhancing measures in AI product design and development. Privacy by design involves incorporating privacy considerations into the design and architecture of AI systems, such as minimizing data collection, anonymizing or pseudonymizing personal data, and implementing privacy-preserving technologies. By adopting privacy by default, organizations ensure that privacy protections are enabled by default settings, such as limiting data access, implementing granular consent mechanisms, and providing users with control over their personal data. By adopting these principles, organizations can minimize the risk of privacy violations, protect user privacy, and build trust with users and stakeholders.

Moreover, the section delves into the strategies and methodologies for implementing privacy by design and default in AI product development. These strategies encompass a range of technical, organizational, and legal measures aimed at ensuring privacy and data protection throughout the AI product lifecycle. Technical measures include implementing encryption, access controls, and data minimization techniques to protect sensitive data and prevent unauthorized access or disclosure. Organizational measures include establishing privacy policies, procedures, and training programs to raise awareness of privacy risks and responsibilities among employees and stakeholders. Legal measures include conducting privacy impact assessments, obtaining user consent, and complying with privacy regulations and standards.

Furthermore, the section explores the challenges and opportunities for organizations in implementing privacy by design and default in AI product development. While privacy by design and default principles offer significant benefits in terms of privacy protection and user trust, they also present technical, operational, and legal challenges for organizations.

Technical challenges include integrating privacy-enhancing technologies into AI systems, ensuring interoperability and scalability, and addressing the trade-offs between privacy and functionality. Operational challenges include aligning privacy practices with business objectives, managing resource constraints, and fostering a culture of privacy awareness and accountability. Legal challenges include navigating the complex regulatory landscape, addressing compliance requirements, and mitigating the risk of legal liability or reputational harm for privacy violations.

In addition to addressing challenges, the section explores the opportunities for organizations to leverage privacy by design and default as a strategic advantage in the marketplace. Organizations that prioritize privacy and data protection can differentiate themselves from competitors, attract users who value privacy and trust, and build long-term relationships based on transparency and integrity. By embedding privacy protections into their AI products, organizations can demonstrate their commitment to privacy and data protection, enhance user trust, and mitigate the risk of privacy-related harm or regulatory sanctions.

Privacy by design and default principles are integral to compliance with privacy regulations and user trust in AI products. By understanding the importance of these principles, adopting privacy-enhancing measures, and addressing the challenges and opportunities of privacy by design and default, organizations can protect user privacy, foster trust with users and stakeholders, and promote responsible AI development and deployment. Ultimately, privacy by design and default are not only legal requirements but also ethical imperatives for organizations seeking to uphold user privacy, data protection, and ethical standards in AI innovation.

Cross-Border Data Transfer Considerations

Cross-border data transfers have emerged as a significant regulatory challenge in the digital age, with implications for privacy, security, and compliance with data protection laws. This section embarks on a comprehensive exploration of the complex considerations surrounding international data transfers and the diverse regulatory landscape governing cross-border data flows. By examining these considerations in detail, AI practitioners gain valuable insights into the strategies required to navigate cross-border data transfer challenges effectively, mitigate compliance risks, and ensure the lawful and ethical handling of data across borders.

At the core of the discussion lies the recognition of the global nature of data flows and the need to reconcile divergent regulatory frameworks governing data protection and privacy. As organizations increasingly rely on cross-border data transfers to support global operations, collaboration, and innovation, they must address the challenges posed by regional data protection laws, data sovereignty requirements, and regulatory expectations regarding data transfers. By adopting a proactive approach to cross-border data transfer considerations, organizations can minimize the risk of regulatory non-compliance, protect user privacy, and maintain the trust and confidence of users and stakeholders.

One of the key themes explored in this section is the impact of regional data protection laws on cross-border data transfers. Laws such as the General Data Protection Regulation (GDPR) in the European Union (EU), the California Consumer Privacy Act (CCPA) in the United States, and the Personal Information Protection Law (PIPL) in China impose strict requirements for the lawful transfer of personal data across borders. These laws prescribe conditions for data transfers, such as obtaining user consent, implementing adequate safeguards, and ensuring an adequate level of protection for transferred data. By understanding the requirements of regional data protection laws, organizations can assess the legality of cross-border data transfers and implement appropriate measures to ensure compliance.

Moreover, the section delves into the strategies and mechanisms for navigating cross-border data transfer challenges while ensuring compliance with diverse regulatory requirements. These strategies encompass a range of technical, organizational, and legal measures aimed at protecting data privacy, ensuring data security, and maintaining regulatory compliance in cross-border data transfers. Technical measures include implementing encryption, pseudonymization, and data localization techniques to protect data during transit and storage. Organizational measures include establishing data transfer policies, procedures, and contractual agreements to govern cross-border data flows and ensure compliance with regulatory requirements. Legal measures include conducting data protection impact assessments, obtaining regulatory approvals, and entering into data transfer agreements or binding corporate rules to legitimize international data transfers.

Furthermore, the section explores the challenges and opportunities for organizations in navigating cross-border data transfer considerations. While cross-border data transfers offer significant benefits in terms of global collaboration, innovation, and business expansion, they also present technical, operational, and legal challenges for organizations. Technical challenges include ensuring data interoperability, compatibility, and integrity across different jurisdictions and systems. Operational challenges include managing data sovereignty requirements, cultural differences, and language barriers in international data transfers. Legal challenges include interpreting and complying with diverse regulatory requirements, addressing the risk of regulatory enforcement actions or fines for non-compliance, and ensuring accountability and transparency in cross-border data transfer practices.

In addition to addressing challenges, the section explores the opportunities for organizations to leverage cross-border data transfers as a strategic advantage in the marketplace. Organizations that effectively navigate cross-border data transfer considerations can unlock opportunities for global expansion, collaboration, and innovation while ensuring compliance with regulatory requirements and protecting user privacy. By adopting best practices for cross-border data transfers, organizations can demonstrate their commitment to responsible data stewardship, enhance user trust, and differentiate themselves in the global marketplace.

Cross-border data transfer considerations are complex and multifaceted, requiring organizations to navigate diverse regulatory requirements, technical challenges, and operational considerations. By understanding the impact of regional data protection laws, adopting appropriate strategies and mechanisms, and addressing the challenges and opportunities of cross-border data transfers, organizations can ensure compliance, protect user privacy, and maintain the trust and confidence of users and stakeholders in an increasingly interconnected and data-driven world. Ultimately, effective management of cross-border data transfer considerations is not only a legal requirement but also a strategic imperative for organizations seeking to leverage the benefits of global data flows while upholding ethical standards and regulatory compliance in data protection and privacy.

Legal and Ethical Aspects of AI

The exploration of legal and ethical aspects of AI encompasses a multifaceted examination of the evolving landscape surrounding artificial intelligence. This chapter delves into the dynamic interplay between legal frameworks, potential liability concerns, and the ethical imperatives guiding AI development. By delving into these dimensions in detail, AI practitioners gain valuable insights into the strategies required to navigate the complex legal and ethical terrain, mitigate risks, and foster responsible AI innovation.

At the heart of the discussion lies the recognition of the profound impact of AI on society, individuals, and organizations, and the need to reconcile legal requirements with ethical considerations to ensure that AI technologies are developed and deployed responsibly. As AI technologies continue to evolve and proliferate across various domains, they raise a host of legal and ethical questions regarding accountability, transparency, fairness, and human rights. By addressing these questions, organizations can proactively address potential legal challenges, mitigate liability risks, and build public trust in AI technologies.

One of the key themes explored in this chapter is the evolving legal landscape surrounding AI, including potential liability issues and legal frameworks that may impact AI development. Laws and regulations governing AI vary across jurisdictions and may encompass areas such as data protection, intellectual property, privacy, cybersecurity, and consumer protection. Organizations developing AI technologies must navigate these legal frameworks to ensure compliance and mitigate the risk of legal challenges or regulatory enforcement actions. By understanding the legal requirements and implications of AI development, organizations can design AI systems that adhere to legal standards and minimize legal risks.

Moreover, the chapter delves into the importance of incorporating ethical considerations into AI practices to align with societal expectations and foster responsible AI development. Ethical considerations in AI encompass a wide range of principles, including transparency, fairness, accountability, privacy, and human rights. Organizations developing AI technologies must prioritize ethical considerations throughout the AI lifecycle, from data collection and algorithm design to deployment and use. By adopting ethical frameworks and guidelines, organizations can ensure that AI technologies are developed and deployed in a manner that respects the rights and dignity of individuals, promotes fairness and equity, and upholds societal values.

Furthermore, the chapter explores the challenges and opportunities for organizations in addressing legal and ethical aspects of AI. While legal and ethical considerations present challenges for AI development and deployment, they also offer opportunities for organizations to demonstrate their commitment to responsible AI innovation, ethical conduct, and societal impact. By proactively addressing legal and ethical concerns, organizations can differentiate themselves in the marketplace, build public trust and confidence in AI technologies, and mitigate the risk of legal and reputational harm.

In addition to addressing challenges, the chapter also examines the role of regulatory bodies, industry associations, and other stakeholders in shaping the legal and ethical landscape of AI. Regulatory bodies may play a crucial role in developing and enforcing regulations governing AI, while industry associations may establish ethical guidelines and best practices for AI development and deployment. By engaging with stakeholders and participating in collaborative efforts to address legal and ethical challenges, organizations can contribute to the development of a responsible and sustainable AI ecosystem.

The exploration of legal and ethical aspects of AI is essential for ensuring that AI technologies are developed and deployed in a manner that respects legal requirements, ethical principles, and societal values. By understanding the evolving legal landscape, incorporating ethical considerations into AI practices, and engaging with stakeholders, organizations can navigate the complex legal and ethical terrain, mitigate risks, and foster responsible AI innovation. Ultimately, the integration of legal and ethical considerations into AI development and deployment is not only a legal requirement but also a moral imperative for organizations seeking to harness the transformative potential of AI while upholding ethical standards and societal values.

Stakeholder Communication and Transparency

Transparent communication with stakeholders serves as a cornerstone for ensuring regulatory compliance and fostering trust in AI systems. This section delves into the multifaceted strategies and methodologies for establishing transparent communication channels with users, customers, and regulatory authorities. By examining these strategies in detail, organizations gain valuable insights into the importance of transparent practices in building trust, enhancing transparency, and demonstrating a commitment to ethical and compliant AI practices.

At the core of the discussion lies the recognition of the pivotal role that transparent communication plays in fostering accountability, promoting user trust, and maintaining regulatory compliance. As AI technologies continue to evolve and impact various aspects of society, organizations must prioritize transparent communication to keep stakeholders informed about compliance efforts, data handling practices, and ethical considerations. By adopting transparent communication practices, organizations can foster a culture of openness, accountability, and trust, and demonstrate their commitment to responsible AI development and deployment.

One of the key themes explored in this section is the importance of proactive and transparent communication about compliance efforts with users, customers, and regulatory authorities. Organizations must keep stakeholders informed about their compliance efforts, data handling practices, and any changes or updates to AI systems that may impact users' rights or interests. Transparent communication involves providing clear and accessible information about how AI systems work, how data is collected, used, and protected, and what measures are in place to ensure compliance with regulatory requirements. By adopting transparent communication practices, organizations can empower stakeholders to make informed decisions about their interactions with AI systems and build trust and confidence in the organization's commitment to ethical and compliant AI practices.

Moreover, the section explores the various strategies and methodologies for communicating compliance efforts to stakeholders effectively. These strategies encompass a range of communication channels and techniques aimed at reaching diverse stakeholders and conveying complex information in a clear and understandable manner. Communication channels may include website disclosures, privacy notices, user agreements, FAQs, user-friendly interfaces, and direct communication with regulatory authorities. Techniques for effective communication may include plain language, visual aids, interactive tools, and educational resources to help stakeholders understand complex concepts and make informed decisions.

Furthermore, the section examines the benefits of transparent communication for building user trust and enhancing transparency in AI systems. Transparent communication fosters a culture of openness and accountability, where organizations are transparent about their AI practices, data handling processes, and compliance efforts. By being transparent, organizations can build trust with users and stakeholders, demonstrate their commitment to ethical and compliant AI practices, and differentiate themselves in the marketplace. Moreover, transparent communication promotes transparency in AI systems, where users have visibility into how their data is used, how decisions are made, and what measures are in place to protect their privacy and rights.

In addition to addressing the benefits of transparent communication, the section also explores the challenges and opportunities for organizations in implementing transparent communication practices. While transparent communication offers significant benefits in terms of trust-building and transparency, it also presents challenges for organizations, such as ensuring the accuracy and completeness of information, addressing stakeholder concerns and expectations, and managing the volume and complexity of information communicated. However, by overcoming these challenges, organizations can leverage transparent communication as a strategic advantage, enhancing stakeholder engagement, building trust and confidence, and demonstrating leadership in responsible AI development and deployment.

Transparent communication with stakeholders is vital for regulatory compliance and trust-building in AI systems. By adopting transparent communication practices, organizations can keep stakeholders informed about compliance efforts, data handling practices, and ethical considerations, empower stakeholders to make informed decisions, and build trust and confidence in the organization's commitment to ethical and compliant AI practices. Ultimately, transparent communication is not only a legal requirement but also a moral imperative for organizations seeking to foster accountability, transparency, and trust in AI systems and promote responsible AI development and deployment.

Collaboration with Regulatory Authorities

Collaboration with regulatory authorities represents a proactive and strategic approach to ensuring compliance with evolving legal and regulatory frameworks governing AI technologies. This section delves into the multifaceted strategies and advantages of engaging with regulatory bodies, seeking guidance, and actively participating in industry discussions. By examining these collaborative efforts in detail, organizations gain valuable insights into the benefits of regulatory engagement, the opportunities for shaping regulatory frameworks, and the importance of ensuring alignment between AI practices and evolving compliance expectations.

At the heart of the discussion lies the recognition of the pivotal role that collaboration with regulatory authorities plays in fostering transparency, promoting regulatory compliance, and shaping the future of AI regulation. As AI technologies continue to advance and intersect with various industries and sectors, regulatory bodies play a crucial role in developing and enforcing regulations to safeguard public interests, protect consumer rights, and ensure ethical and responsible AI innovation. By actively engaging with regulators, organizations can stay abreast of regulatory developments, seek guidance on compliance requirements, and contribute to the development of regulatory frameworks that support innovation while mitigating risks and protecting societal interests.

One of the key themes explored in this section is the benefits of engaging with regulatory authorities, seeking guidance, and participating in industry discussions. Collaboration with regulators offers organizations valuable insights into regulatory expectations, emerging trends, and best practices for compliance. By building constructive relationships with regulatory authorities, organizations can gain access to regulatory guidance, clarifications, and interpretations of legal requirements, helping them navigate complex regulatory landscapes and mitigate compliance risks. Moreover, participation in industry discussions allows organizations to share insights, exchange best practices, and contribute to the development of industry standards and guidelines that promote ethical and responsible AI practices.

Moreover, the section explores the various mechanisms and forums for collaborating with regulatory authorities and participating in industry discussions. These mechanisms may include regulatory consultations, public hearings, stakeholder meetings, industry associations, and working groups focused on specific AI-related topics. By actively participating in these forums, organizations can engage directly with regulators, share their perspectives, and influence the development of regulatory frameworks that balance innovation with regulatory oversight. Furthermore, collaboration with industry associations and working groups allows organizations to collaborate with peers, share knowledge and experiences, and develop industry-wide standards and best practices for AI development and deployment.

Furthermore, the section examines the opportunities for organizations in shaping regulatory frameworks and ensuring alignment between AI practices and evolving compliance expectations. By actively engaging with regulators and participating in industry discussions, organizations can contribute to the development of regulatory frameworks that support innovation while addressing societal concerns and ethical considerations. Moreover, collaboration with regulatory authorities allows organizations to proactively address regulatory challenges, seek regulatory approvals for AI products and services, and build credibility and trust with regulators, stakeholders, and the public.

In addition to addressing the benefits and opportunities of collaboration with regulatory authorities, the section also explores the challenges and considerations for organizations in engaging with regulators and participating in industry discussions. These challenges may include navigating regulatory complexity, managing competing interests and priorities, and balancing the need for innovation with regulatory compliance. However, by overcoming these challenges and adopting a collaborative approach to compliance, organizations can leverage regulatory engagement as a strategic advantage, enhance regulatory compliance, and foster trust and confidence in AI technologies.

Collaboration with regulatory authorities is essential for ensuring compliance with evolving legal and regulatory frameworks governing AI technologies. By actively engaging with regulators, seeking guidance, and participating in industry discussions, organizations can gain valuable insights into regulatory expectations, shape regulatory frameworks, and ensure alignment between AI practices and evolving compliance expectations. Ultimately, collaboration with regulatory authorities is not only a legal requirement but also a strategic imperative for organizations seeking to foster transparency, promote ethical and responsible AI innovation, and build trust and confidence in AI technologies.

Future Trends in AI Compliance

Concluding with a forward-looking perspective, this section delves into the anticipated future trends in AI compliance, recognizing the dynamic and evolving nature of regulatory landscapes surrounding artificial intelligence. By exploring emerging legal frameworks, global standards, and evolving regulatory expectations, AI practitioners gain valuable insights into the trajectory of AI compliance and the strategic approaches required to navigate forthcoming challenges.

At the core of this discussion lies the recognition of the imperative for AI practitioners to anticipate and adapt to evolving regulatory requirements. As AI technologies continue to advance and permeate various sectors, regulatory bodies worldwide are increasingly focusing on establishing comprehensive frameworks to govern AI development, deployment, and use. These frameworks aim to safeguard privacy, mitigate risks, and promote ethical and responsible AI innovation. By staying abreast of emerging legal frameworks and global standards, AI practitioners can proactively align their practices with evolving regulatory expectations and position themselves as leaders in compliance and responsible AI development.

One of the key themes explored in this section is the emergence of new legal frameworks and regulatory initiatives designed to address the unique challenges posed by AI technologies. These initiatives may include sector-specific regulations, such as those governing healthcare, finance, and transportation, as well as broader legislative efforts aimed at regulating AI across multiple industries. Additionally, governments and regulatory bodies are increasingly focusing on AI-specific regulations, guidelines, and standards to address issues such as transparency, accountability, bias mitigation, and algorithmic fairness. By anticipating these emerging legal frameworks, AI practitioners can prepare to adapt their practices and ensure compliance with evolving regulatory requirements.

Moreover, the section examines the growing importance of global standards and harmonization efforts in AI compliance. Recognizing the global nature of AI technologies and data flows, efforts are underway to develop international standards and guidelines that promote interoperability, consistency, and transparency in AI practices. Organizations such as the International Organization for Standardization (ISO), the Institute of Electrical and Electronics Engineers

(IEEE), and the Organization for Economic Co-operation and Development (OECD) are actively involved in developing standards and guidelines for AI governance, ethics, and compliance. By aligning with these global standards, AI practitioners can demonstrate their commitment to responsible AI development and enhance their credibility and competitiveness in the global marketplace.

Furthermore, the section explores the evolving regulatory expectations surrounding AI compliance and the strategic measures AI practitioners can adopt to address these expectations. Regulatory bodies are increasingly emphasizing the importance of transparency, accountability, and ethical considerations in AI development and deployment. They are also placing greater scrutiny on AI systems' data handling practices, algorithmic decision-making processes, and impact on individuals and society. By adopting proactive measures such as implementing robust governance structures, conducting ethical impact assessments, and fostering a culture of responsible AI development, organizations can build secure, trustworthy, and compliant AI products that meet the expectations of users and regulators alike.

In addition to addressing compliance challenges, the section also examines the opportunities for innovation and competitive advantage that arise from embracing AI compliance. Organizations that proactively invest in compliance initiatives and adopt best practices for responsible AI development can differentiate themselves in the marketplace, build trust and confidence with users and stakeholders, and mitigate legal and reputational risks. Moreover, compliance with emerging legal frameworks and global standards can open up new markets, foster international collaborations, and position organizations as leaders in ethical and responsible AI innovation.

Anticipating future trends in AI compliance is essential for AI practitioners to navigate the evolving regulatory landscape and ensure the responsible development and deployment of AI technologies. By staying informed about emerging legal frameworks, global standards, and regulatory expectations, AI practitioners can proactively adapt their practices and build secure, trustworthy, and compliant AI products that meet the expectations of users and regulators alike. Ultimately, by aligning with established frameworks, staying informed about evolving regulations, and adopting proactive measures, AI practitioners can position themselves for success in an increasingly regulated and competitive AI landscape.

9. THE CONTINUOUS LEARNING ORGANIZATION

CULTIVATING A LEARNING CULTURE IN PRODUCT MANAGEMENT

In the dynamic landscape of product management, the ability to adapt, innovate, and stay ahead of the curve is paramount. This chapter explores the concept of a continuous learning organization, emphasizing the importance of fostering a culture where learning is embedded in the fabric of product management practices. From embracing new technologies to staying informed about market trends, this chapter delves into strategies, frameworks, and best practices to cultivate a learning-centric environment that propels product management teams toward sustained success.

The Imperative of Continuous Learning in Product Management

The significance of continuous learning in product management cannot be overstated, especially in the face of rapid technological advancements, evolving market dynamics, and shifting user expectations. This chapter embarks on an exploration of the fundamental role that ongoing learning plays in the realm of product management, emphasizing its pivotal importance as a cornerstone for sustained success rather than merely a tool for adaptation.

At its core, this discussion underscores the ever-changing nature of the product management landscape. With technological innovations reshaping industries at an unprecedented pace and consumer preferences evolving rapidly, product managers must proactively engage in continuous learning to stay ahead of the curve. By embracing a mindset of perpetual learning, product managers not only adapt to the current environment but also anticipate future trends, seize opportunities, and navigate challenges with agility and foresight.

Furthermore, the chapter delves into the multifaceted aspects of continuous learning in product management. It encompasses not only technical skills related to product development, but also strategic insights into market trends, user behavior, and competitive dynamics. Product managers must continually expand their knowledge base, refine their skill sets, and hone their decision-making abilities to effectively lead product teams and drive innovation.

Moreover, the discussion highlights the diverse sources of learning available to product managers. From formal education and professional development courses to industry conferences, networking events, and online resources, there are myriad opportunities for product managers to acquire new knowledge, gain fresh perspectives, and stay informed about emerging trends and best practices. By actively seeking out these learning opportunities, product managers can enrich their understanding of the ever-evolving product management landscape and enhance their ability to deliver value to their organizations and customers.

In addition to individual learning initiatives, the chapter also explores the importance of fostering a culture of continuous learning within product teams and organizations. By promoting a collaborative environment where knowledge sharing, experimentation, and innovation are encouraged, organizations can harness the collective intelligence of their teams and drive continuous improvement across the product development lifecycle. This collaborative approach to learning not only enhances team cohesion and morale but also fosters a culture of innovation and adaptability that is essential for staying competitive in today's fast-paced business environment.

Furthermore, the chapter examines the strategic implications of continuous learning for product management. By continuously expanding their knowledge base and staying abreast of industry trends, product managers can identify emerging opportunities, anticipate market shifts, and develop innovative solutions that meet the evolving needs of customers. Moreover, continuous learning enables product managers to make informed decisions, mitigate risks, and drive strategic initiatives that drive business growth and competitive advantage.

The imperative of continuous learning in product management cannot be overstated. In a rapidly changing business landscape characterized by technological disruptions and shifting consumer preferences, product managers must embrace a mindset of perpetual learning to stay ahead of the curve. By actively seeking out learning opportunities, fostering a culture of continuous learning within their teams, and leveraging their newfound knowledge to drive strategic initiatives, product managers can position themselves and their organizations for sustained success in an increasingly competitive marketplace.

Embracing Technological Advancements

In today's rapidly evolving landscape, technology stands as a powerful catalyst for innovation and transformation within product management. This section delves into the multifaceted strategies for product managers to not only embrace but also effectively leverage technological advancements. From the integration of AI and machine learning to the exploration of blockchain and other emerging technologies, this discussion underscores the pivotal role of continuous learning in enabling product managers to navigate and harness the potential of these advancements.

At its essence, this exploration emphasizes the imperative for product managers to remain agile and adaptive in the face of technological disruption. With advancements such as AI and machine learning revolutionizing data analysis, automation, and decision-making processes, product managers must cultivate a deep understanding of these technologies to unlock their full potential within their product development initiatives. By staying abreast of the latest technological trends and developments through continuous learning, product managers can identify opportunities to enhance efficiency, improve user experiences, and drive innovation within their products and organizations.

Moreover, the section delves into the diverse applications and implications of emerging technologies within product management. For instance, AI and machine learning hold immense promise for enhancing product personalization, predictive analytics, and user engagement. By leveraging these technologies, product managers can gain deeper insights into user behavior, anticipate customer needs, and deliver tailored experiences that drive customer satisfaction and loyalty. Similarly, blockchain technology offers opportunities for enhancing transparency, security, and traceability within product ecosystems, enabling product managers to streamline supply chain processes, mitigate risks, and foster trust among stakeholders.

Furthermore, the discussion explores the role of continuous learning in enabling product managers to effectively integrate technological advancements into their product development strategies. Beyond simply acquiring technical skills, continuous learning empowers product managers to cultivate a broader understanding of the strategic implications, ethical considerations, and potential risks associated with emerging technologies. By engaging in ongoing education, attending industry conferences, and participating in relevant training programs, product managers can enhance their ability to evaluate, prioritize, and implement technology-driven initiatives that align with organizational goals and deliver tangible value to customers.

In addition to individual learning initiatives, the section also highlights the importance of fostering a culture of innovation and experimentation within product teams and organizations. By encouraging cross-functional collaboration, knowledge sharing, and experimentation with new technologies, organizations can create an environment where product managers feel empowered to explore innovative solutions and drive positive change. Moreover, by providing access to resources, tools, and support networks, organizations can facilitate continuous learning and skill development among their product teams, enabling them to adapt and thrive in an ever-changing technological landscape.

Embracing technological advancements is essential for product managers seeking to drive innovation and remain competitive in today's dynamic marketplace. By staying abreast of emerging technologies, cultivating a culture of continuous learning, and effectively integrating these advancements into their product development strategies, product managers can unlock new opportunities, drive value creation, and position their organizations for long-term success in the digital age.

Staying Informed About Market Trends

In the dynamic and competitive landscape of product management, staying ahead necessitates more than just reacting to market shifts—it demands a proactive approach to understanding and leveraging market trends. This section delves into comprehensive methodologies for monitoring, analyzing, and responding to market trends, consumer behavior dynamics, and industry shifts. It highlights the indispensable role of a continuous learning mindset in empowering product managers to anticipate market changes and strategically align product strategies with evolving market dynamics.

At its core, this exploration underscores the critical importance of market intelligence in informing product strategy and decision-making processes. By harnessing a diverse array of data sources, analytics tools, and market research methodologies, product managers can gain deep insights into customer preferences, competitor strategies, and emerging trends that shape the competitive landscape. From analyzing customer feedback and conducting user surveys to tracking industry publications and monitoring social media sentiment, product managers must adopt a holistic approach to gathering and synthesizing market intelligence.

Moreover, the section delves into the multifaceted dimensions of market trends analysis, encompassing both quantitative and qualitative methodologies. While quantitative data provides valuable insights into market size, growth rates, and demographic trends, qualitative data offers nuanced insights into consumer preferences, pain points, and emerging needs. By leveraging a combination of quantitative metrics and qualitative insights, product managers can develop a holistic understanding of market trends and tailor product strategies to meet the evolving needs and preferences of their target audience.

Furthermore, the discussion explores the role of technology in enhancing market trends analysis and decision-making processes. With the proliferation of data analytics tools, machine learning algorithms, and predictive modeling techniques, product managers have access to unprecedented levels of data-driven insights and foresight. By harnessing the power of data analytics, product managers can identify patterns, forecast trends, and make informed decisions about product development, pricing strategies, and go-to-market initiatives.

Additionally, the section emphasizes the importance of continuous learning in enabling product managers to stay abreast of evolving market trends and dynamics. In today's fast-paced business environment, market trends can change rapidly, driven by factors such as technological advancements, regulatory changes, and shifts in consumer behavior. By investing in continuous education, attending industry conferences, and participating in relevant training programs, product managers can enhance their ability to anticipate market changes, identify emerging opportunities, and adapt their product strategies accordingly.

In addition to individual learning initiatives, the section also highlights the value of fostering a culture of knowledge sharing and collaboration within product teams and organizations. By encouraging cross-functional collaboration, sharing market insights, and conducting regular strategy sessions, organizations can leverage the collective intelligence of their teams to stay ahead of market trends and drive innovation. Moreover, by providing access to market research resources, competitive intelligence tools, and trend analysis reports, organizations can empower product managers to make data-driven decisions and respond effectively to changing market dynamics.

Staying informed about market trends is essential for product managers seeking to drive strategic product decisions and maintain a competitive edge in the marketplace. By adopting comprehensive methodologies for monitoring and analyzing market trends, leveraging technology to enhance decision-making processes, and fostering a culture of continuous learning and collaboration, product managers can position their organizations for success in today's dynamic and ever-evolving business landscape.

Customer-Centric Learning

In the realm of product management, customer-centricity is not just a buzzword—it's a guiding principle for success. This section delves deeply into customer-centric learning strategies, recognizing the invaluable role of customer insights in driving product success. By exploring a range of methodologies, from gathering user feedback and conducting surveys to harnessing the power of data analytics, product managers can cultivate a deep understanding of user needs and preferences, thereby refining products and enhancing user satisfaction.

At its core, customer-centric learning is about putting the needs and preferences of users at the forefront of product development efforts. By actively soliciting feedback from users, product managers gain firsthand insights into how customers interact with their products, what features resonate most strongly, and where there may be opportunities for improvement. Whether through direct user interviews, usability testing sessions, or online feedback channels, product managers must adopt a proactive approach to gathering and synthesizing customer insights.

Moreover, the section delves into the multifaceted dimensions of customer-centric learning, encompassing both qualitative and quantitative methodologies. While qualitative research methods, such as user interviews and focus groups, offer rich insights into user attitudes, motivations, and pain points, quantitative data analysis provides valuable insights into user behavior, usage patterns, and performance metrics.

By leveraging a combination of qualitative and quantitative methodologies, product managers can develop a comprehensive understanding of user needs and preferences, enabling them to make data-driven decisions that drive product success.

Furthermore, the discussion highlights the importance of data analytics in unlocking actionable insights from customer data. With the proliferation of data analytics tools and techniques, product managers have access to vast amounts of data that can provide valuable insights into user behavior, preferences, and trends. By leveraging techniques such as cohort analysis, user segmentation, and predictive modeling, product managers can identify patterns, uncover hidden correlations, and forecast future trends, thereby informing product strategy and decision-making processes.

Additionally, the section emphasizes the role of continuous learning in enabling product managers to stay attuned to evolving customer needs and preferences. In today's fast-paced business environment, user preferences and market trends can change rapidly, driven by factors such as technological advancements, cultural shifts, and competitive pressures. By investing in continuous education, attending industry conferences, and participating in relevant training programs, product managers can enhance their ability to anticipate customer needs, identify emerging opportunities, and adapt their product strategies accordingly.

In addition to individual learning initiatives, the section underscores the value of fostering a culture of customer-centricity within product teams and organizations. By encouraging cross-functional collaboration, sharing customer insights, and prioritizing user feedback, organizations can create an environment where every team member is empowered to contribute to the collective understanding of user needs and preferences. Moreover, by providing access to customer feedback platforms, analytics tools, and user research resources, organizations can facilitate the continuous learning and improvement of their product teams.

Customer-centric learning is indispensable for product managers seeking to drive product success and enhance user satisfaction. By adopting comprehensive methodologies for gathering and analyzing customer insights, leveraging data analytics to unlock actionable insights, and fostering a culture of continuous learning and customer-centricity, product managers can position their organizations for sustained success in today's competitive marketplace.

Agile Methodologies for Adaptive Learning

Agile methodologies have become synonymous with adaptability and responsiveness in the realm of product management. This section embarks on an in-depth exploration of the pivotal role that agile practices play in fostering a culture of continuous learning within product management teams. By examining the principles and practices that underpin agile methodologies, this discussion illuminates how iterative development, frequent feedback loops, and agile principles contribute to adaptive learning, enabling teams to respond effectively to evolving requirements and market dynamics.

At its core, agile methodology is rooted in the principles of flexibility, collaboration, and customer-centricity. By embracing an iterative approach to development, product teams can break down complex projects into smaller, manageable increments, allowing for rapid iteration and experimentation. This iterative process not only enables teams to deliver value to customers more quickly but also facilitates ongoing learning and improvement. By soliciting feedback early and often from stakeholders, product managers can gain valuable insights into user preferences, market trends, and emerging opportunities, enabling them to adapt their product strategies in real-time.

Moreover, the section delves into the key principles and practices that define agile methodologies, such as Scrum, Kanban, and Lean. While each methodology has its unique approach and terminology, they share common principles such as prioritizing customer value, embracing change, and fostering cross-functional collaboration. By adopting agile practices such as daily stand-up meetings, sprint planning sessions, and retrospective reviews, product teams can create a culture of transparency, accountability, and continuous improvement, enabling them to adapt quickly to changing market conditions and customer needs.

Furthermore, the discussion explores the role of agile methodologies in enabling teams to respond effectively to evolving requirements and market dynamics. In today's fast-paced business environment, product requirements and customer preferences can change rapidly, necessitating a flexible and adaptive approach to product development. By embracing agile principles such as prioritizing customer value, embracing change, and fostering cross-functional collaboration, product teams can pivot quickly in response to changing requirements, iterate on their product offerings, and deliver value to customers more effectively.

Additionally, the section highlights the importance of organizational support and leadership in fostering a culture of agile learning within product management teams. By providing resources, training, and support for agile adoption, organizations can empower product teams to embrace agile practices and reap the benefits of adaptive learning. Moreover, by fostering a culture of experimentation, innovation, and continuous improvement, organizations can create an environment where product teams feel empowered to take risks, learn from failures, and iterate on their product offerings to drive success.

Agile methodologies play a pivotal role in fostering a culture of adaptive learning within product management teams. By embracing agile principles and practices, product teams can create a culture of transparency, collaboration, and continuous improvement, enabling them to respond effectively to evolving requirements and market dynamics. Moreover, by providing organizational support and leadership for agile adoption, organizations can empower product teams to embrace agile practices and drive success in today's fast-paced business environment.

Learning from Failures and Iterative Improvement

Innovation often comes hand in hand with failure, but within that failure lies invaluable opportunities for growth and improvement. This section delves deeply into the concept of learning from failures and embracing an iterative improvement mindset within product management. By examining strategies for conducting post-mortems, analyzing failures constructively, and leveraging insights to refine product strategies, this discussion illuminates how continuous learning through failure can contribute to resilience and long-term success.

At its essence, learning from failures is about reframing setbacks as opportunities for growth and learning. By embracing a growth mindset and viewing failures not as obstacles but as stepping stones to success, product managers can cultivate a culture of resilience and innovation within their teams. This section explores methodologies for conducting post-mortems following a failure, allowing teams to dissect what went wrong, identify root causes, and extract valuable lessons for future improvement. By fostering a blame-free environment where failures are viewed as learning opportunities, product managers can empower their teams to embrace experimentation, take calculated risks, and drive innovation.

Moreover, the discussion delves into the importance of constructive failure analysis in driving iterative improvement. Rather than dwelling on past mistakes or assigning blame, product teams must approach failure analysis with a focus on extracting actionable insights and identifying areas for improvement. By engaging in open and honest discussions, soliciting diverse perspectives, and leveraging data-driven insights, product managers can uncover underlying issues, address systemic challenges, and implement corrective actions to prevent similar failures in the future.

Furthermore, the section highlights the role of iterative improvement in driving product success and innovation. In today's fast-paced business environment, the ability to adapt and iterate quickly is paramount to staying ahead of the competition and meeting evolving customer needs. By adopting an iterative approach to product development, product managers can break down complex projects into smaller, manageable increments, allowing for rapid experimentation, feedback, and refinement. This iterative process not only enables teams to deliver value to customers more quickly but also facilitates ongoing learning and improvement, driving innovation and driving long-term success.

Additionally, the discussion underscores the importance of organizational support and leadership in fostering a culture of learning from failures and iterative improvement. By providing resources, training, and support for failure analysis and iterative improvement, organizations can empower product teams to embrace experimentation and innovation. Moreover, by fostering a culture of psychological safety, where team members feel comfortable taking risks and sharing ideas openly, organizations can create an environment where failure is viewed as a natural part of the innovation process and opportunities for growth and improvement are embraced.

Learning from failures and embracing an iterative improvement mindset are essential for driving innovation and success within product management. By reframing failures as opportunities for growth, conducting constructive failure analysis, and fostering a culture of experimentation and innovation, product managers can empower their teams to adapt, iterate, and thrive in today's fast-paced business environment.

Professional Development and Skill Enhancement

The pursuit of knowledge and skill enhancement is an ongoing journey, especially in the realm of product management where the landscape is constantly evolving. This section delves into the professional development of product managers, illuminating strategies for continuous skill enhancement and career growth. By examining a variety of methodologies, including training programs, workshops, and mentorship initiatives, this discussion underscores the importance of investing in individual skill development to foster a culture of continuous learning and collective knowledge within the product management team.

At its core, professional development in product management is about empowering individuals to unlock their full potential and excel in their roles. By providing access to training programs and educational resources, organizations can equip product managers with the knowledge, tools, and techniques needed to thrive in today's dynamic business environment. This section explores the myriad of training programs available to product managers, ranging from formal certifications to online courses and workshops. Whether it's mastering agile methodologies, refining stakeholder management skills, or honing data analytics capabilities, product managers have access to a wealth of resources to enhance their skillset and stay ahead of the curve.

Moreover, the discussion delves into the transformative power of mentorship in driving professional growth and development. By pairing less experienced product managers with seasoned mentors, organizations can facilitate knowledge transfer, skill development, and career advancement. Mentorship programs provide aspiring product managers with invaluable guidance, feedback, and support as they navigate the complexities of product management. Through regular one-on-one meetings, coaching sessions, and collaborative projects, mentors can share insights, offer advice, and help mentees develop the skills and competencies needed to excel in their roles.

Furthermore, the section explores the importance of fostering a culture of continuous learning and skill enhancement within the product management team. By encouraging ongoing skill development, organizations can create an environment where individuals feel empowered to take ownership of their professional growth and pursue opportunities for learning and development. This may involve allocating time and resources for self-directed learning, encouraging participation in industry conferences and events, and promoting knowledge sharing and collaboration within the team.

Additionally, the discussion underscores the role of leadership in championing professional development initiatives and fostering a culture of learning within the organization. By providing support, encouragement, and recognition for ongoing learning efforts, leaders can demonstrate their commitment to the growth and development of their teams. Moreover, by leading by example and actively participating in learning initiatives themselves, leaders can inspire and motivate others to prioritize their own professional development.

Professional development and skill enhancement are essential components of success in product management. By investing in training programs, workshops, mentorship initiatives, and fostering a culture of continuous learning and skill enhancement, organizations can empower product managers to excel in their roles, drive innovation, and achieve long-term success in today's competitive business landscape.

Cross-Functional Collaboration for Learning

Collaboration is not just a buzzword—it's a cornerstone of effective learning and growth within product management teams. This section delves deeply into the critical role of cross-functional collaboration in fostering a culture of continuous learning and knowledge sharing. By examining the importance of bringing together diverse perspectives, interdisciplinary expertise, and collaborative problem-solving, this discussion illuminates how cross-functional collaboration enriches the learning experience and enables product managers to gain a holistic understanding of the challenges and opportunities in product management.

At its essence, cross-functional collaboration is about leveraging the collective wisdom and expertise of individuals from diverse backgrounds and disciplines to tackle complex challenges and drive innovation. By bringing together stakeholders from different departments—such as engineering, design, marketing, and sales—product managers can gain fresh insights, challenge assumptions, and identify creative solutions to problems. This section explores the various ways in which cross-functional collaboration can enrich the learning experience, from brainstorming sessions and collaborative workshops to joint problem-solving exercises and interdisciplinary projects.

Moreover, the discussion delves into the transformative power of diverse perspectives in driving innovation and creativity within product management teams. By engaging with individuals from different disciplines and backgrounds, product managers can gain new insights, challenge conventional thinking, and explore alternative approaches to problem-solving. This diversity of thought not only fosters a culture of innovation but also enriches the learning experience, allowing product managers to gain a more comprehensive understanding of the challenges and opportunities in product management.

Furthermore, the section explores the importance of interdisciplinary knowledge sharing in driving continuous learning within product management teams. By creating opportunities for knowledge exchange and collaboration across departments, organizations can break down silos, foster a culture of openness and transparency, and facilitate the sharing of best practices and lessons learned. Whether through cross-functional workshops, lunch-and-learn sessions, or collaborative projects, product managers can learn from their colleagues' experiences, gain new skills, and broaden their perspectives on product management.

Additionally, the discussion underscores the role of collaborative problem-solving in driving innovation and driving continuous improvement within product management teams. By bringing together individuals with diverse expertise and perspectives, product managers can approach challenges from multiple angles, identify creative solutions, and drive positive change. Through collaborative problem-solving exercises, product managers can learn from each other's strengths, leverage collective knowledge, and develop innovative solutions to complex problems.

Cross-functional collaboration is essential for driving continuous learning, innovation, and growth within product management teams. By leveraging diverse perspectives, interdisciplinary knowledge sharing, and collaborative problem-solving, product managers can gain a more comprehensive understanding of product management challenges and opportunities, drive innovation, and achieve long-term success in today's competitive business landscape.

Knowledge-Sharing Platforms and Tools

Knowledge sharing lies at the heart of fostering continuous learning within product management teams. This section delves into the critical role played by knowledge-sharing platforms, internal wikis, and collaborative tools in facilitating the exchange of insights, ideas, and best practices among team members. By examining the various features and benefits of these tools, this discussion highlights how creating a robust knowledge-sharing ecosystem can enhance collective learning, foster collaboration, and accelerate innovation within product management teams.

At its core, knowledge-sharing platforms serve as centralized repositories for storing, organizing, and disseminating information within an organization. Whether it's an internal wiki, a shared drive, or a dedicated collaboration platform, these tools provide a digital space where product managers can access, contribute to, and learn from a wealth of resources, including project documentation, best practices, lessons learned, and user feedback. This section explores the diverse range of knowledge-sharing platforms available to product management teams, from popular tools like Confluence and SharePoint to custom-built solutions tailored to specific organizational needs.

Moreover, the discussion delves into the transformative impact of knowledge-sharing platforms in driving collaboration and collective learning within product management teams. By providing a centralized hub for accessing and sharing information, these platforms break down silos, facilitate cross-team collaboration, and promote a culture of openness and transparency. Product managers can leverage knowledge-sharing platforms to document and share their insights, collaborate on projects in real-time, and tap into the collective wisdom of the team to solve problems and drive innovation.

Furthermore, the section explores the various features and functionalities of knowledge-sharing platforms that enhance their effectiveness as tools for continuous learning. From customizable templates and robust search functionality to version control and commenting capabilities, these platforms offer a wide range of features designed to streamline knowledge sharing and promote collaboration. By harnessing these features, product managers can create and curate a wealth of valuable resources, making it easier for team members to find relevant information, share their expertise, and contribute to the collective knowledge of the team.

Additionally, the discussion underscores the importance of fostering a culture of knowledge sharing and collaboration within product management teams. By encouraging team members to actively contribute to knowledge-sharing platforms, recognize each other's contributions, and engage in open and constructive dialogue, organizations can create an environment where learning is valued, collaboration is encouraged, and innovation thrives. This culture of knowledge sharing not only enhances individual learning and development but also drives collective intelligence, enabling product management teams to achieve greater success and drive innovation in today's competitive business landscape.

Knowledge-sharing platforms play a crucial role in fostering continuous learning, collaboration, and innovation within product management teams. By providing a centralized hub for accessing and sharing information, these platforms enable product managers to tap into the collective knowledge of the team, collaborate on projects more effectively, and drive innovation. By leveraging the features and capabilities of knowledge-sharing platforms and fostering a culture of knowledge sharing and collaboration, organizations can create an environment where learning thrives, innovation flourishes, and product management teams achieve greater success.

Continuous Learning Leadership
Continuous learning leadership is not just about managing tasks and projects—it's about cultivating an environment where growth, curiosity, and innovation thrive. This section delves into the multifaceted role of leadership in fostering a culture of continuous learning within product management teams. By examining the key attributes and practices of continuous learning leadership, this discussion highlights how effective leaders can inspire, motivate, and empower their teams to embrace lifelong learning and drive innovation.

At its core, continuous learning leadership is about leading by example. Effective leaders understand that they set the tone for the entire organization, and they actively demonstrate their commitment to learning and development. This means staying curious, seeking out new opportunities for growth, and being open to feedback and new ideas. By modeling a growth mindset and a willingness to learn, leaders inspire their teams to do the same, creating a culture where continuous learning is valued and encouraged.

Moreover, the discussion explores the importance of creating a psychologically safe environment where team members feel empowered to take risks, experiment, and learn from their mistakes. Effective leaders understand that learning often involves taking risks and stepping outside of one's comfort zone, and they create an environment where failure is viewed as a natural part of the learning process, rather than something to be feared or avoided. By fostering a culture of psychological safety, leaders enable their teams to innovate, collaborate, and push the boundaries of what's possible.

Furthermore, the section delves into the role of continuous learning leadership in promoting a growth mindset within the product management team. A growth mindset is the belief that abilities and intelligence can be developed through dedication and hard work, rather than being fixed traits. Effective leaders cultivate a growth mindset within their teams by providing regular feedback, recognizing effort and progress, and celebrating learning and improvement. By promoting a growth mindset, leaders empower their teams to embrace challenges, learn from setbacks, and continuously strive for excellence.

Additionally, the discussion explores the importance of setting clear expectations and providing opportunities for learning and development within the product management team. Effective leaders communicate the importance of continuous learning and growth, and they provide their teams with the resources, support, and encouragement they need to succeed. This may involve offering training programs, workshops, and mentorship opportunities, as well as creating opportunities for cross-functional collaboration and knowledge sharing.

Continuous learning leadership is essential for fostering a culture of innovation, collaboration, and growth within product management teams. By leading by example, creating a psychologically safe environment, promoting a growth mindset, and providing opportunities for learning and development, leaders can empower their teams to embrace lifelong learning, drive innovation, and achieve greater success in today's fast-paced business environment.

Learning Metrics and Key Performance Indicators (KPIs)

Learning metrics and key performance indicators (KPIs) serve as vital tools for evaluating the effectiveness of continuous learning initiatives within product management teams. This section delves into the intricate world of learning metrics and KPIs, exploring their definition, measurement, and significance in driving organizational success. By examining the various types of learning metrics and KPIs commonly used in product management, this discussion sheds light on how tracking learning outcomes can provide valuable insights for refining learning strategies and optimizing performance.

At its essence, learning metrics and KPIs are quantitative and qualitative measures used to assess the impact of learning initiatives on individual and organizational performance. These metrics may include indicators such as the number of training hours completed, the percentage of employees who have participated in learning activities, or the improvement in specific skills or competencies over time. By tracking these metrics, product management teams can gauge the effectiveness of their learning programs, identify areas for improvement, and measure the return on investment of their learning initiatives.

Moreover, the discussion delves into the importance of aligning learning metrics and KPIs with organizational goals and objectives. Effective learning metrics should be directly linked to key business outcomes, such as product quality, customer satisfaction, and market share. By aligning learning initiatives with strategic objectives, product management teams can ensure that their learning efforts are focused on driving tangible business results and delivering value to the organization.

Furthermore, the section explores the different types of learning metrics and KPIs that product management teams may use to assess the impact of continuous learning initiatives. These metrics may include both leading indicators, such as employee engagement in learning activities and completion rates of training programs, and lagging indicators, such as improvements in job performance or product quality. By tracking a combination of leading and lagging indicators, product management teams can gain a comprehensive understanding of the effectiveness of their learning initiatives and make data-driven decisions to optimize their learning strategies.

Additionally, the discussion examines the process of measuring learning outcomes and their influence on product success. This involves collecting and analyzing data on learning activities, performance metrics, and business outcomes to identify correlations and trends. By conducting rigorous data analysis, product management teams can gain insights into the impact of learning initiatives on key performance indicators such as time to market, product adoption rates, and customer satisfaction. These insights can then be used to refine learning strategies, allocate resources more effectively, and drive continuous improvement within the organization.

Learning metrics and KPIs are essential tools for assessing the impact of continuous learning initiatives within product management teams. By aligning learning metrics with organizational goals, tracking a combination of leading and lagging indicators, and measuring the influence of learning outcomes on product success, product management teams can gain valuable insights into the effectiveness of their learning programs and drive continuous improvement within the organization.

Incentivizing and Recognizing Learning Achievements
Incentivizing and recognizing learning achievements within the product management team is crucial for fostering a

culture of continuous improvement and development. This section delves into various strategies and approaches for incentivizing and recognizing learning achievements, highlighting their importance in motivating team members and reinforcing the value of continuous learning.

At its core, incentives and recognition serve as powerful tools for encouraging participation in learning initiatives and acknowledging the efforts and accomplishments of individuals within the team. This can take various forms, ranging from financial rewards and bonuses to non-monetary incentives such as extra time off, access to special projects or opportunities, or personalized career development plans. By offering tangible rewards and incentives for learning achievements, organizations demonstrate their commitment to investing in the growth and development of their employees, which in turn fosters motivation and engagement.

Moreover, the discussion explores the importance of creating a culture of recognition where learning achievements are celebrated and valued. This involves acknowledging and publicly recognizing individuals who demonstrate a commitment to continuous learning, whether through formal awards ceremonies, peer-to-peer recognition programs, or public commendations from leadership. By shining a spotlight on learning achievements, organizations reinforce the message that learning is a valued and integral part of the company culture, which further encourages participation and engagement in learning initiatives.

Furthermore, the section delves into the role of personalized recognition and rewards in incentivizing learning achievements. Recognizing individuals' unique learning journeys and accomplishments, such as completing a challenging training program, earning a professional certification, or mastering a new skill, demonstrates that their efforts are seen and appreciated. This personalized approach to recognition not only reinforces the value of continuous learning but also strengthens the emotional connection between employees and the organization, fostering a sense of belonging and loyalty.

Additionally, the discussion explores the use of gamification techniques to incentivize learning achievements and make the learning process more engaging and enjoyable. This may involve incorporating elements such as badges, points, leaderboards, and challenges into learning platforms and activities to create a sense of competition, achievement, and progress. By gamifying the learning experience, organizations can motivate team members to actively participate in learning initiatives, track their progress, and strive for continuous improvement.

Incentivizing and recognizing learning achievements within the product management team is essential for fostering a culture of continuous learning and development. By offering tangible rewards and incentives, creating a culture of recognition, personalizing recognition efforts, and leveraging gamification techniques, organizations can motivate team members to actively engage in learning initiatives, strengthen their skills and competencies, and drive continuous improvement and innovation within the organization.

Cultural Factors in Continuous Learning

Cultural factors play a pivotal role in shaping the learning environment within product management teams. This section delves into the multifaceted nature of organizational culture and its profound influence on continuous learning practices. By examining key cultural factors that impact learning, such as openness to experimentation, tolerance for failure, and a shared commitment to innovation, this discussion sheds light on the importance of cultivating a learning-centric culture for the sustained success of product management teams.

At its essence, organizational culture encompasses the shared values, beliefs, norms, and practices that define the identity and behavior of individuals within an organization. In the context of continuous learning, organizational culture sets the tone for how learning is perceived, valued, and integrated into everyday practices. A culture that fosters curiosity, experimentation, and a growth mindset creates an environment where individuals feel empowered to take risks, explore new ideas, and embrace learning as a lifelong journey.

Openness to experimentation is a fundamental cultural factor that influences continuous learning within product management teams. Organizations that encourage experimentation and innovation create a safe space for team members to explore new approaches, test hypotheses, and learn from both successes and failures. By fostering a culture of experimentation, organizations empower individuals to challenge the status quo, think creatively, and push the boundaries of what's possible, which in turn fuels innovation and drives continuous improvement.

Tolerance for failure is another critical cultural factor that shapes continuous learning practices within product management teams. In cultures where failure is stigmatized or punished, individuals may be hesitant to take risks or try new things, which can stifle innovation and hinder learning. Conversely, in cultures that embrace failure as a natural part of the learning process, individuals feel empowered to take calculated risks, learn from their mistakes, and iterate on their ideas. By fostering a culture of psychological safety where failure is viewed as an opportunity for growth and learning, organizations create an environment where individuals feel comfortable taking risks, experimenting, and pushing the boundaries of what's possible.

Furthermore, a shared commitment to innovation is a cultural factor that drives continuous learning within product management teams. Organizations that prioritize innovation and encourage a culture of creativity and collaboration create an environment where individuals feel inspired to learn, adapt, and innovate. By fostering a culture of innovation, organizations create a sense of purpose and excitement that motivates individuals to engage in continuous learning, explore new ideas, and drive meaningful change within the organization.

Cultural factors profoundly influence continuous learning practices within product management teams. By fostering a culture of experimentation, tolerance for failure, and a shared commitment to innovation, organizations create an environment where individuals feel empowered to learn, grow, and innovate. By cultivating a learning-centric culture, organizations can drive continuous improvement, foster innovation, and achieve sustained success in today's dynamic and competitive business landscape.

Building Learning into Product Management Processes

Integrating learning seamlessly into product management processes is vital for fostering a culture of continuous improvement and innovation. This section delves into the strategies and methodologies for embedding learning into various stages of product development, release planning, and decision-making processes. By examining the iterative refinement of processes based on insights gained from continuous learning, organizations can ensure an adaptive and innovative approach that drives long-term success.

At its core, building learning into product management processes involves incorporating learning activities, feedback loops, and knowledge-sharing mechanisms into existing workflows and methodologies. This ensures that learning becomes an integral part of the product development lifecycle, rather than an isolated activity. By embedding learning into everyday practices, organizations create an environment where continuous improvement is not only encouraged but expected.

One key aspect of building learning into product management processes is incorporating learning activities into product development cycles. This may involve conducting regular retrospectives, post-mortems, or debriefs to reflect on past experiences, identify lessons learned, and capture insights for future iterations. By institutionalizing these learning rituals, organizations create a structured framework for continuous improvement and ensure that knowledge gained from each iteration is leveraged to inform future decisions and actions.

Moreover, integrating learning into release planning processes ensures that insights gained from continuous learning are used to inform product roadmap priorities and feature development. This may involve conducting user research, analyzing customer feedback, and monitoring market trends to identify emerging opportunities and challenges. By incorporating learning-driven insights into release planning, organizations can prioritize initiatives that deliver the most value to customers and align with strategic objectives.

Additionally, weaving learning into decision-making processes ensures that data-driven insights and lessons learned from continuous learning activities are used to inform strategic and tactical decisions. This may involve establishing decision-making frameworks that emphasize evidence-based decision-making, leveraging data analytics and business intelligence tools to inform decision-making, and fostering a culture of experimentation and innovation. By integrating learning into decision-making processes, organizations can make more informed decisions, mitigate risks, and seize opportunities for growth and innovation.

Furthermore, the iterative refinement of processes based on insights gained from continuous learning ensures that product management practices evolve and adapt over time. This may involve regularly reviewing and updating processes, soliciting feedback from stakeholders, and incorporating lessons learned into process improvements. By embracing a mindset of continuous improvement, organizations can ensure that their product management processes remain agile, adaptive, and responsive to changing market dynamics and customer needs.

Building learning into product management processes is essential for driving continuous improvement and innovation within organizations. By embedding learning activities into product development cycles, release planning processes, and decision-making frameworks, organizations can leverage insights gained from continuous learning to inform strategic decisions, prioritize initiatives, and drive long-term success. By embracing a culture of continuous improvement and adaptation, organizations can remain agile, innovative, and competitive in today's dynamic business landscape.

Future Trends in Continuous Learning for Product Management

Concluding the discussion, this section delves into the exciting realm of future trends in continuous learning for product management. By examining emerging technologies, methodologies, and learning modalities, we can anticipate the transformative changes that will shape the landscape of continuous learning in the field of product management. By staying abreast of these trends, product management teams can proactively adapt their learning strategies to remain at the forefront of innovation and drive sustained success.

Emerging technologies are set to revolutionize the way product management teams approach continuous learning. Artificial intelligence (AI) and machine learning (ML) algorithms, for example, have the potential to personalize learning experiences by analyzing individual learning styles and preferences, recommending relevant content, and predicting future learning needs. Similarly, virtual reality (VR) and augmented reality (AR) technologies can create immersive learning environments, allowing product management professionals to simulate real-world scenarios, experiment with new ideas, and collaborate with peers in virtual spaces.

Furthermore, new methodologies and frameworks are poised to enhance the effectiveness of continuous learning initiatives in product management. Agile methodologies, for instance, are evolving to incorporate principles of continuous learning, with concepts such as "inspect and adapt" and "continuous improvement" becoming integral to Agile practices. Similarly, design thinking methodologies emphasize a user-centric approach to problem-solving, encouraging product management teams to empathize with end-users, ideate innovative solutions, and iterate based on feedback.

Moreover, the future of continuous learning for product management will be characterized by a diverse range of learning modalities. Traditional classroom-based training will continue to evolve, with an increasing emphasis on interactive, experiential learning activities that promote active engagement and knowledge retention. E-learning platforms and online courses will become more personalized and adaptive, leveraging AI algorithms to deliver customized learning experiences tailored to individual needs and preferences. Additionally, microlearning, gamification, and social learning platforms will gain popularity, offering bite-sized learning modules, game-based learning experiences, and collaborative learning communities.

As we look ahead, it is clear that continuous learning will be essential for product management teams to thrive in an ever-evolving business landscape. By embracing emerging technologies, methodologies, and learning modalities, product management professionals can enhance their skills, expand their knowledge, and drive innovation within their organizations. By remaining adaptable, proactive, and open to new learning opportunities, product management teams can position themselves for success in the dynamic and competitive world of product management.

UPSKILLING TEAMS FOR AI INTEGRATION

In the rapidly evolving landscape of product management, upskilling teams for AI integration is not just a strategic imperative but a transformative necessity. This chapter explores the multifaceted dimensions of upskilling within the context of AI integration. From understanding foundational AI concepts to mastering advanced implementation techniques, this chapter provides a comprehensive guide on cultivating a learning culture that empowers product management teams to harness the full potential of artificial intelligence.

The Strategic Imperative of AI Upskilling

Kicking off the discussion, this chapter delves into the strategic imperative of upskilling teams to effectively integrate AI technologies into product management practices. It delves into the transformative potential that AI brings to the field of product management and emphasizes the necessity for a proactive approach to continuous learning. The central theme underscores the realization that upskilling is not merely about maintaining relevance but also about unlocking new avenues for innovation and growth within the organization.

AI technologies are poised to revolutionize product management by providing unprecedented insights, automating tasks, and enabling predictive analytics. From enhancing customer experiences to optimizing business operations, AI has the power to drive significant improvements across various facets of product management. However, harnessing the full potential of AI requires product management teams to possess the requisite knowledge, skills, and capabilities to leverage these technologies effectively.

Moreover, the chapter explores how upskilling teams for AI integration involves more than just acquiring technical skills. It entails developing a deep understanding of AI concepts, methodologies, and applications, as well as cultivating critical thinking, problem-solving, and creative skills necessary to harness AI's capabilities to address complex business challenges. Additionally, it involves fostering a culture of experimentation, collaboration, and continuous learning within the organization to encourage innovation and adaptation in the AI-driven landscape.

Furthermore, the strategic imperative of AI upskilling extends beyond individual skill development to organizational readiness and transformation. It involves aligning organizational structures, processes, and strategies to leverage AI effectively, as well as fostering a supportive environment that encourages experimentation and risk-taking. Additionally, it requires investing in infrastructure, tools, and resources to facilitate AI adoption and implementation across the organization.

As organizations navigate the increasingly AI-driven landscape, the chapter emphasizes the importance of taking a proactive approach to continuous learning and upskilling. This involves investing in training programs, workshops, and certifications to equip product management teams with the necessary skills and knowledge to thrive in the AI era. It also entails fostering a culture of curiosity, adaptability, and lifelong learning, where employees are encouraged to explore new ideas, experiment with new technologies, and embrace change.

The strategic imperative of AI upskilling underscores the critical role that continuous learning plays in preparing product management teams for the challenges and opportunities of the AI-driven future. By investing in upskilling initiatives, organizations can empower their teams to leverage AI technologies effectively, drive innovation, and maintain a competitive edge in today's rapidly evolving business landscape.

Understanding Foundational AI Concepts

Establishing a solid foundation in artificial intelligence (AI) concepts is paramount for product management teams looking to integrate AI effectively into their practices. This section initiates the discussion by delving into the fundamental principles of AI, providing an in-depth exploration of key concepts essential for understanding and harnessing AI technologies.

At the core of AI lies machine learning, a subset of AI that empowers systems to learn from data and improve performance over time without explicit programming. This section delves into various machine learning algorithms, including supervised learning, unsupervised learning, and reinforcement learning, elucidating their respective applications and underlying mechanisms. Additionally, it explores deep learning, a subset of machine learning that mimics the structure and function of the human brain through artificial neural networks, discussing its role in powering advanced AI applications such as image recognition, natural language processing (NLP), and autonomous vehicles.

Moreover, the section examines the principles of neural networks, the building blocks of deep learning algorithms. It provides a comprehensive overview of neural network architectures, including convolutional neural networks (CNNs), recurrent neural networks (RNNs), and transformer-based architectures, elucidating their roles in various AI tasks and applications. Furthermore, it delves into the nuances of NLP, a branch of AI concerned with enabling computers to understand, interpret, and generate human language, discussing the challenges and opportunities associated with processing textual data.

In addition to exploring AI concepts in-depth, this section also discusses strategies for fostering a common understanding of AI within the product management team. It emphasizes the importance of providing comprehensive training, resources, and educational materials to equip team members with the knowledge and skills needed to leverage AI effectively. Moreover, it advocates for fostering a culture of continuous learning and knowledge sharing, where team members are encouraged to collaborate, ask questions, and explore new ideas related to AI integration.

By ensuring that product management teams possess a foundational understanding of AI concepts, organizations can lay the groundwork for successful AI integration initiatives. Armed with this knowledge, teams can effectively collaborate with data scientists, engineers, and other stakeholders to develop AI-driven solutions that address business challenges, drive innovation, and deliver value to customers. Ultimately, a solid understanding of AI concepts empowers product management teams to navigate the complexities of the AI landscape with confidence and clarity.

Navigating the AI Technology Landscape

Navigating the intricate AI technology landscape requires a comprehensive understanding of the diverse array of technologies encompassed within the AI domain. This section embarks on a detailed exploration of the multifaceted AI landscape, shedding light on the breadth and depth of technologies such as supervised and unsupervised learning, deep learning, reinforcement learning, and beyond. By providing an in-depth analysis, product management teams can gain insight into the nuanced strengths and diverse applications of these AI technologies, enabling informed decision-making and strategic planning.

At the forefront of the AI landscape lie supervised and unsupervised learning algorithms, which form the bedrock of machine learning. Supervised learning algorithms learn from labeled data, wherein they are trained on input-output pairs to predict future outcomes accurately. Conversely, unsupervised learning algorithms operate on unlabeled data, extracting patterns and structures to uncover hidden insights and relationships within the data. By delving into the nuances of supervised and unsupervised learning, product management teams can discern the most suitable approach for addressing specific business challenges and opportunities.

Furthermore, this section delves into the realm of deep learning, a subset of machine learning characterized by artificial neural networks with multiple layers of interconnected nodes. Deep learning algorithms excel in processing complex data types such as images, audio, and text, enabling advanced capabilities like image recognition, natural language understanding, and speech synthesis. By exploring the intricacies of deep learning architectures such as convolutional neural networks (CNNs), recurrent neural networks (RNNs), and transformers, product management teams can identify opportunities to leverage these powerful algorithms to drive innovation and enhance product capabilities.

Moreover, the discussion extends to reinforcement learning, an AI paradigm wherein agents learn to make decisions by interacting with an environment and receiving feedback in the form of rewards or penalties. Reinforcement learning algorithms excel in scenarios characterized by sequential decision-making and uncertainty, such as autonomous driving and game playing. By understanding the principles and applications of reinforcement learning, product management teams can explore opportunities to incorporate these adaptive learning mechanisms into their products to optimize performance and user experiences.

In addition to these core AI technologies, the landscape also encompasses a myriad of ancillary tools, frameworks, and platforms designed to facilitate AI development and deployment. From development frameworks like TensorFlow and PyTorch to cloud-based AI services like Amazon Web Services (AWS) and Google Cloud AI, product management teams must navigate a vast ecosystem of tools and technologies to orchestrate successful AI initiatives.

By providing product management teams with a comprehensive understanding of the AI technology landscape, this section empowers them to make informed decisions, develop effective strategies, and capitalize on the transformative potential of AI to drive business growth and innovation. Armed with this knowledge, product management teams can navigate the complexities of the AI landscape with confidence and clarity, ensuring that they harness the right mix of technologies to achieve their objectives and deliver value to customers.

Developing Data Literacy and Data Management Skills

Developing robust data literacy and proficient data management skills are paramount for harnessing the transformative power of AI. This section delves into the critical role that data plays as the lifeblood of AI initiatives, underscoring the imperative for product management teams to cultivate a deep understanding of data-related concepts and practices. By embarking on a comprehensive exploration of data literacy and management skills, teams can lay the foundation for successful AI integration initiatives, enabling them to harness data effectively to drive innovation and achieve strategic objectives.

Data literacy encompasses a broad spectrum of competencies, ranging from basic understanding of data concepts to advanced data analysis and interpretation skills. This section advocates for a holistic approach to data literacy, wherein product management teams develop a nuanced understanding of data sources, formats, and structures. By fostering a data-driven mindset within the organization, teams can empower individuals to leverage data as a strategic asset, enabling informed decision-making and driving business growth.

Furthermore, the section delves into the intricacies of data management, emphasizing the importance of implementing robust data governance practices to ensure data quality, integrity, and security. It explores strategies for establishing data governance frameworks, including data classification, access controls, and data lifecycle management. Additionally, it discusses the role of data management platforms and tools in streamlining data workflows, facilitating data integration, and enabling efficient data discovery and analysis.

Moreover, this section underscores the significance of understanding the role of data in training AI models. It explores the process of data preprocessing, including data cleaning, normalization, and feature engineering, as crucial steps in preparing data for AI model training. By equipping product management teams with the knowledge and skills to curate high-quality training datasets, organizations can enhance the performance and reliability of AI models, ensuring that they deliver accurate and actionable insights.

In addition to technical proficiency, this section also emphasizes the importance of ethical considerations in data management. It explores principles of data privacy, security, and ethical data use, advocating for responsible data stewardship practices that uphold user trust and comply with regulatory requirements. By integrating ethical considerations into data management processes, organizations can mitigate risks associated with data misuse and enhance the ethical integrity of their AI initiatives.

By prioritizing the development of data literacy and management skills within product management teams, organizations can unlock the full potential of their data assets and drive innovation in AI. Armed with a comprehensive understanding of data concepts and practices, teams can navigate the complexities of the data landscape with confidence, leveraging data to inform strategic decisions, optimize processes, and deliver value to customers.

Mastering AI Implementation Techniques

Mastering AI implementation techniques is essential for organizations seeking to harness the full potential of artificial intelligence in their operations. This section delves into the intricacies of advanced AI implementation, providing product management teams with a comprehensive understanding of the techniques and methodologies required to successfully integrate AI solutions into their workflows. By exploring the nuances of AI implementation, teams can navigate the complexities of model training, fine-tuning, deployment, and monitoring with confidence, ensuring that AI initiatives deliver tangible value and drive business growth.

At the heart of AI implementation lies model training, a process wherein algorithms are trained on labeled datasets to learn patterns and make predictions. This section delves into the intricacies of model training techniques, exploring methodologies such as supervised, unsupervised, and reinforcement learning. It discusses the importance of selecting the appropriate training algorithms and hyperparameters, optimizing model architectures, and tuning performance metrics to achieve desired outcomes.

Furthermore, the section delves into the challenges and considerations associated with deploying AI models in real-world environments. It explores deployment techniques such as containerization, microservices architecture, and serverless computing, discussing the advantages and trade-offs of each approach. Additionally, it examines strategies for managing model deployment at scale, ensuring reliability, scalability, and security in production environments.

Moreover, the section addresses the critical aspect of model monitoring and maintenance. It explores techniques for monitoring model performance, detecting drift, and retraining models to adapt to changing data distributions and business requirements. By implementing robust monitoring and maintenance processes, organizations can ensure the continued effectiveness and relevance of AI models over time, mitigating risks associated with model decay and obsolescence.

In addition to technical considerations, this section also explores organizational and operational aspects of AI implementation. It discusses the importance of cross-functional collaboration, stakeholder engagement, and change management in driving successful AI initiatives. Moreover, it explores strategies for fostering a culture of experimentation and innovation, enabling teams to iterate rapidly and adapt to evolving business needs.

By mastering AI implementation techniques, product management teams can unlock the transformative potential of artificial intelligence, driving innovation, and competitive advantage. Armed with a deep understanding of model training, deployment, monitoring, and maintenance, teams can navigate the complexities of AI implementation with confidence, ensuring that AI initiatives deliver tangible value and impact across the organization.

Integrating AI with Product Development Processes

Integrating artificial intelligence (AI) seamlessly into product development processes is not merely a challenge but a strategic imperative for organizations seeking to leverage AI to drive innovation and competitive advantage. This section delves into the complexities of integrating AI initiatives with product management workflows, providing comprehensive insights and strategies for navigating this intricate process effectively.

At the outset, the section emphasizes the importance of aligning AI initiatives with the strategic objectives and priorities of the organization. It explores methodologies for identifying opportunities for AI integration within existing product development processes, including market analysis, user research, and competitive benchmarking. By aligning AI initiatives with business goals, product management teams can ensure that AI investments deliver tangible value and support overarching strategic objectives.

Furthermore, the section delves into the nuances of creating cross-functional collaboration across diverse teams and stakeholders. It explores strategies for fostering alignment and synergy between product management, data science, engineering, and other relevant departments. By establishing clear communication channels, defining roles and responsibilities, and fostering a collaborative culture, organizations can harness the collective expertise and insights of cross-functional teams to drive successful AI integration.

Moreover, the section delves into the practical aspects of embedding AI into the iterative cycles of product development. It discusses methodologies such as agile and lean product development, exploring how AI initiatives can be seamlessly integrated into sprint planning, backlog prioritization, and user story mapping processes. By incorporating AI-driven features and functionalities into product roadmaps, organizations can ensure that AI initiatives align with user needs and market demands, driving product innovation and differentiation.

In addition to technical considerations, this section also addresses organizational and cultural factors that impact the integration of AI with product development processes. It explores strategies for overcoming resistance to change, fostering a culture of experimentation and learning, and promoting buy-in from key stakeholders. By cultivating a supportive and adaptive organizational culture, organizations can navigate the complexities of AI integration more effectively, driving successful outcomes and maximizing the value of AI investments.

By examining the strategic, organizational, and operational dimensions of integrating AI with product development processes, organizations can unlock the full potential of AI to drive innovation and competitive advantage. Armed with comprehensive insights and strategies, product management teams can navigate the complexities of AI integration with confidence, ensuring that AI initiatives are seamlessly integrated into product development workflows and deliver tangible value to customers and stakeholders.

Leveraging AI Tools and Platforms

In the contemporary landscape of product management, leveraging AI tools and platforms has become indispensable for organizations striving to innovate and stay ahead of the curve. This section embarks on a comprehensive exploration of the vast array of AI tools and platforms available, offering insights into their functionalities, applications, and potential impact on streamlining product development processes.

The section begins by elucidating the transformative power of AI tools and platforms in simplifying complex tasks across the product development lifecycle. It delves into the diverse categories of AI tools, ranging from cloud-based platforms to specialized development environments, each offering unique capabilities tailored to meet the evolving needs of product management teams.

Within the realm of cloud-based platforms, the section explores leading providers such as Amazon Web Services (AWS), Google Cloud Platform (GCP), and Microsoft Azure, which offer a myriad of AI services, including machine learning, natural language processing, and computer vision. It discusses how these platforms enable product management teams to harness the scalability, flexibility, and cost-effectiveness of cloud computing, empowering them to build and deploy AI-powered solutions with ease.

Furthermore, the section delves into specialized development environments and toolkits designed to cater to specific use cases and industries. It explores platforms such as TensorFlow, PyTorch, and scikit-learn, which provide comprehensive libraries and frameworks for developing and training machine learning models. Additionally, it examines AI-driven analytics tools, such as Tableau and Power BI, which enable product management teams to derive actionable insights from vast volumes of data, informing strategic decision-making and product optimization.

Moreover, the section discusses how product management teams can leverage AI tools and platforms to streamline AI integration, reduce development cycles, and enhance overall productivity. It explores use cases across various domains, including predictive analytics, customer segmentation, and personalized recommendations, highlighting the transformative impact of AI on accelerating innovation and driving business growth.

In addition to technical considerations, the section addresses organizational and cultural factors that influence the successful adoption of AI tools and platforms. It explores strategies for fostering a culture of experimentation, learning, and collaboration, enabling teams to harness the full potential of AI to drive innovation and competitive advantage.

By examining the diverse landscape of AI tools and platforms and their potential applications in product management, organizations can gain valuable insights into how to effectively leverage these technologies to streamline processes, enhance productivity, and unlock new opportunities for growth and innovation. Armed with comprehensive knowledge and strategic insights, product management teams can navigate the complexities of AI integration with confidence, driving successful outcomes and delivering tangible value to customers and stakeholders.

Cross-Functional AI Collaboration

Cross-functional collaboration lies at the heart of successful AI integration, serving as the linchpin that unites diverse skill sets and perspectives to drive innovation and achieve strategic objectives. This section embarks on a comprehensive exploration of the importance of cross-functional collaboration in AI integration, offering insights into the strategies and best practices that enable product managers, data scientists, engineers, and other stakeholders to collaborate effectively and leverage their collective expertise to drive successful AI initiatives.

The section begins by elucidating the transformative impact of cross-functional collaboration on AI integration efforts. It highlights how collaboration between product managers, data scientists, engineers, and other stakeholders fosters synergy, innovation, and creativity, enabling organizations to harness the full potential of AI to solve complex problems, seize new opportunities, and drive business growth.

Moreover, the section delves into the diverse skill sets and perspectives that each stakeholder brings to the table, emphasizing the importance of leveraging these complementary strengths to achieve common goals. It explores how product managers contribute domain expertise, market insights, and strategic vision, while data scientists bring analytical prowess, statistical expertise, and machine learning proficiency, and engineers provide technical expertise, software development skills, and infrastructure knowledge.

Furthermore, the section discusses strategies for creating a collaborative environment where cross-functional teams can thrive. It explores methodologies such as agile and lean product development, which emphasize iterative, collaborative, and customer-centric approaches to problem-solving. It also discusses the role of leadership in fostering a culture of collaboration, trust, and accountability, empowering teams to work together effectively towards shared objectives.

In addition to technical considerations, the section addresses organizational and cultural factors that influence cross-functional collaboration. It explores strategies for overcoming silos, fostering open communication, and promoting knowledge sharing and learning across teams and departments. By cultivating a collaborative culture that values diversity, inclusivity, and continuous improvement, organizations can unlock the full potential of cross-functional collaboration to drive successful AI integration.

By examining the importance of cross-functional collaboration in AI integration and offering insights into the strategies and best practices that enable effective collaboration, organizations can navigate the complexities of AI integration with confidence, drive innovation, and achieve strategic objectives. Armed with a collaborative mindset and a shared vision, cross-functional teams can leverage their collective expertise to harness the transformative power of AI and drive business success.

Ethical Considerations in AI Upskilling

Ethical considerations serve as a cornerstone in the realm of AI upskilling, weaving a crucial thread throughout the fabric of learning initiatives. This section embarks on a comprehensive exploration of the ethical dimensions inherent in AI upskilling efforts, delving into the multifaceted issues surrounding bias, fairness, transparency, and the cultivation of responsible AI practices. By addressing these ethical considerations, upskilling initiatives can ensure that the integration of AI aligns harmoniously with societal values and expectations, fostering trust and accountability in the development and deployment of AI technologies.

The section begins by elucidating the pervasive influence of ethics in AI upskilling, highlighting its profound implications for individuals, organizations, and society at large. It underscores the importance of instilling ethical awareness and responsibility within the workforce, empowering learners to navigate the ethical complexities inherent in AI development and deployment.

Furthermore, the section delves into the multifaceted issue of bias in AI, exploring the various forms it can take, from algorithmic bias to data bias, and its far-reaching implications for fairness and equity. It examines strategies for mitigating bias through ethical data collection, algorithmic transparency, and inclusive design practices, ensuring that AI systems uphold principles of fairness and impartiality.

Moreover, the section explores the concept of transparency in AI upskilling, emphasizing the importance of clear communication and accountability in the development and deployment of AI technologies. It discusses the role of transparency in fostering trust and understanding among stakeholders, enabling informed decision-making and promoting responsible AI practices.

In addition to bias and transparency, the section addresses the broader ethical considerations inherent in AI upskilling, such as privacy, security, and accountability. It examines the ethical implications of data privacy and the importance of safeguarding sensitive information in AI systems. It also discusses the ethical responsibilities of AI practitioners in ensuring the security and integrity of AI technologies, mitigating risks of misuse or harm.

Furthermore, the section explores the concept of responsible AI practices, advocating for a holistic approach that considers not only technical considerations but also ethical, social, and legal implications. It discusses frameworks and guidelines for ethical AI development, such as the IEEE Global Initiative for Ethical Considerations in Artificial Intelligence and

561

Autonomous Systems, and the importance of integrating ethical principles into the fabric of AI upskilling initiatives.

By addressing ethical considerations in AI upskilling, organizations can foster a culture of responsible AI development and deployment, ensuring that AI technologies serve the common good and uphold societal values and expectations. Armed with ethical awareness and a commitment to responsible AI practices, upskilled professionals can navigate the complexities of AI with integrity, empathy, and accountability, driving positive impact and innovation in the digital age.

Continuous Learning Pathways for AI Upskilling

Continuous learning serves as an ever-evolving journey, particularly in the dynamic landscape of AI upskilling. This section embarks on an extensive exploration of continuous learning pathways meticulously crafted to cater to the unique demands of AI upskilling initiatives. It delves into the multifaceted role of various educational avenues, such as training programs, workshops, online courses, and certifications, in furnishing product management teams with structured and comprehensive learning opportunities aimed at augmenting their proficiency in AI.

First and foremost, the section underscores the imperative of structured learning pathways in facilitating effective AI upskilling. It emphasizes the importance of adopting a strategic approach to continuous learning, wherein individuals and organizations meticulously chart out learning trajectories tailored to their specific objectives, skill sets, and learning preferences. By delineating clear learning pathways, product management teams can navigate the vast expanse of AI knowledge with purpose and direction, maximizing the efficacy of their upskilling endeavors.

Moreover, the section delves into the diverse array of educational resources available for AI upskilling, ranging from traditional training programs to modern online courses and certifications. It expounds upon the benefits of each learning modality, highlighting their unique strengths and suitability for different learning styles and preferences. For instance, while training programs and workshops offer hands-on, interactive learning experiences conducive to skill acquisition, online courses and certifications provide flexibility and accessibility, enabling learners to engage with course materials at their own pace and convenience.

Furthermore, the section delves into the intricacies of designing and implementing effective training programs and workshops tailored for AI upskilling. It explores best practices for curriculum development, instructional design, and delivery methods, emphasizing the importance of aligning learning objectives with organizational goals and learner needs. Additionally, it discusses the significance of incorporating real-world case studies, practical exercises, and project-based learning opportunities to enhance the relevance and applicability of training programs to real-world scenarios.

Additionally, the section delves into the burgeoning landscape of online learning platforms and resources dedicated to AI upskilling. It provides an overview of popular platforms, such as Coursera, Udemy, and edX, offering a plethora of AI-related courses and certifications curated by leading experts and institutions. It discusses the advantages of online learning, including flexibility, scalability, and the ability to access high-quality educational content from anywhere in the world.

Moreover, the section explores the role of certifications in validating AI competencies and enhancing the credibility of upskilling efforts. It delves into industry-recognized certifications, such as those offered by professional organizations like the AI Institute and the Association for Computing Machinery (ACM), and discusses the criteria for certification eligibility, examination formats, and continuing education requirements.

The section emphasizes the importance of continuous learning pathways in facilitating effective AI upskilling for product management teams. By leveraging a diverse array of educational resources, including training programs, workshops, online courses, and certifications, organizations can empower their teams with the knowledge, skills, and competencies needed to navigate the complexities of AI with confidence and proficiency, driving innovation and success in the digital era.

AI Upskilling Leadership

Leadership stands at the helm of AI upskilling initiatives, steering them towards success in the ever-evolving landscape of technological advancements. This section embarks on an in-depth exploration of the indispensable attributes of leadership that underpin effective AI upskilling endeavors. It delves into the multifaceted role of leadership in championing, facilitating, and sustaining the process of upskilling, elucidating key principles and practices essential for driving transformative change and fostering a culture of continuous learning within organizations.

First and foremost, the section underscores the paramount importance of leadership buy-in in catalyzing AI upskilling initiatives. It emphasizes the pivotal role of organizational leaders in endorsing and championing upskilling efforts, aligning them with broader strategic objectives, and allocating the necessary resources and support to ensure their success. Leadership buy-in serves as a catalyst for driving cultural transformation and instilling a collective sense of purpose and commitment to AI upskilling across all levels of the organization.

Moreover, the section delves into the crucial role of leadership in creating a supportive learning culture conducive to AI upskilling. It explores the characteristics of a learning-centric culture, such as psychological safety, openness to experimentation, and a growth mindset, and discusses how effective leadership fosters an environment where curiosity, exploration, and continuous improvement are celebrated and encouraged. By nurturing a culture that values learning and growth, leaders can inspire and empower employees to embrace upskilling as a lifelong journey of personal and professional development.

Furthermore, the section examines the role of leadership in fostering an environment where experimentation and learning are valued and rewarded. It discusses the importance of cultivating a culture of innovation, where failure is viewed as a learning opportunity rather than a setback, and experimentation is encouraged as a means of driving progress and innovation. Effective leaders create space for creativity and risk-taking, providing teams with the autonomy and support needed to explore new ideas, technologies, and approaches to problem-solving.

Additionally, the section explores the significance of inclusive leadership in ensuring the success of AI upskilling initiatives. It emphasizes the importance of diversity and inclusion in driving innovation and creativity, and discusses how inclusive leadership practices, such as active listening, empathy, and collaboration, foster a sense of belonging and empowerment among team members from diverse backgrounds and perspectives. By championing diversity and inclusion, leaders can harness the collective intelligence and creativity of their teams, driving innovation and excellence in AI upskilling efforts.

The section underscores the pivotal role of leadership in driving successful AI upskilling initiatives. By demonstrating commitment to upskilling, fostering a supportive learning culture, encouraging experimentation and innovation, and championing diversity and inclusion, leaders can inspire and empower their teams to embrace continuous learning and drive transformative change in the digital age. Leadership is not only essential for navigating the complexities of AI upskilling but also for unlocking the full potential of organizations and individuals in the pursuit of excellence and innovation.

Measuring AI Upskilling Impact

Measuring the impact of AI upskilling initiatives is a multifaceted endeavor that demands a nuanced approach to evaluation and assessment. This section embarks on a comprehensive exploration of the methodologies, metrics, and key performance indicators (KPIs) essential for gauging the effectiveness and success of upskilling programs tailored for product management teams. It delves into the intricacies of measuring the impact of AI upskilling initiatives, providing insights into the diverse range of metrics and KPIs that enable organizations to track progress, assess skill development, and quantify the tangible outcomes and benefits derived from upskilling efforts.

First and foremost, the section delves into the importance of defining clear and measurable objectives for AI upskilling initiatives. It emphasizes the need for alignment between upskilling goals and organizational priorities, ensuring that objectives are specific, measurable, achievable, relevant, and time-bound (SMART). By establishing clear objectives, organizations can effectively track progress, measure success, and evaluate the impact of upskilling programs on key business outcomes.

Moreover, the section explores the diverse array of metrics and KPIs that organizations can leverage to measure the impact of AI upskilling initiatives. It delves into quantitative metrics, such as skills assessments, certification completion rates, and proficiency levels, which provide tangible indicators of skill development and competency enhancement among product management teams. Additionally, it discusses qualitative metrics, including employee feedback, satisfaction surveys, and performance reviews, which offer valuable insights into the perceived value and effectiveness of upskilling programs from the perspective of participants.

Furthermore, the section examines the role of performance indicators in evaluating the impact of AI upskilling on product management outcomes. It discusses how organizations can track KPIs related to product innovation, time-to-market, customer satisfaction, and business performance to assess the direct impact of upskilling initiatives on organizational success. By correlating upskilling efforts with key business metrics, organizations can demonstrate the tangible value of AI upskilling in driving strategic objectives and achieving sustainable competitive advantage.

Additionally, the section explores the importance of ongoing monitoring and evaluation in measuring the long-term impact of AI upskilling initiatives. It emphasizes the need for continuous feedback loops, regular assessments, and iterative refinement of upskilling programs to ensure their effectiveness and relevance in a rapidly evolving technological landscape. By adopting a data-driven approach to measurement and evaluation, organizations can continuously optimize their upskilling efforts to meet the evolving needs and challenges of the digital age.

The section underscores the importance of measuring the impact of AI upskilling initiatives as a critical component of strategic workforce development. By defining clear objectives, leveraging a diverse range of metrics and KPIs, and adopting a data-driven approach to evaluation, organizations can effectively assess the success and value of upskilling programs and drive continuous improvement in product management capabilities. Measurement is not only essential for demonstrating the ROI of upskilling efforts but also for informing future investments and ensuring the long-term success and competitiveness of organizations in the digital era.

Addressing Challenges in AI Upskilling

Navigating the multifaceted landscape of AI upskilling presents organizations with a myriad of challenges, each demanding careful consideration and strategic intervention. This section embarks on an in-depth exploration of the common challenges encountered in the AI upskilling journey, offering insights into the underlying complexities and potential solutions for overcoming these obstacles.

One of the foremost challenges in AI upskilling initiatives is overcoming resistance to change. As organizations endeavor to embrace AI technologies and cultivate a culture of continuous learning, they often encounter resistance from employees who may be apprehensive about the perceived threats to job security or the daunting prospect of acquiring new skills. This section delves into the root causes of resistance to change, such as fear of the unknown, skepticism about the value of upskilling, and concerns about the disruption of established workflows. It discusses strategies for addressing resistance to change, including transparent communication, stakeholder engagement, and change management initiatives aimed at fostering a positive and supportive upskilling environment.

Another significant challenge in AI upskilling is managing resource constraints, including budgetary limitations, time constraints, and competing priorities. Organizations may struggle to allocate sufficient resources, such as funding, time, and personnel, to support comprehensive upskilling initiatives effectively. This section explores the impact of resource constraints on the scalability and effectiveness of upskilling programs, highlighting the importance of prioritization, resource optimization, and strategic alignment with organizational goals. It discusses strategies for maximizing the impact of upskilling efforts within resource constraints, such as leveraging technology-enabled learning platforms, partnering with external training providers, and adopting agile methodologies to iteratively refine and adapt upskilling initiatives based on available resources.

Moreover, this section addresses the challenge of ensuring the relevance and effectiveness of upskilling programs in a rapidly evolving technological landscape. As AI technologies continue to advance and new skills become increasingly in demand, organizations must continuously adapt their upskilling strategies to meet changing needs and priorities. It discusses the importance of ongoing needs assessment, skills gap analysis, and curriculum refinement to ensure that upskilling initiatives remain aligned with emerging trends and industry developments. Additionally, it explores the role of flexible learning pathways, personalized training experiences, and modularized curricula in catering to diverse learning preferences and addressing individual skill gaps effectively.

Furthermore, the section examines the challenge of fostering a culture of lifelong learning and continuous improvement within organizations. In many cases, entrenched mindsets, institutional barriers, and resistance to change may hinder efforts to cultivate a learning-centric culture that embraces experimentation, innovation, and knowledge sharing. This section discusses strategies for overcoming cultural barriers to upskilling, including leadership buy-in, role modeling by senior executives, and the establishment of learning communities and peer-to-peer networks. It emphasizes the importance of creating a supportive environment where employees feel empowered to take ownership of their learning journey and pursue opportunities for growth and development.

This section underscores the importance of addressing challenges effectively in the AI upskilling journey to unlock the full potential of workforce transformation. By understanding the root causes of resistance to change, managing resource constraints strategically, adapting to evolving technological trends, and fostering a culture of continuous learning, organizations can navigate the complexities of the upskilling landscape and drive sustainable success in the digital age. Challenges are not insurmountable obstacles but opportunities for innovation, resilience, and growth, paving the way for organizations to thrive in an AI-driven future.

Inclusive AI Upskilling

the organization. It delves into the multifaceted nature of inclusivity, acknowledging the importance of fostering an environment where every individual, regardless of their background or level of expertise, has equitable access to upskilling opportunities and resources.

One of the key aspects of inclusive AI upskilling is recognizing and addressing the unique needs and challenges faced by individuals from diverse backgrounds. This includes considering factors such as socioeconomic status, educational background, age, gender, ethnicity, and cultural heritage. By acknowledging and accommodating these differences, organizations can create tailored upskilling programs that resonate with a wide range of learners. For example, providing flexible learning pathways, offering language support, and incorporating culturally relevant content can help ensure that upskilling initiatives are accessible and inclusive for all employees.

Moreover, this section explores the importance of accommodating diverse learning styles and preferences in AI upskilling efforts. Individuals have different ways of acquiring and processing information, ranging from visual and auditory learners to kinesthetic learners who prefer hands-on, experiential learning activities. By offering a variety of learning modalities, such as interactive workshops, online courses, peer-to-peer mentoring, and hands-on projects, organizations can cater to the diverse learning needs and preferences of their workforce. Additionally, incorporating universal design principles into upskilling materials and platforms ensures that they are accessible to individuals with disabilities, further promoting inclusivity.

Furthermore, the section addresses the challenge of bridging the skills gap for individuals with varying levels of expertise in AI and related technologies. While some employees may already possess a strong foundation in data science, machine learning, or programming, others may be relatively new to these concepts. This section discusses strategies for accommodating learners at different skill levels, such as offering beginner, intermediate, and advanced-level courses, providing pre-requisite modules for foundational concepts, and offering personalized learning paths based on individual skill assessments. By scaffolding learning experiences and providing targeted support, organizations can empower employees at all levels to develop their AI capabilities and contribute meaningfully to the organization's AI initiatives.

Moreover, this section explores the importance of fostering a culture of psychological safety and belonging in AI upskilling programs. Individuals are more likely to engage in learning activities and take risks in their learning journey when they feel supported, valued, and respected by their peers and leaders. This includes creating opportunities for open dialogue, soliciting feedback, and recognizing and celebrating diverse perspectives and contributions. By nurturing a culture of inclusion and belonging, organizations can create an environment where every employee feels empowered to participate in AI upskilling initiatives and contribute their unique insights and talents to the organization's success.

Inclusive AI upskilling is not just about providing access to learning opportunities; it is about creating an environment where every individual feels valued, supported, and empowered to participate in the organization's AI journey. By acknowledging and accommodating diverse backgrounds, learning styles, and skill levels, organizations can foster a culture of inclusion and belonging that drives innovation, creativity, and collaboration. Inclusivity is not just a moral imperative; it is also a strategic advantage that enables organizations to harness the full potential of their diverse workforce and thrive in an increasingly complex and interconnected world.

STAYING AHEAD IN A RAPIDLY EVOLVING LANDSCAPE

In the ever-changing landscape of product management, the ability to stay ahead is contingent on cultivating a culture of continuous learning. This chapter explores strategies, frameworks, and best practices for product management teams to remain at the forefront of innovation, adapt to emerging trends, and navigate the challenges posed by a rapidly evolving environment.

The Strategic Imperative of Continuous Learning

The Strategic Imperative of Continuous Learning

The chapter initiates by illuminating the strategic necessity of continuous learning within the realm of product management, underlining its indispensable role in navigating the ever-evolving landscape of technology, market dynamics, and user preferences. It delves into the profound impact of rapid technological advancements, emphasizing the transformative influence they exert on product development processes and customer interactions. Furthermore, it underscores the dynamic nature of market trends, highlighting the imperative for product managers to remain agile and responsive to shifting consumer demands and competitive forces.

Moreover, the chapter elucidates the significance of evolving user expectations, emphasizing the pivotal role of continuous learning in enabling product managers to anticipate and adapt to changing customer needs and preferences. It explores how the relentless pursuit of knowledge and skill enhancement empowers product management professionals to not only meet but exceed customer expectations, fostering loyalty and driving business growth.

Furthermore, the chapter delves into the broader strategic implications of continuous learning, emphasizing its role in fostering innovation and driving organizational success. It discusses how a culture of continuous learning enables companies to stay ahead of the curve, identify emerging opportunities, and proactively address challenges. By embracing a mindset of lifelong learning, product management teams can unlock new possibilities for innovation, differentiation, and sustained competitive advantage in an increasingly dynamic and unpredictable business environment.

Additionally, the chapter examines the multifaceted nature of continuous learning, acknowledging that it encompasses not only technical skills but also soft skills such as communication, collaboration, and leadership. It underscores the importance of cultivating a holistic approach to learning that encompasses both technical expertise and interpersonal capabilities, enabling product managers to effectively navigate complex organizational dynamics and drive cross-functional collaboration.

Moreover, the chapter explores the strategic implications of continuous learning for organizational culture and talent development. It discusses how a commitment to continuous learning fosters a culture of curiosity, resilience, and adaptability, attracting top talent and retaining high-performing employees. By investing in the professional development of their workforce, organizations can build a sustainable competitive advantage and position themselves as employers of choice in the highly competitive marketplace.

The chapter emphasizes that continuous learning is not just a strategic option but a fundamental imperative for product management professionals seeking to thrive in today's fast-paced and increasingly complex business environment. By embracing a mindset of lifelong learning and prioritizing skill enhancement, product managers can position themselves and their organizations for long-term success in an ever-changing world.

Agile Adaptation to Technological Advancements

Agile Adaptation to Technological Advancements

In the fast-paced realm of product management, where innovation is the norm, the ability to adapt to technological advancements with agility is paramount. This section embarks on an in-depth exploration of the strategies and practices that empower product management teams to swiftly integrate emerging technologies into their processes, products, and services.

First and foremost, it's essential to acknowledge the dynamic nature of technological advancements. From breakthroughs in artificial intelligence and machine learning to developments in blockchain, IoT, and beyond, the technological landscape is constantly evolving. As such, product management professionals must cultivate a mindset of continuous learning and vigilance to stay abreast of the latest innovations.

Moreover, the section underscores the importance of proactive engagement with emerging technologies. This entails not only monitoring industry trends and attending conferences but also actively seeking out opportunities to experiment with new tools, platforms, and frameworks. By fostering a culture of experimentation and innovation, product management teams can gain valuable insights into the potential applications and implications of emerging technologies.

Furthermore, the section delves into the role of agile methodologies in facilitating rapid adaptation to technological advancements. Agile frameworks such as Scrum and Kanban provide product management teams with the flexibility and responsiveness needed to iterate quickly, validate hypotheses, and pivot in response to changing market conditions. By embracing agile principles, teams can accelerate the pace of innovation and reduce time-to-market for new products and features.

Additionally, the section explores the concept of technology assessment and evaluation. Not all technological advancements are equally relevant or applicable to every product or business context. Therefore, product management teams must develop robust criteria for assessing the potential impact, feasibility, and scalability of new technologies. This may involve conducting proof-of-concept experiments, engaging in pilot projects, or collaborating with external partners and experts.

Moreover, the section emphasizes the importance of cross-functional collaboration in driving agile adaptation to technological advancements. Product managers must work closely with engineering, design, marketing, and other stakeholders to align on priorities, identify opportunities, and overcome implementation challenges. By fostering a culture of collaboration and knowledge sharing, organizations can leverage the diverse expertise of their teams to drive innovation and achieve strategic objectives.

The section highlights that agile adaptation to technological advancements is not just a reactive process but a proactive and strategic imperative for product management teams. By staying informed, embracing experimentation, leveraging agile methodologies, conducting technology assessments, and fostering cross-functional collaboration, organizations can position themselves to thrive in an ever-evolving technological landscape.

Proactive Monitoring of Market Trends

Proactive Monitoring of Market Trends

In the dynamic and competitive landscape of product management, staying ahead of the curve necessitates not only reacting to current market trends but also proactively anticipating future shifts. This section delves into comprehensive strategies for proactive monitoring and analysis of market trends, empowering product management teams to maintain a strategic advantage in their respective industries.

To begin with, it's crucial to emphasize the multifaceted nature of market trends. These trends encompass not only changes in consumer preferences and behaviors but also broader shifts in technology, regulations, economic conditions, and competitive dynamics. Therefore, effective market trend monitoring requires a holistic approach that encompasses diverse sources of information and perspectives.

One key strategy explored in this section is continuous market intelligence. Product management teams must establish robust mechanisms for collecting, synthesizing, and analyzing data from various sources, including market research reports, customer feedback, social media, industry publications, and competitor analysis. By leveraging advanced analytics tools and techniques, teams can extract actionable insights from vast amounts of data, enabling them to identify emerging trends and patterns.

Moreover, the section delves into the importance of trend analysis and forecasting. Product management professionals must not only identify current market trends but also assess their potential impact and longevity. This involves conducting rigorous trend analysis, identifying underlying drivers, and developing predictive models to forecast future developments. Scenario planning, wherein teams simulate various hypothetical scenarios based on different trend trajectories, can also provide valuable insights into potential future outcomes.

Furthermore, the section explores the role of cross-functional collaboration in proactive trend monitoring. Product managers must work closely with sales, marketing, research and development, and other departments to gather diverse perspectives and insights. By fostering a culture of collaboration and knowledge sharing, organizations can

577

enhance their ability to detect and respond to market trends effectively.

Additionally, the section highlights the importance of agility and responsiveness in proactive trend monitoring. Market trends can emerge rapidly and evolve unpredictably, requiring product management teams to be agile in their response. Agile methodologies, such as iterative development and frequent feedback loops, enable teams to adapt quickly to changing market conditions and adjust their strategies accordingly.

Proactive monitoring of market trends is a strategic imperative for product management teams seeking to maintain a competitive edge in today's dynamic business environment. By embracing continuous market intelligence, trend analysis, scenario planning, cross-functional collaboration, and agility, organizations can position themselves to anticipate market shifts and capitalize on emerging opportunities.

Customer-Centric Learning and Feedback Loops

Customer-Centric Learning and Feedback Loops

In the realm of product management, understanding and meeting customer needs is paramount to success. This section delves deeply into the concept of customer-centric learning strategies, highlighting the importance of leveraging real-time feedback loops, comprehensive user surveys, and advanced data analytics to continuously improve products and services.

Real-time feedback loops are essential components of customer-centric learning. By establishing mechanisms for collecting and processing feedback from users in real-time, product management teams can gain valuable insights into user experiences, preferences, and pain points. This may involve implementing features such as in-app feedback forms, live chat support, or social media listening tools to capture and analyze customer feedback as it occurs. Moreover, the section emphasizes the significance of actively listening to customer feedback, responding promptly to inquiries, and incorporating user suggestions into product development cycles.

User surveys serve as another cornerstone of customer-centric learning. Through carefully crafted surveys and questionnaires, product managers can gather structured feedback from a representative sample of users, enabling them to identify trends, uncover hidden insights, and validate hypotheses. Furthermore, the section explores best practices for survey design, including the use of clear and concise questions, the implementation of randomized response options, and the solicitation of both quantitative and qualitative feedback to gain a comprehensive understanding of user sentiment.

Data analytics play a crucial role in augmenting customer-centric learning efforts. By harnessing the power of advanced analytics tools and techniques, product management teams can extract actionable insights from vast troves of data, including user interactions, engagement metrics, and demographic information. This may involve employing techniques such as cohort analysis, user segmentation, and predictive modeling to identify patterns, predict future behavior, and personalize user experiences. Additionally, the section explores the importance of data privacy and security considerations in handling sensitive user data, emphasizing the need for robust data governance frameworks and compliance with regulatory requirements.

Furthermore, the section delves into the iterative nature of customer-centric learning. Product managers must continuously iterate and refine their products based on insights gleaned from customer feedback and data analytics. This iterative process involves prioritizing feature enhancements, conducting A/B testing experiments, and monitoring key performance indicators to assess the impact of product changes on user satisfaction and business outcomes. Additionally, the section discusses the importance of fostering a culture of experimentation and innovation within product management teams, encouraging risk-taking and learning from failures to drive continuous improvement.

Customer-centric learning and feedback loops are essential components of effective product management. By embracing real-time feedback mechanisms, conducting user surveys, leveraging data analytics, and adopting an iterative approach to product development, organizations can gain valuable insights into customer needs and preferences, driving innovation and delivering exceptional user experiences.

Iterative Improvement and Learning from Setbacks

Iterative Improvement and Learning from Setbacks

In the ever-evolving landscape of innovation, setbacks are not just occasional stumbling blocks but integral components of the learning process. This section delves into the notion of iterative improvement and the invaluable lessons gleaned from setbacks. It sheds light on the dynamic interplay between resilience, adaptability, and the relentless pursuit of progress.

Setbacks, whether minor hiccups or major challenges, provide invaluable opportunities for growth. By embracing a culture of iterative improvement, product management teams can transform setbacks into stepping stones toward success. This involves reframing setbacks not as failures but as opportunities for learning and innovation.

One of the key strategies discussed in this section is conducting post-mortems or retrospective analyses following setbacks. These sessions provide a structured framework for reflecting on what went wrong, why it happened, and how similar issues can be prevented in the future. By engaging in open and honest discussions, product management teams can uncover root causes, identify areas for improvement, and develop actionable strategies for mitigating risks.

Moreover, the section emphasizes the importance of analyzing setbacks constructively. Rather than dwelling on past mistakes, product managers should approach setbacks with a growth mindset, viewing them as valuable sources of insight and learning. This involves reframing setbacks as opportunities to experiment, iterate, and refine product strategies based on real-world feedback.

Additionally, the section explores the concept of continuous learning through setbacks. By adopting an iterative approach to problem-solving, product management teams can leverage setbacks as catalysts for innovation and improvement. This involves embracing a mindset of experimentation, encouraging risk-taking, and learning from both successes and failures.

Furthermore, the section discusses the role of resilience in navigating setbacks. Resilience is not just about bouncing back from adversity but about bouncing forward, leveraging setbacks as opportunities for growth and transformation. This may involve fostering a supportive team culture, providing psychological safety for experimentation, and celebrating both successes and failures as part of the learning journey.

Iterative improvement and learning from setbacks are essential components of effective product management. By embracing setbacks as opportunities for growth, conducting constructive analyses, and fostering a culture of resilience and continuous learning, product management teams can navigate challenges with confidence and drive innovation in the face of adversity.

Fostering a Culture of Curiosity and Exploration

A thriving culture of curiosity is not just a luxury but a strategic imperative for product management teams striving to stay ahead in today's rapidly evolving landscape. This section delves into the multifaceted nature of curiosity and explores how it can be cultivated and harnessed to drive innovation, creativity, and continuous improvement within teams.

Curiosity is the fuel that ignites the flames of exploration and innovation. It compels individuals to ask questions, seek new perspectives, and push the boundaries of what is known. In the context of product management, a culture of curiosity is characterized by a relentless pursuit of understanding, a willingness to challenge the status quo, and an eagerness to explore uncharted territories.

One of the key strategies discussed in this section is the encouragement of team members to explore new ideas and experiment with innovative solutions. By providing opportunities for hands-on exploration and creative problem-solving, product management teams can unleash the full potential of their members' curiosity. This may involve setting aside dedicated time for brainstorming sessions, hackathons, or innovation workshops where team members can freely explore new concepts and prototype novel solutions.

Moreover, the section emphasizes the importance of embracing a mindset of continuous curiosity. Curiosity is not just a fleeting emotion but a habit of mind that can be cultivated and nurtured over time. Product management teams can foster a culture of continuous curiosity by celebrating curiosity-driven inquiry, rewarding risk-taking and experimentation, and providing avenues for ongoing learning and professional development.

Additionally, the section explores the role of leadership in fostering a culture of curiosity and exploration. Leaders play a critical role in setting the tone for the team culture and modeling the behaviors they wish to see in others. By demonstrating a genuine curiosity for new ideas, encouraging open dialogue, and creating a psychologically safe environment for sharing and experimentation, leaders can inspire and empower their teams to embrace curiosity as a driving force for innovation.

Furthermore, the section discusses the benefits of interdisciplinary collaboration in fostering curiosity and exploration. By bringing together individuals with diverse backgrounds, perspectives, and areas of expertise, product management teams can stimulate cross-pollination of ideas, spark creative insights, and foster a culture of continuous learning and discovery.

Fostering a culture of curiosity and exploration is essential for product management teams seeking to stay ahead in today's fast-paced and ever-changing business landscape. By encouraging curiosity-driven inquiry, embracing a mindset of continuous learning, empowering team members to experiment and explore, and fostering interdisciplinary collaboration, product management teams can unlock new opportunities, drive innovation, and create value for their customers and stakeholders.

Embracing Cross-Functional Collaboration

Cross-functional collaboration lies at the heart of adaptability and innovation within product management teams. In today's complex and rapidly evolving business landscape, the ability to seamlessly integrate diverse perspectives, skills, and expertise is essential for driving successful outcomes. This section delves into the critical role of cross-functional collaboration in fostering adaptability and driving innovation, offering insights into strategies for breaking down silos, promoting interdisciplinary collaboration, and creating a shared understanding that accelerates problem-solving and innovation.

1. Breaking Down Silos: Silos can hinder communication, stifle creativity, and impede progress within organizations. This section explores strategies for breaking down silos and fostering a culture of collaboration across functional boundaries. One approach is to establish cross-functional teams that bring together individuals from different departments or disciplines to work towards common goals. By promoting collaboration and knowledge sharing across these teams, organizations can break down silos and foster a more integrated and cohesive approach to problem-solving.

2. Promoting Interdisciplinary Collaboration: Interdisciplinary collaboration is the cornerstone of innovation. This section discusses the importance of promoting collaboration between product managers, designers, engineers, marketers, and other stakeholders involved in the product development process. By bringing together individuals with diverse skills and expertise, organizations can leverage the collective intelligence of their teams to tackle complex challenges, generate creative solutions, and drive innovation.

3. Creating a Shared Understanding: Effective collaboration requires a shared understanding of goals, priorities, and expectations. This section explores strategies for creating a shared understanding among cross-functional teams, including clear communication, alignment around shared objectives, and regular checkpoints to review progress and address any challenges or concerns. By fostering a shared

understanding, organizations can ensure that all team members are working towards common goals and are empowered to contribute their unique perspectives and insights.

4. Accelerating Problem-Solving and Innovation: Cross-functional collaboration enables organizations to tap into a diverse range of perspectives, skills, and experiences, which can accelerate problem-solving and drive innovation. This section examines how collaboration can lead to more creative solutions, faster decision-making, and greater adaptability in the face of changing market conditions or customer needs. By harnessing the collective intelligence of cross-functional teams, organizations can stay ahead of the competition and drive sustainable growth and success.

Embracing cross-functional collaboration is essential for driving adaptability and innovation within product management teams. By breaking down silos, promoting interdisciplinary collaboration, creating a shared understanding, and accelerating problem-solving and innovation, organizations can leverage the full potential of their teams and drive meaningful results that create value for customers and stakeholders alike.

Monitoring and Adopting Emerging Technologies

In today's fast-paced technological landscape, product managers must continuously monitor and adopt emerging technologies to stay competitive and meet evolving customer demands. This section delves into comprehensive strategies for effectively navigating the dynamic landscape of emerging technologies, emphasizing the proactive pursuit of innovation through dedicated teams, technology scouting initiatives, and collaborative partnerships.

1. Establishing Dedicated Teams: One effective strategy for monitoring and adopting emerging technologies is to establish dedicated teams tasked with scouting and evaluating new innovations. These teams, composed of experts from various disciplines such as engineering, design, and business development, are responsible for staying informed about the latest technological trends, conducting in-depth assessments of their potential impact, and recommending actionable strategies for integration into product development processes.

- Roles and Responsibilities: These dedicated teams are responsible for conducting research, analyzing market trends, and evaluating emerging technologies based on their relevance, feasibility, and potential impact on product offerings. By dedicating resources to this endeavor, organizations can ensure that they are well-positioned to capitalize on emerging opportunities and maintain a competitive edge in the market.

- Continuous Learning and Skill Development: Continuous learning and skill development are essential for dedicated teams to effectively monitor and adopt emerging technologies. This may involve participating in training programs, attending industry conferences, and collaborating with external experts to stay up-to-date on the latest advancements in technology and innovation.

2. Technology Scouting Initiatives: Technology scouting initiatives involve actively seeking out new technologies and innovations that have the potential to disrupt or enhance existing product offerings. This proactive approach to monitoring emerging technologies allows product managers to identify promising opportunities early on and develop strategic plans for their adoption.

- Scanning the Technological Landscape: Technology scouting involves scanning the technological landscape for promising innovations across various domains, including artificial intelligence, blockchain, augmented reality, and more. By leveraging data analytics, market research, and industry insights, product managers can identify emerging technologies that align with their organization's strategic objectives and product roadmap.
-
- Engaging with Startups and Innovation Hubs: Collaborating with startups, research institutions, and innovation hubs can provide valuable insights into emerging technologies and facilitate potential partnerships or investment opportunities. By engaging with external stakeholders, product managers can access cutting-edge technologies, gain early access to innovative solutions, and stay ahead of the competition.

3. Collaborative Partnerships: Collaborative partnerships with technology vendors, academic institutions, and industry experts can accelerate the adoption of emerging technologies and foster a culture of innovation within organizations.

- Strategic Alliances: Forming strategic alliances with technology vendors allows organizations to gain access to specialized expertise, resources, and technologies that may not be available internally. These partnerships can facilitate joint research and development efforts, co-innovation initiatives, and the co-creation of new products and services.

- Open Innovation Platforms: Open innovation platforms enable organizations to collaborate with external stakeholders, such as customers, suppliers, and industry partners, to co-create solutions and address common challenges. By leveraging the collective intelligence of a diverse ecosystem of contributors, organizations can accelerate the pace of innovation and drive meaningful outcomes.

Monitoring and adopting emerging technologies require a proactive approach that involves establishing dedicated teams, implementing technology scouting initiatives, and fostering collaborative partnerships. By staying abreast of the latest technological trends, evaluating emerging opportunities, and strategically integrating new innovations into product development processes, organizations can position themselves for long-term success and maintain a competitive edge in the market.

Learning from Industry Thought Leaders and Best Practices

In the dynamic landscape of product management, staying informed about industry trends and best practices is essential for driving innovation and maintaining a competitive edge. This section delves into the significance of learning from industry thought leaders, experts, and best practices, highlighting actionable strategies for continuous improvement and professional development.

1. Engaging with Industry Thought Leaders: Industry thought leaders possess invaluable expertise and insights that can inform and inspire product managers in their professional journey. Engaging with thought leaders through various channels allows product managers to gain fresh perspectives, stay informed about emerging trends, and expand their knowledge base.

• Following Thought Leaders: Actively following thought leaders on social media platforms, industry blogs, and professional networks enables product managers to access timely updates, thought-provoking articles, and insightful commentary on relevant topics. By curating a diverse set of thought leaders to follow, product managers can benefit from a broad range of perspectives and expertise.

•

- Attending Industry Conferences and Events: Participating in industry conferences, seminars, and webinars provides opportunities for product managers to learn from thought leaders firsthand, engage in thought-provoking discussions, and network with peers. These events often feature keynote speeches, panel discussions, and workshops led by industry luminaries, offering valuable insights into emerging trends and best practices.

•

- Joining Professional Associations and Forums: Joining professional associations and online forums dedicated to product management allows product managers to connect with industry thought leaders, exchange ideas, and participate in knowledge-sharing activities. These communities serve as valuable platforms for learning from experienced practitioners, accessing resources, and building professional networks.

2. Studying Best Practices and Case Studies: Analyzing best practices and real-world case studies provides product managers with practical insights into successful product management strategies, methodologies, and implementation approaches.

- Reading Industry Publications: Regularly reading industry publications, whitepapers, and case studies enables product managers to stay updated on the latest best practices, success stories, and lessons learned from leading organizations. By studying real-world examples of successful product launches, market strategies, and innovation initiatives, product managers can glean actionable insights and apply them to their own projects.

- Participating in Peer Learning Circles: Peer learning circles facilitate collaborative learning and knowledge exchange among product management professionals. These small-group discussions, facilitated by experienced facilitators or industry experts, provide a forum for sharing best practices, discussing challenges, and brainstorming solutions in a supportive environment.

- Enrolling in Continuous Learning Programs: Enrolling in continuous learning programs, such as online courses, workshops, and certification programs, allows product managers to deepen their knowledge, acquire new skills, and stay updated on evolving industry trends. These programs often feature curated content, expert-led sessions, and interactive learning experiences designed to enhance professional development and advance career growth.

Learning from industry thought leaders and best practices is essential for continuous improvement and professional development in product management. By engaging with thought leaders, attending industry events, studying best practices, and participating in peer learning activities, product managers can stay informed, inspired, and equipped to drive innovation and success in their roles.

Embracing Change as a Continuous Learning Opportunity

In the fast-paced and ever-changing landscape of product management, embracing change is not just a necessity but a strategic imperative. This section delves into the mindset of viewing change as a continuous learning opportunity, exploring actionable strategies for cultivating adaptability, resilience, and a positive attitude toward change within product management teams. By embracing change as a catalyst for ongoing learning and innovation, product managers can navigate uncertainty with confidence and drive sustainable success.

1. Recognizing Change as an Inevitable Reality: The first step in embracing change is acknowledging its inevitability. Change is a constant in today's dynamic business environment, driven by technological advancements, market shifts, and evolving customer preferences. By recognizing change as an inherent aspect of the product management landscape, teams can adopt a proactive stance and prepare themselves to respond effectively to emerging challenges and opportunities.

2. Fostering a Growth Mindset: Cultivating a growth mindset is essential for embracing change as a learning opportunity. A growth mindset is characterized by a belief in one's ability to learn and grow through experience, challenges, and feedback. Product management teams can foster a growth mindset by encouraging experimentation, promoting risk-taking, and reframing failures as valuable learning experiences. By viewing setbacks as opportunities for growth rather than obstacles, team members can approach change with resilience and optimism.

3. Building Adaptive Capacity: Adaptive capacity refers to the ability of individuals and teams to respond effectively to change and uncertainty. Product management teams can enhance their adaptive capacity by developing flexible processes, fostering open communication, and encouraging cross-functional collaboration. By establishing agile frameworks, conducting regular scenario planning exercises, and empowering team members to voice their ideas and concerns, organizations can build resilience and agility in the face of change.

4. Embracing a Continuous Learning Mindset: Change presents opportunities for continuous learning and skill

development. Product management teams can embrace a continuous learning mindset by seeking out new knowledge, staying informed about industry trends, and actively pursuing professional development opportunities. By investing in training programs, attending industry conferences, and participating in peer learning activities, team members can expand their expertise and adapt to evolving requirements.

5. Encouraging Experimentation and Innovation: Change creates opportunities for experimentation and innovation. Product management teams can leverage change as a catalyst for creativity by encouraging experimentation, embracing diversity of thought, and fostering a culture of innovation. By providing resources, support, and recognition for innovative ideas, organizations can harness the potential of change to drive breakthroughs and competitive advantage.

Embracing change as a continuous learning opportunity requires a proactive mindset, a commitment to growth, and a culture of innovation. By recognizing change as a catalyst for learning and innovation, product management teams can navigate uncertainty with confidence, drive sustainable success, and stay ahead in today's rapidly evolving business landscape.

Leveraging Online Learning Platforms and Resources
Harnessing the Power of Online Learning Platforms and Resources for Continuous Development

In today's digital age, online learning platforms have revolutionized the way individuals acquire knowledge and skills. This section delves into the multifaceted role of online learning platforms, courses, and resources in facilitating continuous learning and professional development within product management teams. By leveraging these platforms effectively, teams can stay ahead of the curve, adapt to evolving industry trends, and enhance their capabilities.

1. Accessible and Diverse Learning Materials: Online learning platforms offer a vast array of courses, tutorials, webinars, and resources covering diverse topics relevant to product management. From foundational concepts to advanced techniques, these platforms provide accessible and flexible learning materials that cater to the varying needs and interests of team members. Whether it's mastering data analysis techniques, honing project management skills, or delving into emerging technologies like artificial intelligence and blockchain, online platforms offer a wealth of resources to support continuous learning.

2. Flexible Learning Modalities: One of the key advantages of online learning platforms is their flexibility. Team members can access course materials at their own pace and schedule, allowing for personalized learning experiences that fit into busy work schedules. Whether it's through self-paced courses, live webinars, or interactive workshops, online platforms offer a variety of learning modalities to accommodate different learning styles and preferences. This flexibility enables team members to engage with content in a way that best suits their individual needs, promoting deeper understanding and retention of knowledge.

3. Opportunities for Skill Acquisition and Development: Online learning platforms serve as valuable resources for skill acquisition and development. Product management teams can leverage these platforms to acquire new skills, enhance existing competencies, and stay updated on the latest industry best practices. Whether it's mastering project management methodologies, refining communication and leadership skills, or learning how to navigate emerging technologies, online courses provide practical and actionable insights that empower team members to excel in their roles.

4. Stay Updated on Industry Trends and Best Practices: The field of product management is constantly evolving, with new

technologies, methodologies, and market trends emerging at a rapid pace. Online learning platforms serve as a conduit for staying updated on industry trends and best practices. Through curated courses, expert-led webinars, and industry-specific resources, product management teams can gain valuable insights into emerging trends, innovative strategies, and real-world case studies that inform their decision-making and drive business success.

5. Community and Networking Opportunities: Many online learning platforms offer community forums, discussion boards, and networking opportunities that facilitate knowledge sharing and collaboration among peers. Product management professionals can connect with like-minded individuals, share experiences, and exchange ideas in virtual communities dedicated to their field. These networking opportunities not only enrich the learning experience but also foster a sense of camaraderie and support among team members, creating a collaborative learning ecosystem.

Online learning platforms play a pivotal role in facilitating continuous learning and professional development within product management teams. By harnessing the power of these platforms, teams can access diverse learning materials, acquire new skills, stay updated on industry trends, and connect with peers in a collaborative learning environment. As digital learning continues to evolve, product management professionals have unprecedented opportunities to expand their knowledge, enhance their capabilities, and drive innovation in their organizations.

Establishing Learning Metrics and Key Performance Indicators (KPIs)

In the dynamic landscape of product management, measuring the effectiveness of continuous learning initiatives is paramount. This section delves into the intricate process of establishing robust learning metrics and key performance indicators (KPIs) tailored to the unique needs and objectives of product management teams. By defining clear metrics and KPIs, organizations can gain valuable insights into the impact of learning initiatives, track progress, and refine strategies to optimize outcomes.

1. Defining Learning Outcomes and Objectives: The first step in establishing learning metrics and KPIs is to define clear learning outcomes and objectives aligned with the organization's goals. This involves identifying the specific knowledge, skills, and competencies that product management teams aim to develop through continuous learning initiatives. Whether it's enhancing technical proficiency, improving leadership capabilities, or fostering innovation and creativity, clearly defined learning objectives provide a roadmap for measuring progress and success.

2. Quantifying Skill Development and Proficiency: Learning metrics and KPIs should encompass both qualitative and quantitative measures of skill development and proficiency. This may include assessments, evaluations, and performance reviews to gauge the acquisition and mastery of key competencies relevant to product management roles. By quantifying skill development, organizations can track individual and team progress over time, identify areas for improvement, and tailor learning interventions to address specific needs.

3. Measuring Learning Impact on Product Success: Ultimately, the effectiveness of continuous learning initiatives should be evaluated based on their impact on product success. This involves tracking KPIs related to product performance, customer satisfaction, and business outcomes influenced by the knowledge and skills acquired through learning initiatives. By correlating learning outcomes with product success metrics, organizations can assess the tangible benefits of

investing in employee development and make data-driven decisions to optimize future learning strategies.

4. Tracking Engagement and Participation: Another critical aspect of learning metrics is tracking engagement and participation in learning activities. This may include metrics such as course completion rates, attendance at training sessions, participation in workshops, and engagement with learning resources. By monitoring engagement metrics, organizations can assess the level of interest, motivation, and commitment among team members and identify opportunities to enhance participation and involvement in continuous learning initiatives.

5. Feedback and Performance Reviews: Incorporating feedback mechanisms and performance reviews into learning metrics allows for ongoing assessment and refinement of learning strategies. Regular feedback from participants, managers, and stakeholders provides valuable insights into the effectiveness of learning initiatives, areas for improvement, and emerging training needs. Performance reviews serve as an opportunity to recognize achievements, address challenges, and align individual development goals with organizational objectives.

6. Continuous Improvement and Iterative Evaluation: Learning metrics and KPIs should support a culture of continuous improvement and iterative evaluation. Organizations should regularly review and refine their learning metrics based on evolving needs, feedback, and changing business priorities. By adopting an iterative approach to evaluation, organizations can adapt learning strategies in real time, optimize resource allocation, and ensure alignment with strategic objectives.

Establishing comprehensive learning metrics and KPIs is essential for evaluating the impact of continuous learning initiatives on product management teams. By defining clear objectives, quantifying skill development, measuring learning impact on product success, tracking engagement, soliciting feedback, and embracing a culture of continuous improvement, organizations can effectively assess the effectiveness of their learning initiatives and drive continuous growth and innovation.

Nurturing a Culture of Collaboration and Knowledge Sharing

In the fast-paced realm of product management, the power of collaboration and knowledge sharing cannot be overstated. This section delves into the multifaceted strategies aimed at nurturing a robust culture of collaboration and knowledge sharing within product management teams, thereby enhancing learning outcomes and driving collective growth and innovation.

1. Creating Internal Forums for Idea Exchange: Internal forums serve as invaluable platforms for fostering collaboration and facilitating the exchange of ideas, insights, and best practices among team members. Whether it's through virtual discussion boards, dedicated Slack channels, or regular team meetings, creating spaces where team members can openly share their thoughts, experiences, and challenges fosters a sense of community and encourages collaborative problem-solving.

2. Utilizing Collaborative Tools for Seamless Communication: In today's digital age, collaborative tools play a pivotal role in promoting real-time communication and collaboration among geographically dispersed teams. Platforms such as Microsoft Teams, Google Workspace, and Asana provide features for document sharing, task management, and project collaboration, enabling seamless communication and collaboration across product management teams. By leveraging these tools effectively, teams can streamline

workflows, enhance productivity, and facilitate knowledge sharing in a virtual environment.

3. Establishing Shared Repositories for Knowledge Management: Shared repositories serve as centralized repositories for storing, organizing, and accessing knowledge assets such as project documentation, best practices, and lessons learned. Whether it's through wikis, document management systems, or knowledge bases, establishing shared repositories ensures that valuable insights and institutional knowledge are documented and readily accessible to all team members. This promotes cross-functional collaboration, accelerates onboarding of new team members, and prevents knowledge silos within the organization.

4. Encouraging Peer Learning and Mentorship: Peer learning and mentorship programs provide opportunities for mutual learning and skill development among team members. Pairing junior team members with more experienced mentors fosters knowledge transfer, skill acquisition, and professional growth. Additionally, organizing peer-led learning sessions, lunch-and-learn sessions, or brown bag sessions on relevant topics encourages team members to share their expertise, learn from each other, and strengthen bonds within the team.

5. Promoting Communities of Practice: Communities of practice bring together individuals with shared interests or expertise to collaborate, learn from each other, and drive innovation within specific domains or areas of focus. Whether it's a community focused on agile methodologies, user experience design, or data analytics, fostering communities of practice provides a platform for deepening domain knowledge, sharing best practices, and tackling common challenges collaboratively. By encouraging active participation and knowledge sharing within these communities, organizations can harness collective

intelligence and foster continuous learning across product management teams.

6. Recognizing and Rewarding Knowledge Sharing Behaviors: Recognizing and rewarding knowledge sharing behaviors reinforces the value of collaboration and incentivizes team members to actively contribute to the collective learning culture. Whether it's through formal recognition programs, peer-to-peer awards, or performance incentives tied to knowledge sharing outcomes, acknowledging and celebrating individuals who demonstrate a commitment to knowledge sharing fosters a culture where sharing knowledge is not only encouraged but also celebrated and valued.

Nurturing a culture of collaboration and knowledge sharing within product management teams is essential for driving continuous learning, fostering innovation, and achieving collective success. By creating internal forums for idea exchange, utilizing collaborative tools for seamless communication, establishing shared repositories for knowledge management, encouraging peer learning and mentorship, promoting communities of practice, and recognizing and rewarding knowledge sharing behaviors, organizations can cultivate a dynamic learning ecosystem that empowers team members to thrive and excel in today's rapidly evolving business landscape.

Leadership's Role in Fostering Continuous Learning

Leadership serves as the cornerstone in cultivating and sustaining a culture of continuous learning within an organization. This section delves into the multifaceted attributes and actions that define effective leadership in driving ongoing learning initiatives, empowering teams to thrive amidst the ever-evolving business landscape.

1. Leadership Buy-In and Commitment to Learning: Leadership buy-in is fundamental to the success of any continuous learning initiative. When leaders actively champion the value of ongoing learning and demonstrate a personal commitment to their own development, it sets a powerful example for the rest of the organization. By prioritizing learning and dedicating resources towards skill development programs, leaders send a clear message that continuous improvement is not just encouraged but ingrained in the organizational culture.

2. Setting a Learning-Focused Vision: Visionary leadership plays a crucial role in shaping the organizational culture towards continuous learning. Leaders who articulate a compelling vision for the future, one that emphasizes the importance of adaptability, innovation, and lifelong learning, inspire and motivate their teams to embrace change and seek out new opportunities for growth. By communicating a clear and compelling vision that aligns with the organization's goals and values, leaders foster a sense of purpose and direction that energizes teams to pursue excellence through continuous learning.

3. Providing Resources for Skill Development: Effective leaders recognize that investing in their people is an investment in the organization's future success. They allocate resources, whether it's time, budget, or access to learning opportunities, to support ongoing skill development and professional growth. This may involve providing access to training programs, workshops, conferences, online courses, or mentorship opportunities tailored to the needs of individual team members. By equipping employees with the tools and resources they need to continuously learn and upskill, leaders empower them to adapt to changing demands and excel in their roles.

4. Creating a Psychological Safe Environment: Leadership plays a crucial role in creating a psychological safe environment where team members feel comfortable taking risks, sharing ideas, and experimenting with new approaches. Leaders who foster an inclusive and supportive culture, one where failures are viewed as learning opportunities rather than setbacks, encourage innovation and creativity among their teams. By promoting open communication, constructive feedback, and a growth mindset, leaders create an environment where continuous learning thrives and individuals feel empowered to stretch beyond their comfort zones.

5. Leading by Example: Perhaps the most powerful way that leaders drive continuous learning is by leading by example. When leaders demonstrate a genuine curiosity, a hunger for knowledge, and a willingness to learn from their mistakes, it sets a powerful precedent for the rest of the organization. By actively participating in learning initiatives, sharing their own experiences and insights, and acknowledging their own areas for improvement, leaders inspire a culture of humility, resilience, and continuous self-improvement throughout the organization.

The leadership plays a pivotal role in fostering a culture of continuous learning within an organization. By championing learning initiatives, setting a learning-focused vision, providing resources for skill development, creating a psychologically safe environment, and leading by example, leaders empower their teams to thrive amidst change, adapt to new challenges, and drive innovation in an increasingly dynamic business environment.

Future-Forward Learning Strategies

As we draw this chapter to a close, we embark on an exploration of future-forward learning strategies tailored to equip product management teams with the skills and knowledge needed to navigate the ever-evolving landscape of technology and industry demands. By anticipating emerging trends, embracing innovative learning modalities, and aligning with evolving industry expectations, product management teams can proactively position themselves for success in the dynamic future ahead.

1. Embracing Emerging Technologies: One of the key pillars of future-forward learning strategies is the proactive embrace of emerging technologies. Product management teams must stay abreast of cutting-edge innovations such as artificial intelligence, blockchain, augmented reality, and the Internet of Things. By investing in training programs, workshops, and hands-on experiences that explore the potential applications and implications of these technologies, teams can gain a competitive edge and drive innovation within their organizations.

2. Adopting Agile Learning Modalities: In the fast-paced digital age, traditional learning approaches are no longer sufficient. Future-forward product management teams must adopt agile learning modalities that emphasize flexibility, interactivity, and real-time feedback. This may involve leveraging micro-learning platforms, gamified simulations, virtual reality training, and collaborative learning environments to deliver dynamic and engaging learning experiences that cater to the diverse needs and preferences of modern learners.

3. Cultivating a Culture of Lifelong Learning: Lifelong learning is the cornerstone of future success in product management. Organizations must foster a culture where continuous learning is not just encouraged but ingrained into the fabric of everyday operations. By promoting a growth mindset, providing opportunities for skill development, and recognizing and rewarding learning achievements,

organizations can create an environment where employees are motivated to pursue excellence and adapt to change proactively.

4. Harnessing Data-Driven Insights: Data analytics and insights play a crucial role in shaping future-forward learning strategies. Product management teams can leverage data-driven approaches to identify learning gaps, measure the effectiveness of training programs, and tailor learning experiences to individual preferences and performance metrics. By harnessing the power of data analytics, teams can optimize their learning initiatives and drive continuous improvement in skill development and knowledge acquisition.

5. Fostering Collaboration and Knowledge Sharing: Collaboration and knowledge sharing are essential components of future-forward learning strategies. Product management teams must create opportunities for cross-functional collaboration, peer-to-peer mentoring, and knowledge exchange to capitalize on the collective expertise and insights within the organization. By fostering a culture of collaboration and knowledge sharing, teams can leverage diverse perspectives, co-create innovative solutions, and accelerate learning and innovation across the organization.

Future-forward learning strategies are essential for equipping product management teams with the skills, knowledge, and mindset needed to thrive in an increasingly dynamic and competitive business landscape. By embracing emerging technologies, adopting agile learning modalities, cultivating a culture of lifelong learning, harnessing data-driven insights, and fostering collaboration and knowledge sharing, organizations can empower their teams to navigate future challenges with confidence and drive sustainable growth and innovation.

10. CASE STUDIES AND SUCCESS STORIES

REAL-WORLD EXAMPLES OF AI-ENHANCED PRODUCT MANAGEMENT

In this chapter, we delve into real-world case studies and success stories that exemplify the transformative impact of AI on product management. These narratives showcase diverse industries, innovative applications, and the tangible benefits that organizations have achieved through the integration of artificial intelligence into their product management practices.

Case Study 1: Optimizing User Experience with AI-Powered Personalization

Introduction:
In this case study, we delve into the transformative impact of AI-powered personalization on user experience within a prominent e-commerce platform. By harnessing the capabilities of artificial intelligence, the platform revolutionized its approach to customer engagement, driving significant improvements in satisfaction, conversion rates, and revenue generation.

Background:
The e-commerce platform, a leader in its industry, recognized the growing importance of delivering personalized experiences to its users. With an extensive catalog of products and a diverse customer base, the platform sought to

leverage AI algorithms to tailor recommendations and content to individual preferences and behaviors.

Implementation:
The implementation process began with a comprehensive analysis of user data, encompassing browsing history, purchase patterns, demographic information, and engagement metrics. Leveraging advanced machine learning algorithms, the platform developed a sophisticated recommendation system capable of understanding and predicting user preferences with remarkable accuracy.

The AI-powered recommendation system was seamlessly integrated into the platform's user interface, delivering personalized product suggestions, curated content, and targeted promotions in real-time. Through continuous learning and refinement, the system adapted to evolving user preferences, ensuring relevance and effectiveness over time.

Results:
The impact of the AI-powered personalization initiative was profound, yielding tangible benefits across key performance metrics:

1. Enhanced User Satisfaction: By presenting users with personalized recommendations tailored to their interests and preferences, the platform witnessed a notable increase in user satisfaction and engagement. Customers appreciated the curated shopping experience, leading to higher levels of brand loyalty and repeat purchases.

2. Improved Conversion Rates: The personalized recommendation system proved to be a powerful driver of conversion, guiding users towards products that aligned with their needs and preferences. As a result, the platform experienced a significant uptick in conversion rates, with

more users completing purchases and adding items to their carts.

3. Boost in Revenue: The implementation of AI-powered personalization had a direct impact on the platform's bottom line, driving substantial revenue growth. By delivering targeted recommendations and promotions, the platform was able to capitalize on cross-selling and upselling opportunities, increasing average order values and overall sales revenue.

Conclusion:
This case study highlights the transformative potential of AI-powered personalization in enhancing user experience and driving business outcomes within the e-commerce domain. By leveraging advanced machine learning algorithms to deliver tailored recommendations and content, the platform successfully increased user satisfaction, conversion rates, and revenue, solidifying its position as a leader in the industry. As organizations continue to prioritize personalization and customer-centricity, AI-powered solutions will play an increasingly pivotal role in shaping the future of e-commerce.

Case Study 2: Streamlining Product Development with Predictive Analytics

Introduction:
In this case study, we examine how a forward-thinking software development company utilized predictive analytics to optimize its product development processes. By harnessing the power of predictive models and AI-driven insights, the organization achieved significant improvements in project timeline estimation, resource allocation, and time-to-market for new products.

Background:

The software development company faced the common challenge of accurately estimating project timelines and effectively allocating resources across multiple projects. In an industry characterized by tight deadlines and evolving customer demands, the company sought to leverage data-driven approaches to streamline its product development lifecycle and enhance efficiency.

Implementation:
The implementation process began with the collection and analysis of historical data related to previous projects, including timelines, resource utilization, project scope, and performance metrics. Leveraging advanced predictive analytics techniques, the organization developed AI-driven models capable of forecasting project timelines and identifying potential bottlenecks in the development process.

The predictive models were integrated into the company's project management system, allowing project managers to access real-time insights and recommendations for optimizing resource allocation and scheduling. By leveraging historical data and machine learning algorithms, the organization was able to anticipate project delays, allocate resources more effectively, and proactively mitigate risks.

Results:
The implementation of predictive analytics had a transformative impact on the company's product development processes, yielding significant improvements across key performance indicators:

1. Accurate Project Timeline Estimation: The AI-driven predictive models provided project managers with accurate forecasts of project timelines, enabling better planning and allocation of resources. By leveraging historical data and advanced algorithms, the organization reduced the

uncertainty associated with project deadlines, leading to more reliable delivery schedules.

2. Optimized Resource Allocation: Predictive analytics allowed the organization to optimize resource allocation based on project requirements, skill sets, and availability. By identifying potential bottlenecks and resource constraints in advance, the company ensured that projects were adequately staffed and equipped to meet deadlines, resulting in improved productivity and efficiency.

3. Reduced Time-to-Market: With more accurate project timeline estimation and optimized resource allocation, the company experienced a notable reduction in time-to-market for new products and features. By streamlining the product development lifecycle and minimizing delays, the organization was able to respond more swiftly to market demands and gain a competitive edge.

Conclusion:
This case study demonstrates the transformative impact of predictive analytics on product development efficiency within the software development industry. By leveraging AI-driven predictive models to forecast project timelines, optimize resource allocation, and reduce time-to-market, the organization achieved tangible improvements in productivity, efficiency, and competitiveness. As the pace of innovation accelerates, predictive analytics will continue to play a critical role in driving success in the software development landscape.

Case Study 3: AI-Enhanced Agile Methodologies in a Technology Startup
In this case study, we explore how a technology startup embraced AI to enhance its agile development methodologies. By integrating AI algorithms into the sprint planning process, the startup improved the accuracy of time

estimations, identified potential roadblocks proactively, and optimized the allocation of development resources. The outcome was a more efficient and adaptable agile framework that accelerated product iterations.

Case Study 4: Revolutionizing Healthcare with AI-Driven Product Management

Introduction:
In this case study, we explore how a healthcare technology company leveraged AI-driven product management to revolutionize healthcare delivery. By integrating AI-powered tools into their product development processes, the company achieved significant improvements in patient outcomes, clinical decision-making, and overall efficiency in healthcare delivery.

Background:
The healthcare industry faces numerous challenges, including the need to provide high-quality care while managing costs and improving patient outcomes. In response to these challenges, the healthcare technology company sought to harness the power of AI to enhance their product offerings and drive innovation in healthcare delivery.

Implementation:
The implementation process began with the development and deployment of AI-powered tools designed to analyze patient data, predict disease outcomes, and optimize treatment plans. Leveraging advanced machine learning algorithms and natural language processing techniques, the company created sophisticated AI models capable of extracting insights from vast amounts of healthcare data.

These AI-driven tools were integrated into the company's product management processes, allowing healthcare providers to access real-time insights and recommendations for clinical decision-making. By leveraging AI-driven insights, healthcare professionals were able to make more informed treatment decisions, personalize care plans, and improve patient outcomes.

Results:
The integration of AI into product management processes had a transformative impact on healthcare delivery, yielding significant improvements across key performance indicators:

1. Improved Patient Outcomes: By leveraging AI-powered tools for analyzing patient data and predicting disease outcomes, healthcare providers were able to identify high-risk patients, intervene proactively, and personalize treatment plans. This resulted in improved patient outcomes, reduced hospital readmissions, and enhanced quality of care.

2. Enhanced Clinical Decision-Making: AI-driven insights provided healthcare professionals with valuable information to support clinical decision-making. By analyzing patient data, identifying patterns, and recommending optimal treatment options, AI-powered tools empowered healthcare providers to make more informed decisions, leading to better outcomes for patients.

3. Increased Efficiency in Healthcare Delivery: The integration of AI into product management processes streamlined healthcare delivery, reducing administrative burdens, and optimizing resource allocation. By automating routine tasks, prioritizing patient needs, and improving workflow efficiency, healthcare organizations were able to deliver care more effectively and efficiently.

Conclusion:
This case study demonstrates the transformative impact of AI-driven product management on healthcare delivery. By leveraging AI-powered tools to analyze patient data, predict

disease outcomes, and optimize treatment plans, the healthcare technology company achieved significant improvements in patient outcomes, clinical decision-making, and overall efficiency in healthcare delivery. As AI continues to evolve, its role in driving innovation and improving healthcare outcomes will become increasingly essential.

Case Study 5: Enhancing Data-Driven Decision-Making in Financial Services

Introduction:
In this case study, we explore how a banking institution embraced AI to revolutionize data-driven decision-making in product management. By harnessing the power of machine learning models to analyze customer financial behaviors and market trends, the bank transformed its product offerings, personalized customer experiences, and gained a competitive advantage in the dynamic financial services industry.

Background:
The financial services industry is undergoing rapid transformation, driven by advancements in technology, changing customer expectations, and evolving regulatory requirements. In response to these challenges, the banking institution recognized the need to leverage AI to unlock insights from vast amounts of data, optimize its product portfolio, and deliver superior customer experiences.

Implementation:
The implementation process began with the development and deployment of machine learning models capable of analyzing diverse datasets, including customer transaction histories, demographic information, and market trends. Leveraging advanced algorithms and predictive analytics techniques, the bank created AI-driven models to identify

patterns, predict customer preferences, and optimize product offerings.

These machine learning models were integrated into the bank's product management processes, enabling data-driven decision-making across various business functions. By leveraging AI-driven insights, product managers were able to tailor product features, pricing strategies, and marketing campaigns to meet the specific needs and preferences of individual customers.

Results:
The integration of AI into product management processes had a transformative impact on the banking institution, yielding significant improvements across key performance indicators:

1. Enhanced Customer Experiences: By analyzing customer financial behaviors and preferences, the bank was able to personalize product offerings and deliver tailored experiences to individual customers. This resulted in increased customer satisfaction, loyalty, and engagement with the bank's products and services.

2. Optimized Product Portfolio: AI-driven insights enabled product managers to identify emerging trends, assess market demand, and optimize the bank's product portfolio accordingly. By launching new products, refining existing offerings, and discontinuing underperforming products, the bank maintained a competitive edge in the market and maximized revenue opportunities.

3. Improved Risk Management: Machine learning models provided the bank with valuable insights into customer creditworthiness, fraud detection, and risk assessment. By leveraging AI-driven analytics, the bank was able to mitigate

risks, detect anomalies, and prevent fraudulent activities, ensuring the security and integrity of its financial operations.

Conclusion:
This case study illustrates the transformative impact of AI-driven data analytics on data-driven decision-making in the financial services industry. By harnessing the power of machine learning models to analyze customer behaviors, predict market trends, and optimize product offerings, the banking institution achieved significant improvements in customer experiences, product portfolio optimization, and risk management. As AI continues to evolve, its role in driving innovation and competitive advantage in financial services will become increasingly critical.

Case Study 6: Hyper-Personalization in a Retail Giant

Introduction:
In this case study, we delve into how a retail giant utilized AI to achieve hyper-personalization in its product offerings. By leveraging AI-driven algorithms to analyze customer demographics, purchase history, and online behavior, the retailer transformed its approach to personalized shopping experiences. This resulted in heightened customer loyalty, elevated average order values, and a significant increase in overall revenue.

Background:
The retail industry is undergoing a digital revolution, with customers increasingly expecting personalized experiences tailored to their preferences and needs. Recognizing this trend, the retail giant sought to leverage AI technologies to enhance its ability to deliver personalized shopping experiences at scale. By harnessing the power of machine learning and predictive analytics, the retailer aimed to create tailored recommendations and promotions for each individual customer.

Implementation:
The implementation process began with the collection and analysis of vast amounts of customer data, including demographic information, purchase history, browsing behavior, and interactions with the retailer's website and mobile app. Leveraging advanced AI algorithms, the retailer developed personalized recommendation engines capable of identifying patterns, predicting preferences, and delivering targeted product suggestions to customers in real-time.

These AI-driven recommendation engines were seamlessly integrated into the retailer's online platform, allowing customers to receive personalized product recommendations based on their unique preferences and shopping behaviors. By leveraging machine learning models, the retailer was able to continuously refine its recommendations, ensuring relevance and accuracy for each individual customer.

Results:
The implementation of hyper-personalization strategies yielded significant results for the retail giant:

1. Enhanced Customer Loyalty: By providing personalized shopping experiences tailored to each customer's preferences, the retailer fostered deeper connections with its customer base. This led to increased customer loyalty, with shoppers returning to the retailer's platform for their future shopping needs.

2. Higher Average Order Values: Personalized product recommendations encouraged customers to explore additional items relevant to their interests, resulting in higher average order values. By presenting customers with relevant cross-selling and upselling opportunities, the retailer was able to maximize the value of each transaction.

3. Substantial Revenue Growth: The combination of enhanced customer loyalty and higher average order values contributed to a significant boost in overall revenue for the retail giant. By leveraging AI-driven hyper-personalization, the retailer was able to capture additional sales opportunities and drive sustainable revenue growth over time.

Conclusion:
This case study highlights the transformative impact of AI-driven hyper-personalization in the retail industry. By harnessing the power of machine learning algorithms to analyze customer data and deliver personalized shopping experiences, the retail giant achieved remarkable results, including increased customer loyalty, higher average order values, and substantial revenue growth. As AI continues to evolve, its role in enabling hyper-personalized experiences will become increasingly essential for retailers seeking to thrive in an increasingly competitive landscape.

Case Study 7: AI-Driven Collaboration in a Global Tech Corporation

Introduction:
In this case study, we explore how a global technology corporation utilized AI to revolutionize collaboration within its product management teams. By integrating AI-driven communication and project management tools, the corporation aimed to enhance cross-functional collaboration, optimize information sharing, and expedite the product development lifecycle. The result was a substantial increase in team efficiency, a reduction in time-to-market, and the successful launch of innovative products.

Background:
Effective collaboration is essential for large, globally distributed organizations, especially in the fast-paced technology sector. Recognizing the need to streamline

collaboration processes and improve communication across its product management teams, the global tech corporation embarked on a journey to leverage AI technologies. The corporation sought to harness the power of AI-driven tools to facilitate seamless communication, foster collaboration, and drive innovation within its product development teams.

Implementation:
The implementation process began with a comprehensive assessment of the corporation's collaboration challenges and pain points. By identifying areas where communication bottlenecks and inefficiencies existed, the corporation gained valuable insights into the specific needs of its product management teams. Leveraging this knowledge, the corporation selected and implemented AI-driven communication and project management tools tailored to address these challenges.

These AI-driven tools encompassed a range of capabilities, including natural language processing (NLP) for sentiment analysis, machine learning algorithms for task prioritization, and predictive analytics for resource allocation. By analyzing communication patterns, identifying critical tasks, and predicting potential roadblocks, these tools enabled the product management teams to work more efficiently and collaboratively.

Results:
The implementation of AI-driven collaboration tools yielded significant results for the global tech corporation:

1. Increased Team Efficiency: By streamlining communication and automating routine tasks, the AI-driven tools enhanced team efficiency, allowing product management teams to focus on high-priority tasks and strategic initiatives. The reduction in manual effort and administrative overhead

resulted in more time allocated to value-added activities, ultimately driving productivity gains across the organization.

2. Reduced Time-to-Market: The improved collaboration facilitated by AI-driven tools led to a significant reduction in time-to-market for new products and features. By enabling faster decision-making, smoother coordination between cross-functional teams, and quicker resolution of issues, the corporation was able to accelerate the product development lifecycle and bring innovations to market more rapidly.

3. Successful Product Launches: The enhanced collaboration and improved communication resulting from AI-driven tools contributed to the successful launch of new products and features. By fostering a culture of innovation and collaboration, the corporation was able to capitalize on market opportunities, meet customer needs more effectively, and drive business growth.

Conclusion:
This case study illustrates the transformative impact of AI-driven collaboration in a global technology corporation. By leveraging AI technologies to enhance communication, streamline collaboration, and accelerate the product development lifecycle, the corporation achieved significant improvements in team efficiency, reduced time-to-market, and successful product launches. As AI continues to evolve, its role in facilitating collaboration within organizations will become increasingly essential for driving innovation and maintaining competitiveness in the global marketplace.

Case Study 8: Addressing Ethical Considerations in AI Product Management

Introduction:
This case study explores how a tech startup took proactive steps to address ethical considerations in its AI-driven

product management practices. Recognizing the potential risks associated with AI, including biases and lack of transparency, the startup prioritized ethical considerations to build trust with users and ensure responsible AI implementation.

Background:
As AI technology becomes increasingly prevalent in product management, concerns about ethics and fairness have come to the forefront. Biases in AI algorithms, lack of transparency, and unintended consequences can undermine user trust and lead to ethical dilemmas. To mitigate these risks, the tech startup made ethics a central focus of its AI product management strategy.

Implementation:
The startup adopted a multifaceted approach to address ethical considerations in its AI-driven product management practices:

1. Fairness-Aware Algorithms: The startup implemented fairness-aware algorithms designed to mitigate biases and ensure equitable outcomes. These algorithms were trained on diverse datasets and subjected to rigorous testing to identify and mitigate potential biases based on factors such as race, gender, and socioeconomic status.

2. Ethical Audits: The startup conducted regular ethical audits to evaluate the impact of AI algorithms on users and identify areas for improvement. These audits involved examining algorithmic decision-making processes, assessing the fairness of outcomes, and soliciting feedback from users and stakeholders.

3. Stakeholder Engagement: The startup actively involved diverse stakeholders, including users, domain experts, and ethicists, in decision-making processes related to AI product

management. By soliciting input from a range of perspectives, the startup gained valuable insights into ethical considerations and ensured that its AI products aligned with societal values and expectations.

Results:
The implementation of ethical considerations in AI product management yielded positive results for the tech startup:

1. Building Trust: By prioritizing ethics and transparency, the startup built trust with users, demonstrating its commitment to responsible AI practices. Users were reassured that the AI-driven products were designed with fairness and integrity in mind, leading to increased confidence and engagement.

2. Mitigating Biases: The adoption of fairness-aware algorithms helped mitigate biases in AI decision-making processes, ensuring that outcomes were equitable across diverse user groups. By proactively addressing biases, the startup reduced the risk of discrimination and unfair treatment, enhancing the integrity of its AI products.

3. Strengthening Reputation: The startup's proactive approach to addressing ethical considerations enhanced its reputation as a responsible AI innovator. Customers, investors, and regulatory authorities recognized the startup's commitment to ethical practices, further solidifying its position as a leader in the AI industry.

Conclusion:
This case study highlights the importance of addressing ethical considerations in AI product management. By implementing fairness-aware algorithms, conducting regular ethical audits, and involving diverse stakeholders in decision-making processes, the tech startup demonstrated its commitment to responsible AI practices. As AI technology continues to evolve, prioritizing ethics will be essential for

building trust with users and ensuring the responsible deployment of AI-driven products.

Case Study 9: Continuous Learning for Innovation in a Software Development Firm

Introduction:
This case study delves into how a software development firm embraced continuous learning to drive innovation in product management. Recognizing the rapid pace of technological evolution and the need to stay ahead in a competitive market, the firm prioritized a culture of learning to foster innovation and adaptability.

Background:
In the fast-paced software development industry, innovation is key to maintaining a competitive edge. To fuel innovation, the software development firm recognized the importance of continuous learning for its product management teams. By encouraging ongoing skill development and knowledge acquisition, the firm aimed to empower its teams to adapt to emerging technologies and industry trends.

Implementation:
The software development firm implemented various strategies to promote continuous learning and foster innovation:

1. Establishing a Culture of Curiosity: The firm cultivated a culture of curiosity, encouraging team members to explore new ideas, experiment with innovative solutions, and embrace a mindset of lifelong learning. This culture of curiosity fostered an environment where team members felt empowered to question the status quo and seek out new opportunities for innovation.

2. Ongoing Training Programs: The firm provided ongoing training programs and professional development opportunities for its product management teams. These programs covered a wide range of topics, including emerging technologies, industry best practices, and leadership skills. By investing in the continuous development of its employees, the firm ensured that its teams were equipped with the latest knowledge and skills needed to drive innovation.

3. Incentivizing Learning Achievements: The firm incentivized learning achievements by recognizing and rewarding team members who demonstrated a commitment to continuous learning. This could include completing training courses, earning certifications, or contributing to knowledge-sharing initiatives within the organization. By incentivizing learning achievements, the firm reinforced the value of continuous learning and encouraged a culture of continuous improvement.

Results:
The implementation of continuous learning initiatives yielded positive results for the software development firm:

1. Adaptability to Emerging Technologies: By prioritizing continuous learning, the firm's product management teams remained adaptable and responsive to emerging technologies. Team members were able to quickly learn new skills and techniques, enabling them to leverage emerging technologies to drive innovation in product development.

2. Stay Ahead of Industry Trends: Continuous learning empowered the firm's product management teams to stay ahead of industry trends and best practices. By staying informed about the latest developments in the software development industry, teams were able to anticipate market changes and proactively adjust their strategies to capitalize on emerging opportunities.

3. Consistent Delivery of Innovative Products: The firm's commitment to continuous learning resulted in a culture of innovation where team members were encouraged to experiment and think creatively. This culture of innovation fueled the consistent delivery of innovative products that met the evolving needs of customers and outpaced competitors in the market.

Conclusion:
This case study highlights the transformative impact of continuous learning on innovation in product management within a software development firm. By establishing a culture of curiosity, providing ongoing training programs, and incentivizing learning achievements, the firm created an environment where innovation flourished, enabling it to maintain a competitive edge in the dynamic software development industry.

Case Study 10: Future-Forward AI Integration in an Automotive Manufacturer

Introduction:
This case study explores how an automotive manufacturer embraced future-forward AI integration in its product management practices to stay ahead in the competitive automotive industry. By leveraging AI across various facets of its operations, the manufacturer aimed to enhance operational efficiency, improve product quality, and maintain a competitive edge in the rapidly evolving market.

Background:
As the automotive industry undergoes rapid transformation driven by technological advancements and changing consumer preferences, manufacturers face the challenge of staying relevant and competitive. Recognizing the potential of AI to drive innovation and efficiency, the automotive

manufacturer embarked on a journey to integrate AI into its product management practices.

Implementation:
The automotive manufacturer implemented future-forward AI integration initiatives across different areas of its operations:

1. Product Design: AI was integrated into the product design process to optimize vehicle performance, enhance safety features, and improve fuel efficiency. By leveraging AI algorithms to analyze vast amounts of data on vehicle design, aerodynamics, and materials, the manufacturer was able to design vehicles that met the evolving needs and preferences of consumers while adhering to regulatory standards.

2. Manufacturing Processes: AI was utilized to optimize manufacturing processes and improve production efficiency. By implementing AI-driven predictive maintenance systems, the manufacturer was able to anticipate equipment failures, schedule maintenance activities proactively, and minimize downtime on the production line. Additionally, AI-powered quality control systems were deployed to detect defects and ensure the consistency and accuracy of the manufacturing process.

3. Predictive Maintenance: AI was employed to enable predictive maintenance of vehicles, allowing the manufacturer to identify potential issues before they escalate into costly repairs or breakdowns. By analyzing sensor data from vehicles in real-time, AI algorithms could detect anomalies and predict when components were likely to fail, enabling proactive maintenance interventions to be carried out.

Results:
The implementation of future-forward AI integration initiatives yielded significant results for the automotive manufacturer:

1. Operational Efficiency: By leveraging AI to optimize manufacturing processes and enable predictive maintenance, the manufacturer achieved greater operational efficiency, reduced downtime, and minimized production disruptions. This led to increased productivity and cost savings across the manufacturing operations.

2. Improved Product Quality: AI-driven quality control systems enhanced the accuracy and consistency of the manufacturing process, resulting in improved product quality and fewer defects. This, in turn, translated to higher customer satisfaction and reduced warranty claims for the manufacturer.

3. Competitive Edge: By embracing AI integration in product management practices, the automotive manufacturer gained a competitive edge in the rapidly evolving automotive industry. Its ability to deliver innovative, high-quality vehicles efficiently positioned it as a leader in the market and enabled it to meet the demands of discerning consumers.

Conclusion:
This case study demonstrates the transformative impact of future-forward AI integration in product management practices within an automotive manufacturer. By leveraging AI across product design, manufacturing processes, and predictive maintenance, the manufacturer achieved operational efficiency, improved product quality, and maintained a competitive edge in the dynamic automotive industry landscape.

LESSONS LEARNED FROM INDUSTRY LEADERS

In this chapter, we dive deep into compelling case studies and success stories from industry leaders that exemplify the transformative impact of AI on product management. Each narrative is a rich source of lessons learned, shedding light on the challenges faced, innovative solutions implemented, and the overarching principles that have guided these organizations toward success in their AI-enhanced product management endeavors.

Lessons from Case Study 1: Optimizing User Experience
The first case study underscores the importance of understanding user behavior and preferences. The lesson learned is that AI-powered personalization can significantly enhance user experience, leading to increased customer satisfaction and revenue. Key takeaways include the need for robust data analytics, continuous refinement of recommendation algorithms, and a commitment to delivering tailored experiences that resonate with individual users.

Lessons from Case Study 2: Streamlining Product Development
The second case study highlights the value of predictive analytics in streamlining product development processes. The key lesson is that AI-driven insights can empower organizations to make informed decisions, allocate resources efficiently, and reduce time-to-market. The chapter emphasizes the importance of leveraging historical data, implementing predictive models, and fostering a culture of data-driven decision-making.

Lessons from Case Study 3: Agile Methodologies Enhanced by AI

The third case study delves into the integration of AI with agile methodologies. The lesson learned is that AI can amplify the effectiveness of agile practices, particularly in sprint planning and resource allocation. Key takeaways include the benefits of iterative improvement, the importance of real-time data in decision-making, and the need for flexibility to adapt to changing project dynamics.

Lessons from Case Study 4: Transformative Impact in Healthcare

In the healthcare-focused case study, the lesson is drawn from the transformative impact of AI on clinical decision-making and patient outcomes. The key takeaway is the potential of AI to revolutionize healthcare practices, emphasizing the need for ethical considerations, robust data security, and interdisciplinary collaboration between healthcare professionals and AI experts.

Lessons from Case Study 5: Data-Driven Decision-Making in Finance

The fifth case study highlights the significance of data-driven decision-making in the financial services sector. The lesson learned is that AI can provide valuable insights into customer behaviours and market trends, enabling organizations to tailor their product offerings effectively. Key takeaways include the importance of leveraging AI for competitive advantage, maintaining regulatory compliance, and prioritizing data security.

Lessons from Case Study 6: Hyper-Personalization Strategies

The hyper-personalization case study emphasizes the impact of AI on tailoring customer experiences in retail. The lesson learned is that AI-driven personalization can foster customer loyalty and substantially increase revenue. Key takeaways include the need for comprehensive customer data analysis, responsible use of personalization algorithms, and the alignment of hyper-personalization with customer expectations.

Lessons from Case Study 7: AI-Driven Collaboration in Tech
The seventh case study explores the role of AI in enhancing collaboration within global tech corporations. The lesson learned is that AI can streamline communication, project management, and cross-functional collaboration. Key takeaways include the integration of AI tools, the promotion of transparent communication, and the establishment of collaborative frameworks that align with organizational goals.

Lessons from Case Study 8: Addressing Ethical Considerations
The case study focused on ethical considerations in AI product management offers a critical lesson. The key takeaway is that organizations must proactively address ethical challenges in AI, incorporating fairness-aware algorithms and conducting regular ethical audits. Key considerations include transparency, diversity in decision-making, and an ongoing commitment to responsible AI practices.

Lessons from Case Study 9: Continuous Learning for Innovation
The ninth case study underscores the significance of continuous learning in fostering innovation. The lesson learned is that a culture of curiosity, supported by ongoing training programs and incentives for learning achievements, contributes to a team that consistently adapts to emerging technologies and stays ahead of industry trends.

Lessons from Case Study 10: Future-Forward AI Integration in Automotive

The final case study highlights the importance of future-forward AI integration in the automotive industry. The lesson learned is that incorporating AI into product design, manufacturing processes, and predictive maintenance can lead to operational efficiency and a competitive edge. Key takeaways include a commitment to staying abreast of emerging technologies, fostering interdisciplinary collaboration, and aligning AI strategies with long-term industry trends.

A SYNTHESIS

This section synthesizes cross-cutting lessons and themes derived from the diverse case studies. It identifies overarching principles that can guide organizations embarking on AI-enhanced product management journeys. Common themes include the importance of data-driven decision-making, the need for ethical considerations, the value of interdisciplinary collaboration, and the transformative potential of continuous learning.

Key Considerations for Successful AI Integration

This concludes by distilling key considerations for organizations seeking successful AI integration into their product management practices. These considerations encompass strategic data utilization, ethical AI implementation, collaborative frameworks, and a commitment to ongoing learning. The chapter encourages organizations to leverage these insights as they navigate the complex landscape of AI-enhanced product management.

This section serves as a comprehensive guide for product management professionals, offering actionable lessons learned from industry leaders who have successfully integrated AI into their practices. By drawing inspiration from these case studies and distilling the key principles, organizations can navigate the challenges, harness the transformative power of AI, and chart a course toward innovative and successful product management in the evolving digital landscape.

FAILURES AND PIVOT POINTS - LEARNING FROM SETBACKS

In this chapter, we shift the focus from triumphs to tribulations, exploring case studies and success stories that delve into failures, setbacks, and the pivotal moments that led to course corrections. By examining these instances of adversity, product management professionals can gain invaluable insights into the challenges of integrating AI into their practices and learn from the resilience and adaptability demonstrated by organizations facing setbacks.

Navigating Setbacks: The Uncharted Terrain

We begin by acknowledging that setbacks are an inevitable part of the innovation journey, especially when incorporating AI into product management. It emphasizes the importance of viewing failures as opportunities for learning and growth. The narrative sets the stage for case studies that candidly discuss challenges faced, strategies employed to navigate setbacks, and the subsequent pivot points that led to eventual success.

Case Study 1: Revisiting AI-Driven User Experience Enhancement

Introduction:
This case study revisits a scenario where an attempt to enhance user experience through AI-driven personalization did not yield the expected results. It delves into the challenges faced, the lessons learned, and the subsequent adjustments made to improve user engagement.

Background:
The company, a leading e-commerce platform, had initially implemented AI-driven personalization algorithms to enhance

user experience and drive engagement. However, despite the initial optimism, the results fell short of expectations. Users were not responding as anticipated, and engagement metrics were below target.

Challenges Faced:
1. Misjudging User Preferences: One of the key challenges was misjudging user preferences. The AI algorithms, based on historical data, failed to accurately predict user behavior and preferences, leading to personalized recommendations that did not resonate with users.

2. Lack of Continuous User Feedback: Another challenge was the lack of continuous user feedback. The company relied solely on historical data to train the AI algorithms, overlooking the importance of real-time user feedback in refining personalization strategies.

3. Inflexible Algorithms: The AI algorithms lacked flexibility to adapt to changing user preferences and market dynamics. As a result, the personalized recommendations became stale over time, failing to keep pace with evolving user needs.

Lessons Learned:
1. Importance of Continuous User Feedback: The failure highlighted the importance of continuous user feedback in refining personalization strategies. The company realized the need to actively solicit feedback from users and incorporate it into the AI algorithms to improve relevance and accuracy.

2. Flexibility and Adaptability: The experience underscored the importance of building flexibility and adaptability into AI algorithms. Rather than relying solely on historical data, the company recognized the need to incorporate real-time data and dynamic user preferences into the algorithms.

3. User-Centric Approach: The failure prompted a shift towards a more user-centric approach to personalization. Instead of relying solely on data-driven insights, the company began prioritizing user preferences and feedback, ensuring that personalized recommendations were aligned with user expectations.

Adjustments Made:
1. Integration of Real-Time Feedback: The company implemented mechanisms to collect real-time user feedback and incorporated it into the AI algorithms. This allowed for more accurate and relevant personalized recommendations based on current user preferences.

2. Dynamic Personalization Algorithms: The AI algorithms were redesigned to be more flexible and adaptive, capable of adjusting to changing user preferences and market trends in real-time. This ensured that personalized recommendations remained relevant and engaging over time.

3. Emphasis on User-Centric Design: The company adopted a more user-centric approach to personalization, prioritizing user preferences and feedback in the development of personalized recommendations. This led to a more intuitive and engaging user experience, driving increased user engagement and satisfaction.

Results:
The adjustments made based on the lessons learned from the initial failure yielded significant improvements in user engagement and satisfaction:

1. Increased User Engagement: The integration of real-time user feedback and dynamic personalization algorithms resulted in increased user engagement with the platform. Users responded more positively to personalized recommendations that were aligned with their preferences.

2. Improved User Satisfaction: The emphasis on a user-centric approach to personalization led to improved user satisfaction. Users appreciated the platform's ability to deliver relevant and engaging recommendations tailored to their individual preferences.

3. Higher Conversion Rates: The improved user engagement and satisfaction translated into higher conversion rates for the company. Users were more likely to make purchases and return to the platform for future transactions, driving increased revenue and profitability.

Conclusion:
This case study illustrates the importance of learning from failures and continuously refining strategies to achieve success. By revisiting the initial failure in AI-driven user experience enhancement, the company was able to identify key lessons, make necessary adjustments, and ultimately achieve improved user engagement and satisfaction. It serves as a testament to the value of continuous learning and adaptation in driving business success.

Case Study 2: Unforeseen Challenges in Predictive Analytics

Introduction:
This case study delves into a scenario where a company encountered unforeseen challenges while implementing predictive analytics in its product development lifecycle. It explores the hurdles faced, the lessons learned, and the strategies employed to overcome obstacles.

Background:
The company, a software development firm, sought to leverage predictive analytics to streamline its product

development processes. However, during the implementation phase, several unforeseen challenges emerged, hindering the expected progress.

Challenges Faced:
1. Data Accuracy Issues: One of the primary challenges was data accuracy. The company realized that the quality of the data used for training predictive models was not as reliable as initially assumed. This led to inaccuracies in the predictions generated by the models, undermining their effectiveness.

2. Model Training Complexity: The complexity of training predictive models posed another challenge. The company underestimated the time and resources required to train models effectively, leading to delays in the implementation timeline. Additionally, fine-tuning the models to achieve optimal performance proved to be a daunting task.

3. Unforeseen External Factors: External factors, such as changes in market conditions or regulatory requirements, also presented challenges. These unforeseen variables impacted the accuracy and relevance of the predictive models, necessitating constant adjustments to maintain effectiveness.

Lessons Learned:
1. Thorough Feasibility Assessments: The experience highlighted the importance of conducting thorough feasibility assessments before embarking on predictive analytics initiatives. Assessing data quality, model complexity, and potential external factors upfront can help anticipate challenges and mitigate risks.

2. Iterative Model Refinement: The need for iterative model refinement became evident during the implementation process. Instead of expecting perfect predictions from the

outset, the company learned to embrace an iterative approach, continuously refining models based on feedback and real-world data.

3. Building Resilience: The experience taught the importance of building resilience in the face of unexpected obstacles. By maintaining flexibility and adaptability, the company was able to pivot quickly in response to changing circumstances, ensuring that predictive analytics initiatives remained on track.

Strategies Employed:
1. Data Quality Improvement: The company implemented measures to improve the quality of its data, including data cleaning, validation, and enrichment processes. This helped enhance the accuracy and reliability of the predictive models.

2. Iterative Model Training: Instead of aiming for perfection in the initial model training phase, the company adopted an iterative approach to model training and refinement. This allowed for continuous improvement and adaptation to evolving data patterns.

3. Scenario Planning: To address unforeseen external factors, the company implemented scenario planning techniques. By anticipating potential scenarios and their impact on predictive models, the company was better prepared to adjust strategies accordingly.

Results:
Despite the initial challenges, the company's efforts to overcome obstacles in implementing predictive analytics yielded positive results:

1. Improved Predictive Accuracy: The measures taken to enhance data quality and refine predictive models led to improved accuracy in predictions. This resulted in more

reliable insights for decision-making in the product development lifecycle.

2. Streamlined Development Processes: The iterative approach to model refinement and scenario planning helped streamline development processes. The company was able to adapt quickly to changing conditions, reducing delays and improving overall efficiency.

3. Enhanced Resilience: By building resilience into its predictive analytics initiatives, the company became better equipped to handle unforeseen challenges in the future. This resilience fostered confidence among stakeholders and positioned the company for continued success.

Conclusion:
This case study illustrates the importance of anticipating and addressing unforeseen challenges in predictive analytics initiatives. By learning from the hurdles encountered, the company was able to refine its approach, build resilience, and ultimately achieve success in leveraging predictive analytics to streamline its product development lifecycle. It underscores the value of adaptability, iteration, and resilience in navigating complex data-driven initiatives.

Case Study 3: Adapting Agile Methodologies Amidst Turbulence

Introduction:
This case study examines a scenario where the integration of AI with agile methodologies encountered turbulence and resistance within a product management team. It explores the challenges faced, the strategies employed to overcome obstacles, and the lessons learned from the experience.

Background:

The product management team, tasked with integrating AI into its agile development processes, encountered resistance and challenges due to the inherent differences between AI initiatives and traditional agile practices.

Challenges Faced:
1. Alignment with Agile Principles: One of the primary challenges was aligning AI initiatives with agile principles. Traditional agile methodologies emphasize incremental development and iterative feedback loops, which may not seamlessly accommodate the complexities of AI projects, such as longer development cycles and uncertainty in outcomes.

2. Resistance to Change: Resistance to change within the team posed another challenge. Some team members were accustomed to traditional agile practices and were hesitant to adopt new methodologies or adjust their way of working to accommodate AI initiatives.

3. Collaboration Hurdles: The integration of AI introduced collaboration hurdles within the team. Cross-functional collaboration, essential for successful AI implementation, was hindered by siloed workflows, communication breakdowns, and differing perspectives on how to incorporate AI into agile processes.

Lessons Learned:
1. Effective Change Management: The experience underscored the importance of effective change management when introducing AI into agile environments. Clear communication, stakeholder engagement, and addressing concerns proactively are essential for overcoming resistance and fostering buy-in from team members.

2. Flexibility in Agile Practices: The need for flexibility in agile practices became evident. While adhering to agile principles

is crucial, teams must be willing to adapt methodologies to accommodate the unique requirements of AI projects. This may involve adjusting sprint lengths, redefining user stories, or incorporating dedicated AI-focused ceremonies into agile rituals.

3. Emphasis on Collaboration: Collaboration emerged as a key factor in overcoming challenges. Encouraging open communication, fostering a culture of transparency, and breaking down silos between teams are essential for facilitating cross-functional collaboration and alignment on AI initiatives.

Strategies Employed:
1. Education and Training: The team invested in education and training to increase awareness and understanding of AI concepts and their integration with agile methodologies. This helped alleviate concerns and build confidence among team members in embracing AI initiatives.

2. Pilot Projects: The team initiated pilot projects to test the integration of AI with agile methodologies on a smaller scale. This allowed for experimentation, learning from failures, and refining processes before scaling AI initiatives across the organization.

3. Iterative Adaptation: Adopting an iterative approach, the team continuously adapted its agile practices to better accommodate AI projects. This involved soliciting feedback, identifying pain points, and making incremental adjustments to workflows, ceremonies, and team dynamics.

Results:
Despite the initial challenges, the team's efforts to adapt agile methodologies to accommodate AI initiatives yielded positive results:

1. Improved Collaboration: By addressing collaboration hurdles and fostering a culture of openness, the team achieved improved cross-functional collaboration and alignment on AI projects.

2. Enhanced Flexibility: The team demonstrated enhanced flexibility in its agile practices, allowing for the seamless integration of AI initiatives without compromising the core principles of agility.

3. Successful AI Implementation: Through effective change management, education, and iterative adaptation, the team successfully integrated AI into its agile development processes, achieving improved outcomes and driving innovation.

Conclusion:
This case study highlights the importance of effectively managing change, fostering collaboration, and adapting agile methodologies to accommodate AI initiatives. By learning from challenges, embracing flexibility, and emphasizing collaboration, product management teams can successfully integrate AI into their agile practices and drive innovation in an increasingly complex landscape.

Case Study 4: Ethical Dilemmas in Healthcare AI Integration

Introduction:
This case study delves into the ethical dilemmas encountered by a healthcare technology company during the integration of AI into clinical decision-making processes. It sheds light on the unforeseen biases in AI models and the ethical considerations that were initially overlooked, highlighting the importance of ethical audits, stakeholder involvement, and responsible AI practices.

Background:
The healthcare technology company embarked on integrating AI into its clinical decision-making processes to improve patient outcomes, streamline workflows, and enhance healthcare delivery. However, during the implementation phase, unforeseen ethical dilemmas arose, challenging the company's ethical framework and testing its commitment to responsible AI practices.

Ethical Dilemmas Faced:
1. Unforeseen Biases in AI Models: The company discovered unforeseen biases in the AI models used for clinical decision-making. These biases resulted in disparities in treatment recommendations, diagnostic accuracy, and patient outcomes, raising concerns about fairness, equity, and patient safety.

2. Overlooking Ethical Considerations: The initial implementation of AI failed to adequately consider ethical considerations, such as fairness, transparency, and accountability. This oversight led to unintended consequences, eroding trust among healthcare professionals, patients, and regulatory authorities.

3. Impact on Patient Care: The ethical dilemmas surrounding AI integration had a direct impact on patient care. Patients received inconsistent or inaccurate treatment recommendations, leading to suboptimal outcomes, patient dissatisfaction, and potential harm.

Lessons Learned:
1. **Importance of Ethical Audits:** The experience underscored the importance of conducting thorough ethical audits throughout the AI development lifecycle. Ethical audits help identify biases, disparities, and unintended consequences early on, enabling proactive mitigation strategies and ensuring responsible AI practices.

2. Diverse Stakeholder Involvement: Involving diverse stakeholders, including healthcare professionals, ethicists, patients, and regulatory authorities, is essential for addressing ethical dilemmas effectively. Diverse perspectives help identify blind spots, evaluate potential risks, and ensure that AI solutions align with ethical principles and societal values.

3. Ongoing Commitment to Responsible AI: Achieving ethical AI integration requires an ongoing commitment to responsible AI practices. This involves continuous monitoring, evaluation, and refinement of AI models to mitigate biases, enhance transparency, and uphold ethical standards throughout the product lifecycle.

Strategies Employed:
1. Ethical Review Boards: The company established ethical review boards comprised of multidisciplinary experts to assess the ethical implications of AI integration. These boards provided oversight, guidance, and recommendations for addressing ethical dilemmas and ensuring alignment with ethical principles.

2. Bias Mitigation Techniques: Implementing bias mitigation techniques, such as fairness-aware algorithms, data preprocessing, and model interpretability, helped mitigate biases and disparities in AI models. These techniques aimed to ensure fairness, transparency, and accountability in clinical decision-making processes.

3. Stakeholder Engagement: Engaging stakeholders through workshops, focus groups, and feedback sessions facilitated open dialogue, consensus-building, and collaboration on ethical considerations. Stakeholder input informed decision-making processes and enhanced the ethical robustness of AI solutions.

Results:
Despite the initial ethical dilemmas, the company's proactive approach to addressing ethical considerations yielded positive outcomes:

1. Improved Ethical Compliance: By conducting ethical audits, involving diverse stakeholders, and implementing bias mitigation techniques, the company achieved improved ethical compliance in AI integration.

2. Enhanced Trust and Transparency: Transparency about the ethical challenges faced and proactive efforts to address them enhanced trust among healthcare professionals, patients, and regulatory authorities.

3. Optimized Patient Care: The company's commitment to responsible AI practices led to optimized patient care, improved treatment outcomes, and enhanced patient safety in clinical decision-making processes.

Conclusion:
This case study underscores the importance of ethical considerations in AI integration, particularly in healthcare settings. By learning from ethical dilemmas, engaging stakeholders, and implementing responsible AI practices, healthcare technology companies can navigate ethical challenges effectively and ensure that AI solutions uphold ethical principles and benefit patient care.

Case Study 5: Unintended Consequences in Financial Services AI

Introduction:
This case study delves into the unintended consequences encountered in the financial services sector resulting from the integration of AI into data-driven decision-making processes.

It sheds light on the challenges posed by unintended biases in decision algorithms and unanticipated market reactions, highlighting the importance of continuous monitoring, bias mitigation strategies, and proactive approaches to addressing unintended consequences.

Background:
The financial services sector adopted AI-driven technologies to enhance data-driven decision-making, improve operational efficiency, and gain a competitive edge in the market. However, during the implementation phase, unforeseen consequences emerged, challenging the sector's ethical framework and testing its commitment to responsible AI practices.

Unintended Consequences Faced:
1. Unintended Biases in Decision Algorithms: The integration of AI into decision-making processes led to unintended biases in decision algorithms. These biases resulted in disparities in lending practices, investment recommendations, and risk assessments, raising concerns about fairness, equity, and regulatory compliance.

2. Unanticipated Market Reactions: The use of AI-driven algorithms to automate trading strategies and investment decisions resulted in unanticipated market reactions. These reactions contributed to market volatility, liquidity issues, and systemic risks, undermining market stability and investor confidence.

Lessons Learned:
1. Continuous Monitoring: The experience underscored the importance of continuous monitoring of AI-driven systems to detect and address unintended consequences promptly. Continuous monitoring helps identify biases, anomalies, and emerging risks, enabling proactive intervention and mitigation strategies.

2. Bias Mitigation Strategies: Implementing bias mitigation strategies, such as fairness-aware algorithms, diversity in training data, and model interpretability, is essential for mitigating unintended biases in decision algorithms. These strategies aim to ensure fairness, transparency, and accountability in financial decision-making processes.

3. Proactive Approach: Taking a proactive approach to addressing unintended consequences involves anticipating potential risks, conducting scenario analyses, and implementing safeguards to prevent adverse outcomes. Proactive measures help minimize the impact of unintended consequences and uphold ethical standards in AI-driven decision-making.

Strategies Employed:
1. Ethical Review Committees: Establishing ethical review committees comprised of domain experts, ethicists, and regulatory advisors facilitated ethical assessments of AI-driven decision-making processes. These committees provided oversight, guidance, and recommendations for addressing unintended consequences and ensuring compliance with ethical standards.

2. Algorithmic Audits: Conducting algorithmic audits and impact assessments helped identify biases, anomalies, and unintended consequences in decision algorithms. These audits involved evaluating algorithmic outputs, assessing their impact on diverse stakeholder groups, and implementing corrective measures to mitigate risks.

3. Stakeholder Engagement: Engaging stakeholders, including regulators, industry associations, and consumer advocacy groups, facilitated transparency, accountability, and collaboration in addressing unintended consequences.

Stakeholder input informed decision-making processes and enhanced the ethical robustness of AI-driven systems.

Results:
Despite the initial unintended consequences, the financial services sector's proactive approach to addressing ethical challenges yielded positive outcomes:

1. Improved Ethical Compliance: By implementing bias mitigation strategies, conducting ethical audits, and engaging stakeholders, the sector achieved improved ethical compliance in AI-driven decision-making.

2. Enhanced Market Stability: Proactive measures to address unintended consequences contributed to enhanced market stability, reduced volatility, and increased investor confidence in financial markets.

3. Regulatory Compliance: The sector's commitment to responsible AI practices and proactive engagement with regulators ensured compliance with regulatory requirements and ethical standards in AI integration.

Conclusion:
This case study highlights the importance of addressing unintended consequences in AI-driven decision-making processes, particularly in the financial services sector. By learning from unintended consequences, implementing bias mitigation strategies, and taking a proactive approach to ethical challenges, the sector can navigate risks effectively and ensure that AI solutions uphold ethical principles while delivering value to stakeholders.

Case Study 6: Struggling with Hyper-Personalization in Retail

Introduction:
This case study delves into the challenges encountered by a retail giant while implementing hyper-personalization strategies through AI. It explores the complexities of balancing personalized experiences with user privacy concerns and the potential for information overload. The lessons learned underscore the importance of striking a delicate balance, obtaining user consent, and transparent communication in hyper-personalization efforts.

Background:
The retail giant aimed to enhance customer experiences by leveraging AI to deliver hyper-personalized product recommendations, promotions, and shopping experiences. However, during the implementation process, the company faced challenges related to privacy, user consent, and the effective management of personalized content.

Challenges Faced:
1. Privacy Concerns: Implementing hyper-personalization raised privacy concerns among customers regarding the collection, storage, and usage of their personal data. Customers expressed apprehension about data breaches, unauthorized access, and the potential misuse of their information, leading to distrust and reluctance to engage with personalized experiences.

2. Information Overload: The abundance of personalized content generated by AI-driven algorithms resulted in information overload for customers. Instead of enhancing the shopping experience, excessive personalization overwhelmed users, making it difficult for them to navigate through the vast array of recommendations and promotions effectively.

3. User Consent: Obtaining explicit consent from users to collect and process their personal data for hyper-personalization purposes proved challenging. Many customers were unaware of the extent to which their data was being utilized, leading to concerns about transparency, accountability, and control over their personal information.

Lessons Learned:
1. Balancing Personalization and Privacy: The experience highlighted the importance of striking a delicate balance between delivering personalized experiences and respecting user privacy. Retailers must prioritize data protection, transparency, and user control to build trust and foster positive relationships with customers.

2. Obtaining User Consent: Obtaining explicit consent from users for data collection and processing is essential for ethical hyper-personalization efforts. Retailers should implement transparent consent mechanisms, clearly communicate the purpose and scope of data usage, and empower users to make informed choices about their privacy preferences.

3. Managing Information Overload: Managing information overload requires a thoughtful approach to content curation, relevance filtering, and personalization algorithms. Retailers should tailor personalized experiences to match user preferences, interests, and browsing behaviors while avoiding overwhelming users with irrelevant or redundant content.

Strategies Employed:
1. Transparency and Communication: The retail giant implemented transparent communication strategies to educate users about its hyper-personalization practices, data handling procedures, and privacy safeguards. Clear and

concise privacy policies, cookie notices, and consent forms were designed to enhance transparency and build trust with customers.

2. Preference Management Tools: Providing users with preference management tools empowered them to control the types of personalized content they received, the frequency of communications, and the channels through which they preferred to interact with the brand. Preference centers and opt-in/opt-out mechanisms enabled users to customize their shopping experiences according to their preferences and privacy preferences.

3. Algorithmic Fairness and Diversity: Ensuring algorithmic fairness and diversity in personalized recommendations helped mitigate the risk of unintentional biases and discrimination. The retail giant implemented fairness-aware algorithms, diversity metrics, and bias detection mechanisms to monitor and address potential biases in its hyper-personalization models.

Results:
Despite the initial challenges, the retail giant's proactive approach to addressing privacy concerns and managing information overload yielded positive outcomes:

1. Enhanced Trust and Loyalty: Transparent communication, user consent mechanisms, and preference management tools fostered trust and loyalty among customers, enhancing their confidence in the brand's hyper-personalization efforts.

2. Improved User Engagement: By enabling users to tailor their shopping experiences according to their preferences and privacy preferences, the retail giant increased user engagement, interaction rates, and conversion rates across its digital channels.

3. Compliance with Regulatory Standards: The retail giant's commitment to data protection, privacy compliance, and ethical hyper-personalization practices ensured alignment with regulatory standards and industry best practices, mitigating legal risks and reputational damage.

Conclusion:
This case study highlights the importance of addressing privacy concerns, managing information overload, and obtaining user consent in hyper-personalization efforts. By prioritizing transparency, user control, and algorithmic fairness, retailers can build trust, enhance user engagement, and drive business growth through ethical hyper-personalization strategies.

Case Study 7: Communication Breakdown in Global Tech Corporation

Introduction:
This case study examines a scenario where the adoption of AI-driven collaboration tools resulted in communication breakdowns within a global tech corporation. It explores the challenges faced, the adjustments made, and the lessons learned to foster effective communication amidst technological integration.

Background:
The global tech corporation aimed to enhance collaboration and streamline communication among its geographically dispersed teams by implementing AI-driven collaboration tools. However, the transition to these new tools presented unexpected challenges, leading to misinterpretation, resistance, and breakdowns in communication channels.

Challenges Faced:
1. Misinterpretation: The introduction of AI-driven collaboration tools led to misinterpretation of messages and

instructions due to unfamiliarity with the new platform's features and functionalities. Employees struggled to adapt to the new communication interface, resulting in confusion and misunderstanding in team interactions.

2. Resistance to New Tools: Some employees resisted the adoption of AI-driven collaboration tools due to skepticism about their effectiveness, concerns about job displacement, or reluctance to embrace change. This resistance hindered the smooth integration of the new tools into existing workflows and communication practices.

3. Human Factor in Technology Integration: The human factor, including individual preferences, communication styles, and work habits, posed challenges in effectively leveraging AI-driven collaboration tools. Differences in communication preferences and technological proficiency among team members exacerbated communication breakdowns and hindered collaboration efforts.

Lessons Learned:
1. User Training and Onboarding: Providing comprehensive training and onboarding programs for employees is essential to familiarize them with new AI-driven collaboration tools, build confidence in using the technology, and mitigate resistance to change. Hands-on training sessions, tutorials, and user guides can help employees navigate the features and functionalities of the new platform effectively.

2. Clear Communication Strategies: Implementing clear communication strategies, including guidelines for message clarity, tone, and etiquette, can minimize misinterpretation and facilitate effective communication in virtual environments. Encouraging concise and structured communication practices can enhance clarity and comprehension among team members.

3. Understanding Employee Needs: Recognizing and understanding the diverse needs and preferences of employees is crucial for successful technology integration. Tailoring communication tools and workflows to accommodate different communication styles, work preferences, and technological proficiency levels can foster inclusivity and engagement among team members.

Strategies Employed:
1. Comprehensive Training Programs: The global tech corporation implemented comprehensive training programs and workshops to educate employees about the features and functionalities of the AI-driven collaboration tools. Hands-on training sessions, video tutorials, and user guides were provided to facilitate skill development and familiarity with the new platform.

2. Change Management Initiatives: Change management initiatives were introduced to address employee resistance and foster a culture of openness to technological change. Communication campaigns, town hall meetings, and leadership support initiatives were implemented to communicate the benefits of the new tools and address employee concerns.

3. Feedback Mechanisms: Implementing feedback mechanisms and soliciting input from employees helped identify pain points, address challenges, and refine communication strategies. Regular feedback surveys, focus groups, and open-door policies encouraged employees to voice their opinions, share their experiences, and contribute to continuous improvement efforts.

Results:
The proactive measures taken to address communication breakdowns yielded positive outcomes:

1. Improved Adoption Rates: Comprehensive training programs and change management initiatives increased employee confidence and acceptance of AI-driven collaboration tools, leading to improved adoption rates and engagement levels.

2. Enhanced Communication: Clear communication strategies and feedback mechanisms improved clarity, comprehension, and collaboration among team members. Employees felt more confident in navigating the new tools and leveraging them to communicate effectively with colleagues.

3. Fostered Collaboration: The understanding of employee needs and preferences fostered a culture of collaboration and inclusivity within the organization. Team members embraced the new communication tools and workflows, resulting in increased productivity, efficiency, and synergy across global teams.

Conclusion:
This case study underscores the importance of addressing communication breakdowns and understanding the human factor in technology integration. By providing comprehensive training, implementing clear communication strategies, and fostering a culture of openness to change, organizations can overcome challenges and leverage AI-driven collaboration tools to enhance communication and collaboration in a global context.

Case Study 8: Unforeseen External Factors in Automotive AI

Introduction:
This case study delves into the challenges encountered by an automotive manufacturer as a result of unforeseen external factors affecting AI integration in product management. It examines the impact of regulatory changes, market shifts, and

geopolitical factors on the manufacturer's AI-enhanced product management strategies.

Background:

The automotive manufacturer embarked on a journey to integrate AI into various aspects of its product management processes to enhance efficiency, quality, and innovation. However, unforeseen external factors emerged, presenting challenges that were not initially accounted for in the AI integration plan.

Challenges Faced:

1. Regulatory Changes: The automotive industry operates within a highly regulated environment, with frequent updates to safety standards, emissions regulations, and data privacy laws. Unforeseen regulatory changes posed challenges in compliance, requiring adjustments to AI algorithms, data management practices, and product development processes to ensure adherence to evolving regulations.

2. Market Shifts: Rapid shifts in consumer preferences, economic conditions, and market trends impacted the demand for automotive products and services. Unanticipated changes in market dynamics, such as shifts towards electric vehicles or changes in consumer buying behavior, necessitated modifications to AI-driven product management strategies to align with evolving market needs and trends.

3. *Geopolitical Factors: Geopolitical events, such as trade disputes, tariffs, or geopolitical tensions, can disrupt supply chains, production processes, and market access. Unforeseen geopolitical factors introduced uncertainties and risks, requiring the automotive manufacturer to reassess its AI integration strategy and mitigate potential impacts on product management operations.

Lessons Learned:

1. Scenario Planning: Incorporating scenario planning into AI integration strategies enables organizations to anticipate and prepare for various external factors that may impact product management initiatives. Scenario analysis helps identify potential risks, evaluate their potential impact, and develop contingency plans to mitigate adverse effects on product development and business operations.

2. Adaptability to External Influences: Maintaining flexibility and adaptability in AI-driven product management approaches allows organizations to respond effectively to unforeseen external factors. By continuously monitoring market trends, regulatory changes, and geopolitical developments, organizations can adjust their AI strategies, reallocate resources, and pivot product development efforts to capitalize on emerging opportunities and mitigate risks.

3. Holistic Risk Management: Adopting a holistic approach to risk management involves identifying, assessing, and mitigating risks across various dimensions, including regulatory compliance, market volatility, and geopolitical uncertainties. Implementing robust risk management processes and controls enables organizations to proactively address potential threats to AI integration initiatives and safeguard against adverse impacts on product management operations.

Strategies Employed:
1. Regulatory Compliance Audits: The automotive manufacturer conducted regular regulatory compliance audits to ensure that AI-driven product management practices aligned with evolving regulatory requirements. Compliance teams collaborated with AI engineers and product managers to assess the impact of regulatory changes on AI algorithms, data processing workflows, and product development protocols.

2. Market Intelligence Analysis: The manufacturer invested in market intelligence analysis to monitor consumer trends, competitor activities, and market dynamics. Market intelligence teams provided timely insights and recommendations to product management teams, enabling them to adapt AI strategies, refine product offerings, and capitalize on emerging market opportunities.

3. Geopolitical Risk Assessments: Geopolitical risk assessments were conducted to identify potential geopolitical factors that could impact supply chains, manufacturing operations, and market access. Cross-functional teams collaborated to develop contingency plans, diversify supply chain sources, and mitigate geopolitical risks through strategic sourcing and production planning.

Results:
The proactive measures taken to address unforeseen external factors resulted in several positive outcomes:

1. Enhanced Resilience: The automotive manufacturer demonstrated enhanced resilience in the face of regulatory changes, market shifts, and geopolitical uncertainties. Proactive risk management practices enabled the organization to adapt quickly to external influences, minimize disruptions, and maintain continuity in product management operations.

2. Improved Agility: By incorporating scenario planning and maintaining flexibility in AI-driven product management approaches, the manufacturer improved its agility in responding to changing market conditions and customer demands. Agile decision-making processes enabled the organization to capitalize on emerging opportunities and mitigate risks effectively.

3. Sustained Innovation: Despite external challenges, the automotive manufacturer sustained its focus on innovation and product development. AI-driven product management strategies continued to drive innovation, improve product quality, and enhance customer satisfaction, enabling the organization to maintain its competitive edge in the automotive industry.

Conclusion:
This case study underscores the importance of anticipating and addressing unforeseen external factors in AI integration initiatives. By adopting proactive risk management practices, maintaining adaptability to external influences, and embracing a holistic approach to risk management, organizations can navigate challenges effectively and achieve sustainable success in AI-enhanced product management.

Case Study 9: Overcoming Resistance to Continuous Learning

Introduction:
This case study delves into the challenges faced by a software development firm in overcoming resistance to continuous learning initiatives within its organization. Despite recognizing the importance of continuous learning for innovation and staying competitive in the rapidly evolving tech landscape, the firm encountered resistance from employees reluctant to embrace change.

Background:
The software development firm recognized the need to prioritize continuous learning as a strategic imperative to foster innovation and maintain its competitive edge. However, entrenched cultural norms, fear of change, and skepticism about the value of learning initiatives hindered progress

toward cultivating a culture of curiosity and continuous improvement.

Challenges Faced:
1. Organizational Mindset: The firm struggled to shift the organizational mindset from a traditional, static approach to learning to one that embraced continuous learning as a core value. Resistance to change was prevalent among employees accustomed to established processes and routines, making it challenging to introduce new learning initiatives.

2. Cultural Norms: Deep-rooted cultural norms that favored stability over experimentation and innovation contributed to resistance to continuous learning. Employees were hesitant to step out of their comfort zones and embrace new learning opportunities, fearing failure or disruption to their routines.

3. Perceived Value: Some employees questioned the perceived value of continuous learning initiatives, expressing skepticism about how investing time and resources in learning would translate into tangible benefits for their roles or the organization as a whole.

Strategies Employed:
1. Leadership Support: Leadership played a crucial role in driving the cultural shift toward continuous learning. Executives and managers actively championed learning initiatives, demonstrating their commitment through actions such as participating in training programs, providing resources for skill development, and recognizing and rewarding learning achievements.

2. Incentivizing Learning: The firm implemented incentives and recognition programs to incentivize and motivate employees to participate in continuous learning activities. Rewards such as certifications, promotions, and opportunities for career advancement were offered to employees who

demonstrated a commitment to learning and skill development.

3. Persistent Communication: Clear and persistent communication about the importance of continuous learning and its benefits was essential in overcoming resistance. Regular town hall meetings, internal newsletters, and workshops were used to educate employees about the value of learning, address concerns, and share success stories of individuals who had benefited from learning initiatives.

Lessons Learned:
1. Leadership Alignment: Leadership alignment and support are critical for driving cultural change and overcoming resistance to continuous learning. When leaders actively endorse and participate in learning initiatives, they set a positive example for employees and reinforce the importance of continuous learning as a core organizational value.

2. Tailored Incentives: Tailoring incentives to align with individual and organizational goals can increase engagement and participation in learning activities. Recognizing and rewarding employees who demonstrate a commitment to learning helps reinforce desired behaviors and creates a culture where continuous improvement is valued and celebrated.

3. Persistent Efforts: Overcoming resistance to continuous learning requires persistent efforts and a long-term commitment to cultural change. Building a learning culture is an ongoing process that requires patience, perseverance, and a willingness to address challenges and setbacks along the way.

Results:
1. Cultural Transformation: The persistent efforts to promote continuous learning led to a gradual cultural transformation

within the software development firm. Employees became more receptive to learning opportunities, embraced experimentation and innovation, and demonstrated a willingness to adapt to changing technologies and industry trends.

2. Increased Engagement: Employee engagement in learning activities increased significantly as a result of leadership support, incentivization, and persistent communication efforts. Employees were more proactive in seeking out learning opportunities, participating in training programs, and applying newly acquired skills to their roles.

3. Enhanced Innovation: A culture of continuous learning fostered a spirit of innovation and creativity within the organization. Employees felt empowered to explore new ideas, experiment with emerging technologies, and contribute to product development initiatives, resulting in enhanced innovation and competitiveness in the marketplace.

Conclusion:
This case study highlights the importance of addressing resistance to continuous learning through leadership support, incentivization, and persistent communication. By cultivating a culture of curiosity and continuous improvement, organizations can overcome barriers to learning, drive innovation, and maintain a competitive edge in today's rapidly changing business environment.

EMBRACING THE FUTURE - A CALL TO ACTION

A s we conclude our exploration into the Future of Product Management and AI, it becomes evident that the intersection of these realms holds immense potential for innovation, growth, and transformation. The journey through defining the landscape, tracing the evolution of product management, understanding the rise of artificial intelligence, and delving into the confluence of these domains has revealed a dynamic landscape that demands agility, adaptability, and a commitment to continuous learning.

The confluence of Product Management and AI represents more than a technological evolution; it symbolizes a paradigm shift in how organizations conceive, create, and deliver products to meet the evolving needs of a dynamic market. The case studies, successes, and failures underscore the multifaceted nature of this journey, acknowledging both triumphs and setbacks as integral components of the innovation process.

Embracing Change and Continuous Learning

The rapid pace of technological advancements, market dynamics, and user expectations necessitates a proactive approach to change. Embracing this change involves fostering a culture of continuous learning within product management teams. The ability to adapt to emerging technologies, integrate AI seamlessly, and stay ahead of industry trends becomes a competitive advantage in the digital era.

Human-Centric Design and Ethical Considerations

The chapters on human-centric design and ethical considerations underscore the importance of placing users at the center of AI-driven product development. Balancing automation with the human touch, addressing privacy concerns, and ensuring ethical AI practices are not just ethical imperatives but crucial elements in building trust and sustaining long-term relationships with users.

Agile Methodologies and Data-Driven Decision Making

Agile methodologies, when adapted for AI projects, enhance the iterative development process and provide real-time feedback loops. The chapters on data-driven decision-making shed light on the pivotal role of analytics, metrics, and turning data into actionable strategies. Leveraging big data for product insights empowers organizations to make informed decisions that resonate with user needs and market trends.

Personalization, Customization, and Security

The exploration of personalization and customization in product management unveils the transformative power of AI in tailoring experiences for users. However, this personalization journey must be navigated with careful consideration of privacy concerns and user consent. The chapters on security and trust emphasize the critical need to establish and maintain user trust through robust security measures and compliance with regulatory standards.

Collaboration, Communication, and Continuous Learning Organization

Building cross-functional teams, communicating complex AI concepts to non-technical stakeholders, and overcoming challenges in remote AI product management are essential elements in navigating the collaborative landscape of AI-driven teams. The chapters on the continuous learning organization stress the importance of upskilling teams, cultivating a learning culture, and staying ahead in a rapidly evolving landscape.

Lessons from Setbacks and Pivotal Moments

The chapter on failures and pivotal moments illuminates the reality that setbacks are inherent in the innovation journey. However, these setbacks, when navigated with resilience and adaptability, become pivotal moments for learning and growth. The synthesis of key takeaways offers actionable insights into overcoming challenges, refining strategies, and persevering in the face of adversity.

EMBRACING THE FUTURE: A CALL TO ACTION

As we stand at the crossroads of the future, the call to action resounds with the imperative to embrace the possibilities that AI brings to product management. It urges organizations to foster a culture of innovation, to see setbacks as stepping stones, and to recognize that the journey towards AI-enhanced product management is a continuous evolution.

This is not just a technological evolution; it is a cultural shift. It necessitates a mindset that values learning, adapts to change, and places human needs at the forefront of technological advancements. The call to action implores product management professionals, leaders, and organizations to embark on this journey with a spirit of curiosity, a commitment to ethical practices, and a relentless pursuit of excellence.

In embracing the future of product management and AI, we are not merely adopting new technologies; we are shaping the way we innovate, collaborate, and create value for users. The journey ahead is dynamic, and the potential is boundless. The call to action is an invitation to not only navigate this terrain but to be pioneers, crafting a future where the confluence of product management and AI becomes a beacon of innovation, user-centricity, and continuous evolution.

THE ONGOING JOURNEY OF AI AND PRODUCT MANAGEMENT

As we culminate our exploration into the future of AI and Product Management, we find ourselves at the crossroads of innovation, poised on the precipice of an era defined by the seamless integration of human ingenuity and artificial intelligence. This ongoing journey is not a destination but a perpetual evolution, a dynamic interplay of technology, adaptability, and the ceaseless pursuit of excellence in product management.

A Tapestry of Evolution

Our journey began by defining the landscape, navigating through the evolution of product management, and understanding the rise of artificial intelligence. It is a tapestry woven with threads of innovation, resilience, and the continuous quest to harness the potential of AI in shaping the products of tomorrow. The chapters unfolded as interconnected narratives, each contributing a unique hue to the canvas of this transformative journey.

Navigating the Confluence

The confluence of Product Management and AI represents more than a convergence of technologies; it is a meeting point of creativity and computation. It's where human intuition collaborates with machine intelligence to birth products that not only meet but anticipate user needs. Navigating this confluence demands a nuanced understanding of human-centric design, ethical considerations, and the intricacies of collaboration within AI-driven teams.

Agility and Data-Driven Precision

The chapters on Agile Methodologies and Data-Driven Decision Making revealed the synergies that propel product management into a new realm of efficiency. Agile methodologies, when harmonized with AI, create a symphony of iterative development and real-time feedback loops. Data-driven decision-making, on the other hand, transforms information into actionable strategies, making every decision a precise chord in the symphony of product management.

Personalization, Customization, and Trust

The exploration of personalization and customization illuminated the path to crafting tailored experiences for users, but it came with the caveat of navigating privacy concerns and user consent. Trust emerged as a central theme, underscoring the importance of establishing and maintaining user trust through meticulous attention to security, compliance, and ethical AI practices.

Continuous Learning and Resilience

The journey through the Continuous Learning Organization and Lessons from Setbacks highlighted that setbacks are not roadblocks but stepping stones to growth. A culture of continuous learning, adaptability, and resilience emerges as the cornerstone of success in the ever-evolving landscape of AI and product management.

A Call to Pioneering Action

As we conclude this exploration, the call to action is not just an epilogue but a prelude to what lies ahead. It beckons product management professionals, leaders, and organizations to be pioneers in shaping the future. The ongoing journey of AI and product management is a testament to the human capacity for innovation, learning, and the audacity to embrace change.

An Ongoing Symphony

In essence, the journey of AI and product management is an ongoing symphony, where the melody of human creativity harmonizes with the precision of artificial intelligence. It is a symphony that resonates with the rhythms of change, the melodies of innovation, and the harmonies of collaboration. As we step into the future, let this symphony be a celebration of possibility, a manifestation of our collective ingenuity, and a testament to the enduring spirit of evolution.

The journey is ongoing, the challenges are dynamic, and the future is an open score waiting to be composed. As product management professionals, leaders, and innovators, let us not merely navigate this journey but be the conductors orchestrating a symphony that defines the very essence of AI-enhanced product management – a harmonious blend of technology, humanity, and the perpetual pursuit of excellence.

APPENDIX

GLOSSARY OF KEY TERMS

In the dynamic landscape of AI and Product Management, understanding key terms is essential for effective communication and comprehension. This glossary serves as a reference guide, providing concise definitions for terminology encountered throughout the book.

Agile Methodologies: A set of iterative development methodologies that prioritize flexibility, collaboration, and customer feedback. In AI product management, Agile methodologies are adapted to accommodate the dynamic nature of AI projects.

Artificial Intelligence (AI): The simulation of human intelligence in machines, enabling them to perform tasks that typically require human intelligence. In product management, AI is employed for data analysis, pattern recognition, and decision-making.

Big Data: Extremely large and complex data sets that cannot be easily managed, processed, or analyzed using traditional data processing tools. Big data is utilized in AI product management for extracting valuable insights and patterns.

Continuous Learning: A culture that fosters ongoing learning and adaptation within an organization. In the context of AI and product management, continuous learning involves staying abreast of technological advancements and evolving industry trends.

Data-Driven Decision Making: The practice of making informed decisions based on analysis and interpretation of data. In AI product management, data-driven decision-making involves leveraging data analytics to inform and guide strategic choices.

Ethical Considerations: The evaluation and integration of ethical principles into decision-making processes. In AI product management, ethical considerations involve addressing biases, ensuring fairness, and protecting user privacy.

Human-Centric Design: A design approach that prioritizes the needs, preferences, and experiences of users. In AI product management, human-centric design ensures that AI applications align with user expectations and enhance user experiences.

Machine Learning: A subset of AI that enables systems to learn and improve from experience without being explicitly programmed. In product management, machine learning is utilized for predictive analytics, pattern recognition, and automation.

Predictive Analytics: The use of statistical algorithms and machine learning techniques to identify patterns and make predictions about future events. In AI product management, predictive analytics aids in forecasting trends and optimizing decision-making.

Privacy Concerns: The ethical and legal considerations related to the protection of individuals' personal information. In AI product management, addressing privacy concerns involves implementing measures to secure and responsibly handle user data.

Product Lifecycle: The series of stages a product goes through, from conception and development to launch, maintenance, and eventual discontinuation. In AI product management, understanding the product lifecycle is crucial for effective planning and execution.

Security Concerns: The identification and mitigation of potential risks to the confidentiality, integrity, and availability of data and systems. In AI product management, security concerns involve safeguarding AI models, user data, and the overall product infrastructure.

User Experience (UX): The overall experience a user has while interacting with a product or system. In AI product management, UX is a critical consideration to ensure that AI applications are intuitive, user-friendly, and meet user expectations.

This glossary provides a foundation for comprehending key terms related to AI and product management. As the field continues to evolve, staying familiar with these terms will aid professionals in navigating the intricacies of AI-enhanced product development and management.

RESOURCES FOR FURTHER READING

Expanding your knowledge in the dynamic realms of AI and Product Management requires access to comprehensive and up-to-date resources. The following list encompasses recommended readings, articles, and online platforms that delve deeper into the intricacies of AI, product management, and their confluence.

BOOKS:

1. "AI Superpowers: China, Silicon Valley, and the New World Order" by Kai-Fu Lee
2. "Inspired: How To Create Products Customers Love" by Marty Cagan
3. "Human Compatible: Artificial Intelligence and the Problem of Control" by Stuart Russell
4. "Lean Product and Lean Analytics" by Ben Yoskovitz and Alistair Croll
5. "Artificial Intelligence: A Guide for Thinking Humans" by Melanie Mitchell

ONLINE PLATFORMS AND JOURNALS:

1. [Harvard Business Review](https://hbr.org/)
2. [MIT Sloan Management Review - Artificial Intelligence] (https://sloanreview.mit.edu/topic/artificial-intelligence/)
3. [ProductCoalition](https://productcoalition.com/)
4. [Towards Data Science](https://towardsdatascience.com/) - Medium publication focusing on AI and data science.
5. [AI & Society Journal](https://www.springer.com/journal/146) - A scholarly journal exploring the societal impacts of AI.

ONLINE COURSES AND CERTIFICATIONS:

1. [Coursera - AI For Everyone](https://www.coursera.org/learn/ai-for-everyone)
2. [edX - Essential Mathematics for Artificial Intelligence](https://www.edx.org/professional-certificate/microsoft-essential-math-for-ai)
3. [Product Management Certification - Product School](https://www.productschool.com/product-management-certification/)

BLOGS AND NEWSLETTERS:

1. [ProductCoalition Blog](https://productcoalition.com/)
2. [Towards AI](https://towardsai.net/)
3. [Product Talk - Marty Cagan](https://svpg.com/articles/)

CONFERENCES AND EVENTS:

1. [ProductCamp](https://productcamp.org/) - Unconferences focused on product management.
2. [The AI Summit](https://theaisummit.com/) - Global series of conferences on artificial intelligence.

PODCASTS:

1. [The AI Alignment Podcast](https://www.alignmentforum.org/)
2. [Masters of Scale](https://mastersofscale.com/) - Explores the strategies and tactics of successful entrepreneurs and leaders.

COMMUNITIES:

1. [Product Management Community on Reddit](https://www.reddit.com/r/ProductManagement/)
2. [AI & Machine Learning Community on LinkedIn](https://www.linkedin.com/groups/14017235/)

These resources offer a diverse range of perspectives, insights, and practical knowledge to deepen your understanding of AI and Product Management. Whether you are a seasoned professional or just starting, exploring these materials will contribute to your ongoing learning and professional development.

INDEX

This index provides a quick reference to key topics and terms discussed throughout the book. Use this index to navigate and locate specific information within the text.

PULL QUOTE

"Embark on a transformative journey into the heart of a symphony where the intricate chords of human creativity seamlessly intertwine with the resonant melodies of artificial intelligence. Within this dynamic interplay, innovation transcends mere technological prowess; it becomes a harmonious fusion, sculpting a future characterized by perpetual learning, unwavering adaptability, and a bold embrace of change.

Picture this ongoing symphony as a vibrant tapestry, where each thread represents a commitment to continuous evolution. Here, the alliance of human ingenuity and artificial intelligence becomes the orchestrator of a mesmerizing composition. It is a cultural narrative that transcends boundaries, inviting us to join a collective pursuit of knowledge, growth, and the limitless possibilities woven into the fabric of progress.

As we navigate this symphony of innovation, it unfolds not merely as a technological journey but as a cultural shift—an ever-evolving narrative shaped by the resonance of human curiosity and the precision of artificial intelligence. Every note played and every beat resonates with the spirit of progress, propelling us forward into a realm where the collaboration between human creativity and artificial intelligence orchestrates a captivating symphony of boundless possibilities."

ABOUT THE AUTHOR

Meet Sajjad Ahmad, a luminary Product Manager in the telecom sector with an illustrious 24-year career doing Product Management for 14 years. Having navigated the ever-evolving corridors of telecommunications, Sajjad possesses an in-depth understanding of the industry's nuances, challenges, and innovations.